FLORIDA

ATLANTIC OCEAN

83° 82° 31° 30° 29° 28° 27° 26° 25°

Okefenokee Swamp
441
95
OSCEOLA NATIONAL FOREST
10
Jacksonville
1
St. Augustine
441
129
Florida Nat'l Scenic Trail
A1A
301
Daytona Beach
Gainesville
17
Lake George
OCALA NATIONAL FOREST
CANAVERAL NATIONAL SEASHORE
Ocala
75
4
95
Titusville
Cape Canaveral
19
98
Orlando
19
98
Melbourne
441
1
Tampa
4
Lakeland
Clearwater
Florida's Turnpike
St. Petersburg
F L O R I D A
Fort Pierce
41
Kissimmee
Sarasota
17
27
Lake Okeechobee
West Palm Beach
75
441
Fort Myers
95
Fort Lauderdale
BIG CYPRESS NATIONAL PRESERVE
75
A1A
41
Tamiami Trail
The Everglades
Miami
EVERGLADES NATIONAL PARK
BISCAYNE NATIONAL PARK

1
see Florida Keys inset at left
Key West

EVERGLADES NATIONAL PARK
1
Key Largo
Florida Bay
N
1
Marathon
Florida Keys
ATLANTIC OCEAN

N

Scale in Miles
25   50   100

NATIONAL
AUDUBON
SOCIETY
FIELD GUIDE TO
Florida

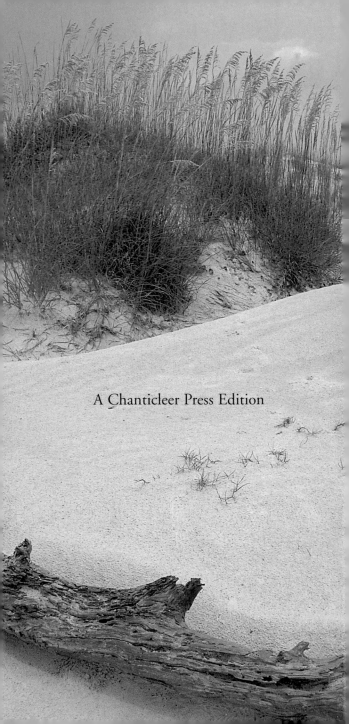

A Chanticleer Press Edition

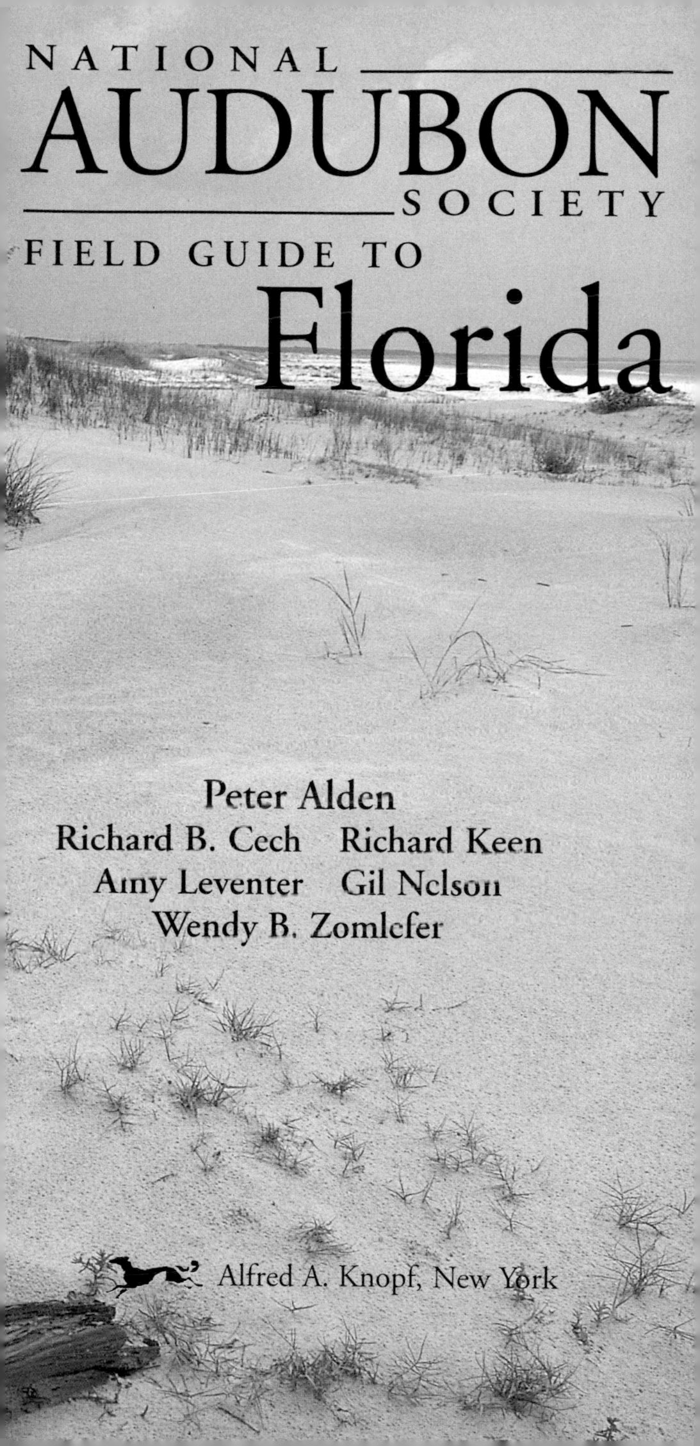

NATIONAL
AUDUBON
SOCIETY
FIELD GUIDE TO
Florida

Peter Alden

Richard B. Cech   Richard Keen

Amy Leventer   Gil Nelson

Wendy B. Zomlefer

Alfred A. Knopf, New York

Prepared and produced by
Chanticleer Press, Inc., New York.

Printed and bound by
Dai Nippon Printing Co., Ltd., Hong Kong.

First Edition
Published May 1998
First Printing

Library of Congress Cataloging-in-Publication Data

National Audubon Society field guide. Florida / Peter Alden . . .
    [et al.]. — 1st ed.
        p.   cm.
    Includes index.
    ISBN 0-679-44677-X
    1. Natural history—Florida.   I. Alden, Peter.   II. National
Audubon Society.
QH105.F6N38   1998
508.759—dc21   97-31242

Front Cover: Great Blue Heron with Bald Cypresses
Spine: Mangrove islet, Florida Bay
Back Cover: Zodiacal light in Leo, Swamp Hibiscus, Roseate Spoonbill, Cayo Costa State Park
Table of Contents: Sea Oats, Canaveral National Seashore; full moon; Little Metalmark
Title Page: Canaveral National Seashore
Pages 8–9: Sunrise over a marsh, Merritt Island National Wildlife Refuge
Page 74–75: White Ibis and Anhingas, A. R. Marshall Loxahatchee National Wildlife Refuge
Pages 378–379: Hillsborough River, Hillsborough River State Park

National Audubon Society

The mission of NATIONAL AUDUBON SOCIETY, founded in 1905, is to conserve and restore natural ecosystems, focusing on birds, other wildlife, and their habitats for the benefit of humanity and the earth's biological diversity.

One of the largest, most effective environmental organizations, Audubon has more than 550,000 members, numerous state offices and nature centers, and 500+ chapters in the United States and Latin America, plus a professional staff of scientists, lobbyists, lawyers, policy analysts, and educators. Through our nationwide sanctuary system we manage 150,000 acres of critical wildlife habitat and unique natural areas for birds, wild animals, and rare plant life.

Our award-winning *Audubon* magazine, published six times a year and sent to all members, carries outstanding articles and color photography on wildlife and nature, and presents in-depth reports on critical environmental issues, as well as conservation news and commentary. We also publish *Field Notes,* a journal reporting on seasonal bird sightings, and *Audubon Adventures,* a children's newsletter reaching 450,000 students. Through our ecology camps and workshops in Maine, Connecticut, and Wyoming, we offer professional development for educators and activists; through Audubon Expedition Institute in Belfast, Maine, we offer unique, traveling undergraduate and graduate degree programs in Environmental Education.

Our acclaimed *Wild!Life Adventures* television documentaries, airing on TBS Superstation and in syndication, deal with a variety of environmental themes, and our children's series for the Disney Channel, *Audubon's Animal Adventures,* introduces family audiences to endangered and threatened wildlife species. Our weekly birding series *All Bird TV,* which airs on Discovery's Animal Planet Channel, provides viewers with birding tips and takes them to some of the greatest bird locations in the United States. Other Audubon film and television projects include conservation-oriented movies, electronic field trips, and educational videos. National Audubon Society also sponsors books and interactive programs on nature, plus travel programs to exotic places like Antarctica, Africa, Australia, Baja California, Galápagos Islands, and Patagonia.

For information about how you can become an Audubon member, subscribe to *Audubon Adventures,* or to learn more about our camps and workshops, please write or call:

NATIONAL AUDUBON SOCIETY
Membership Dept.
700 Broadway
New York, New York 10003
212-979-3000
http://www.audubon.org/

Contents
Part One: Overview

Overview

Natural Highlights

Visitors to Florida have long been captivated by the beauty and abundance that exist within the state's 58,560 square miles. Often thought of as a land of palm trees, sandy beaches, and perpetual summer, the state attracts tourists and retirees by the millions. But what many visitors overlook is the subtle diversity of Florida's many unique natural areas, which undergo constant change and progression throughout the year. This quiet rhythm is a major reason naturalists find Florida fascinating.

John Pennekamp Coral Reef State Park, Key Largo

Coral Reefs

The only place in the continental United States where living coral reefs can be observed is off the Florida coast. Visitors can explore this tropical habitat by scuba diving, snorkeling, or touring in a glass-bottom boat. By any method, the intricacies of the reef and the delicate life it sustains are evident: a colorful array of corals, anemones, sponges, shrimps, squids, and fishes large and small.

Cayo Costa State Park

The Gulf Coast

The shallow waters of the Gulf of Mexico off Florida's western coast provide a rich breeding ground for mollusks, and the relatively gentle tidal activity of the coast here allows shells to wash ashore without excessive battering. These factors come together at such places as Sanibel Island and Cayo Costa, where many species of shells can be found. The aftermath of an ocean storm is considered the best time for shelling, as large numbers of specimens are often carried ashore.

Parks and Refuges

Florida's many parks and wildlife refuges offer visitors a relatively pristine encounter with the state's natural habitats. Many people make their first acquaintance with subtropical wildlife at southern Florida's Everglades National Park. Many parts of the park, including the Anhinga Trail —which runs along Taylor Slough, a watery refuge for many creatures during the dry season—attract interest-

Anhinga Trail, Everglades National Park

ing native species of birds, fish, amphibians, and reptiles (including alligators), as well as a variety of exotic flora, such as Gumbo Limbos and orchids. Among Florida's other outstanding natural areas are St. Marks National Wildlife Refuge and Ocala National Forest, both in northern Florida, and Merritt Island National Wildlife Refuge in central Florida.

Birds and Birding

Early each May a curious spectacle unfolds on Garden Key in the Dry Tortugas, a cluster of small coral islands about 70 miles from Key West: A handful of casually strolling Cattle Egrets share the grassy courtyard of Fort Jefferson (a Civil War–era military prison) with clusters of birders armed with telescopes and binoculars. The birders have come to see rarities, including breeding tropical seabirds such as Sooty Terns and Brown Noddies. The egrets, originally an African species that found its way to Florida in the early 1940s, are now well established. Florida is home to hundreds of bird species and is visited by abundant migrating and breeding birds each year. It is perhaps best known for waterbirds, including Sandhill Cranes, Anhingas, and ibises.

Fort Jefferson, Dry Tortugas

Inland Topography

Florida's highest point, at 345 feet above sea level, is in the Western Highlands of the northern panhandle. From northernmost Florida a backbone of discontinuous uplands extends down the peninsula nearly to Lake Okeechobee. South of Okeechobee, elevations are generally less than 26 feet above sea level. Changes in elevation throughout the state are relatively small but ecologically significant, with high and low ground supporting vastly different flora and fauna. Nearly 8,000 lakes of 10 acres or more, 1,700 rivers and creeks, 300 springs, and an abundance of marshes and swamps within the state's boundaries contain more than 4,000 square miles of water. Additionally, the limestone bedrock is honeycombed with innumerable subterranean caverns, many filled with water.

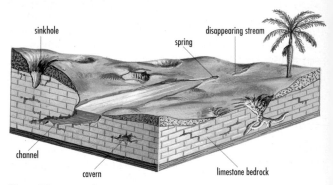

Karst Topography

Karst topography, an irregular landscape shaped over millions of years by the dissolving of calcium-carbonate rocks (such as Florida's limestone bedrock) by groundwater, is characterized by sinkholes, subterranean caverns and channels, underground drainage systems, and "disappearing" streams that detour underground, reappearing miles away as springs. Sinkholes—small, steep depressions in the earth—can form when the roofs of underground caverns become progressively thinner and weaker, and eventually collapse. Most lakes in Florida's Central Highlands occupy basins left by sinkholes.

Manatee Springs State Park

Manatee Springs

Originating in a large underground cave system in the Gulf coastal lowlands of northern Florida (near Chiefland), Manatee Springs, whose waters maintain a constant temperature of 72 degrees Fahrenheit, is visited every winter by Manatees. It is only one of the hundreds of warm, clear springs in Florida, most of which are in the northwest.

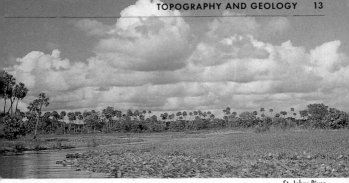

St. Johns River

St. Johns River

At 285 miles in length, the St. Johns is the longest river entirely within Florida. It is also one of the largest in the United States to flow northward, from Brevard County in east-central Florida to the Atlantic northeast of Jacksonville, where the river is several miles wide and estuarine—that is, influenced by the tidal influx of seawater.

Lake Okeechobee

Lake Okeechobee

With an area of about 436,000 acres, Lake Okeechobee, fed by Lake Kissimmee and associated lakes via the Kissimmee River and draining to the sea via the Everglades, is one of the largest freshwater lakes in the United States. Only 15 to 20 feet deep, it is the remnant of an ancient shallow sea. Lake flooding during hurricanes in the late 1920s caused almost 2,500 deaths; subsequently, a dike was built around the lake, disrupting the natural flow of water into the Everglades.

Florida's Ridges

The Brooksville, Trail, Lake Wales, and Atlantic Coastal Ridges are elevated areas that trend north–south through peninsular Florida; all but the last end north of Lake Okeechobee. The Trail Ridge was formed by windblown sand. The other three are erosional features that were shaped by ocean currents along ancient shorelines during times of high sea level.

The Everglades

A 2½-million-acre fresh- to brackish-water marsh covering much of southern Florida, the Everglades is bordered on the west by Big Cypress Swamp and on the east by a low limestone ridge. Although the

Everglades National Park

Everglades appears completely flat, it slopes slightly downhill from north to south, with elevations decreasing from about 18 feet above sea level at its northernmost border with Lake Okeechobee to sea level in the south.

Ocean and Coastal Topography

Florida's 1,200-mile seashore—this figure does not factor in indentations along the shoreline, including bays, lagoons, and the like—the longest of any state besides Alaska, is characterized by generally low wave energy and a small tidal range of up to 6 feet on the eastern coast and a mere 2 feet on the western. Despite the small tidal range, the relatively low slope of the Florida landscape means that a wide swath of coastline is exposed to the rise and fall of the tides, facilitating the creation of salt marshes and mangrove swamps. The shallow slopes of the wide continental shelf in the Gulf of Mexico further reduce wave energy along Florida's western coast, where seashells are gently washed onto beaches. The Gulf coast of Florida is bathed by the Loop Current, a stream of warm water that flows clockwise, entering the Gulf of Mexico between Cuba and the Yucatán Peninsula and exiting between Cuba and the tip of the Florida peninsula as the swiftly flowing Florida Current—the beginning of the Gulf Stream.

Dunes, St. Joseph Peninsula State Park

Sand Dunes

Driftwood and clumps of beach grass in a back beach area interrupt the landward flow of wind and cause beach sand to be deposited in their lee—the start of a dune. Such dunes are usually asymmetric in shape, with the steep downwind side at an angle of 32 degrees from the vertical; termed the "angle of repose," it is the slope beyond which particles will begin to tumble downhill. Dunes will migrate downwind if they are not stabilized by hardy vegetation, such as Sea Oats, that can withstand sea spray and burial by sand. Sand dunes are the mainland's greatest defense against the flooding that often accompanies the tropical storms and hurricanes that visit the Florida coast.

Mangrove islet, Florida Bay

Florida Bay

Florida Bay, which stretches between the Keys and the mainland, is actually a vast patchwork of 4- to 6-foot-deep "lakes" separated by shallow mudbanks exposed at low tide. Marine vegetation, mainly three genera of marine algae with calcareous (calcium-containing) parts that are left behind when the algae die, has been deposited over the past 4,000 years to form the blanket of marine mud that covers the bottom of the bay.

View from Plantation Key to Upper Matecumbe Key

The Florida Keys

When sea levels drop, as during periods of glaciation, and coral reefs are exposed to air, the corals die. Their hard skeletons remain and form limestone, which eventually erodes and forms a soil capable of supporting plant growth. The Florida Keys are a string of more than 100 coral reef and oolitic limestone (see Rocks, below) islands that began forming some 150,000 years ago, when a shallow sea covered most of the Florida peninsula. Stretching about 135 miles from Fowey Rock near Miami to the Dry Tortugas, the Keys, which average less than 10 feet above sea level, separate Florida Bay to the north and west from the deep trough of the Straits of Florida to the south.

Barrier Islands

Barrier islands are sedimentary islands separated from the mainland by bays and lagoons. Some originate as sand spits that are breached during storms, but in Florida most barrier islands were formed during a relatively rapid rise in sea level at the end of the last ice age some 10,000 years ago. Where coasts were very wide and gently sloping, beach ridges and dune lines were cut off from the mainland and left as offshore sandbars as the sea level began to rise. As sea levels continued to rise, these offshore sand bodies migrated landward, following the transgressing shoreline in a tractor-tread–like motion, as sand on the seaward side of the island was washed over and deposited on the landward side, primarily during storms. This process continued until about 4,000 or 5,000 years ago, when sea levels began to stabilize. Barrier islands are still very dynamic, always shifting, migrating, and changing.

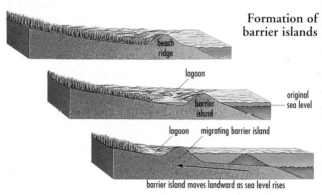

Formation of barrier islands

barrier island moves landward as sea level rises

Florida Platform and Escarpment

The Florida peninsula is the emergent portion of the Florida Platform, a large, relatively flat limestone-based bank covered by water less than 300 feet deep that separates the Atlantic Ocean from the Gulf of Mexico. Florida sits at the eastern edge of the platform; fairly steep slopes plunge to oceanic depths only about 3 or 4 miles off the southeastern coast. To the west the platform extends more than 100 miles before ending in the Florida Escarpment, a steep limestone cliff that in places drops sharply several thousand feet. The Florida Keys form the southern rim of the Florida Platform.

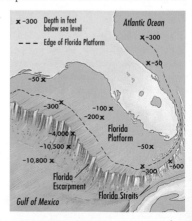

Coral reef with Barrel Sponge, West Palm Beach

Coral Reefs

Coral reefs are built of the skeletal matter of organisms that extract calcium carbonate from sea water and use it to build their skeletons. Although corals are the most conspicuous and largest reef builders, many other organisms contribute to reef formation, including foraminifera, mollusks, bryozoans, polychaete worms, and several kinds of plants. The underlying limestone consists of the remains of these organisms' skeletons ground by wave action and cemented by biological and chemical processes into a solid limestone that in time loses all resemblance to the original skeletons. Corals occur throughout the world's oceans, but reef-building species are restricted to warm, clear, calm, sunlit waters — conditions found in much of southern Florida. The reefs there are of the "fringing" variety; that is, they grow outward from a coastline, remaining more or less continuous with the land they border, and develop mostly in shallow waters. Reefs protect the coastline, absorbing the energy of incoming waves. Patches of reefs occur along much of Florida's coastline (though there are few in the Gulf) but are best developed in the Keys.

Caribbean Life

The Keys host many plant and animal species native to the West Indies. New Caribbean strays turn up regularly in southern Florida, and some establish colonies. The White-crowned Pigeon, a West Indian native, has become an increasingly common resident in semitropical hardwood hammocks on the Keys and lower peninsula. As there was never a land bridge between Florida and the Caribbean islands, the origin of much tropical plant life in the Keys is a matter of speculation.

White-crowned Pigeon

The Interaction of Water and Land

Calcareous beach, Bahia Honda State Park

When the ancient supercontinent of Pangaea began to break apart about 200 million years ago, new continents were created as the Atlantic Ocean started to form. Rock from what is today western Africa was stranded on the western side and became part of the Florida basement (the lowermost rock). Over the next 125 million years or so, parts or all of Florida were alternately above and below sea level, and land-derived sediments, such as quartz sand and clays, and marine sediments were likewise alternately deposited. From about 75 million to 25 million years ago, most of Florida was submerged as a shallow marine environment teeming with life. Many organisms, such as corals, bryozoans, mollusks, and foraminifera, deposited calcareous skeletal parts, which settled to the sea floor. With time, compaction and cementation of the skeletal parts contributed to the formation of the limestone Florida Platform (see Ocean and Coastal Topography, above). Between about 25 and 2 million years ago, an overall drop in global sea level (caused by seawater being stored as ice in Antarctica) again left much of Florida periodically above water, exposing the limestone to the elements. Over the past 2 million years the earth has experienced several glacial expansions and retreats, and sea levels have risen and fallen as much as 500 feet, drastically transforming the shape and extent of Florida's shoreline.

Evolution of Florida's Beaches

Beginning about 30 million years ago and continuing today, rivers and currents have transported southward large amounts of sediments eroded from the Appalachian Mountains of western North Carolina, South Carolina, and Georgia. As these rocks weathered, their constituent quartz was physically but not chemically broken down, and was eventually deposited as quartz sand beaches. The beaches of southernmost Florida—farther from the influx of debris from the north—are calcareous, composed of fragments of old coral, broken shells, sea urchin spines, and coralline algae.

Quartz beach, St. Joseph Peninsula State Park

Florida's Shoreline and Global Warming

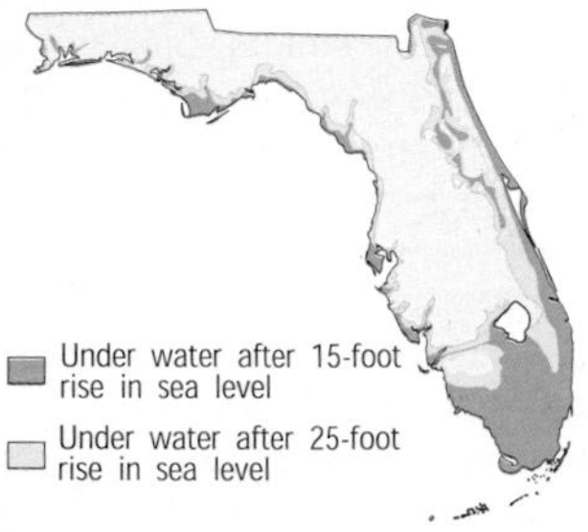

Models of global warming predict a sea level rise due to thermal expansion of water—as water gets warmer, it expands in volume—and melting of polar ice. Since the late 19th century, earth's average surface temperature has risen approximately 1.8 degrees Fahrenheit, and sea levels have risen about 4 to 6 inches over the same period. Florida's low elevation and gentle slope make it particularly susceptible to even minor changes in sea level. Pictured here is Florida's coastline given 15- and 25-foot rises in sea level. Even a 1-foot rise in sea level would cause Florida's high-tide mark to move 200 to 1,000 feet inland.

Under water after 15-foot rise in sea level

Under water after 25-foot rise in sea level

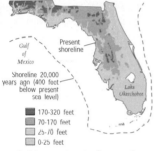

Ancient Shorelines of Florida

During times of maximum glaciation, such as 20,000 years ago, sea level was some 400 feet lower and the Florida peninsula two to three times as wide as it is today. When less ice was present at various times during the past several million years, sea level was as much as 320 feet higher than today, and peninsular Florida probably consisted of a number of islands. Only today's highest elevations would have been above sea level.

Gulf of Mexico

Present shoreline

Shoreline 20,000 years ago (400 foot below present sea level)

Lake Okeechobee

170–320 feet

70–170 feet

25–70 feet

0–25 feet

Formation of the Everglades

The Everglades began to form only 5,000 years ago during a time of rising sea levels, when an increase in rainfall resulted in the flooding of flat, low-lying, and poorly drained southern Florida. Upland vegetation, including pine trees, could not tolerate the standing surface water, and marsh plants took their place. Peat, characteristic in wetlands, began to accumulate and irregularities in surface topography were smoothed over, contributing to the flat terrain of the Everglades today.

Floridan Aquifer System

Aquifers are subsurface rocks with interconnected pore spaces that permit the storage and flow of water. The Floridan Aquifer System, also known as Florida's "rain barrel," is one of the world's most productive, serving as the main source of fresh water for many Florida communities. Formed over millions of years as carbonate sediments were deposited and dissolved, it underlies all of Florida at depths ranging from just a few feet to 1,000 feet below the surface.

Minerals and Natural Resources

Minerals, the building blocks of rocks, are naturally occurring inorganic, crystalline substances with characteristic chemical compositions and structures that determine their appearance. A mineral may be a single native element, such as copper or gold, or a compound of elements. Minerals are recognized by such physical properties as hardness, cleavage (breakage along well-defined planes of weakness) and fracture (any type of rough and uneven breakage), luster (the way the surface reflects light), and crystal structure. Color may be an unreliable identifying feature, as minor impurities can cause significant color variations.

QUARTZ

One of the most common minerals at earth's surface; a building block of Florida's beaches. Generally colorless or white; small-grained; shelly fracture; no cleavage. Glassy luster; cannot be scratched with a knife. Crystals are six-sided, with pyramidal ends. Quartz sand on a beach is well worn down and rounded—finding an actual crystal is extremely unlikely.

LIMONITE

An important iron ore, chemically the same substance as rust. Dull yellowish brown, shapeless, and soft enough to leave a stain on paper or cloth. Very pure deposits found near Chiefland (southwest of Gainesville); less pure deposits found throughout Florida. Mined as iron ore and paint pigment.

Fossil Fuels

Fossil fuels, such as oil, natural gas, and coal, are complex mixtures of hydrocarbons that occur when the organic remains of plants and animals are transformed through time by heat and pressure. Oil fields are present in both southern Florida and in the western pan-

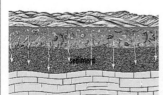

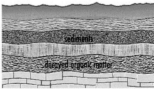

Oil and natural gas begin forming when the remains of tiny marine plants and animals mix with sediments on the bottoms of shallow ocean waters. As time passes the layer of sediments with the decayed organic matter becomes buried as layer after layer of sediment collects on top of it. As water advances and retreats over millions of years and more layers are added, the overlying layers of sediment grow thicker and harder.

PHOSPHATES

A group of minerals found in sedimentary rocks; range in color from white to gray to black. "Land pebble" type occurs as loosely or well-consolidated granular particles; found throughout most of the peninsula; mined commercially (mainly for fertilizer) in two regions: Central Florida Phosphate District of Polk, Hillsborough, Manatee, and Hardee Counties, in west-central Florida; and Northern Phosphate District of Hamilton and Columbia Counties, in north-central part of state. Florida leads U.S. in phosphate production; produces 25 percent of world's supply.

HEAVY MINERALS

Heavy minerals, which include rutile, ilmenite, staurolite, zircon, and tourmaline, are defined as those minerals that are 2.9 times heavier than the same volume of water. In Florida, heavy minerals are mixed in with almost all the quartz and clay sands but are found in economically valuable concentrations only in the northeast. Mined by a floating suction dredge, they have many industrial uses. They may not be easily identified individually due to their small size, but many appear as dark sand grains.

CALCITE

The principle mineral in limestone, made of calcium carbonate. Color varies widely; most often colorless, white, or yellow. Soft enough to be scratched by a knife; will bubble when exposed to acid. Found virtually everywhere in Florida.

handle. The southern Florida fields, centered around Seminole, tap oil found in 135-million-year-old patch reefs located about 12,000 feet below the surface. Panhandle oil is produced from limestones about 150 million years old at a depth of about 15,000 feet.

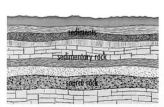
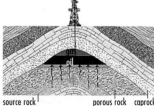

Pressure helps to convert the organic materials (now a layer of rock called the source layer) into gas and oil droplets. Oil and gas travel upward through porous rock until they are trapped by a rock layer called caprock. Gas, oil, and groundwater form a reservoir in the porous rock from which the oil and gas are pumped.

Rocks

A given rock may be composed of only one mineral or it may be an aggregate of different minerals. Rocks provide a tangible record of many geologic processes that are impossible to observe directly—for example, the melting of rocks in earth's interior. The identification of rocks can sometimes be difficult, but clues are provided by their constituent minerals, grain size, and overall texture. All of Florida's surface rocks are sedimentary—that is, they are formed primarily through the consolidation of layers of sediment (fragments of older, weathered rock ranging in size from submicroscopic particles to boulders, and/or organic or chemical matter) deposited at earth's surface, usually in water. For much of its history the peninsula has been submerged, which accounts for Florida's abundance of sedimentary rocks.

Limestone

Limestone, Florida's bedrock, is the most common rock type in the state. A sedimentary rock made of calcium carbonate, it generally forms in marine environments as plants and animals with calcareous body parts die and fall to the seafloor. Limestone can also form when water becomes supersaturated with calcium carbonate—that is, when there are too many calcium and carbonate ions in the water for them all to remain in dissolved form. Colors range from white and yellow to shades of gray. Limestone can be scratched easily with a knife, and often contains fossils. Texture varies among the six major types of Florida limestone: Coquina, Key Largo, Miami, Ocala, Suwannee, and Tampa limestones (these names indicate the area in which the rock was first observed). The differences among types are determined by their constituent grains: coral skeletons, various types of microscopic marine creatures, shells, or other materials.

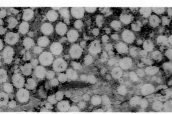

MIAMI LIMESTONE   Oolitic facies   Bryozoan facies

Found in two forms, or facies. **Oolitic facies** are nonbiological in origin; consist mainly of ooids, tiny round grains of calcite that originate as loose, undissolved spherules deposited in shallow, agitated water; eventually become cemented together. Appears whitish, fine-grained; in cross section, displays concentric shells of calcite, like layers of an onion. Found in southern Florida, in Broward, Collier, Dade, and Monroe Counties. **Bryozoan facies** are massive (up to a foot in diameter), irregular, knobby colonies of calcareous skeletons of the bryozoan *Schizoporella floridana.* Common in Everglades and Florida Bay.

COQUINA

Used as building stone in U.S. for more than 400 years; can be seen at Castillo de San Marcos in St. Augustine. Found in about a 3-mile-wide strip from St. Johns County to Palm Beach County along eastern coast. **COMPOSITION** Whole and fragmented shells and quartz sand cemented together with mineral calcite. **APPEARANCE** Generally whitish yellow; coarse, depending on constituent particles.

TAMPA LIMESTONE

A hard, microcrystalline rock exposed in western Florida in Tampa Bay area. **COMPOSITION** Primarily calcite; contains from 20 to 70 percent impurities: quartz sand, clay, and phosphate. **APPEARANCE** Generally whitish to gray, depending on amount of impurities.

KEY LARGO LIMESTONE

Found only in Florida Keys, from Soldier Key to approximately Big Pine Key. **COMPOSITION** Fossilized corals that have been partially dissolved and replaced with crystalline calcite. **APPEARANCE** Coarse textured; white to light gray.

OCALA LIMESTONE

Underlies almost entire state; outcrops found in many areas from northwestern to west-central Florida. **COMPOSITION** Almost pure calcium carbonate; composed almost entirely of tiny shells of foraminifera, a marine zooplankton. **APPEARANCE** Whitish to cream-colored; fine-grained; chalky.

SUWANNEE LIMESTONE

Outcrops in northwestern to west-central Florida. **COMPOSITION** Not as pure as Ocala limestone. About 90 percent or more calcium carbonate from loosely cemented foraminifera, echinoids, and rare mollusks, and a few percent impurities such as quartz sand and clay. **APPEARANCE** Fine- to medium-grained; sometimes denser than Ocala Limestone.

Fossils

A fossil is any indication of past plant or animal life, including petrified wood, animal bones or teeth, shells, footprints, and even molds or casts in the shape of a plant or animal left in rock after the organism itself disintegrated. Almost all fossils are discovered in sedimentary rocks, usually in areas that were once underwater, which explains why many fossils are of aquatic species. Florida, however, has abundant terrestrial fossils as well. While the bones and teeth of extinct terrestrial vertebrates are usually leached and thereby weakened in soils, high concentrations of minerals in Florida's waters assist in their preservation. But fossil hunters are not likely to find dinosaur remains in Florida. Dinosaurs became extinct about 65 million years ago, and Florida's oldest surface rocks are about 45 million years old; any dinosaur fossils would lie well beneath the surface.

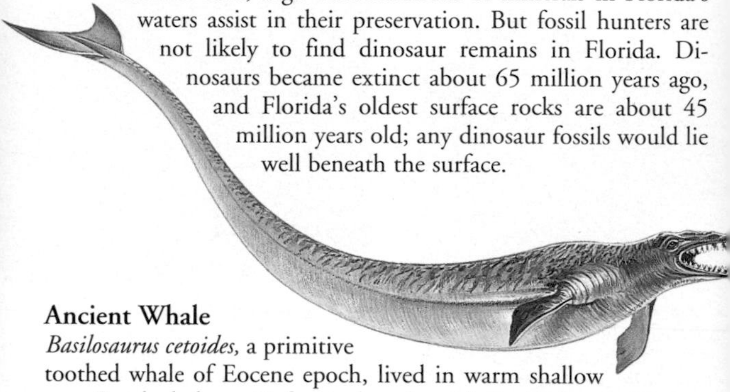

Ancient Whale

Basilosaurus cetoides, a primitive toothed whale of Eocene epoch, lived in warm shallow seas. Reached about 65 feet in length, with forelimbs modified to work as paddles; distinguished by extremely elongated vertebrae in trunk and tail. Basilosaur teeth and vertebrae are rare finds in Ocala limestone, which occurs in outcrops in northwestern to west-central Florida.

Ancient Sharks

Carcharodon species from Eocene to Pleistocene may have reached 45 feet in length, with triangular teeth up to 7 inches long. Fossils, mainly of teeth, found in Bone Valley region (Central Florida Phosphate District, which includes Polk, Hillsborough, Hardee, and Manatee Counties), at Venice Beach, and along Peace and St. Johns Rivers. Genus includes living Great White Shark.

CENOZOIC ERA

TERTIARY		
PALEOGENE		
PALEOCENE	EOCENE	OLIGOCENE
63	55	38

millions of years ago

American Mastodon

A morphologically more primitive contemporary of the mammoth, *Mammut americanum* lived from late Pliocene through Pleistocene. A forest browser with low-crowned cheek teeth consisting of rounded and pointed cones covered in thick enamel. Fossils of teeth and bones found in rivers all over Florida, as well as in ancient dune deposits along both coasts.

Three-toed Horses

Fossilized teeth and leg and foot bones of Miocene three-toed horses, *Cormohipparion* species, distinguish them from larger, one-toed modern horses, *Equus* species, which appeared by late Pliocene. *Cormohipparion* fossils have been found in Withlacoochee River (in Marion and Citrus Counties), in Hawthorne group sediments in northern and central Florida, and in Bone Valley region (see Ancient Sharks).

Equus is characterized by high-crowned cheek teeth with complex enamel pattern and strongly developed single hoof on each foot. *Equus* fossils found in Pleistocene deposits throughout Florida.

WHY DID SO MANY PLEISTOCENE ANIMALS BECOME EXTINCT?

Throughout much of the latter half of the Cenozoic Era, Florida was home to a diverse assemblage of animals, including rhinos, saber-toothed cats, giant tortoises, early horses and camels, ground sloths, armadillos, and mammoths, mastodons, and their relatives. It is thought that many of these animals found refuge in Florida during the Pleistocene Epoch as an escape from the cold and ice of glaciated North America. The cause of their demise, about 10,000 years ago, is still hotly debated among scientists; some speculate that the extinction resulted from changing climate and vegetation at the close of the Ice Age combined with overhunting by early Native Americans.

NEOGENE		QUATERNARY	
MIOCENE	PLIOCENE	PLEISTOCENE	HOLOCENE
24	5	2	.01

Florida Cave Bear

Florida Cave Bear *(Tremarctos floridanus),* common during late Pleistocene, probably survived into Holocene in Florida. Almost exclusively herbivorous. Abundant remains found in cave, sinkhole, and river deposits, including 8,000-year-old skeleton from Devil's Den sinkhole in Levy County.

Saber-toothed Cats

Saber-toothed cats *(Smilodon* species), carnivores with short, powerful limbs, used their long canines to stab prey in neck or belly. Relatively rare in mid- to late Pleistocene deposits in Florida rivers and sinkholes.

Ancient Glyptodon

A stout-limbed, tortoise-like mammal, *Glyptotherium floridanum* reached 6 to 7 feet in length. Carapace (shell) consisted of thousands of thick, polygonal, bony plates, with distinct rosette sculpturing. Lived from late Pliocene through late Pleistocene. Fossilized plates relatively common in rivers and along beaches throughout peninsular Florida.

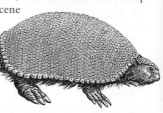

Jefferson's Ground Sloth

Megalonyx jeffersoni, a woodland browser the size of an ox, had very simple, high-crowned teeth that lacked enamel and grew continuously. Lived during mid- to late Pleistocene. Fossils found in rivers throughout Florida and in sinkholes in northern and central parts of state. Genus *Megalonyx,* which means "large claw," was first described in 1797 by Thomas Jefferson.

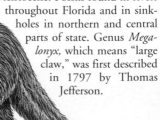

Ancient Scallops

Ancient scallops, such as *Chesapecten jeffersonius,* pictured, and *C. septenarius,* looked much like some modern scallops but larger; common in Pliocene rocks in Florida. Major difference between the two species is fewer number of ribs on *C. septenarius* shells. Good samples in excavations in Sarasota County and along Caloosahatchee River in Hendry County.

Miocene Snail

Turritella subgrundifera, a snail, was distinguished by its long slender shell. Sutures that separate each whorl scarcely impressed on shell; primary whorls marked by finer spirals. Common in Miocene rocks in Calhoun County, in panhandle.

Pliocene Snail

Cancellaria conradiana, a moderate-size snail, had generally rounded whorls, strong oblique ribs, and a broad, notched aperture (the opening in the shell through which the soft parts protrude). Dates from Pliocene; found along Miami Canal and in excavations in Charlotte County.

Ancient Foraminifera

Nummulites was a genus of disk-shaped foraminifera—small, amoeba-like marine organisms that secrete a calcareous shell—that lived in warm shallow seas from Paleocene to Oligocene. Well-preserved fossils found in Ocala limestone, which occurs in west-central and northwestern Florida.

Plant Fossils

Well-preserved wood and leaf fossils are uncommon in Florida; when found with bones and shells, they give paleontologists clues for reconstructing vegetation and climate in which ancient animals once lived. Well-preserved wood fossils found in phosphate mines of Hamilton and Polk Counties and in beds of Suwannee and Sante Fe Rivers in Columbia and Gilchrist Counties.

Habitats

Florida's mild climate and abundant water supply support natural communities of exceptional diversity, yet Florida's ecosystems must also adapt to difficult environmental conditions. Many communities cling insecurely to foundations of hard limestone or sand. In addition, the flat topography makes habitats vulnerable to seemingly small changes in water levels and other climatic factors, which can rapidly unbalance an area's ecology. Against this subtle and shifting background, it is difficult to define Florida's habitats exactly or to generalize as to their distribution. Reefs, tropical hardwood hammocks, mangrove forests, and large marsh systems tend to prevail in the south; lakes, ponds, swamps, prairies, and temperate hardwood forests are more dominant inland, in northern or central Florida; and pinelands, although most prevalent in northern and central regions, can be found nearly everywhere.

Effects of Fire

Fire at Big Cypress National Preserve

Although it is seldom directly observed, fire is a primary factor in shaping Florida's ecosystems, especially dry, well-drained habitats. Dry prairies regularly experience wildfires in a natural state; indeed, fire is instrumental in suppressing the growth of woody plants that would otherwise transform these areas into woodlands. Wet prairies, by comparison, host a specialized set of herbaceous (nonwoody) plant species that can withstand both occasional fires and periodic flooding. Some pinelands, such as the Sand Pine scrub in the panhandle, require periodic fires to trigger the release of their seeds. Habitats such as northern hardwood forests and southern hardwood hammocks are not fire-resistant and can thrive only in locations that offer relative safety from burning.

Hurricane Erin, 1995, Gulf coast

Effects of Wind

Wind has two primary effects on Florida's habitats. First, it carries salt mist and airborne sand particles ashore, which spray and scour coastal habitats. Only communities that can withstand this physical and chemical abuse—mangroves, maritime forests, and dunes stabilized by vegetation—can survive. Second, violent tropical storms destroy most habitats in their path, and any natural community positioned to experience storm damage must be able to regenerate efficiently afterward. Mangroves and maritime forests recover quickly, but hardwood hammocks destroyed by Hurricane Andrew in 1992 will take years to regenerate fully, and habitat managers must struggle in the interim to prevent alien plants such as Melaleucas and Brazilian Peppers from overgrowing these areas.

Saltwater Myrtle Creek,
Little Talbot Island State Park

Effects of Water

The level and salinity of a region's water supply are important in determining the biological communities that can exist there. Naturally, maritime environments, including reefs, salt marshes, and mangrove swamps, require a constant supply of salt water. Freshwater habitats such as wet prairies, marshes, and swamps lack tolerance for salt water and can be killed or damaged by overwashes (such as the "storm surge" caused by hurricanes) or by the infiltration of salt water into underground aquifers. With the diversion of fresh water from the Everglades during the 20th century to support the ever-growing human population, salt-tolerant mangrove forests have extended progressively farther inland.

Effects of Earth

Limestone coastline, Florida Keys

Though much of Florida's geology is based on forms of a single rock, limestone, the relationship between ecosystems and the geological substrate is nonetheless variable and complex. Sandy habitats—dunes, maritime forests, and pinewoods—are widespread, occurring inland as well as along the shore. Such habitats drain rapidly and are susceptible both to dehydration and to the loss of minerals and nutrients through leaching. Stony habitats, in which limestone exists near the surface with little accumulated organic material, include the hardwood hammocks and rimrock pinelands of southern Florida. Tree growth can be limited in these areas because nutrients are in short supply and it is difficult for trees to establish secure root systems. If the rock is particularly porous, lack of water may further limit plant life. Habitats that develop over clay substrates or very fine sand, such as the Everglades, pine flatwoods, and some northerly hardwood forests, retain water, providing favorable conditions for moisture-loving plant communities. Cypress swamps, salt marshes, and mangrove swamps have poorly oxygenated soils dominated by fine silt and "muck" that pose special challenges to plant growth.

Reefs, Keys, and Tropical Seas

Most of the Florida Keys—a low, 135-mile-long archipelago off southern Florida—began as coral reefs, enormous accumulations of calcium carbonate secreted in microscopic increments by colonies of tiny marine invertebrates. Exposed by declining sea levels during global cold spells, the shallower reefs in the chain died, leaving behind a rough limestone platform upon which terrestrial communities took hold. Where the limestone base is more porous, as in the Upper Keys (those east of Big Pine Key), habitats have developed that require less fresh surface water, such as West Indian hardwood hammocks. Where the base consists of less porous rock, as in the Lower Keys, open pine forests similar to those of the mainland rimrock region occur. The only living coral reefs in the continental United States occur off southern Florida and the Keys. Still farther south, beyond the reefs, lie the Straits of Florida, a relatively deep channel separating the Keys from Cuba. Warm currents flowing eastward through the straits combine with other warm currents from the Caribbean to form the northward-flowing Gulf Stream.

Reef Communities

Southern Florida's fringing reefs support ecosystems of great complexity. Some 650 species of fish and 40 species of coral inhabit these reefs, as do a great assortment of sponges, tunicates, marine worms, echinoderms, and other invertebrates. Intricate relationships develop among reef denizens; brightly colored "cleaning shrimp," for instance, attract reef fish, which allow themselves to be inspected for external parasites. At left, a cleaning shrimp tends to a moray eel.

Long-spined Urchin (left), Blade Fire Coral (center), Green Moray (right)

Dangers of the Reef

The stock villains of the coral reef—barracudas, sharks, moray eels, and octopuses—though potentially dangerous, tend to be nonaggressive unless cornered or confused by quick motions. By comparison, many less-notorious reef inhabitants such as sea urchins, with their sharp spines, and Fire Coral, which inflicts a burning rash, are more likely to pose a risk to divers.

Tropical Seas and the Gulf Stream

Tropical waters, such as those that extend northward from the Caribbean toward the southern edge of Florida, are generally not a richly productive habitat. Sea life depends on plankton, which in turn requires nutrients, and nutrients have a tendency to sink to the ocean bottom unless stirred up. The sun-warmed surface waters of tropical seas form a "lid" that traps nutrients in the depths and prevents them from welling up toward the surface. An exception occurs along the turbulent boundaries of ocean currents, such as the Gulf

Stream, which carries warm water (some 6.5 million cubic yards per second) eastward past the Keys and northward into the Atlantic Ocean. Marked by a continuous strand of Floating Sargassum Weed (pictured), the edge of the Gulf Stream is a focal point for much ocean life.

Coral Reef Ecology

Most coral reef colonies form in water at least 20 feet deep, where turbulence and exposure to air are less likely; yet reefs cannot survive at depths much greater than 300 feet, because photosynthetic algae living with the coral don't get enough light at great depths. These algae recirculate coral waste products (mainly phosphorus and nitrogen), thus preventing their loss from the reef ecosystem. They also secrete additional calcium carbonate, which is important in building the reef and holding it together. In some cases the algae secrete toxins that seem to deter predators from eating the coral organisms. In return for these valuable services, the algae profit from the stable environment and exposure to the sun that their coral hosts provide. In this regard, the exceptionally clear waters off southern Florida are particularly favorable for coral growth. A reef off Key Largo is pictured below.

Beaches, Dunes, and Barrier Islands

Many species of animals appear along Florida's beaches, dunes, and barrier islands at some point during the year, adding interest to these unique and distinctive communities. Migrant land birds use coastal habitats as they travel, often taking cover in thickets or maritime forests. However, comparatively few animals reside in dune and dry beach habitats permanently, as the loose mineral soil there does not support large terrestrial communities. Off Florida's Atlantic coastline, strong currents and punishing waves tend to constrain the diversity of inshore habitats. Specialized organisms do best here, such as burrowers that have adapted to the ocean's turbulence.

Sanderlings

Beaches: The Intertidal Zone

During much of the year, a colorful assortment of Coquina clams is momentarily exposed with each wave that hits Florida's beaches. As the wave recedes, small flocks of Sanderlings track the water's edge with choreographed precision, snatching up clams and other small invertebrates before they can dig back into the sand. The ultimate in short-distance migrants, Coquinas can sense shifts in ocean levels: On rising tides they move to the seafloor surface, allowing the waves to carry them up the beach; the process is reversed on falling tides, when the clams ride back to deeper water. As venturing away from

Coquinas

protection in this manner exposes Coquinas to great danger, the evolutionary trade-off seems to be that their "tide-following" behavior keeps the clams in the turbulent part of the surf, where food is most available.

Barrier Islands and Lagoons

Habitat zones on barrier islands—dunes, thickets, maritime forests, and marshes—are shaped by wind (blowing saline mists and blasting sand) and water (tidal activity and over-washes). The Great Southern White

Barrier islands, Canaveral National Seashore

butterfly prefers barrier islands, and seldom occurs far inland except in extreme southern Florida. The lagoons formed between barrier islands and the mainland offer protected habitat for fish and other coastal fauna. These lagoons are often rimmed by salt marshes and, in the south, by mangroves. At low tide their broad mudflats provide feeding grounds for herons, egrets, Roseate Spoonbills, and mixed flocks of shorebirds, each bird using its distinctively shaped bill to forage for a specific type of prey.

Dry Beach and Dunes

Ghost Crab

The dry portions of the beach, above the maximum high-tide line, are fragile habitats, constantly transformed by wind, storms, and tidal activity. Yet these natural forces are withstood by modest-looking plants such as Sea Oats, whose deep anchor roots and extensive network of shallow, root-like rhizomes secure their own habitat. The exposed nature of this zone makes it treacherous for smaller invertebrates, which frequently hide in burrows by day for

Sea Oats, Canaveral National Seashore

protection, venturing out only at night to forage. An example is the elusive, fast-moving Ghost Crab, a terrestrial species that occasionally dips its gills in seawater to keep them moist but would drown if continuously submerged. Dry beaches and dunes provide ideal nesting habitat for coastal bird species, such as gulls, terns, and shorebirds. Finding safety in numbers, these colonial nesters band together to attack intruders.

Maritime Forests

Maritime forests, which include a variety of woodland habitats that occur near the shore, grow in interrupted patches along much of the state's coast, predominantly on the lagoon side of barrier islands. The rigors of the seaside environment enforce certain similarities in these habitats. For one thing, the sandy, highly acidic soils on which they grow are typically deficient in minerals and organic nutrients. As a result, maritime forests frequently contain dense thickets and tangles of vines, which can quickly cycle nutrients into living material before they are permanently lost through leaching or erosion. Along Florida's northern coast, and to a decreasing extent farther south, Live Oaks form dense canopies in maritime forests; tolerance to salt spray makes Live Oaks particularly suited to living along the shore. The slow decomposition of their thick, waxy leaves, which are shed throughout the year rather than all at once in the fall, creates a timed release of minerals that may increase recycling efficiency in the forest ecosystem.

Ancient Live Oak, Canaveral National Seashore

Salt Marshes

A salt marsh is a low-growth habitat made up predominantly of nonwoody plants that is regularly inundated with salt water as a result of tidal action. With each tidal cycle, salt marshes are drained of wastes and then reflooded with nutrients. This flushing action is what makes them one of the richest habitats on earth. They offer protected spawning places for thousands of marine organisms and feeding grounds for a host of aquatic and terrestrial predators. In addition, salt marshes generate excess nutrients that nourish nearby bays and coastal seas. Despite such abundance, saltmarsh life requires many adaptations: to changing water and temperature levels, to high salinity, to silty and poorly oxygenated soil, and to the risks of the food chain. Florida's salt marshes and associated estuaries (brackish river entrances) benefit from the state's warm climate and relatively mild tidal action; they have greater species diversity than similar habitats northward on the Atlantic coast.

Mud Fiddlers

Saltmarsh Communities

Although salt marshes may appear uniform at first glance, they actually have many subtle gradations that affect the distribution of their inhabitants. The seaward edge of the marsh, for example, tends to be more saline than landward areas, which affects local life forms on the basis of their level of salt tolerance. Marsh channels sustain lusher growths of marsh grass and allow aquatic life forms to penetrate the interior of the marsh, especially at high tide. Still, the dominant condition to which saltmarsh life must adapt is constant flux. Fiddler crabs, for example, scuttle along the exposed mudflats to forage at low tide, then retreat to their burrows at high tide. Several species occupy different marsh subhabitats; their names—Sand Fiddler, Mud Fiddler, and Brackish-water Fiddler—reflect their preferred environments.

Life on Salt Pans

Salt pans—irregularly flooded areas in the mud of salt marshes where evaporation has created particularly high salt concentrations—are distinguished by the kinds of plants that can survive there. Saltworts and glassworts, waxy-leaved succulents that can tolerate high levels of salinity, are the dominant vegetation in many salt pans. Caterpillars of the Eastern Pygmy-Blue, the smallest of Florida's butterflies, feed exclusively on these plants; adult butterflies often congregate nearby in large numbers.

Saltwort and Southern Glasswort, Everglades National Park

Needlerush and cordgrasses, St. Marks National Wildlife Refuge

Saltmarsh Grasses

Without hardy plants such as cordgrasses and Needlerush, there would be no salt marshes. These salt-tolerant grasses colonize oxygen-poor mudflats, trapping nutrients and building soil. Their leaves expel excess salt, and their hollow stems conduct oxygen to their roots.

Clapper Rail

Marsh Birds

Although many birds use salt marshes for nesting or feeding, few are as completely associated with this habitat as the Clapper Rail, an elusive skulker that seldom occurs anywhere else. The Saltmarsh Sharp-tailed Sparrow and the Seaside Sparrow are also restricted to coastal marshes. Of two endemic Florida races of Seaside Sparrow, one is threatened (Cape Sable race) and the other recently became extinct (Dusky race).

Seaside Sparrow

Mangrove Swamps

The term "mangrove" is generally applied to species from several families of tropical trees—in Florida, the Red Mangrove, Black Mangrove, and White Mangrove—that share the trait of being specially adapted to tidally flooded coastal banks. Mangrove communities flourish where average annual temperatures exceed 65 degrees Fahrenheit and there are few hard freezes. Florida's central and southern coasts are fringed by some of the world's most extensive mangrove swamps; these are most abundant in the south and southwest, where the gradual slope of the coastline allows the modest tide to cover and uncover an extensive strip of coast, fostering the growth of mangrove swamps several miles wide in the intertidal mud deposits that are protected from large breaking waves. The Ten Thousand Islands are made up of mangroves.

Prop Root Communities

All three Florida mangroves have exposed roots that "breathe" through pores, facilitating oxygen uptake in a submerged habitat. In the Red Mangrove these roots originate as dangling aerial roots that eventually grow down, forming large, intertangled loops called prop roots. These distinctive, maze-like prop roots create a complex microhabitat, important in providing sanctuary for young marine organisms, many of which are commercially valuable as adults. Juvenile West Indies Spiny Lobsters, for example, remain among Red Mangrove prop roots for the first two years of life. Black (and often White) Mangroves have conspicuous "breathing roots," erect finger-like branches of the underground roots that often make mangrove swamps impenetrable.

Red Mangrove prop roots

Mangrove Propagation

Mangroves do not propagate using ordinary means of dispersal. Rather, young plants begin to grow while still attached to the parent tree, developing into propagules that drop into the water and float along until an appropriate substrate is encountered. The germinating fruits of the Red Mangrove are quite spectacular: pendulous, torpedo-like seedlings dangling from the branches. The lima-bean–like pods of the Black Mangrove split almost

Red Mangrove propagules

Ten Thousand Islands, Everglades National Park

immediately when the fruit falls. And though they are not as visible, the spongy-coated, ribbed fruits of the White Mangrove often sprout as soon as they are stranded in soil. Propagules of all three mangroves take root mainly in sheltered areas or on shorelines with relatively low wave energy, which can be found throughout much of the southwestern and southern parts of the state.

Mangrove Swamp Ecology

The ecology of mangrove swamps closely parallels that of salt marshes: Salt-tolerant mangroves extend out from protected shores, trapping detritus and stabilizing land as they spread. And, as with marshes, the daily flushing and replenishment of the tides is critical to the swamps' survival. Mangroves limit their internal salt concentration by screening out salt as they absorb water and/or by excreting it through specialized glands in their leaves. Though mangroves can survive in fresh water, they generally cannot compete with hardier plants that grow there.

Bird Life of Mangrove Overwash Islands

In the shifting, regularly inundated world of mangrove overwash islands (small mangrove-covered islets that are periodically flooded by tides) in the Keys and Florida Bay, mangrove thickets provide unique roosting and nesting sites for herons, egrets, White Ibises,

Nesting Magnificent Frigatebirds, Dry Tortugas National Park

Brown Pelicans, and Magnificent Frigatebirds. A few species of birds are closely associated with mangroves, including the Golden race of the Yellow Warbler, the Black-whiskered Vireo, and the elusive Mangrove Cuckoo, which skulks in the dense understory of mangroves and tropical hardwood hammocks.

Rivers, Swamps, and Lakes

More than any other state in the lower 48, Florida is a land of water, a description that applies equally well to its inland habitats as to those along the coast. The state's flat topography, porous bedrock, and abundant rainfall create a complex array of aquatic habitats, including rivers, swamps (forested wetlands), and persistent openwater habitats such as lakes, springs, and ponds with depths greater than 6'7" (beyond the range of emergent vegetation). Aquatic habitats such as these are biologically rich, supporting numerous species of fish, legions of aquatic invertebrates, turtles, water snakes, and amphibians, abundant aquatic birds, and several distinctive mammals, including the endangered Manatee.

Bald Cypress, Withlacoochee River

River Swamps and Bay Galls

Ecologists distinguish many categories of swampland in Florida, and though much of this habitat has been lost, swamps as a whole still account for some 10 percent of the state's total land area. Especially in the north, river floodplains, or bottomlands, support particularly diverse swampy forests composed of Bald Cypress, Red Maple, tupelos, and other flood-tolerant species. Rarely more than a few miles wide, these riparian swamps are useful in dispersing the runoff from storms by absorbing excess flows. They are also home to a wide variety of wildlife, including Northern River Otters, Wood Ducks, American Alligators, Barred Owls, Prothonotary Warblers, and many other distinctive species. Bay galls are a specialized class of swamp that occur in low-lying wooded habitats, such as pine flatwoods, where the water table is near the surface. These swamps are generally limited in size but nevertheless support distinctive flora.

Little Blue Heron, Corkscrew Swamp

Lakes and Ponds

The porous limestone that lies beneath much of Florida gradually dissolves in contact with water; as a result, vast underground waterways have formed beneath much of the state. The eventual subsidence of such underground cavities results in sinkholes or in shallow lakes. Few of Florida's lakes and ponds are very deep; the average depth of most is between 15 and 20 feet, including Lake Okeechobee, despite its enormous surface area. The surfaces of some lakes and ponds are concealed by rafts of floating lily pads, Water Lettuce, Duckweed, or other vegetation. About 40 native fish species, including the Bluegill and the Largemouth Bass, breed in Florida lakes, along with about 20 introduced species. To date, nonnative fish have been less successful in invading Florida's lakes than its rivers and canals.

Springs and Rivers

Florida's many springs and rivers are surface evidence of the state's active and complex water table. Some springs produce enormous quantities of clear, warm mineral water—hundreds of millions of gallons a day in some cases. Their mild temperatures and consistent flow make some of Florida's springs important wintering grounds for the Manatee and other species of aquatic wildlife. There are dozens of clear springs between Tampa and Tallahassee. Florida's rivers, which host a diverse

Cypress Springs

assemblage of fish and freshwater mollusks, are at significant risk from pollution and other disturbances.

Cypress dome, Everglades National Park

Cypress Swamps

Of Florida's swamplands, cypress swamps may be the most distinctive. The towering Bald Cypresses and somewhat shorter Pond Cypresses are conifers that lose their foliage during the winter dry season. Because their seeds cannot germinate underwater, cypresses require habitats that are at least periodically dry. They grow in several distinct settings around the state: on bits of elevated terrain in sawgrass marshes, where they may form characteristic domes; in mucky terrain, where they form long, narrow formations called "strands"; and in swamps along river floodplains. Cypresses create a habitat for many other species, including such colorful epiphytes (air plants) as bromeliads, orchids, and ferns, which grow on their trunks and branches.

Freshwater Marshes

If there is a single habitat that symbolizes Florida's wild lands in the public mind, it is most likely the Everglades, an immense freshwater marsh covering about 4,000 square miles in the southern tip of the state (originally it was three times this size). Many smaller marshes occur throughout Florida, byproducts of the state's flat topography and high water table. By definition, marshes are shallow wetlands with low, emergent, soft-stemmed vegetation, few or no trees, and standing water throughout most of the year. They usually form around lakes or river borders, where nonporous, clay-based subsoils prevent rapid seepage. A healthy marsh can support abundant life, including lush stands of sawgrass up to 10 feet tall, immense flocks of wading birds, fish, exotic plants, alligators, and much more.

Freshwater marsh, Big Cypress National Preserve

The Everglades

The Everglades, a vast "river of grass" called *pa-hay-okee* ("grassy waters") by the Seminoles, begins as an overflow from Lake Okeechobee. It meanders southward on a very shallow gradient into Florida Bay; kept above the water table by a layer of clay-based soil, it finally dissipates in brackish mangrove forests as it approaches the coast. Along this route to the sea, the Everglades consists of mile upon mile of sawgrass marsh interrupted occasionally by hardwood hammocks that develop where the ground is slightly elevated.

American Alligator and heron at Taylor Slough

Sloughs

Florida's marshes are typically shallow and often seasonal—they can dry out completely during severe winter droughts. The deepest and most permanent areas in a marsh are referred to as sloughs. In winter they serve as concentration points for much of a marsh's wildlife, sustaining its populations until rains return. A well-known example is Taylor Slough in Everglades National Park; Anhinga Trail, which runs along its edge, has long been a prime observation site for wintering birds and other marsh life, including alligators.

Freshwater marsh, Fakahatchee Strand State Park

Emergent Abundance

Freshwater marshes produce an abundance of emergent vegetation (plants whose leaves or stems rise above the water surface from a submerged rootstock). The decaying remains of these plants form deep layers of peat and other organic soils. A main constituent of this organic residue in many of the state's marshes is Sawgrass—actually a sedge, not a grass—whose leaf edges are quite saw-like. The primary plant in non-Sawgrass marshes may be a cattail, water-lily, or iris. Species diversity can be especially great where a single, dominant species such as Sawgrass does not crowd out potential competitors.

Gator Holes

Alligators play an important role in Florida's wetland ecology. To escape the severe droughts that periodically affect the state's wetlands, some alligators burrow in the mud and remain dormant, but others thrash actively, creating a depression that fills with groundwater. While such "gator holes" are not limited

Gator hole, Everglades National Park

to marsh habitats, during prolonged dry spells they are critical to the survival of many aquatic species that inhabit Florida's marshes, and so are legally protected in Everglades National Park.

Apple Snail Ecology

Florida Apple Snail

Sawgrass marshes are a productive habitat, but they are sometimes difficult for terrestrial herbivores to exploit. An ideal grazer in this semiaquatic environment is the Florida Apple Snail, a colorful gastropod that thrives on sawgrass. This snail is a primary food for a number of avian predators, including the Limpkin and the Snail Kite. Because the Florida Apple Snail prefers specific water levels, its predators are often required to move from place to place as conditions fluctuate.

Prairies

Florida's prairies, among the state's most distinctive wild areas, are generally grassy expanses dominated by low-growth vegetation. They exhibit considerable variation and bear only a distant relationship to prairies found elsewhere on the continent. Ecologists recognize two general types: wet prairies, inundated during some portion of the year (typically from 50 to 150 days), and dry prairies, inundated only after heavy rains. Although both kinds of prairie found in Florida have certain features in common—for example, low herbaceous vegetation, dependence on regular wildfires to maintain that low-growth character, and periodic inundation—authorities generally consider dry prairies to be more closely related to pine flatwoods and wet prairies to be more closely related to marshes than either kind of prairie is to the other. Each prairie type has characteristic plant and animal communities.

Sandhill Crane

Dry Prairies

Situated on sandy, acidic soil, dry prairies are typically dominated by wiregrasses, broomsedges, or similar species. These nearly treeless expanses, which occur widely throughout mid-central Florida, generally have a low water table, causing them to be dry in nature, yet they also have a hardpan substrate that deters drainage, causing them to flood easily during rainy periods. The ecology and appearance of many dry prairies have been altered over the decades by grazing and other disturbances, and a great deal of prairie habitat has been lost to agriculture and development. But considerable tracts of this habitat persist at sites such as Myakka River State Park, southeast of Sarasota.

Dry-prairie Birds

Several isolated bird populations occur in Florida's dry prairies, hundreds of miles from their nearest relatives. Many, such as the non-migratory Florida race of Sandhill Crane, are not considered full species. But as techniques for tracing the evolutionary relationships among populations improve, some of these races are now being regarded as separate species. The Florida Scrub Jay, for example, was recently split from the Western Scrub Jay partly on the basis of differences in social behavior. Other distinctive animals of Florida's dry prairies are the Crested Caracara, the Burrowing Owl, the Hispid Cotton Rat, the Eastern Harvest Mouse, and the Eastern Spotted Skunk.

Wet Prairies

Prairie grasses, Lake Kissimmee State Park

Wet prairies occupy a middle position between freshwater marshes and dry prairies, and occur mostly in the middle of the state. Generally at lower elevations than surrounding habitats, they are wet and boggy for much of the year, yet the flora retains definite terrestrial characteristics, such as an inability to survive continual immersion. Wet prairies abound in moisture-loving herbaceous plants such as sundews, sedges, and meadow beauties, and are among the best places anywhere to observe reptiles and amphibians. Paynes Prairie, south of Gainesville, is noted for its abundant populations of frogs and snakes.

Insectivorous Plants and Herb Bogs

Among the most interesting wet-prairie plants are those that supplement their diet in nutrient-poor environments by capturing and ingesting insects. Four general types

Trumpet Pitcher Plants, Apalachicola National Forest

are represented in Florida: bladderworts, sundews, butterworts, and pitcher plants. Each has a distinct method for capturing prey. For example, the leaves of pitcher plants are modified into vats, or "pitchers," in which water collects. The leaves produce a chemical that lures crawling insects to the rim of the vat; once inside, the insects cannot maintain their footing on the interior leaf walls, which are covered with loose, waxy scales and stiff, short, downward-pointing hairs. Eventually the prey plunges into the pitcher below, where it is digested. Large stands of Trumpet Pitcher Plants can be found in "herb bogs" of the panhandle, which occur in seepage zones between pinewoods and swamps or streams.

Bear Country

When people think of "Black Bear country," they may imagine Maine's north woods or the Great Smoky Mountains, but the Black Bear is equally at home in Florida's wet prairies. (A marauding Black Bear, Ol' Slewfoot, was a central character

Black Bears

in Marjorie Kinnan Rawlings's *The Yearling,* set in central Florida in the late 1800s.) Wet prairies contain a wide assortment of plants and small animals on which bears can feed; of equal importance, prairie pools offer cooling relief for the large, fur-covered mammals during Florida's hot summers.

Upland Wooded Areas

Florida's upland wooded habitats occur on elevated ground that is not regularly inundated—though given the state's high water table, even upland woods can at times be quite sloshy. These woodlands are a diverse collection of habitats. In the south, the tropical influence of the West Indies is apparent, whereas the north has temperate forests typical of the southeastern United States. A variety of distinct intermediate woodland forms exist in between.

Slash Pine and wiregrass community,
Apalachicola National Forest

Pinelands and Scrub

Well adapted to dry, sandy soil conditions, pinelands and pine scrub are prominent features of Florida's interior landscape. Ecologists recognize many categories of pinelands, although the differences among them—defined by such factors as drainage, elevation, fire resistance, soil composition, and acidity—can be difficult to discern. Pineland habitats are maintained by fire, without which they would transform to hardwood communities. Most of the major pinewood types can be seen at Ocala National Forest in the north.

Pine Flatwoods

Pine flatwoods, low-lying pinelands that grow on sandy, relatively poorly drained soil, are Florida's most extensive ecosystem, occupying about half the total land area. Although pine flatwoods are seasonally moist, and sometimes flooded, dry-season fires are necessary

Saw Palmetto and Slash Pines, Osceola
National Forest

to maintain them as pinewoods rather than allowing them to transform into hardwood forests. The overstory—consisting principally of Longleaf Pines, Pond Pines, and Slash Pines—varies from nearly closed to open and savanna-like. Undisturbed pine flatwoods tend to have an open understory composed of palmetto and shrubs such as Wax Myrtle, Tar Flower, Gallberry, and Fetterbush; after a fire, the understory is usually grassy for a period of time. With the suppression of fire in recent years, many pine flatwoods have lost their open understory and now resemble flatwood scrub. Flat-

Florida Panther

wood inhabitants include the Pine Woods Tree Frog, Eastern Fox Squirrel, Brown-headed Nuthatch, and Florida Panther.

Scrub

The term "scrub" is applied to several different habitats in Florida, including Sand Pine, oak, and coastal scrub, as well as to flatwood scrub, a transitional habitat between pine flatwoods and true scrub. The harsh conditions of scrub environments tend to limit the development of trees, which often amount to no more than a stunted overstory of Sand Pines. In its most selective sense, true scrub refers to an exceptionally dry oak or pine-oak habitat found along the

Scrub, Lake Wales Ridge

state's central ridge line, growing over a deep layer of well-drained, nutrient-poor quartz sand. Prime examples include Big Scrub of Ocala National Forest and relict scrublands of the Lake Wales Ridge. Scrub habitat is maintained by periodic intense fires, which occur every 20 to 80 years.

Florida's Refugias

Several times during the last 2 million years, central and southern Florida were mostly underwater, except for a few isolated bits of elevated land that remained above sea level. These biological islands, called refugias, served as lifeboats for terrestrial plants and animals, dozens of which evolved into new species during their isolation and are now unique to central Florida. The scrub habitat that now occupies these sites is among Florida's most distinctive ecosystems, similar in many ways to the deserts of the Southwest (the two locations have a number of plant and animal groups in common). Florida has an exceptionally large number of endemic plant species—perhaps 11 percent of its plants occur only in Florida—and a majority of these occur in scrub habitats. Many are listed by the federal or state government as threatened or endangered. The refugias also created an array of animal scrub specialists such as the Florida Mouse, Florida Scrub Jay, Florida Scrub Lizard, and several skinks and snakes.

Rimrock pines, Long Pine Key

Rimrock Pines

This unique pinewood community grows on a thin layer of soil atop a rough, pitted base of limestone, or rimrock. It occurs only in southern Florida, on islands such as Big Pine Key, and at such sites as Long Pine Key, an elevated pinewood "island" in the Everglades. Slash Pine tends to dominate these open woodlands, which are interspersed with ankle-twisting cavities in the dissolving limestone. The Key Deer, a tiny endangered race of White-tailed Deer, lives in the rimrock forests of Big Pine Key.

High Pinelands

Another form of upland pinewoods are the high pines, including sandhills and clayhills. Sandhills, typically open and almost park-like in character, have an overstory of tall, widely spaced Longleaf Pines and an understory primarily of wiregrasses interspersed with low shrubs. The understory is somewhat denser in clayhills (found in the northern panhandle), owing to their clay-based subsoil. High pine habitats are maintained by rather frequent low-intensity fires, occurring once every one to ten years.

High pine sandhill, Osceola National Forest

Longleaf Pines are highly fire-adapted, even as saplings, and individual trees may live to be more than 500 years old. High pines support a relatively large number of bird species, including the Pine Warbler, Brown-headed Nuthatch, Red-headed and Red-cockaded Woodpeckers, and Bachman's Sparrow.

Gopher Tortoise Ecology

Burrowing species are prominent in habitats that are sufficiently elevated and well drained. Florida's high pinelands are home to a number of burrowers, including Southeastern Pocket Gophers and scarab beetles, both of which are important in mixing the soil. The quintessential burrower, however, is the Gopher Tortoise, whose methodically constructed tunnels are the focal point of an entire mini-ecosystem. Not only are its burrows home to the declining Gopher Frog and Eastern race of Indigo Snake, but 300 other species of vertebrates use or rely on the burrows for shelter or food. Despite its

Gopher Tortoise

pivotal importance to this array of commensal species, the tortoise is itself declining. While hunting was banned in 1987, loss of habitat and transformation of the woodland understory due to fire control continue to reduce its numbers.

Tropical hardwood hammock, Key Largo Hammocks State Botanical Site

Tropical Hardwood Hammocks

In southern Florida, tropical hardwood trees grow on elevated coastal ridges and islands of ground that are slightly above the level of surrounding marshes and other wet habitats, forming what are called hammocks. In the upper Keys and southern peninsula, hardwood hammocks consist of West Indian species such as Gumbo Limbo, Pigeon-plum, Poison-wood, and Mahogany (though much of the latter has been removed), plus many tropical vines and epiphytes. A single hammock may contain scores of different trees that can be difficult to identify because many have leaves with a similar pointed shape that facilitates the shedding of water. A number of colorful tree snails and butter-

Gumbo Limbo

flies are closely associated with tropical hammocks, including Schaus' Swallowtails (endangered), Florida Whites, Ruddy Daggerwings, Florida Purplewings, and Hammock Skippers.

Temperate Hardwood Forests

Live Oak

In northern Florida, above the Cody Escarpment, are hardwood forests that resemble those found in Georgia and northward. Characteristic species include Live Oaks (often draped with Spanish Moss), Sweetgum, hickories, and magnolias. Many of these species cannot tolerate the poorly drained, fire-prone areas lying farther southward. In far northern Florida, the hardwood forests intermix with southeastern pinewoods. Look here for Carolina Chickadees, Oak Toads, Virginia Opossums, and Great Horned Owls.

The Impact of Human Settlement

Little evidence remains of the thousands of years of habitation by Native Americans in Florida, yet it took modern inhabitants only about a century to greatly transform the landscape.

Native Americans in Florida

By the time the Spanish established their first permanent colony at St. Augustine in 1565, Native Americans had already inhabited the peninsula for nearly 12,000 years. Originally hunter-gatherers, many tribes later became skilled agriculturalists, growing corn, squash, beans, tobacco, and other crops. They ate fish and shellfish, sometimes immobilizing the fish in confined pools using poisons extracted from plants. The demise of these early tribes, whose populations probably never exceeded a few hundred thousand, came in the 1700s due to European disease and slave raids. Their place was taken by modern inhabitants, including the Seminole, who are descended from more northerly tribes such as the Creek and Eufala.

European and American Settlement

Royal Palm Hotel, Miami, 1899

Most early European colonists avoided Florida. Few wanted to contend with the wet habitats and often hostile tribes, and the region remained sparsely settled for centuries, serving primarily as a political pawn until coming under U.S. control in 1821. The Everglades were not even explored by Europeans until the 1830s. It was not until after the Civil War that development began in earnest, centered from the outset on tourism, as coastal communities became popular with wealthy northern vacationers. Forests were clear-cut to make way for massive new settlements, and rivers were dredged to create farmland for citrus and sugar cane. An east-coast rail line was built with luxury resorts at each stop—most notably in Miami, which by the turn of the century was booming. Be-

Construction of East Coast Railway, Overseas Extension, Long Pine Key

tween 1920 and 1924 alone, Miami's population more than tripled, from 30,000 to 100,000. Before World War II Florida ranked 27th among the states in population; by 1960 it had risen to 10th and in 1990 it was fourth, with a population of nearly 13 million. The impact of this activity on Florida's habitats, and on vulnerable plants and animals living in the state, has been enormous.

Citrus grove, 1890s

Diversion of Water Flows

In the 1920s a pair of hurricanes killed thousands of people living south of Lake Okeechobee. These disasters, along with escalating demands from farmers, ranchers, and developers, spurred a series of huge water-control projects. Excess fresh water once crept slowly southward from the Kissimmee marshlands into Lake Okeechobee each summer, spilling over the southern rim of the lake and on to the Everglades. The U.S. Army Corps of Engineers channeled the lake's feeder rivers, diverted its water, and constructed massive dikes along the lakeshore. The environmental consequences of these actions quickly became apparent. With its wetlands nearly 80 percent

Original and straightened portions of Kissimmee River

destroyed, the Kissimmee River basin sustained a 93 percent drop in waterfowl use. Without wetland buffers to moderate the impact of agricultural pollutants, the lake became overrun with oxygen-depleting plant growth. Wading bird populations in the Everglades dropped more than 90 percent, from an estimated 1½ million in 1935 to a mere 70,000 in 1972. Reduced freshwater flow through the Everglades also dangerously increased the salinity of Florida Bay, fostering an invasion of algae that killed the bay's Turtle Grass, a plant relied upon by young Tarpons and Bonefish, both classified as threatened. Without adequate freshwater flows to maintain the area's underground aquifers, some aquifers began to subside or to experience saltwater inflows. A series of remedial steps has been initiated in recent years, including a gradual reversal of channelization of the Kissimmee River, acquisition of more wetlands around the Everglades, and curtailment of agricultural runoff.

The Price of Progress

Florida's staggering population growth combined with its suitability for various types of agriculture have placed severe demands on natural resources. Millions of acres of prime habitat have been destroyed to make room for condominiums, malls, marinas, resorts, citrus groves, and fields of sugar cane. Massive water-control projects and pollution runoff have caused extensive damage to the environment, particularly to wetlands and their wildlife.

Tamiami Trail, 1927 (left), 1990s (right)

Resorts, Roads, and Urban Areas

Much of the development of the last 50 years has removed environmentally sensitive habitats near the coast—such as maritime forests, hardwood hammocks, and mangroves—or biologically valuable, "scenic" upland habitats—sandhill pinewoods, for example. To accommodate their new human neighbors, coastal marshes have been drained, sprayed, and flooded in an effort to control mosquito populations. In Tampa Bay, 81 percent of the original seagrass was destroyed by 1991. Ambitious road-building projects have been undertaken to answer the travel needs of the state's growing population, starting with the Tamiami Trail, the first east–west auto road across the Everglades, which opened in 1928. More than 100,000 miles of state, local, and interstate roadways now exist in Florida. As these roads invade sensitive habitats, the incidence of automobile collisions with wildlife, including rare species such as the Florida Panther and Key Deer, has increased.

Cane fields, Lake Okeechobee

Agriculture

Florida's long growing season—all year in the south—makes it a prime location for many forms of agriculture. About 7.5 million acres in Florida are classified as agricultural. The modern citrus industry began in the early 1800s, probably at the Kingsley Plantation near Jacksonville. Over the years, hard freezes that destroyed groves spurred the southward relocation of citrus plantations. The development of frozen concentrate in 1950, offering extended shelf life and transportability for citrus products, allowed larger-scale production and distribution. Unfortunately, the natural areas most favorable for new citrus groves include central scrub and prairie regions that are home to many of Florida's rarest endemic plant and animal species. Even more than the citrus industry, vegetable farming practices and sugar cane plantations have had a detrimental impact on the natural environment. Many of the wetlands that once provided a natural flow of fresh water through the Everglades were drained to make way for cropland, which depletes the soil of minerals without replacing them. Wood Storks and other wading birds in the south have suffered from the loss of wetland feeding areas, and the runoff of pollutants from sugar cane fields southeast of Lake Okeechobee has caused serious damage to plants and wildlife in the Everglades.

Natural Slash Pine woods (left), Longleaf Pine plantation (right)

Lumbering

Most of Florida's natural woodlands have been lumbered and replaced with "plantations" managed for timber harvest. The effects of these practices have been substantial. Planted timber zones tend to have lower species diversity than natural woodlands, and less-diverse and less-productive undergrowth. The removal of mature trees with nesting cavities seriously limits the prospects of species that depend on such resources, such as the endangered Red-cockaded Woodpecker, which nests in old-growth Longleaf Pines.

Cattle Ranching

When cattle grazing began on a commercial scale in the 1800s, mostly on reclaimed wet prairies north and west of Lake Okeechobee, it was big business. In early times, cows were allowed to roam the prairies and scrublands freely. "Cow hunters" literally tracked the cattle down individually at round-up time, using gunshot-like cracks of the whip to move them along (hence the term "cracker" as a general name for Floridians). Cattle grazing can be highly detrimental, a problem exacerbated in 1952 by the passage of a law that required cattle to be fenced. Such fencing reduces the natural character of rangelands by increasing the potential for overgrazing, and may encourage the replacement of native vegetation with specialized forage grasses. Fortunately, a number of ranchers have allowed their property to retain much of its natural character, thereby permitting threatened species such as the Crested Caracara to persist.

The Impact on Flora and Fauna

Human activity has many unintended but nevertheless deleterious effects on wildlife. Although much of the damage wrought by humans on Florida's environment has been inadvertent, in a few cases harmful activities have been more direct. But with "ecotourist" revenues increasing, there are solid economic as well as esthetic grounds for returning Florida's natural areas to a state of health.

Direct Exploitation

A notorious example of human exploitation of nature was the "plume trade" of the late 1800s and early 1900s, in which Snowy and Great Egrets were hunted nearly to extinction for their ornate breeding feathers, which were used to adorn women's hats. The Florida and National Audubon Societies were formed to combat this practice, and egrets are now fully recovered. Similarly, the American Alligator was

Egret plume hat

reduced to the brink of extinction by the late 1960s, hunted mainly for its hide. Recovery efforts have been highly successful, and there may be more alligators in Florida today than ever before. Far less assured is the fate of several marine turtle species that use Florida's beaches for egg-laying; in the past these huge creatures were slaugh-

Atlantic Ridley

tered for their meat as they came ashore. At present, large-scale illegal poaching of tree snails and epiphytic orchids from hardwood hammocks has reduced or eliminated them from many sites. Some collectors have destroyed hammocks containing unique varieties of tree snails in order to enhance the value of their collections.

Introduced Animals

With its hospitable climate, Florida hosts a wide variety of introduced plants and animals, many of them serious pests. The large and voracious Giant Toad, originally from South America, devours many native organisms. Among introduced reptiles, the Brown Anole has penetrated a wide range of habitats, apparently outcompeting the native Green Anole, as the latter has declined sharply since its Cuban relative colonized the state.

Brown Anole, male

Inadvertent Damage to Wildlife

Population growth and unabated tourism have meant a rise in unintentional damage to wildlife in Florida. Motorboats, for example, account for a high percentage of Manatee deaths; there

Manatee with propeller scars

are at present only 2,000 to 3,000 Manatees left in Florida. Bright lights along coastal strips can disorient marine turtles trying to come ashore to nest and young hatchlings trying to return to the sea. Offshore, illegal anchorage and boat collisions in shallow water damage coral reefs and cause muddying of the water, which chokes coral polyps and screens out light. Additionally, direct contact with the coral by divers can kill off the coral organisms.

Melaleuca

Introduced Plants

More than 1,000 nonnative plant species inhabit Florida, dominating more than 1.5 million acres in the state. The Melaleuca, an Australian import introduced in the early 1900s to help drain wetlands, has proved all too efficient at wetland depletion, and ecologists are battling its spread into the Everglades. The Australian-pine, widely planted along canals, beaches, and near towns as a windbreak, outcompetes native plants, is of little use to native wildlife, forms dense root mats along shorelines that can interfere with nesting turtles and crocodiles, and is difficult to eradicate. Another resistant species is the Brazilian Pepper, a densely vegetated and thicket-forming understory plant that crowds out native vegetation; it is now widespread in southern Florida.

Conservation Activities

Florida has a growing number of devoted conservationists and organizations. Broad conservation initiatives such as the "Save the Everglades" campaign are combined with specific programs to assist particular habitats or species. Large-scale projects are now under way to preserve the badly endangered Florida Panther, to breed the endangered Schaus' Swallowtail butterfly in captivity and release it back into suitable habitats in the Keys and southern mainland, and even to re-establish a colony of Whooping Cranes, former inhabitants of the state extirpated long ago.

Florida Panther

Weather

Florida straddles the indefinite boundary between the tropics and the temperate latitudes, and is subject to the atmospheric currents and storm systems of both climate zones. In summer the weather is undeniably tropical, with humid air wafted in by trade winds off the Atlantic Ocean, while in winter, cold fronts—some bearing mild air, others bringing a brisk chill—sweep the state.

Wind Patterns

Earth's atmosphere is driven into motion as hot tropical air rises and spreads toward the poles and cold polar air sinks and flows toward the equator. Earth's rotation warps this north–south exchange of warm and cold air into vast wind patterns, including the prevailing westerlies, a broad west-to-east current of air that flows over most of the United States and southern Canada, and the trade winds, which blow westward across the tropical Atlantic and other oceans. Florida's climate is influenced by both of these great wind currents.

The Progress of a Frontal Storm System

As a low-pressure storm system starts, a warm front, usually on the east side of the storm center, marks the leading edge of northbound warm air. As it rises over colder, denser air to its north, the warm air produces moderate but steady rain (usually in northern Florida).

West of the storm's center, arctic air plunges south behind a cold front, along which heavier cold air shoves like a wedge beneath the warm, usually moist air. Forced upward, the warm air expands and cools, its moisture condensing into clouds and rain.

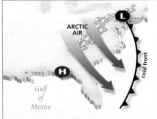

As the center of low pressure passes, generally to the east, the trailing cold front may sweep the entire peninsula, setting off brief but heavy showers, squalls, and thunderstorms. After the storm departs, in-flowing high pressure brings clearing, cooler weather and fair skies.

Highs and Lows

Embedded in the prevailing westerlies are a succession of whirls and eddies: systems of high pressure (fair weather) and low pressure (high humidity, cloudiness, storms) that form and dissipate along fronts, boundaries between warm and cold air masses. Winds blow in a circular pattern around the center of weather systems: In the Northern Hemisphere they blow counterclockwise (as seen from above) in a low-pressure system and clockwise in a high-pressure system. Only occasionally, and mostly in winter, do "lows" pass over Florida, although during late fall, winter, and spring, Florida is often affected by the flow around lows passing far to the north.

Bermuda High and Trade Winds

During summer and early fall, most of Florida lies under the western fringe of the Bermuda High, a massive, semi-permanent high-pressure system covering much of the tropical Atlantic Ocean. Southeasterly trade winds blowing around the Bermuda High fan warm, humid air into the state and keep cold fronts at bay. Nearly every day during summer, heating from the sun sets off scattered afternoon thunderstorms across the peninsula, while sea breezes keep the beaches basking in sunshine. At night the pattern often reverses, and land breezes carry cool night air back out to sea, sometimes setting off storms over the water. Once a week or so, easterly waves (weak areas of low pressure embedded in the broad southeasterly flow) increase shower activity and sometimes trigger downpours.

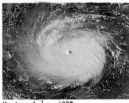

Hurricane Andrew, 1992

Tropical Storms and Hurricanes

Most easterly waves remain no more than disturbed areas of patchy showers and shifting winds; but during their passage over tepid Atlantic, Gulf, or Caribbean waters, the showers may intensify and the winds organize into a circular motion. Some easterly waves develop into tropical storms, low-pressure systems of spiral or circular bands of showers and thunderstorms with winds exceeding gale force (39 m.p.h.). These storms come ashore or pass close to Florida several times a year. If a tropical storm's winds reach 73 m.p.h., it becomes a hurricane; once or twice a year on average, during late summer or early fall, a hurricane rides the trade winds into Florida.

Easterly wave in trade winds

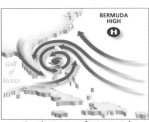

Easterly wave intensifies into tropical storm

Florida's climate ranges from tropical in the south to temperate in the north, giving the state plenty of varied and extreme weather.

Rain

Florida's rain may fall as an all-day soaker, a sudden thunderstorm downpour, a brief sun shower, or a torrential deluge associated with a tropical storm or hurricane. Annual rainfall averages 54 inches statewide, ranging from 40 inches in the Keys to 64 inches in the panhandle and in inland sections of southeastern Florida. The rainfall is highly variable, however; locally, wet years often provide twice as much rain as dry years.

Rare snow, Christmas 1989

Snow

Florida is not known for its snow, but the white stuff does occasionally fall. Flurries and light dustings of an inch or less occur every few years in the panhandle, but across the Florida peninsula snow is very rarely seen. The state's southernmost recorded snowfall (a trace, too little to measure) fell at Homestead (Dade County) on January 19, 1977.

Waterspout, Key Largo

Tornadoes and Waterspouts

On average, 46 tornadoes per year touch down in Florida, a frequency that rivals that of the core of Tornado Alley in the central United States. Florida actually suffers more tornadoes per square mile than any other state in the country, although many of these are small, brief, and weak tornadoes that form beneath small thunderstorms and towering cumulus clouds. Tornadoes can touch down anywhere in Florida, and occur all months of the year. Along the coast, and especially in the Florida Keys, waterspouts—tornadoes that touch down over water—are frequently sighted during the summer.

Thunder and Lightning

Lightning is an electrical discharge between one part of a cloud and another, between two clouds, or between a cloud and the earth. In a typical year, lightning strikes Florida more than a million times; perhaps ten times as many flashes arc across the skies without striking the ground. The annual strike rate reaches 50 per square mile in the central Florida peninsula, about three times the national average. Thunder is caused by the explosive expansion of air heated by lightning along a narrow channel within or extending from a cumulonimbus cloud, and is therefore often associated with heavy rain, hail, high winds, or tornadoes. Most locations in Florida average more than 100 thunderstorms per year, with a peak frequency of 130 per year at Lakeland, in central Florida; the national average is about 50 per year. In summer, storms occur somewhere in the state nearly every day.

Green Flash

A green flash is an exceedingly brief, brilliant, greenish (rarely bluish) light seen on the horizon just as the last of the solar disk disappears at sunset (or immediately before it appears at sunrise). It is a weak prismatic effect caused by atmospheric refraction, or bending, of light (blue and green light refract more strongly than yellow and red). A greenish fringe appears on the upper edge of the sun and remains momentarily after the rest of the sun dips below the horizon. Florida, especially the Keys, provides viewers excellent opportunities to glimpse this elusive phenomenon, which requires a low, flat horizon and a clear, cloudless sight line to the sun.

Record-setting Florida Weather

DEADLIEST HURRICANE September 17, 1928. More than 1,800 people drowned along Lake Okeechobee when extreme winds sent the lake's waters over surrounding levees.

COSTLIEST HURRICANE August 24, 1992. Hurricane Andrew caused $23 billion in damage, mostly in Dade County.

MOST POWERFUL HURRICANE Labor Day, 1935. Winds estimated at 200 m.p.h. on Long Key.

HIGHEST TEMPERATURE June 29, 1931. 109° F at Monticello.

LOWEST TEMPERATURE February 13, 1899. –2° F at Tallahassee.

MOST RAIN IN 24 HOURS September 5–6, 1950. 38.7 inches at Yankeetown.

GREATEST SNOWSTORM January 10, 1800. 5 inches near mouth of St. Marys River, along Florida–Georgia border.

Seasons

Seasonal changes in Florida are most pronounced in the north, where the highest and lowest temperatures of the year usually span a 70- or 80-degree range (Florida's highest and lowest temperatures have been recorded in the central panhandle). Temperature ranges on the peninsula are moderated by the surrounding water masses. In southernmost Florida the climate is considered tropical, and seasons are marked more by differences in rainfall than in temperature.

Seasons result from the changing angle of sunlight striking the ground over the course of a year. As earth moves around its orbit, its 23½-degree tilt on its axis means that for half the year the Northern Hemisphere is inclined toward the sun and the sun's rays shine on it more directly; for half the year it is tilted away from the sun and the sun's rays are more oblique. The latitude that receives the greatest heat from the sun is farther north during the summer months (though earth's surface—land and sea—takes a while to warm up, so that early August is actually hotter than late June). Atmospheric currents, such as the prevailing westerlies, Bermuda High, and trade winds, in turn shift to the north.

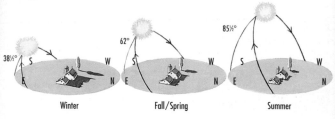

Winter   Fall/Spring   Summer

At 28° N (the latitude of Tampa), the noontime sun at the winter solstice rises only 38½° above the horizon; in summer the noontime sun has an altitude above the horizon of 85½°.

Spring

Spring officially begins on or about March 21, called the spring (or vernal) equinox, when the sun appears directly overhead at noon at the equator. Cold fronts still sweep across Florida in spring, triggering showers and thunderstorms (a few of which may spawn tornadoes), but the high-pressure systems that follow in the wake of the fronts are much milder than those of winter. Showers usually pass quickly, and spring is the sunniest season of the year across the state.

Flowering Dogwood

Summer

The sun reaches its peak over the Northern Hemisphere around June 21, the longest day (that is, daylight period) of the year, known as the summer solstice. Cold fronts all but disappear from Florida's weather, and the Bermuda High expands in-

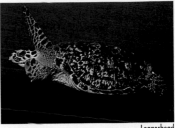
Loggerhead

land from the Atlantic Ocean. Around the Bermuda High's southern flank, southeasterly trade winds bring in a steady flow of heat and humidity. Most days the only relief comes from cooling sea breezes along the coast or thunderstorms bred from the humid air; along the Atlantic coast, southeasterly winds may blow the storms inland, leaving the beaches and coastal towns sunny while showers prevail just a few miles inland. Although summer is the "rainy season," enough sunshine gets through to raise average daytime temperatures to about 90 degrees Fahrenheit across most of Florida.

Blue winged Teal

Fall

As it did at the spring equinox, the sun "crosses" the equator at the fall (or autumnal) equinox, around September 22. With persistent heat and almost daily rain, September is another summer month, weatherwise, but the northern half of the state enjoys a marked dry-

ing-out in October as the southeasterly trade winds weaken and occasional cold fronts break the heat. Hurricanes or tropical storms may hit the coastline in August, September, or October. By November, the hurricane threat diminishes, and the entire state enjoys frequent mild, sunny days and cool nights.

Winter

Winter arrives on December 21, the winter solstice. As long winter nights settle in over the Arctic, cold fronts increase, bringing frost to northern Florida and cool, breezy days across the peninsula. Average daytime temperatures in January are in the 60s Fahrenheit north of Orlando, the 70s to the south. For most of Florida, winter is the dry season—some locations around the Everglades receive only a tenth as much rain in December as they do in June. But in the panhandle, cold fronts occasionally stall over the Gulf of Mexico in winter and generate coastal storms with all-day rains.

Manatees

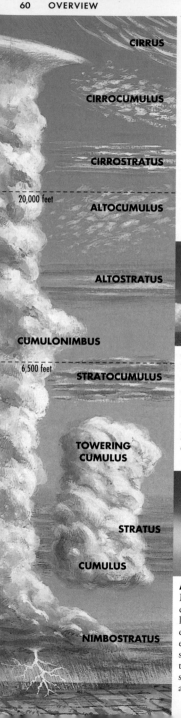

CIRRUS

CIRROCUMULUS

CIRROSTRATUS

20,000 feet

ALTOCUMULUS

ALTOSTRATUS

CUMULONIMBUS

6,500 feet

STRATOCUMULUS

TOWERING CUMULUS

STRATUS

CUMULUS

NIMBOSTRATUS

Typical Clouds

Clouds form when moist air is cooled, causing water molecules to condense into water droplets or ice crystals. While most types of clouds can be spotted over Florida, the ones described here are among the most common or significant. The illustration at left shows the relative common altitudes of cloud types; distances are not shown to scale.

CUMULONIMBUS

Tallest of all cloud types; commonly called thunderheads. Lower part composed of water droplets; fuzzy, fibrous top—the "anvil"—made of ice crystals. Produce lightning, thunder, heavy rain, and sometimes hail, high winds, or tornadoes. Most common from May to September.

ALTOSTRATUS

Middle-level clouds, mainly of water droplets; usually appear as featureless gray sheet covering sky. Thickening, low altostratus from west, especially in winter, often bring steady widespread rain within hours; thickening altostratus from east or south in summer or fall may mean an approaching tropical storm.

CUMULUS
Water-droplet clouds formed at tops of rising air currents set in motion by uneven heating of ground by sun. Domed tops, like bright white heads of cauliflower. Typical clouds of fine summer days, but can occur any time of year. More common inland than along coast or offshore.

TOWERING CUMULUS
Cumulus clouds grow into towering, or swelling, cumulus if atmospheric moisture is sufficient and it is much warmer at ground level than in the air aloft. May produce light showers, which in turn can develop into thunderstorms—watch for rapid billowing in tops.

STRATOCUMULUS
Low, flat-based, white to gray water-droplet clouds, usually covering most of sky and arranged in rows or patches, from which light rain may fall. Most common along Gulf coast, especially in winter, and particularly when wind is blowing onshore.

CIRRUS
High (5 miles or more), thin, wispy clouds composed of ice crystals; may be seen in any season and anywhere in Florida. In winter, cirrus thickening from west or south may signal approaching rain or snow; however, cirrus often come and go without bringing any lower clouds or rain.

FOG
Clouds formed at ground level; occurs 20–50 days per year inland, fewer than 10 along coast. Advection fog: forms when humid air overruns cold surfaces; rare in Florida. Radiation fog: caused by overnight cooling of still air; burns off as sun rises; more common inland and in coastal marshes.

HURRICANE SQUALL
Low, rapidly moving clouds bearing heavy rains and strong, gusty winds associated with spiral bands of clouds circling center of a hurricane. As hurricane approaches, squalls alternate with lulls until strongest winds, in eye wall, arrive, followed by calm conditions in eye, then strong winds from other side.

Our Solar System

The sun, the nine planets that revolve around it, and their moons make up our solar system. Venus, Mars, Jupiter, and Saturn are easily visible to the naked eye; Mercury, Uranus, Neptune and Pluto are more difficult to see. Other objects are transient: the wide orbits of comets make them rare visitors near earth, and meteors flash brightly for only seconds before disappearing.

Observing the Sky in Florida

Florida's southerly location enables stargazers to see notable celestial objects such as the Southern Cross, not visible north of Florida. The air can be calm and steady, which is favorable for telescope-viewing, allowing such details as Saturn's rings and Jupiter's cloud bands to stand out. Haze, humidity, and lights in heavily populated areas often brighten the night sky, making it more difficult to see stars and planets.

FULL MOON

The full moon rises at sunset and sets at dawn. It is highest in the sky in December, when it may pass directly overhead in central and southern Florida (in summer, it rises only about 40 degrees). Some lunar features show up best when the moon is full: the dark "seas" (hardened lava flows) and the "rays" of bright material splattered from craters. Craters and mountain ranges are best seen before and after full moon, when the angle of sunlight throws them into relief; look especially near the terminator, the dividing line between the moon's day and night sides. Because the moon is locked in earth's gravitational grip, the same side of the moon always faces us.

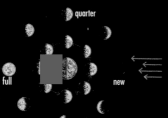

quarter

full

new

quarter

PHASES OF THE MOON

As the moon makes its monthly orbit around earth, the illuminated lunar surface area appears to grow (wax), shrink (wane) and even disappear (at new moon). The center of the illustration shows the phases with sunlight coming from the right. The outer drawings show how the moon looks from our perspective on earth.

VENUS

Cloud-shrouded Venus alternates between being our "morning star" and "evening star," depending on where it is in its orbit. This brilliant planet usually outshines everything in the sky except for the sun and moon. As it circles the sun, Venus displays phases, which can be viewed through a small telescope or high-power binoculars.

Venus (left) and the moon

MARS

Every 25½ months, when earth is aligned between Mars and the sun, Mars is closest to us and at its brightest and most colorful, appearing orange-red to the naked eye. At this time, called opposition (opposite in the sky from the sun), Mars rises at sunset and remains in the sky all night. Bright, white polar caps and dusky surface markings may be glimpsed through a small telescope at opposition. Mars rivals Jupiter in brightness at opposition, but fades somewhat at other times.

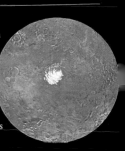

JUPITER

Visible in our morning sky for about five months at a stretch and in our evening sky for five months, Jupiter appears brighter than any star in the night sky at all times. The largest planet in our solar system, it has a diameter of 88,850 miles, 11.2 times that of earth. Jupiter's four largest moons—Ganymede, Io, Europa, and Callisto—can often be spotted with binoculars.

Jupiter (top) and moons

SATURN

Visible most of the year, Saturn appears to the naked eye as a slightly yellowish, moderately bright star. A small telescope reveals its rings, composed mainly of rocky chunks of ice, and the two largest (Titan and Rhea) of its more than 20 known moons.

METEORS

These "shooting stars" are typically chips ranging from sand-grain to marble size that are knocked off asteroids (tiny planets) or blown off comets and burn up as they strike our atmosphere. The strongest annual meteor showers are the Perseids, which peak around August 12, and the Geminids, which peak around December 13.

COMETS

Comets are irregular lumps of ice and rock left over from the formation of the solar system. Once or twice a decade, a notable comet approaches the sun from the outer regions that it travels in its far-ranging elliptical orbit. The sun's energy vaporizes the comet's surface, generating a tail of gas and dust that may be millions of miles long.

Comet Hale-Bopp, 1997

ZODIACAL LIGHT

Florida is an ideal location to observe the subtle glow of zodiacal light, a dim, cone-shaped band of light caused by the reflection of sunlight off billions of minute dust particles orbiting the sun in the same plane as the planets. Also known as "false dusk" or "false dawn," the light is best seen from a dark-sky location just after dusk, and is brightest where the sun went down.

Stars and Deep-sky Objects

As earth orbits the sun in its annual cycle, our planet's night side faces in steadily changing directions, revealing different stars, constellations, and views of our own Milky Way. People in ancient times named constellations after mythological figures and familiar creatures whose shapes they saw outlined by the stars. The best known of these constellations lie along the ecliptic, the imaginary line that traces the apparent annual path of the sun through the sky. Earth, our moon, and the other planets orbit in nearly the same plane, all traveling along a band roughly 16 degrees wide centered on the ecliptic and called the zodiac. (The zodiac is traditionally divided into 12 segments, but 13 constellations actually intersect it.)

Modern constellations are simply designated regions of the celestial sphere, like countries on a map. Most constellations bear little resemblance to their namesakes. Beyond the approximately 6,000 stars visible to the naked eye lie other fascinating deep-sky objects—star clusters, galaxies, nebulas (gas clouds)—that can be seen, some with the naked eye and others with binoculars or a small telescope.

The Zodiac

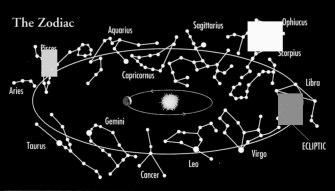

Seasonal Star Maps

The following pages show star maps for each of the four seasons drawn at a latitude of 25 degrees north (Miami) for the specific times and dates indicated. (If you wish to observe at a different time or date, note that the same stars appear two hours earlier each month, or one hour earlier every two weeks.) The map for each season is divided into four quadrants: northeast, northwest, southeast, and southwest. Start by facing the direction in which you have the clearest view; if your best view is northeastward, use the northeast map. The maps plot the constellations and major stars; the wavy, pale blue areas represent the band of the Milky Way; the zenith, the point directly overhead, is indicated. The key to finding your way around the sky is to locate distinctive constellations or star groups and then to use them to find others. The maps do not chart the planets of our solar system, whose positions change continually; their locations are often listed in the weather section of newspapers.

WINTER: ORION

On winter nights, we look outward through a spiral arm of our disk-shaped galaxy. Many hot, young blue or white stars (such as Sirius, Rigel, and Procyon), along with some older, cooler yellow and reddish stars (Capella, Aldebaran, Betelgeuse, and Canopus), dominate the sky. New stars are being born in the Orion Nebula, a mixture of new stars, gases, and dust visible to the naked eye as a fuzzy area in Orion's sword, which hangs from his belt.

SPRING: SOUTHERN CROSS

By looking due south on a clear night, sky-watchers south of Fort Myers/Palm Beach may see the constellation Crux, the Southern Cross. The best time to see it is from April 1 (at midnight/1 a.m. DST) to May 1 (11 p.m. DST). The bright stars alpha Centauri (at 4.3 light years away, the nearest bright star to our solar system) and beta Centauri can be seen in the same area of sky just above the horizon.

SUMMER: MILKY WAY

During the summer months, earth's dark side faces toward the bright center of the Milky Way, making that hazy band of light a dominant feature in the sky. A scan with binoculars through the Milky Way from Cygnus to Sagittarius and Scorpius reveals dozens of star clusters and nebulas. High to the northeast, the hot, white stars of the Summer Triangle—Vega, Deneb, and Altair—are usually the first stars visible in the evening.

FALL: ANDROMEDA GALAXY

On autumn evenings, earth's night side faces away from the plane of our galaxy, allowing us to see other, more distant ones. The Andromeda Galaxy can be found northeast of the Great Square of Pegasus, just above the central star on the dimmer northern "leg" of Andromeda. (On the Fall Sky: Southeast map, the galaxy is near the first D in Andromeda.) Appearing as an elongated patch of fuzzy light, it is 2.5 million light years away.

The Winter Sky

The chart is drawn for these times and dates but can be used at other times during the season

ERIDANUS TAURUS Aldebaran
Zenith
Pleiades
AURIGA
Capella
LYNX
Mira
CETUS
Algol
ARIES
PERSEUS
URSA MAJOR
TRIANGULUM
CAMELOPARDALIS
PISCES
ANDROMEDA CASSIOPEIA Polaris
URSA MINOR
PEGASUS
CEPHEUS
AQUARIUS
LACERTA
DRACO
WEST
NORTH

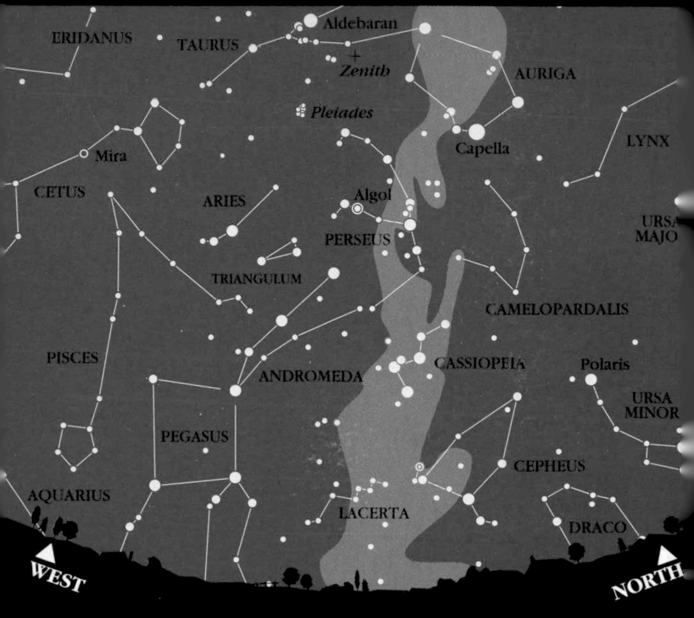

NORTHWEST

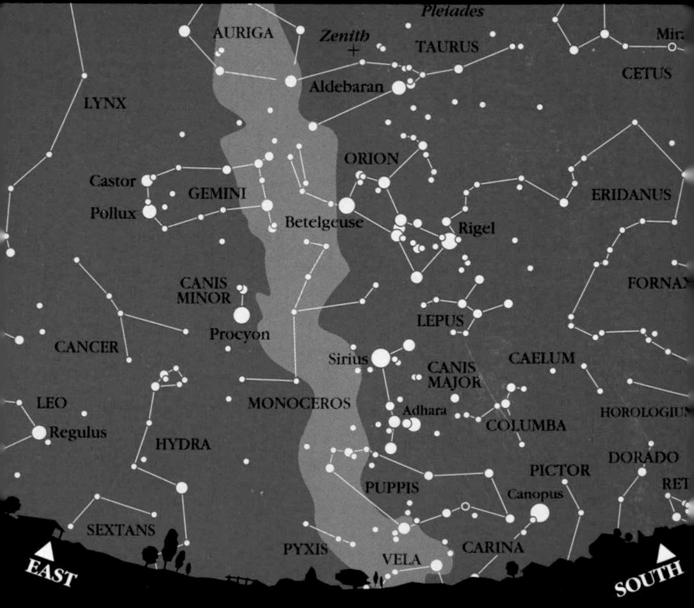

Pleiades
AURIGA *Zenith* TAURUS Mira
CETUS
Aldebaran
LYNX
ORION
Castor GEMINI ERIDANUS
Pollux Betelgeuse Rigel
CANIS MINOR
FORNAX
Procyon LEPUS
CANCER CAELUM
Sirius
LEO CANIS MAJOR
Regulus Adhara COLUMBA HOROLOGIUM
MONOCEROS
HYDRA PICTOR DORADO
PUPPIS Canopus RET
SEXTANS CARINA
PYXIS VELA
EAST SOUTH

SOUTHEAST

December 1, midnight; January 1, 10 P.M.; February 1, 8 P.M.

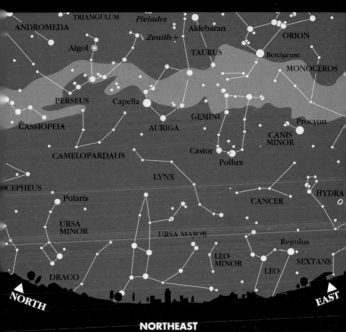

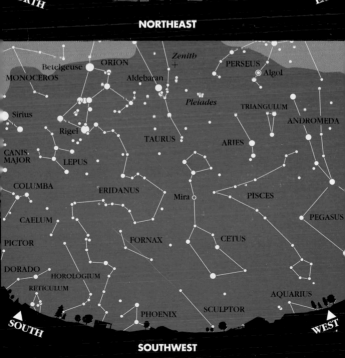

The Spring Sky

NORTHWEST

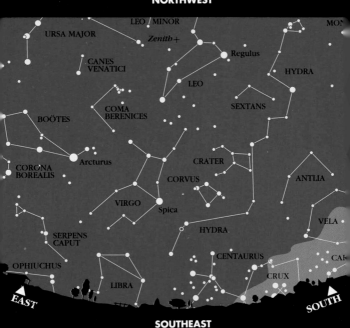

SOUTHEAST

March 1, midnight; April 1, 10 P.M. (11 P.M. DST); May 1, 8 P.M.
(9 P.M. DST)

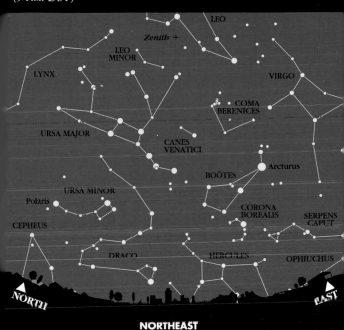

NORTHEAST

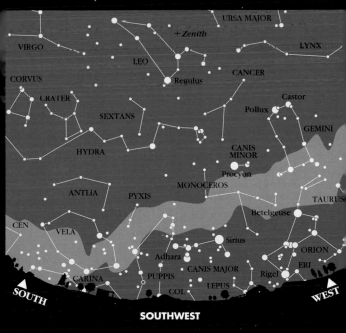

SOUTHWEST

The Summer Sky

The chart is drawn for these times and date but can be used at other times during the seaso

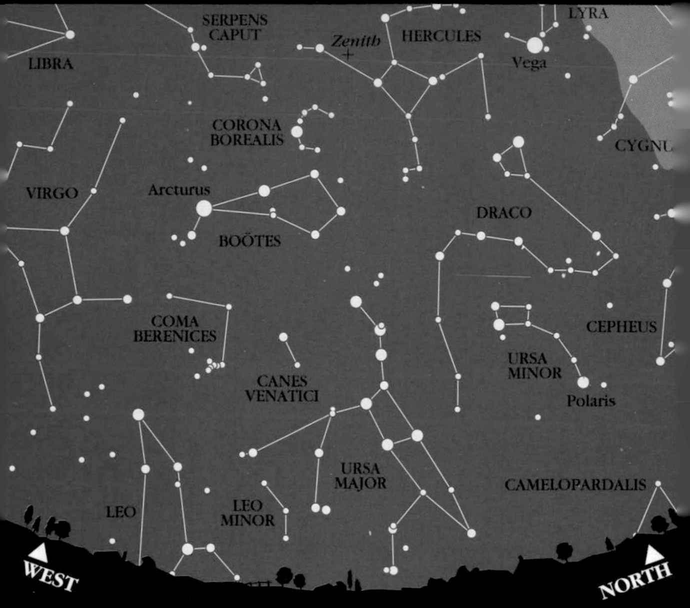

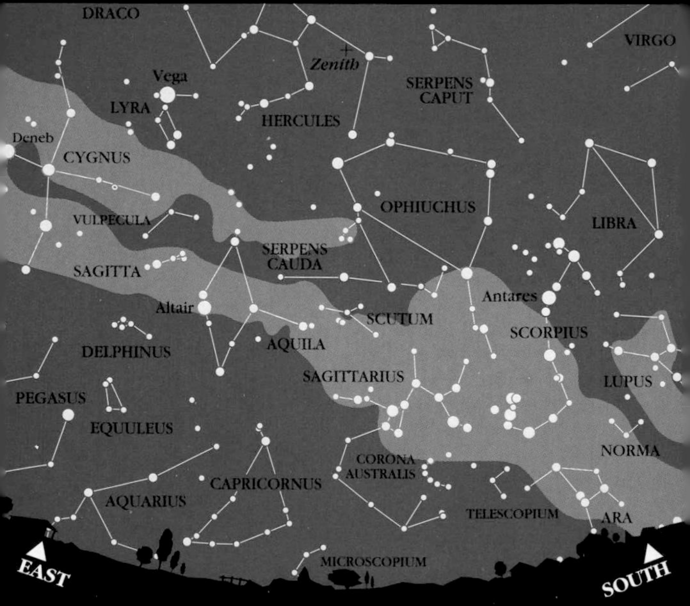

June 1, midnight (1 A.M. DST); July 1, 10 P.M. (11 P.M. DST);
August 1, 8 P.M. (9 P.M. DST).

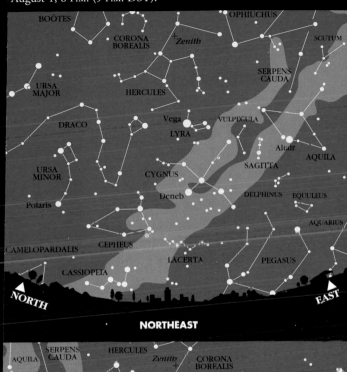

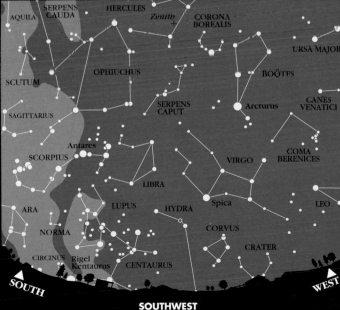

The Fall Sky

The chart is drawn for these times and date but can be used at other times during the seaso...

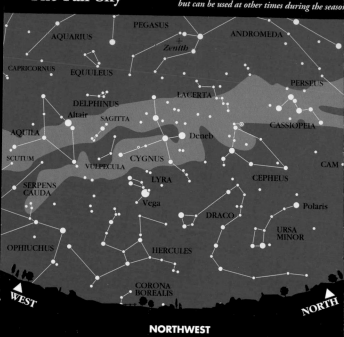

NORTHWEST

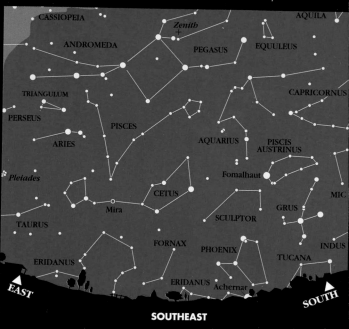

SOUTHEAST

September 1, midnight (1 A.M. DST); October 1, 10 P.M. (11 P.M. DST); November 1, 8 P.M.; December 1, 6 P.M.

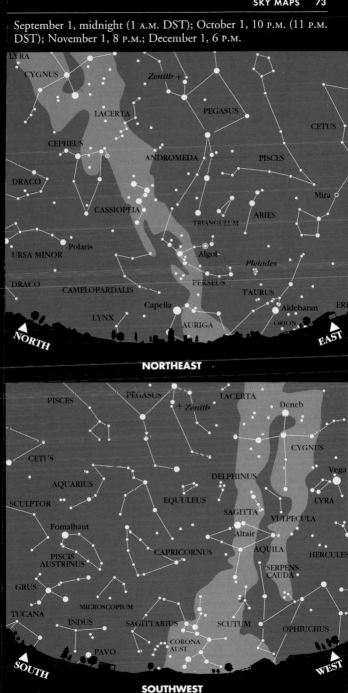

Flora and Fauna

How to Use the Flora and Fauna Section

Part Two of this book presents approximately 1,000 of the most common species found in Florida, beginning with mushrooms, algae, lichens, ferns, and other spore plants, and continuing with large and small trees, wildflowers, invertebrates (mostly seashore creatures and insects), fishes, amphibians, reptiles, birds, and mammals. Flora species are presented alphabetically by English family name. Fauna species are sequenced according to their taxonomy, or scientific classification. The classification and the names of species in this guide are based on authoritative sources when these exist for a given group.

Introductions and Other Essays

Most major sections of Part Two—for example, trees, wildflowers, marine invertebrates, birds—have an introduction, and some groups within the larger sections are also described in brief essays. The introductions should be read along with the species accounts that follow, as they present information that is fundamental for understanding the plants or animals in question. For groups without introductory essays, shared features are sometimes given in the opening sentence of the first species in the sequence.

Names

Each account begins with the common name of the species. Common names can change and may differ in other sources; if a species has a widely used alternate name, that is also given, within quotation marks, directly below the common name. The scientific species name, shown below the common name, is italicized (alternate scientific names are also sometimes listed). In a few cases (some flowers and invertebrates), organisms are best known on the genus level and are presented as such here. For example, the Cicadas are presented as a group: the *Tibicen* species. Below the scientific name is the name of the group (class, order, family) with which the species is most commonly associated.

Description

The species accounts are designed to permit identification of species in the field. An account begins with the organism's typical mature or adult size: length (L), height (H), diameter (D), tail length (T), and/or wingspan (WS). The size is followed by the species' physical characteristics, including color and distinctive markings. We use the abbreviations "imm." (immature) and "juv." (juvenile). The term "morph" describes a distinctive coloration that occurs in some individuals.

Other Information

For every species, the typical habitat is described. Other information may also be given, such as seasonality (bloom times of flowers or periods of activity for mammals) or the need for caution (species that can cause irritation, illness, or injury). Similar species are sometimes described at the end of an account. The range (the area in which the species lives) is not stated if the species occurs through-

male (left), immature (right)

Names

AMERICAN ROBIN
Turdus migratorius
THRUSH SUBFAMILY

Description

10″. Male breast and sides rufous-orange; back and wings gray-brown; head blackish, with broken white eye ring; throat striped; bill yellow; tail black, with tiny white corners; vent white. Female head and back duller brown. Tail fairly long. In spring and summer, an earthworm specialist; in fall and winter, roams in berry-searching flocks, forms large communal roosts. **VOICE** Song: prolonged, rising and falling *cheery-up cheery-me*. Calls: *tut tut tut* and *tseep*.

Other
Information

HABITAT Woods, shrubs, lawns. **RANGE** Mar.–Oct.: rare breeder n FL. Oct.–Apr.: all FL.

out Florida; the one exception to this rule is the birds, for which the range is always given. The term "local" means that a species occurs in spotty fashion over a large area, but not throughout the entire area. In describing the geographic range of species, we use the abbreviations e (east), w (west), n (north), s (south), c (central), and combinations of these (sc for south-central). Note that when the range is given as "n FL," this includes the panhandle.

Color, shape, and size may vary within plant and animal species, depending on environmental conditions and other factors. Bloom, migration, and other times can vary with the weather, latitude, and geography.

Classification of Living Things

Biologists divide living organisms into major groups called kingdoms, the largest of which are the plant and animal kingdoms. Kingdoms are divided into divisions (for plants) or phyla (for animals); these are then divided into classes, classes into orders, orders into families, families into genera (singular: genus), and genera into species. The species is the basic unit of classification and is generally what we have in mind when we talk about a "kind" of plant or animal. The scientific name of a species consists of two Latin or Latinized words. The first is the genus; the second is the species, often describing the appearance or geographical distribution of the species. The scientific name of the Florida Mouse is *Podomys floridanus*. *Podomys* is the genus, and *floridanus* is the species.

Species are populations or groups of populations that are able to interbreed and produce fertile offspring themselves; they usually are not able to breed successfully or produce fertile offspring with members of other species. Many widespread species have numerous races (subspecies)—populations that are separated from one another geographically; races within a species may differ in appearance and behavior from other populations of that species.

Flora

The flora section of this guide includes flowering and nonflowering plants as well as algae and mushrooms, which are no longer considered part of the plant kingdom. Botanists are developing new classification systems that place most algae outside of the green plants group. Mushrooms are covered here because they are somewhat plant-like in appearance and are often found on plants or plant matter.

The first part of the flora section begins with mushrooms, followed by algae and lichens. The next group is the nonflowering spore plants such as liverworts, mosses, clubmosses, horsetails, and ferns. Trees follow, beginning with conifers, then large broadleaf trees, and finally small broadleaf trees and shrubs. Wildflowers, including flowering vines, grasses, and water plants in addition to terrestrial herbaceous plants, end the flora section.

In most of the flora subsections, species are grouped by family. The families are sequenced alphabetically by the English family name. Within each family, the species are sequenced alphabetically by Latin species name. The measurements given in the species accounts are typical mature sizes in Florida. Colors, shapes, and sizes may vary within a species depending on environmental conditions. Bloom times vary throughout the region, especially north to south, along the coast, and at different elevations. The geographic range is specified only when the species is not found throughout the state.

Users of this guide are warned against eating or otherwise consuming any plants or parts of a plant (including fiddleheads or berries or other fruits) or any mushrooms based on the information supplied in this guide.

Mushrooms

The organisms known as fungi—including molds, yeasts, mildews, and mushrooms—range from microscopic forms to mammoth puffballs. Unlike plants, they do not carry out photosynthesis, and thus must obtain food from organic matter, living or dead. The fungi in this book are of the type commonly known as mushrooms.

Most mushrooms that grow on the ground have a stalk and a cap. The stalks of different species vary in shape, thickness, and density. There is sometimes a skirt-like or bracelet-like ring midway up or near the top of the stalk, and the stalk base is often bulbous or sometimes enclosed by a cup at or just below the surface of the ground. Bracket (or shelf) mushrooms, which grow on trunks or logs, are often unstalked or short-stalked. A mushroom's cap may be smooth, scaly, warty, or shaggy, and its shape may be round, flat, convex (bell- or umbrella-shaped), or concave (cup- or trumpet-shaped). The caps of many species change as they mature, from closed and egg-shaped to open and umbrella-like; the cap color may also change with age.

Fungi reproduce through the release of single-celled bodies called spores. Many mushrooms bear their microscopic, spore-producing structures on the underside of the cap, either on radiating blade-like gills or within tiny tubes that terminate in pores. In others, the spore-producing structures line the inside of a cup-shaped cap or are located in broad wrinkles or open pits on the sides or top of the cap. Puffball mushrooms produce their spores within a ball-shaped body; the spores are released when the mature ball breaks open at the top or disintegrates.

In the accounts that follow, sizes given are typical heights (for stalked species) and cap widths of mature specimens.

Caution

Of the many hundreds of mushroom species occurring in Florida, at least 10 are deadly poisonous to eat, even in small amounts, and many others cause mild to severe reactions. The brief descriptions and few illustrations in this guide are not to be used for determining the edibility of mushroom species. Inexperienced mushroom-hunters should not eat any species they find in the wild.

Parts of a Mushroom

CAESAR'S AMANITA
Amanita caesarea
AMANITA FAMILY
H 7"; W 7". Cap flat, sticky, red or red-orange, with yellow edge. Stalk slender, hollow, pale yellow; tapers toward cap; has skirt-like ring and white bulbous base. Gills pale yellow. **SEASON** June–Oct. **HABITAT** On ground in mixed woods.

FLY AMANITA
Amanita muscaria
AMANITA FAMILY

H 6″; W 6″. Cap umbrella-shaped, dull to pale orange, with yellowish warts. Stalk stout, hollow, white to pale yellow; usu. has skirt-like ring, bulbous base. Gills white. **CAUTION** Poisonous. **SEASON** Nov.–Feb. **HABITAT** On ground in mixed woods.

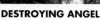

DESTROYING ANGEL
Amanita virosa
AMANITA FAMILY

H 8″; W 4″. Entire mushroom white. Cap umbrella-shaped, ragged-edged. Stalk tall; has tattered, skirt-like ring, bulbous base. **CAUTION** Deadly poisonous. **SEASON** June–Sept. **HABITAT** On ground in oak-pine woods.

OLD-MAN-OF-THE-WOODS
Strobilomyces floccopus
BOLETUS FAMILY

H 4¾″; W 6″. Cap flat, gray-black, with dry pointed scales. Underside has spongy pores. Stalk tough, black-netted or shaggy; often has enlarged base. **SEASON** June–Nov. (probably year-round). **HABITAT** On ground in oak-pine woods.

CHANTERELLE
Cantherellus cibarius
CHANTERELLE FAMILY

H 3″; W 4″. Entire mushroom orange-yellow to vivid yellow; darkens brownish when bruised. Cap usu. trumpet-shaped, wavy-edged. Stalk thick, tapers toward base. Gills thick, ridge-like, blunt, branched; extend down stalk. **SEASON** Aug.–Nov. **HABITAT** On ground in oak-pine woods.

SHAGGY MANE
Coprinus comatus
INKY CAP FAMILY

H 6"; W 2⅜". Cap bell-shaped, light brown, with upcurled, shaggy, brown scales; dissolves at maturity. Stalk tall, hollow, white. Gills pink to purple-black. **SEASON** Year-round. **HABITAT** On plant debris in woods and pastures.

LITTLE INKY CAP
"Mica Cap"
Coprinus micaceus
INKY CAP FAMILY

H 3"; W 2". Cap bell-shaped, yellowish to yellow-brown, thin, shiny; dissolves at maturity. Stalk slender, hollow, brittle, white, slightly powdery. Gills pink to purple-black. Usu. in large clusters. **SEASON** Year-round. **HABITAT** Around old stumps of broadleaf trees or buried wood in lawns or fields.

PARASOL MUSHROOM
Lepiota procera
LEPIOTA FAMILY

H 15¾"; W 6". Cap light brown, scaly, umbrella-shaped. Stalk tall, slender, scaly; has bracelet-like ring, swollen base. Gills white to pinkish. **SEASON** June–Oct. **HABITAT** On ground in pastures, lawns.

MEADOW MUSHROOM
Agaricus campestris
MEADOW MUSHROOM FAMILY

H 2⅜"; W 4". Cap flat, white, smooth or silky-scaled, ragged-edged. Stalk short, often tapers toward base, with ragged skirt-like ring. Gills dark brown. **SEASON** Apr.–Oct. **HABITAT** On ground in meadows, lawns, pastures.

BEEFSTEAK POLYPORE
Fistulina hepatica
POLYPORE FAMILY

W 12". Cap large, flat, reddish brown, fleshy; often sticky, with red sap. Underside cream-colored; stains pink when bruised; has tube-like pores. Stalk absent or very short, thick, attached to side of cap. SEASON June–Nov. HABITAT On logs, stumps, dead or living trees (esp. oaks).

PURPLE-SPORED PUFFBALL
"Cup-shaped Puffball"
Calvatia cyathiformis
PUFFBALL FAMILY

H 8"; W 6". Round to pear-shaped, light brown ball narrows to stalk-like base; has cracked surface. Top breaks up and falls off to release spores. SEASON June–Nov. HABITAT On ground in meadows, lawns, open woods.

TAWNY MILKCAP
"Orange-brown Lactarius"
Lactarius volemus
RUSSULA FAMILY

H 4"; W 4". Brittle; has copious milky sap. Cap tawny brown to orange-yellow, flat to funnel-shaped. Stalk stout, smooth or wrinkly. Gills whitish to cream-colored; stain brown when bruised; extend down stalk. SEASON July–Sept. HABITAT On ground in woods and shaded lawns with oaks.

JACK-O'-LANTERN MUSHROOM
Omphalotus illudens
TRICHOLOMA FAMILY

H 8"; W 6". Cap flat to funnel-shaped, with curled-under edges; orange to yellow-orange. Gills extend down stalk; glow in the dark. Grows in clusters. CAUTION Poisonous. SEASON Aug.–Nov. HABITAT Bases of living trees, on stumps, buried wood.

OYSTER MUSHROOM
Pleurotus ostreatus
TRICHOLOMA FAMILY

W 10". Bracket. Cap fan-shaped, often lobed; white to grayish or brownish. Stalk absent or very short, curved, whitish, attached to one side of cap, velvety at base. Gills whitish, extend down stalk. Forms overlapping clusters. SEASON Year-round. HABITAT On various dead broadleaf trees.

Algae

Algae are a diverse array of organisms ranging from microscopic unicellular forms to large seaweeds. Two groups of algae are included in this guide: yellow-brown algae and green algae. Yellow-brown algae occur almost exclusively in salt water. Green algae most often live in fresh water but are also found in salt water and on land. In fact, land plants evolved from certain kinds of green algae.

The selected algae in this guide are all sizable marine plants commonly known as seaweeds. Most have stalks, leaf-like structures called *fronds* (sometimes with air bladders that keep them afloat), and a pad-, disk-, or root-like structure called a *holdfast* with which they attach to a *substrate* such as sand, rock, shells, a pier, or some other surface. Some species tend to become detached from the substrate and float freely. In the accounts that follow, sizes given are lengths of mature specimens.

SEA LETTUCE
Ulva lactuca
GREEN ALGAE
24″. Bright green. Fronds thin ruffled sheets, roundish to irreg. in outline. Attached to rock, mangrove roots, coral, and other substrates; sometimes free-floating. HABITAT Intertidal zone.

ATTACHED SARGASSUM WEED
Sargassum filipendula
YELLOW-BROWN ALGAE
6′6″. Dark brown. Branched stalks with toothed, lance-shaped to linear fronds and round air bladders. Attached by large lobed holdfast to natural limestone and jetty rock. HABITAT Deep offshore waters.

FLOATING SARGASSUM WEED
Sargassum fluitans
YELLOW-BROWN ALGAE
30″. Golden brown. Smooth to spiny, branched stalk with toothed lanceolate fronds and round air bladders. Free-floating. HABITAT Deep offshore waters; floats inshore.

Lichens

A lichen is a remarkable dual organism made up of a fungus and a colony of microscopic green algae or cyanobacteria ("blue-green algae"). Such a relationship—dissimilar organisms living in intimate association—is known as *symbiosis* and may be detrimental to one of the participants (parasitism) or beneficial to both (mutualism). In a lichen, the fungus surrounds the algae and absorbs water, minerals, and organic substances from the substrate (soil, rock, tree bark) it is growing on; the algae supply carbohydrates produced by photosynthesis. It is not definitely known whether symbiosis in lichens is mutually beneficial or mildly to wholly parasitic.

Lichens occur in a wide range of habitats, including some of the harshest environments on earth, such as deserts and the Arctic (where they serve as the primary food of reindeer and caribou), and can also be found in forests, along roadsides, on buildings and other man-made structures, and on mountaintops. They can withstand extreme variations in temperature and other harsh conditions. During droughts they dry up but do not die; they rapidly absorb water when it does become available, springing back to life. Lichens range widely in color, occurring in white, black, gray, and various shades of red, orange, brown, yellow, or green. Their color often varies dramatically with moisture content.

Most lichens grow extremely slowly, about ¹⁄₂₅ inch to ½ inch per year, and can have extremely long lifetimes. Many lichens have special structures for vegetative reproduction: tiny fragments that break off easily or powdery spots that release powdery balls of algae wrapped in microscopic fungal threads. In others, the fungal component produces spores carried on conspicuous fruiting bodies, which may be cup-like, disk-like, or globular.

In the accounts that follow, sizes given are typical heights and/or widths of mature specimens.

RED BLANKET LICHEN
Herpothallon (Chiodecton) rubrocinta

W 4″ (individuals). Young individuals are flat, greenish-white circles with red edges. Older plant bodies redden and coalesce into large, irregularly shaped colonies. Texture somewhat felt-like. **HABITAT** On tree trunks and branches (esp. of oaks) in hammocks and scrub.

DOG LICHEN
Peltigera canina

W 8″. Blue-gray (dry) to brown (wet) rosette of leathery crinkled lobes; underside felt-like, with tufts of root-like strands. Fruiting bodies brown, saddle-shaped structures at edges. **HABITAT** On moist sandy ground of shady ravines and riversides. **RANGE** n FL.

BEARD LICHEN
Usnea strigosa

H 3″. Yellowish-green, shrubby, intricately branched, bristly stalks hang down from tree branches; stiff when dry, spongy when wet; attached by pad. Fruiting bodies plate-like, at branch ends. **HABITAT** Usu. on ground in sandhills and scrub.

Spore Plants

Spore plants are green land plants such as mosses, clubmosses, and ferns (ferns are introduced separately on page 86) that reproduce from spores rather than seeds. Among the earliest evolved land plants still present on earth, these plants do not produce flowers or fruits. The most conspicuous part of their reproduction is the *spore,* a reproductive cell that divides and eventually develops the structures producing the sperm and egg, which fuse to form a new adult plant. Mosses are feathery, mat-forming plants often found in shady, damp to wet habitats. When "fruiting," their spores are released from a lidded capsule often elevated on a wiry brown fertile stalk. Mosses typically absorb water and nutrients directly from the environment, as they lack a sophisticated vascular system for conducting water and nutrients internally. Clubmosses often look like upright green pipe cleaners or tiny conifers rising from the ground in shady woodlands. When fruiting, their spores are produced in tiny but visible sacs, called *sporangia,* between the leaves. In some species the leaves and sporangia are densely clustered into a long, narrow, cone-like structure. In the accounts that follow, sizes given are typical heights of mature specimens.

SILVER MOSS
Bryum argenteum
MOSS CLASS

H 1″ (when fruiting). Green to bright silver-gray mats of short, densely leafy stalks. Fertile stalks red, leafless, each topped with dark red, cylindrical capsule. **HABITAT** Dry fields, paths, sidewalk crevices, roofs.

HAIRCAP MOSS
"Goldilocks"
Polytrichum commune
MOSS CLASS

H 18″. Green carpet of tall erect stalks with stiff pointed leaves. Fertile stalks reddish, each topped with red-brown, cylindrical capsule. **HABITAT** Soil or rocks in wet areas; edges of bogs and coniferous swamps.

FOXTAIL CLUBMOSS
"Foxtail Bog Clubmoss"
Lycopodium alopecuroides
CLUBMOSS FAMILY

L 23″; H 18″ (when fruiting). Yellow-green. Stalks arched to prostrate, few-branched, densely covered with small, spreading, needle-like leaves. Fertile stalks erect, each topped with bushy tail. **HABITAT** Bogs, ditches, pinewoods. **RANGE** n to sc FL.

Ferns

Ferns, the largest group of seedless vascular plants still found on earth, are diverse in habitat and form. In Florida they occur mainly in shady forests and near fresh water, but several fern species thrive in open sunny areas. Most ferns grow in soil, often in clumps or clusters; some species grow on rocks or trees, and a few float on water.

Ferns have a stem called a *rhizome* that is typically thin and long and grows along the surface or below the ground. The rhizome bears the roots and leaves, and lives for many years. Fern leaves, called *fronds,* are commonly compound and may be *pinnate* (divided into *leaflets*), *bipinnate* (subdivided into *subleaflets*), or even *tripinnate* (divided again into *segments*).

Frond types

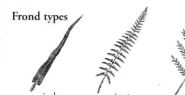

simple   pinnate   bipinnate   tripinnate

Ferns reproduce through the release of spores from tiny sacs called *sporangia,* which commonly occur in clusters *(sori)* on the underside of the frond. The sori may cover the entire frond underside, may form dots or lines, may occur only beneath the frond's curled-under edges, or may be covered by specialized outgrowths of the frond. Fronds that bear sporangia are called fertile fronds; those that do not are called sterile fronds. In some species the sterile and fertile fronds differ in size and shape.

Some ferns are evergreen, but the foliage of many ferns dies back each year. Each spring the rhizome gives rise to coiled tender young fronds called *fiddleheads.* Fiddleheads of some ferns are popular delicacies, but identification is difficult: the shoots of some deadly poisonous flowering plants (including various poison hemlocks) can be mistaken for fern fiddleheads, and many fiddleheads are edible at certain stages and poisonous at others. Only local experts should collect fiddleheads for consumption.

In the accounts that follow, sizes given are typical mature heights or lengths. For illustrations of leaf shapes, see page 136.

segment

sori

Parts of a Fern

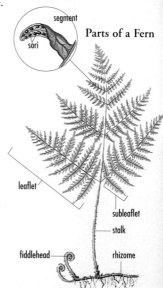

leaflet

subleaflet

stalk

fiddlehead

rhizome

BRACKEN
Pteridium aquilinum
BRACKEN FAMILY
24". Stalks erect, rigid. Fronds divided into 3 broadly triangular, bi- or tripinnate leaflets, each with many pinnate subleaflets. Sori on curled-under leaflet edges. **HABITAT** Dry thickets and hammocks, pinewoods, pastures, roadsides.

VIRGINIA CHAIN FERN
Woodwardia virginica
CHAIN FERN FAMILY
4". Stalks erect. Fronds pinnate, with many oblong to lanceolate deeply lobed leaflets. Sori form chain-like pattern on frond undersides. **HABITAT** Bogs, swamps, marshes, moist woods.

GIANT LEATHER FERN
Acrostichum danaeifolium
MAIDENHAIR FERN FAMILY
13' Stalks erect, stout. Fronds pinnate, with 20–30 narrowly lanceolate leaflets. Fertile fronds taller, with felt-like undersides covered with sporangia. **HABITAT** Edges of brackish and freshwater marshes, lakes, canals. **RANGE** nc to s FL.

LADDER BRAKE
Pteris bahamensis (longifolia)
MAIDENHAIR FERN FAMILY
28". Stalks rigid, wiry. Fronds lanceolate, pinnate, with narrowly linear leaflets. Fertile fronds have smaller leaflets lined with sori on curled-under edges. **HABITAT** On rocks in pinewoods. **RANGE** s FL.

MARSH FERN
Thelypteris palustris
MARSH FERN FAMILY
3'6". Stalks slender. Fronds pinnate, with about 12 lanceolate leaflets, each pinnately divided into several lobes. Sori in rows on frond undersides near midvein, each under a kidney-shaped flap; partly covered by curled-under leaflet edges. **HABITAT** Marshes, swamps, riversides, ditches, wet woods.

STRAP FERN
Campyloneurum phyllitides
POLYPODY FERN FAMILY

3′. Forms clusters on tree trunks. Stalks short. Fronds strap-shaped, undivided, shiny, pendulous; undersides have several rows of sori alongside midrib. **HABITAT** On tree trunks, logs, mossy hammocks; swamps. **RANGE** Peninsular FL.

RESURRECTION FERN
Polypodium polypodioides
POLYPODY FERN FAMILY

8″. Forms huge mats on trees. Stalks slender, scaly. Fronds oblong to lanceolate, leathery, evergreen; pinnate, with linear, wavy-edged leaflets. Sori in row on each side of leaflet midrib. **HABITAT** Hammocks; often on branches of Live Oak, other trees, stumps, logs, rocks.

CINNAMON FERN
Osmunda cinnamomea
ROYAL FERN FAMILY

4′6″. Stalks covered with cinnamon-brown, wooly hairs. Fronds bipinnate, with oblong, pinnately many-lobed leaflets. Fertile fronds precede sterile fronds; have club-shaped, seed-like clusters of sori. **HABITAT** Streamsides, swamps, bogs.

ROYAL FERN
Osmunda regalis var. *spectabilis*
ROYAL FERN FAMILY

4′. Stalks erect. Fronds bipinnate, with 6 or more pairs of leaflets, each with several oblong subleaflets. Fertile leaflets contracted, with brown sori; form conspicuous clusters atop fronds. **HABITAT** Swamps, bogs, streamsides.

SHOESTRING FERN
Vittaria lineata
SHOESTRING FERN FAMILY

L 3′. Forms crowded tufts on tree trunks. Stalks short. Fronds long, ribbon-like, flexible, pendulous. Sori reddish brown; line curled-under edges of frond undersides. **HABITAT** Usu. on Cabbage Palmettos; pinewoods, hammocks, swamps. **RANGE** Peninsular FL.

Trees and Shrubs

Trees and shrubs are woody perennial plants. Trees typically have a single trunk and a well-developed crown of foliage, and grow to at least 16 feet tall; some attain heights of more than 100 feet. Shrubs are usually less than 20 feet tall and often have several woody stems rather than a single trunk. This book covers two major categories of trees and shrubs. Gymnosperms (including conifers) begin on page 92. Broadleaf trees begin on page 96.

Individual tree size varies according to age and environmental factors. The heights given in the following sections are for average mature individuals in Florida; younger trees and those exposed to harsh conditions are smaller; older specimens may attain greater heights in optimal conditions. Trunk diameter, which also varies greatly within a species, is cited only for very large species.

Identifying a Tree

Trees can be identified by three key visual characteristics: crown shape, bark color and texture, and leaf shape and arrangement (illustrated on page 136). Below are common crown shapes for mature conifers and broadleaf trees. These shapes are idealized and simplified for illustrative purposes. The first line of each species account describes tree shape in these terms.

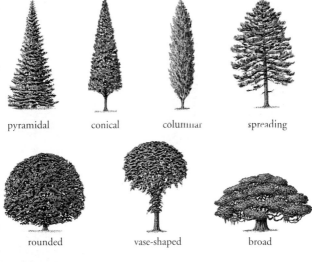

pyramidal   conical   columnar   spreading

rounded   vase-shaped   broad

The roots, trunk, and branches of most trees and shrubs are covered in bark, a protective layer consisting mainly of dead cells. (There are a number of Florida trees—including the palms—that do not have bark or wood.) The bark of young trees often differs in color and texture from mature bark. As a tree grows, the bark splits, cracks, and peels. In some trees, such as birches, the bark peels horizontally. In many trees the bark may develop furrows, ridges, or fissures, may break up into plates, or may flake off. The species accounts describe mature bark unless otherwise noted.

Beneath the bark is the wood, most of which is dense, dark, dead tissue (heartwood) that provides structural support for the plant. Between the heartwood and the bark are many pale, thin layers of living tissue (including sapwood) that transport water and minerals, and produce new wood and bark. Concentric rings, each representing a period (often a year) of growth, are visible in cut trunks and branches.

Shapes of Common Florida Trees

Following are illustrations of the shapes of 36 common Florida species. These represent individuals growing in good conditions and with plenty of space. The shapes of individual trees vary tremendously; those growing in a grove or forest, for instance, may not have these shapes at all.

Slash Pine   Longleaf Pine   Pond Pine   Loblolly Pine

American Beech   Laurel Oak   Basket Oak   Water Oak

Live Oak   Water Tupelo   Black Tupelo   Common Persimmon

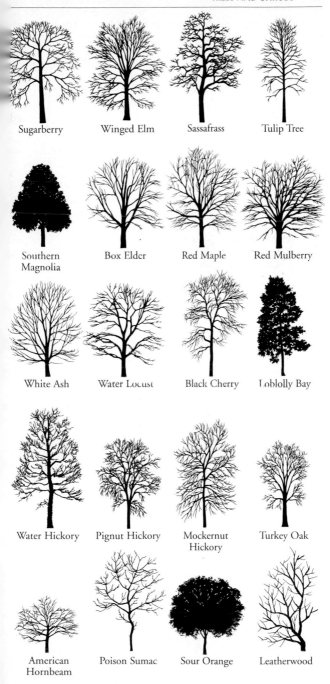

Sugarberry

Winged Elm

Sassafrass

Tulip Tree

Southern
Magnolia

Box Elder

Red Maple

Red Mulberry

White Ash

Water Locust

Black Cherry

Loblolly Bay

Water Hickory

Pignut Hickory

Mockernut
Hickory

Turkey Oak

American
Hornbeam

Poison Sumac

Sour Orange

Leatherwood

American Holly   Crape-myrtle   Chinaberry   Green Hawthorn

Gymnosperms

Gymnosperms ("naked seeds") are trees and shrubs that produce exposed seeds, usually in cones, rather than seeds that are enclosed in an ovary, as in the angiosperms (flowering plants). Conifers, ginkgos, and cycads are all gymnosperms. All of the gymnosperms covered in this guide are conifers, with one exception—the Coontie, a shrubby, fern-like plant that does not produce wood.

Commonly called "evergreens" and known in the timber industry as "softwoods," conifers are the most numerous and widespread gymnosperms found on earth. Their leaves are needle-like (long and slender) or scale-like (small and overlapping), typically evergreen, and well adapted for drought and freezing temperatures, thanks to a thick waxy coating and other protective features.

A distinctive characteristic of conifers is the cone, a reproductive structure comprised of a central axis with spirally arranged scales bearing pollen or seeds. A single tree usually has both pollen-bearing (male) and seed-bearing (female) cones; males are usually carried on lower branches, or lower down on the same branches as females. Male cones appear in spring, shed pollen, and soon fall from the tree. Female cones are larger, more woody, and have scales that protect the seeds until the cones expand to release them; this often occurs in the autumn of the second year after the formation and pollination of the cones. Unless otherwise specified, the cones described in this guide are female.

Of the relatively few conifer species occurring in Florida, the most common include members of the pine and cypress families. Pines found in Florida bear long needles in bundles of two to five; their cones vary widely among different species. Most cypresses have narrow, scale-like leaves covering their branches; their small cones are round and bell-shaped or, in the junipers, fleshy and berry-like.

Typical tree shapes are illustrated on page 89, and leaf shapes, including the needles and scale-like leaves of conifers, are shown on page 136. Unless otherwise noted in the individual species description, needle or scale color is green, fading to yellowish or brown when shedding, and cone color is brown.

SOUTHERN RED CEDAR
"Coastal Red Cedar"
Juniperus virginiana var. *silicicola*
CYPRESS FAMILY

30′. Crown flat to conical. Scales tiny, bluish green, overlapping, cover twigs. Cones tiny, berry-like, bluish. Bark cinnamon brown, thin, shreddy. **HABITAT** Fields, open woods, coastal hammocks, dunes. **RANGE** n to c FL.

BALD CYPRESS
Taxodium distichum
CYPRESS FAMILY

130′. Crown conical to irregularly flat-topped; trunk enlarged at base, often with conical "knees." Needles ¾″, bases twisted; in feather-like arrangement. Cones 1½″, round. Bark dark reddish brown to light brown, furrowed into thin strips. **HABITAT** Swamps, lakesides, floodplains, riversides.

POND CYPRESS
Taxodium distichum var. *imbricarium (T. ascendens)*
CYPRESS FAMILY

100′. Crown conical to irregularly flat-topped; trunk enlarged at base, sometimes with short rounded "knees." Needles ½″, overlapping, cover twigs. Cones 1½″, round. Bark brown to light gray, deeply furrowed into thick vertical plates. **HABITAT** Flatwood ponds. **RANGE** Mainly coastal.

SAND PINE
Pinus clausa
PINE FAMILY

65'. Crown rounded to irreg.; trunk profusely branched. Needles 4", yellowish to dark green, in bundles of 2. Cones 3", egg-shaped. Bark furrowed into narrow ridges, gray to gray-brown. **HABITAT** Dunes, sandhills, sand scrub.

SLASH PINE
Pinus elliottii
PINE FAMILY

130'. Crown rounded to flat-topped. Needles 8", yellow-green to blue-green, in bundles of 2–3. Cones 6", egg-shaped. Bark orange-brown to purple-brown, furrowed into unevenly rectangular, papery, scaly plates. **HABITAT** Flatwoods.

LONGLEAF PINE
Pinus palustris
PINE FAMILY

150'. Crown rounded; branches spreading, up-curved at tips. Needles 12", yellow-green, in bundles usu. of 3. Cones 10", egg-shaped to cylindrical; each scale has sharp, downward-pointing prickle. Bark orange-brown, rectangular, scaly plates. **HABITAT** Sandy uplands, sandhills, flatwoods. **RANGE** n to sc FL.

POND PINE
Pinus serotina
PINE FAMILY

80′. Crown broadly rounded to flat, often ragged. Needles 8″, yellow-green, in bundles of 3. Cones 3″, roundish. Bark red-brown, furrowed into rectangular scaly plates. **HABITAT** Flatwoods, bogs, swamps, shallow ponds. **RANGE** n to nc FL.

LOBLOLLY PINE
Pinus taeda
PINE FAMILY

150′. Crown broadly conical to rounded. Needles 8″, deep yellow-green, in bundles of 2–3. Cones 4″, narrowly egg-shaped. Bark red-brown, scaly, squarish to rectangular plates. **HABITAT** Woods, uplands, old fields. **RANGE** n to nc FL.

COONTIE
"Florida Arrowroot" "Indian Breadroot"
Zamia integrifolia
SAGO-PALM FAMILY

3′. Fern-like or palm-like, with short, stout trunk. Leaves 3′, pinnately compound, with stiff 7″ leaflets. Cones 8″, cylindrical, rusty-brown to purplish, velvety, atop plant. Becoming rare in wild as habitats are destroyed. **HABITAT** Hammocks, pine-oak woods, scrub, shell mounds, towns. **RANGE** Peninsular FL.

Broadleaf Trees and Shrubs

Trees belonging to the angiosperm (flowering plants) group are called broadleaf trees because their leaves are generally broad and flat, in contrast to the needle-like leaves of most conifers. Whereas the seeds of conifers and other gymnosperms are exposed, those of angiosperms are enclosed in an ovary that ripens into a fruit. The fruit may take the form of an edible drupe or berry, such as a cherry or blueberry, a hard-cased nut, the paired winged seeds (key) of a maple, or a dried-out seedpod, such as that of a redbud tree.

In Florida, one of the warmer regions of North America, many broadleaf species (known in the timber industry as "hardwoods") maintain active green leaves year-round. Some tree species, especially those in northern Florida (such as maples), are deciduous, shedding their leaves for the brief and relatively mild winter because the leaves cannot survive freezing temperatures, even for a short period.

Tree species that grow in Florida may look much different than their northern counterparts. The Elderberry, for example, commonly has bipinnately compound leaves in Florida, but always has pinnately compound leaves in the northern United States. Florida's Flowering Dogwood blooms long before its leaves appear, and the leaves mature as the fruit ripens. The Tulip Tree has smaller flowers and more shallowly lobed leaves in Florida. Our Red Maples produce their red flowers in midwinter instead of spring, and the immature red leaves and immature red keys appear soon after. The mature leaves are often three-lobed, whereas north of Florida they are five-lobed.

The individual species descriptions in this guide note leaf color only if it is not green. The various types of leaf arrangements and shapes mentioned in the species descriptions are illustrated on page 136, between the trees and wildflowers sections. As most broadleaf trees bear their leaves in an alternate arrangement, only exceptions are noted in the species descriptions. Leaf measurements indicate length unless otherwise stated. Leaflet measurements are given for compound leaves.

Illustrations of flower types and parts, and a discussion of the structure and function of flowers, are given on pages 137–138, before the wildflowers section. The species accounts generally omit flower information for trees that bloom rather inconspicuously. In Florida, many trees bloom year-round; for such species the typical peak months are given. Fruits of broadleaf trees emerge weeks or months after the flowers; months of maturation are given only for edible fruit.

To facilitate identification, we have grouped descriptions of large broadleaf trees (which begin on page 97) separately from small broadleaf trees and shrubs (which begin on page 110).

POND APPLE
Annona glabra
ANNONA FAMILY

50′. Crown rounded, spreading; trunk short, buttressed. Leaves 5″, elliptical to ovate, leathery, evergreen. Bark dark reddish brown, shallowly fissured. Flowers 1″, cup-shaped, creamy white to pale yellow, nodding; bloom Apr.–June. Fruit 5″, roundish, yellow; edible, ripe Sept.–Nov. HABITAT Swamps, wet hammocks, streamsides. RANGE c FL and south.

AUSTRALIAN-PINE
"Australian Oak" "She-oak" "Horsetail Tree"
Casuarina equisetifolia
AUSTRALIAN-PINE FAMILY

100′. Pine-like, with shaggy open crown. Leaves tiny, scale-like, whorled on jointed, quill-like twigs. Bark dark brown to light gray, furrowed into thin strips. Fruit ¾″, yellowish-brown, woody balls. Introduced from Australia; a very serious pest replacing native plants. HABITAT Beaches, pinelands, disturbed areas. RANGE Coastal peninsular FL.

AMERICAN BEECH
Fagus grandifolia
BEECH FAMILY

100′. Crown narrow to spreading, rounded; trunk tall; branches upright. Leaves 5½″, elliptical to ovate, toothed; turn yellow in fall. Bark light gray, often mottled, smooth. Fruit spiny, orange-green burs; each contain a pair of ¾″, triangular, yellowish-brown beechnuts. HABITAT Hammocks, bluffs. RANGE n FL.

SOUTHERN RED OAK
"Spanish Oak"
Quercus falcata
BEECH FAMILY

100'. Crown rounded; branches wide-spreading. Leaves 8", broadly oval, with 3–7 deep, bristle-tipped lobes, hairy below. Bark fissured, dark brown to blackish. Acorns ½", round; cap shallow. **HABITAT** Upland woods. **RANGE** n to c FL.

LAUREL OAK
"Diamond-leaf Oak"
Quercus laurifolia
BEECH FAMILY

100'. Crown rounded. Leaves 4", opposite, oblanceolate to obovate, leathery, semi-evergreen. Bark furrowed in flat ridges, dark brown. Acorns 1", egg-shaped; cap deep. **HABITAT** Moist woods, hammocks, river and streamsides, bay-tree swamps.

BASKET OAK
"Swamp Chestnut Oak" "Cow Oak"
Quercus michauxii
BEECH FAMILY

100'. Crown compact, rounded; branches stout; trunk thick. Leaves 8¾", obovate, toothed or shallowly lobed, hairy below. Bark light gray, furrowed, scaly. Flowers minute; males in greenish-yellow, pendulous 4" catkins; females in short reddish catkins; bloom Apr.–May. Acorns 1½", egg-shaped; cap deep, bumpy. **HABITAT** Hammocks, limestone ravines. **RANGE** n to nc FL.

WATER OAK
Quercus nigra
BEECH FAMILY

80'. Crown broad, rounded; trunk tall. Leaves 4", obovate, sometimes 3- or 5-lobed. Bark grayish black, furrowed, scaly-ridged. Acorns ¾", round; cap very shallow. **HABITAT** Moist mixed woods. **RANGE** Mainly n to c FL.

LIVE OAK
Quercus virginiana
BEECH FAMILY

H 65'; D 7'. Crown broad, rounded; trunk buttressed; main branches stout, spreading. Leaves 5", elliptical to oblong, wavy-edged; shiny above, hairy below; evergreen. Bark dark brown, ridged and furrowed into small scales. Acorns 1", egg-shaped; cap shallow. **HABITAT** Moist woods, roadsides, city lots.

BLACK MANGROVE
Avicennia germinans
BLACK MANGROVE FAMILY

60'; thicket-forming shrub in n FL. Crown dense, rounded; roots erect, knee-like. Leaves 5", opposite, elliptical to lanceolate, leathery, evergreen. Bark scaly, gray to brown. Flowers ½", funnel-shaped, white, in conical clusters; bloom May–July (year-round). **HABITAT** Tidal swamps. **RANGE** Coastal FL.

PIGEON-PLUM
"Dove-plum" "Tie-tongue"
Coccoloba diversifolia
BUCKWHEAT FAMILY

65'. Crown rounded; branches dense, spreading. Leaves 4", ovate to lanceolate, evergreen. Bark peeling, gray mottled with brown. Fruit ½", berry-like, dark red. **HABITAT** Coastal hammocks. **RANGE** sc FL and south.

WATER TUPELO
Nyssa aquatica
DOGWOOD FAMILY

115'. Trunk buttressed. Leaves 12", ovate to oblong, leathery. Bark dark brown, furrowed. Flowers minute, greenish; bloom Apr.–May. Fruit 1", berry-like, blue-black. Flowers a nectar source of tupelo honey. **HABITAT** Floodplain woods, swamps, pondsides and lakesides. **RANGE** nw FL.

BLACK TUPELO
"Sourgum"
Nyssa sylvatica var. *sylvatica*
DOGWOOD FAMILY

130'. Crown rounded; branches slender, horizontal. Leaves 6", obovate to elliptical-oblong, wavy-edged, often crowded at branchlet ends; turn reddish in fall. Bark light brown, furrowed in scaly ridges. Fruit ½", berry-like, blue-black. **HABITAT** Uplands. **RANGE** n to nc FL.

COMMON PERSIMMON
Diospyros virginiana
EBONY FAMILY

65'. Crown broad, rounded; trunk short; branches stout, spreading; thicket-forming. Leaves 6", lanceolate to broadly elliptical, leathery; turn yellow Aug–Sept. Bark brown to blackish, roughly square-plated. Flowers tiny, greenish yellow. Berries 2½", orange; edible, ripe Aug.–Oct. **HABITAT** Pinelands, moist woods, fields.

SUGARBERRY
"Hackberry"
Celtis laevigata
ELM FAMILY

90'. Crown rounded; branches spreading to drooping. Leaves 6", lanceolate. Bark gray, warty. Fruit ⅓", berry-like, orangish to brownish red. **HABITAT** Wet mixed woods, upland woods, old fields.

WINGED ELM
Ulmus alata
ELM FAMILY

65'. Crown rounded, spreading; branches stout; twigs corky-winged. Leaves 4", lanceolate to broadly elliptical, toothed. Bark reddish brown to gray, furrowed, scaly. Fruit tiny, flat, oval, brown, hairy-fringed. **HABITAT** Woods. **RANGE** n to nc FL.

RED BAY
Persea borbonia
LAUREL FAMILY

65'. Shrubby tree; crown dense, rounded; trunk often leaning; branches upright. Leaves 8", elliptical, leathery, evergreen, spicy-aromatic when crushed. Bark reddish brown to brownish gray, irregularly furrowed. Fruit ½", berry-like, blue-black. **HABITAT** Hammocks, dry woods, coastal dune-scrub.

SASSAFRAS
Sassafras albidum
LAUREL FAMILY

100'. Crown open, flat; trunk stout; branches spreading. Leaves 6"; 1-, 2-, or 3-lobed. Bark furrowed, reddish to brown. Fruit ½", berry-like, blue-black, with thick, bright red stem. **HABITAT** Moist woods, thickets, old fields. **RANGE** n to nc FL.

TULIP TREE
"Yellow Poplar"
Liriodendron tulipifera
MAGNOLIA FAMILY

100′. Crown broadly conical. Leaves 5″, saddle-shaped, 4- or 6-lobed. Bark grayish to brown, furrowed. Flowers 3½″, tulip-shaped, bright green with orange basal splotch; bloom Apr.–May. Fruit 3″, brown, cone-like clusters of winged seeds. **HABITAT** Rich woods, streamsides. **RANGE** n to nc FL.

SOUTHERN MAGNOLIA
"Bull Bay"
Magnolia grandiflora
MAGNOLIA FAMILY

100′. Crown conical; trunk tall, straight. Leaves 8″, elliptical, leathery, rusty-haired below, evergreen. Bark brown or gray, rough, with small plates. Flowers 8″, cup-shaped, white, fragrant; bloom Apr.–Aug. Fruit 5″, egg-shaped, cone-like, rusty brown or pinkish, with fleshy red seeds suspended by hair-like threads. **HABITAT** Hammocks, upland woods, towns. **RANGE** n to c FL.

SWEET BAY
"Swamp Magnolia"
Magnolia virginiana
MAGNOLIA FAMILY

100′. Crown narrowly conical; branches short. Leaves 6″, elliptical, leathery, silvery below, evergreen. Bark grayish, furrowed. Flowers 2¾″, cup-shaped, white, fragrant; bloom Apr.–Oct. Fruit 2″, cone-like, pinkish to rusty brown. **HABITAT** Wet woods, swamps, bogs.

BOX ELDER
"Ash-leaved Maple"
Acer negundo
MAPLE FAMILY

65′. Crown broad, irreg.; trunk often crooked; branches wide-spreading. Leaves 5″, opposite, pinnately compound, with 3–5 ovate or elliptical, toothed, 4″ leaflets. Bark light brown to gray, furrowed. Key 1½″, red-brown. **HABITAT** Moist woods, streamsides, floodplains. **RANGE** n to c FL.

RED MAPLE
Acer rubrum
MAPLE FAMILY

90′. Crown rounded. Leaves 5″, opposite, variable in shape, often palmately 3- to 5-lobed, toothed; turn red, yellow, or orange in fall. Bark dark gray, furrowed. Flowers tiny, red, in bunches; bloom Dec.–Jan. (before leaves). Key 1″, red. **HABITAT** Wet woods, swamps.

SILVER MAPLE
Acer saccharinum
MAPLE FAMILY

80′. Crown rounded. Leaves 6″, opposite, deeply palmately lobed, toothed, silvery below; turn yellow or orange. Bark gray, forms long scaly plates. Flowers tiny, greenish yellow to red, in dense clusters; bloom Jan.–Feb. (before leaves). Key 1½″, light brown. **HABITAT** Wet woods, floodplains. **RANGE** n to nc FL.

STRANGLER FIG
"Golden Fig"
Ficus aurea
MULBERRY FAMILY

65′. Crown broadly rounded; trunks multiple; branches stout, with hanging roots. Leaves 5″, elliptical to ovate, thick, evergreen. Bark small, ash-gray to blackish plates. Figs ¾″, round, red or yellow. Matures from vine-like shrub "strangling" host tree (often Cabbage Palmetto). **HABITAT** Hammocks, coastal islands. **RANGE** c FL and south (usu. coastal).

RED MULBERRY
Morus rubra
MULBERRY FAMILY

65′. Crown rounded; trunk stout; branches spreading. Leaves 4″, heart-shaped, toothed, white-hairy below. Bark reddish brown, ridged, fissured. Flowers tiny, greenish; males in pendulous 2″ spikes, females in thick 1″ spikes; bloom Apr.–June. Fruit 1¼″, blackberry-like, red to dark purple; edible, ripe July–Aug. **HABITAT** Hammocks, pinelands, thickets, towns.

WHITE ASH
Fraxinus americana
OLIVE FAMILY

80′. Crown rounded to pyramidal; branches stout. Leaves 12″, pinnately compound, with 5–9 (usu. 7) ovate to oblong, 6″ leaflets. Bark dark brown to gray, fissured. Flowers minute, greenish yellow; males in dense bunches, females in branched clusters. Key 2½″, brown, 1-winged. **HABITAT** Floodplains, hammocks. **RANGE** n FL.

Palms

The palm family (*Arecaceae* or *Palmae*) is a large, distinctive group of flowering plants comprised of about 200 genera and 2,800 species. Palms occur naturally in tropical as well as subtropical to warm temperate zones. As many as 19 species of palms occur naturally in Florida (some are native while others were introduced and have become naturalized); the Cabbage Palmetto is the state tree.

Palms differ from gymnosperms and broadleaf trees in several ways. The trunks of palms rarely branch. Because the trunk tissue consists of fibers and soft tissue rather than true wood, a palm trunk typically achieves its maximum girth before growing taller, and does not increase significantly in diameter with age, as other trees do. Palms lack true bark, and the trunks are often scarred by leaf stalks that have fallen off.

Palm leaves are the largest among plants and grow in tufts at the top of the trunk. Palms are commonly divided into two groups: those with feather-like leaves (long and pinnately divided into numerous segments) and those with fan-shaped leaves (shallowly or deeply palmately divided into segments). In some fan palms, such as the Cabbage Palmetto, the leafstalk extends into the blade, forming an intermediate leaf type (costapalmate). The segments of all palm leaves are folded lengthwise or corrugated. Palm flowers are borne in huge sprays near the top of the trunk, among or directly below the leaves. Most people envision the huge coconut as the archetypal palm fruit, but native Florida species have large colorful clusters of small, round to egg-shaped, berry-like, inedible fruits.

EVERGLADES PALM
"Paurotis Palm" "Saw Cabbage"
Acoelorrhaphe wrightii
PALM FAMILY

35'. Trunks slender (6"), clustered, covered with reddish-brown leaf-stalk bases. Leaves 3', fan-shaped, deeply palmately divided into folded, linear segments; leafstalk spiny-edged, orange-tinged. **HABITAT** Wet areas, towns. **RANGE** Cultivated in s FL; grows wild only in Everglades N.P.

FLORIDA SILVER PALM
"Silver Thatch Palm"
Coccothrinax argentata
PALM FAMILY

25'. Trunk slender (6"), smooth. Leaves 30", fan-shaped, deeply palmately divided into linear segments, densely silvery-hairy below. Endangered. **HABITAT** Rocky pinelands, coastal dunes. **RANGE** Extreme s FL.

COCONUT PALM
Cocos nucifera
PALM FAMILY

80'. Trunk tall, swollen at base, curved or leaning; gray-brown, with conspicuous rings and vertical cracks. Leaves 23', feather-like, pinnately divided into linear-lanceolate segments. Coconuts 16"; year-round. **HABITAT** Beaches, disturbed areas, towns. **RANGE** Coastal s FL.

FLORIDA ROYAL PALM
Roystonea regia
PALM FAMILY

130'. Trunk tall, light gray, smooth. Leaves 15', feather-like, pinnately divided into linear segments in 4 rows. Flowers white, in clusters of 2 males and 1 female; males ⅓", with 3 spreading petals; females tiny, bud-like. Endangered in wild; widely cultivated. **HABITAT** Marshes, towns. **RANGE** Extreme s FL; Everglades N.P.

CABBAGE PALMETTO
"Cabbage Palm" "Swamp Cabbage"
Sabal palmetto
PALM FAMILY

65'. Trunk tall, light gray, upper part latticed with old leaf bases. Leaves 6', somewhat fan-shaped (costapalmate), with folded linear segments. Often in large groups. Leaf bud at treetop is a delicacy called heart of palm. FL state tree. **HABITAT** Pinelands, hammocks, swamps. **RANGE** Mainly coastal.

SAW PALMETTO
Serenoa repens
PALM FAMILY

6'. Clump-forming. Trunks sprawling, covered with reddish leafstalk bases and brown fibers. Leaves 3', fan-shaped, deeply palmately divided into folded linear segments; leafstalks prickle-edged. **HABITAT** Pinelands, hammocks, coastal dunes, sandhills.

WASHINGTON PALM
"Petticoat Palm"
Washingtonia robusta
PALM FAMILY

100'. Trunk tall, gray, with shaggy skirt of old leaves. Leaves 6', fan-shaped, accordion-pleated, irregularly palmately divided into linear segments with orange-brown, spiny-edged stalks. **HABITAT** Disturbed areas (old homesites, vacant lots), **RANGE** Cultivated throughout FL; naturalized mainly in s FL.

BAHAMA LYSILOMA
"Wild Tamarind"
Lysiloma latisiliquum
PEA FAMILY

65'. Crown umbrella-like; branches zigzag. Leaves 7", semi-evergreen, bipinnately compound, with many ovate to oblong, ½" leaflets. Bark gray to brown, smooth to scaly. Flowers minute, in ¾", pincushion-like, greenish-white heads; bloom Mar.–Aug. Fruit 8" flat black pods. **HABITAT** Hammocks. **RANGE** Extreme s FL.

TAMARIND
"Indian-date"
Tamarindus indica
PEA FAMILY

H 65'; D 5'. Crown dense, rounded; trunk massive, often twisted. Leaves 5", evergreen; pinnately compound, with 20–30 elliptical, ¾" leaflets. Bark dark brown to blackish, rough. Flowers 1", star-shaped, pale yellow, in long clusters; bloom Apr.–June. Fruit 6", bean-like, brown; pulp edible, ripe May–July. **HABITAT** Hammocks, yards. **RANGE** Coastal, from c FL south.

WATER LOCUST
Gleditsia aquatica
PEA FAMILY

80′. Crown broad, flat; trunk short, often thorny; branches thorny. Leaves 8″, feather-like, with many ovate 1″ leaflets. Bark grayish brown to blackish, furrowed or warty. Flowers ⅓″, cup- to star-shaped, greenish white, in slender 4″ clusters; bloom Apr.–June. Fruit 2″, oval, flat, green to red-brown pods. **HABITAT** Hammocks, swamps, riversides, wet woods. **RANGE** n to c FL.

BLACK CHERRY
"Wild Cherry"
Prunus serotina
ROSE FAMILY

100′. Crown rounded. Leaves 6″, oblong, toothed. Bark reddish brown to black, fissured, scaly. Flowers tiny, white, in 6″ clusters; bloom Apr.–May. Cherries ½″, purple-black. **HABITAT** Woods, thickets, old fields. **RANGE** n to c FL.

AMERICAN SYCAMORE
"Plane Tree" "Buttonwood"
Platanus occidentalis
SYCAMORE FAMILY

H 115′; D 3′4″ (wild specimens narrower). Crown broad, open, irreg.; trunk massive. Leaves 10″, maple-like, shallowly palmately 3- to 7-lobed, toothed; turn yellow in fall. Bark smooth; light gray base overlaid with peeling patches of tan, green, or white. Fruit 1¼″ brown balls. **HABITAT** Mainly towns; also floodplains, streamsides. **RANGE** n FL.

LOBLOLLY BAY
Gordonia lasianthus
TEA FAMILY

80'. Crown compact, conical to columnar; branches erect, stout. Leaves 6", elliptical, toothed, leathery, evergreen. Bark dark gray, furrowed. Flowers 3", white, finely fringed, fragrant; bloom May–Aug. **HABITAT** Swamps, bay-tree swamps, bogs. **RANGE** All FL, ex. extreme south.

GUMBO LIMBO
Bursera simaruba
TORCHWOOD FAMILY

80'. Crown spreading, rounded; branches large, crooked; trunk stout. Leaves 8", pinnately compound, with 5–9 ovate, 3" leaflets. Bark reddish brown to green, peeling in papery sheets; resinous, with turpentine odor. Flowers tiny, creamy to greenish white, in 4" clusters; bloom Feb.–Apr. **HABITAT** Hammocks, shell mounds. **RANGE** c FL and south (mainly coastal).

WATER HICKORY
"Bitter Pecan"
Carya aquatica
WALNUT FAMILY

115'. Crown narrowly rounded; trunk tall; branches upright. Leaves 12", pinnately compound, with 7–17 lanceolate, curved, toothed, 4" leaflets. Bark light brown, scaly. Fruit 1½", pear- to egg-shaped, yellowish-brown husks; contain thin-shelled nuts. **HABITAT** Swamps, floodplain forests. **RANGE** All FL, ex. extreme south.

PIGNUT HICKORY
Carya glabra
WALNUT FAMILY

130'. Crown broad, cylindrical; branches spreading. Leaves 16", pinnately compound, with 5–7 variably shaped, toothed, 6" leaflets. Bark gray, ridged, furrowed. Fruit 2", roundish, green to dark brown husks; contain thick-shelled nuts. **HABITAT** Woods. **RANGE** n to c FL.

MOCKERNUT HICKORY
Carya tomentosa
WALNUT FAMILY

115'. Crown narrow to broadly rounded. Leaves 16", pinnate, with usu. 7 ovate to oblong, toothed, hairy, 9" leaflets. Bark gray, ridged, furrowed. Fruit 2", roundish, green to reddish-brown husks; contain thick-shelled nuts. **HABITAT** Upland woods, dry bluffs. **RANGE** n to nc FL.

SWEETGUM
Liquidambar styraciflua
WITCH-HAZEL FAMILY

130'. Crown pyramidal; trunk tall. Leaves 7", maple-like, deeply palmately 5- to 7-lobed, long-pointed, toothed; turn orange to red in fall. Bark dark gray, ridged, furrowed. Flowers minute, in dense, yellow-green or green, round ⅜" heads; bloom May–June. Fruit prickly, green to brown, 1¼" balls. **HABITAT** Moist broadleaf woods, floodplains. **RANGE** n to c FL.

Small Broadleaf Trees and Shrubs

To facilitate identification, we have separated most small broadleaf trees and shrubs from the large broadleaf trees. The species in this section generally reach an average mature height of 40 feet or less.

Although the growth habits of trees and shrubs often intergrade, trees typically have a single woody trunk and a well-developed crown of foliage, whereas shrubs usually have several woody stems growing in a clump. Many of Florida's small trees and shrubs have beautiful and conspicuous flowers and/or colorful fruits. Flower and leaf arrangements and shapes are illustrated on pages 136–137. Evergreens are noted as such.

FLORIDA GROUNDSEL BUSH
"Silverling" "Sea Myrtle"
Baccharis halimifolia
ASTER FAMILY

13'. Many-branched shrub with resinous stems. Leaves 2½", obovate to oblanceolate, evergreen. Flowers in brushy, yellowish or whitish, ½" heads; bloom Aug.–Dec. HABITAT Open woods, marshes, disturbed areas, beaches.

WAX-MYRTLE
"Southern Bayberry"
Myrica cerifera
BAYBERRY FAMILY

40'. Multi-trunked shrub or small, many-branched tree; crown narrow, rounded; branches slender, upright. Leaves 3", oblanceolate, toothed, evergreen. Bark light gray, smooth. Flowers minute, brownish green, in conical clusters; bloom Apr.–June. Fruit tiny, berry-like, covered with bluish-white, waxy bumps. Whole plant aromatic HABITAT Hammocks, pinelands, marshes, flatwoods, bogs, fields, towns.

BAY-CEDAR
Suriana maritima
BAY-CEDAR FAMILY

30'. Clump-forming shrub to small tree. Crown conical; trunk short. Leaves 1½", linear-oblanceolate, grayish green, hairy, fleshy, evergreen. Bark dark gray or brown, cracked or shaggy, peeling in ragged strips. Flowers ½", yellow; bloom year-round. HABITAT Dunes, beaches, coastal scrub, sandy thickets. RANGE Coastal, from c FL south.

ALLEGHENY CHINQUAPIN
Castanea pumila
BEECH FAMILY
50′. Shrub to small tree; crown rounded; trunk(s) short; branches slender. Leaves 6″, elliptical, toothed, leathery, white-hairy below. Bark gray to light reddish brown, shallowly furrowed. Fruit 1¼″, spiny, round, green to brown burs; split to release shiny, brown, egg-shaped, edible nut; ripe Aug.–Oct. **HABITAT** Dry woods, disturbed areas. **RANGE** n to nc FL.

CHAPMAN OAK
Quercus chapmanii
BEECH FAMILY
25′. Shrub or shrubby tree. Leaves 3″, oblong to obovate, variably lobed, nearly evergreen; often turn reddish to yellowish in winter. Bark grayish brown, plated. Acorns 1″, oblong; cap deep. **HABITAT** Dry pinelands, oak scrub.

BLUEJACK OAK
Quercus incana
BEECH FAMILY
40′. Shrubby tree. Leaves 4″, lanceolate to elliptical, bluish to grayish green, hairy below. Bark grayish brown to blackish, square-plated. Acorns ½″, round; cap shallow. **HABITAT** Sandhills, dry pinelands. **RANGE** n to c FL.

TURKEY OAK
Quercus laevis
BEECH FAMILY
50′. Crown rounded; trunk short; branches stout. Leaves 8″, oblong, deeply 3- to 7-lobed, leathery, yellow-green, with twisted stalks; turn red. Bark dark gray to blackish, deeply furrowed, scaly-ridged. Acorns ¾″, egg-shaped; cap shallow. **HABITAT** Sandhills, dry pinelands.

MYRTLE OAK
Quercus myrtifolia
BEECH FAMILY

40′. Shrub or shrubby tree. Leaves 2″, oval or elliptical or obovate, leathery, evergreen. Bark dark gray, smooth to rough. Flowers minute; males in yellowish-green 1¼″ catkins. Acorns ½″, round; cap shallow, scaly. **HABITAT** Sandhills, oak scrub, pine flatwoods.

AMERICAN HORNBEAM
"Blue Beech" "Ironwood"
Carpinus caroliniana
BIRCH FAMILY

35′. Crown rounded, bushy; trunk short, often fluted, muscular looking, often crooked; branches slender. Leaves 2½″, ovate, toothed. Bark gray, smooth to rough. Fruit tiny, round nutlets, each with 3-lobed, leaf-like bract; in ¾″ clusters. **HABITAT** Swamps, wet woods, streamsides. **RANGE** n to c FL.

HOP HORNBEAM
"Rough-barked Ironwood"
Ostrya virginiana
BIRCH FAMILY

40′. Crown wide-spreading; branches drooping. Leaves 4″, oblong to elliptical, toothed. Bark brown, plated, peeling in narrow strips. Fruit 2½″ cone-like clusters of many tiny nuts in papery whitish sacs. **HABITAT** Hammocks, floodplains, towns. **RANGE** n to nc FL.

SEA GRAPE
Coccoloba uvifera
BUCKWHEAT FAMILY

50′. Sprawling shrub to compact tree; trunk(s) short, gnarled. Leaves 10″, roundish, pink-veined, leathery, evergreen. Bark light brown with pale blotches, smooth. Fruit ¾″, purplish, in grape-like clusters; used for jam, ripe Aug.–Sept. Planted to control beach erosion; protected by law. **HABITAT** Beaches, hammocks, scrub, dunes, towns. **RANGE** Coastal, from nc FL south.

JAMAICA CAPER TREE
Capparis cynophallophora
CAPER FAMILY
20′. Sprawling shrub to small tree with arched branches. Leaves 4″, elliptical to obovate, leathery; yellow-green above, silvery brown below. Bark dark red-brown, thin, cracked. Flowers ½″, white to bright purple; bloom Apr.–July. Pods 12″, scaly, reddish. **HABITAT** Coastal hammocks, shell mounds. **RANGE** Coastal, from c FL south.

MANGO
Mangifera indica
CASHEW FAMILY
50′. Crown dense, spreading. Leaves 8″, crowded (appear whorled), lanceolate to narrowly elliptical, leathery, evergreen. Bark gray or dark brown, rough. Flowers ⅓″, cup-shaped, yellowish green or greenish white or reddish, in large clusters; bloom Jan.–Mar. Mangoes 6″, red or pink, tinged with yellow or green; edible, ripe May–June. **CAUTION** Touching broken fruit skin may cause rash. **HABITAT** Hammocks, disturbed areas. **RANGE** Local along coast, from c FL south.

POISONWOOD
"Poison Tree"
Metopium toxiferum
CASHEW FAMILY
40′. Shrub to small tree with low broad crown. Leaves 8″, black-spotted, leathery, evergreen, pinnately compound, with 3–7 ovate 3″ leaflets. Bark reddish brown, scaly. Flowers tiny, greenish yellow, in 8″ clusters; bloom Apr.–June (year-round). Fruit ½″, berry-like, orange-yellow. **CAUTION** All parts poisonous to touch. **HABITAT** Pinelands, hammocks, dunes. **RANGE** Coastal s FL.

WINGED SUMAC
"Shining Sumac"
Rhus copallina
CASHEW FAMILY

25'. Slender shrub to small tree; thicket-forming. Leaves 12", pinnately compound, with 9–23 lanceolate to oblong-elliptical, 3" leaflets on winged axis; turn red to orange in fall. Bark brown, rough, with large scales. Fruit tiny, berry-like, dark red, hairy; in dense, pyramidal, 12" clusters. **HABITAT** Dry woods, thickers, roadsides, fields.

BRAZILIAN PEPPER
"Florida Holly"
Schinus terebinthifolius
CASHEW FAMILY

10'. Shrub to small tree with dense uneven crown of arched interlaced branches. Leaves 6", pinnately compound, with 3–11 elliptical to lanceolate, toothed, 2" leaflets; evergreen; exude turpentine odor when crushed. Bark grayish brown, smooth. Fruit tiny, berry-like, red. Introduced; replacing native plants. **HABITAT** Hammocks, mangrove swamps, pinelands, disturbed areas. **RANGE** Peninsular FL.

POISON SUMAC
Toxicodendron vernix
CASHEW FAMILY

25'. Few-branched shrub to small tree. Leaves 14", pinnately compound, with 7–15 oblong to ovate, 4" leaflets on reddish stalks. Bark light gray, smooth. Flowers tiny, yellowish, in arching or drooping 8" clusters; bloom Apr.–June. Fruit tiny, berry-like, white or yellowish. **CAUTION** Do not touch; Poison Ivy relative. **HABITAT** Swamps, bogs, moist woods, thickets. **RANGE** n to c FL.

KEY LIME
"Lime"
Citrus aurantiifolia
CITRUS FAMILY

25′. Shrub to small tree with spiny twigs. Leaves 3″, elliptical to ovate, evergreen. Bark greenish brown, smooth to rough. Flowers 1¼″, star-shaped, white; bloom Mar.–Apr. Limes 2½″, greenish yellow; edible (sour), ripe Aug.–Oct. **HABITAT** Hammocks, shell mounds, disturbed areas. **RANGE** Coastal s FL.

SOUR ORANGE
"Seville Orange"
Citrus aurantium
CITRUS FAMILY

20′. Small tree with rounded crown. Leaves 5″, elliptical to ovate, evergreen; stalks broadly winged. Bark grayish, smooth. Flowers 1½″, star-shaped, white; bloom Mar.–May. Fruit orange-like, 3½″, orange to reddish. **HABITAT** Coastal hammocks, shell mounds, disturbed areas. **RANGE** Local.

COMMON HOPTREE
"Wafer Ash" "Stinking Ash" "Skunkbush"
Ptelea trifoliata
CITRUS FAMILY

25′. Low spreading shrub or small tree with rounded crown. Leaves 6″, palmately compound, with 3 ovate to lanceolate, 6″ leaflets. Bark smooth, gray. Flowers ½″, star-like, yellowish green; bloom Apr.–May. Fruit 1¼″, wafer-like, green. Foul-smelling. **HABITAT** Moist woods. **RANGE** n to c FL.

HERCULES'-CLUB
"Southern Prickly Ash" "Tickle-tongue" "Toothache Tree"
Zanthoxylum clava-herculis
CITRUS FAMILY

35′. Large shrub to small tree; spiny; crown rounded; trunk short; clump-forming. Leaves 8″, pinnately compound, with 7–9 ovate, curved, toothed, 3″ leaflets. Bark light gray, often with corky, spiny knobs. Flowers tiny, greenish yellow, in 4″ clusters; bloom May–June. **HABITAT** Hammocks, riversides, sand dunes; cultivated along fences and hedgerows.

LIME PRICKLY-ASH
"Wild Lime"
Zanthoxylum fagara
CITRUS FAMILY

30'. Shrub to small tree (in s FL); thorny; crown narrow, rounded. Leaves 4", leathery, evergreen, pinnately compound, with usu. 7–9 ovate to oblanceolate, toothed, 1¼" leaflets on winged axis. Bark scaly, gray. Flowers tiny, greenish yellow, along twigs; bloom May–June (year-round). Fruit tiny, round, reddish brown. **HABITAT** Hammocks. **RANGE** nc FL and south.

COCO-PLUM
"Icaco-plum"
Chrysobalanus icaco
COCO-PLUM FAMILY

16'. Spreading shrub to small tree with dense rounded crown. Leaves 3", obovate to round, leathery, erect, in 2 rows, evergreen. Bark smooth, brownish. Flowers ⅓", bell-shaped, whitish, hairy, in short clusters; bloom year-round. Fruit 1½", berry-like, dark purple; used in jam, ripe year-round. **HABITAT** Hammocks, canal edges, beaches. **RANGE** c FL and south (mainly coastal).

FLORIDA ROSEMARY
Ceratiola ericoides
CROWBERRY FAMILY

5'. Rounded shrub with many erect branches. Leaves ½", needle-like, thick, with curled-under edges; seem whorled. Flowers minute, rusty brown, clustered in leaf axils; bloom Mar.–Apr. Fruit tiny, berry-like, greenish yellow. **HABITAT** Sandhills, scrub, dunes.

LEATHERWOOD
"Titi" "Ironwood" "Swamp Cyrilla"
Cyrilla racemiflora
CYRILLA FAMILY

25'. Multi-stemmed shrub or small tree; crown open, rounded; branches spreading. Leaves 4", oblanceolate to elliptical, leathery, semi-evergreen. Bark thin gray scales. Flowers tiny, white, in narrow 6" clusters; bloom May–Aug. **HABITAT** Swamps, wet pinelands, riversides, bogs. **RANGE** n to c FL.

FLOWERING DOGWOOD
Cornus florida
DOGWOOD FAMILY

40′. Small tree with rounded crown. Leaves 4″, opposite, ovate to broadly elliptical; turn bright red. Bark gray to blackish, fissured into small scales. Flowers 4″, each made up of 4 white or pink, petal-like bracts around a dense greenish flower cluster; bloom Apr.–May (before leaves). Fruit ½″, berry-like, bright red. **HABITAT** Woods, towns. **RANGE** n to c FL.

GEIGER TREE
Cordia sebestena
FORGET-ME-NOT FAMILY

30′. Slender shrub to small tree with rounded crown, upright branches. Leaves 6″, heart-shaped, hairy, evergreen. Bark dark brown to blackish, furrowed, scaly. Flowers 1½″, trumpet-shaped, orange-red, in branched clusters; bloom Mar.–Nov. (year-round). Fruit 1¼″, berry-like, white. **HABITAT** Hammocks. **RANGE** s FL.

DEVIL'S WALKING-STICK
"Hercules'-club"
Aralia spinosa
GINSENG FAMILY

25′. Spiny shrub or small tree with open, umbrella-like crown. Leaves 5′, bi- or tripinnately compound, with many ovate, toothed, 4″ leaflets. Bark furrowed, brown. Flowers tiny, white, in round bunches arranged in large branched clusters. Fruit ⅓″, berry-like, purple. **HABITAT** Moist woods, hammocks. **RANGE** n to c FL.

TAR FLOWER
"Fly Catcher"
Befaria racemosa
HEATH FAMILY

8'. Slender shrub; branches few, stiff, erect. Leaves 1½", elliptical to ovate, evergreen. Flowers 2", star-like, fragrant, sticky, with 7 spoon-shaped, white petals, sometimes pink-tinged at tips; bloom Mar.–May. **HABITAT** Pine flatwoods, scrub. **RANGE** Peninsular FL.

DRAGON TREE
"Tree Lyonia" "Rusty Lyonia"
"Poor Grub"
Lyonia ferruginea
HEATH FAMILY

20'. Large shrub to small tree; trunk and branches twisted. Leaves 3", elliptical to oblanceolate, with curled-under edges; leathery, rusty-scaled below, evergreen. Bark reddish brown, furrowed. Flowers tiny, white with rusty scales; bloom Apr.–May. **HABITAT** Dry pinelands, scrub. **RANGE** n to sc FL.

FETTERBUSH
"Shiny Lyonia" "Staggerbush"
Lyonia lucida
HEATH FAMILY

13'. Many-branched shrub with broad crown. Leaves 3", elliptical to obovate, leathery, evergreen. Flowers ⅓", urn-shaped, whitish pink or pink or red, clustered in leaf axils; bloom Apr.–May. **HABITAT** Pinelands, flatwoods, scrub, bogs, wet woods.

WILD AZALEA
Rhododendron canescens
HEATH FAMILY

16'. Erect shrub with irreg. crown. Leaves 4", oblanceolate to elliptical, hairy below. Flowers 1¼", trumpet-shaped, pink, hairy, fragrant, clustered at branch ends; bloom Feb.–Apr. **HABITAT** Flatwoods, hammocks, bluffs, streamsides. **RANGE** n to nc FL.

SWAMP AZALEA
"Clammy Azalea"
"Swamp Honeysuckle"
Rhododendron viscosum
HEATH FAMILY

16'. Open, stiff-branched shrub. Leaves 3", oblanceolate to obovate, hairy. Flowers 2", trumpet-shaped, white, often pink-tinged, sticky, fragrant; bloom May–June. HABITAT Wet woods, swamps, bogs. RANGE n to sc FL.

SPARKLEBERRY
Vaccinium arboreum
HEATH FAMILY

35'. Slender tree with crooked branches, irreg. crown. Leaves 1", obovate to elliptical, evergreen; often turn reddish in fall. Bark grayish brown, often mottled, scaly. Berries ⅓", green to blue-black. HABITAT Hammocks, woods, oak scrub, streamsides, clearings. RANGE n to sc FL.

HIGHBUSH BLUEBERRY
Vaccinium corymbosum
HEATH FAMILY

16'. Shrub with 1 to several erect branching stems. Leaves 3", ovate to elliptical, untoothed. Flowers ½", cylindrical to urn-shaped, white to pinkish, in short bunches; bloom Apr.–May. Berries ½", blue-black; edible, ripe June–July. HABITAT Hammocks, pinelands, swamps, bay-tree swamps.

SHINY BLUEBERRY
Vaccinium myrsinites
HEATH FAMILY

24". Spreading, colony-forming shrub with slender branches and stems. Leaves ½", elliptical to ovate, toothed, evergreen. Flowers tiny, urn-shaped, white to dark pink, in short bunches or branched clusters; bloom Apr.–May. Berries ⅓", blue-black; edible, ripe May–June. HABITAT Pine flatwoods, sandhills, scrub.

DAHOON HOLLY
Ilex cassine
HOLLY FAMILY
30'. Shrub to small tree with rounded crown, short trunk, slender branches. Leaves 4", lanceolate to oblanceolate, evergreen. Bark smooth, dark gray. Flowers tiny, white, in small branched clusters; bloom Apr.–June (year-round). Fruit 1/3", berry-like, red, orange-red, or yellow. **HABITAT** Flatwoods, bogs; pond-, swamp-, and streamsides.

POSSUM HAW
"Winterberry"
Ilex decidua
HOLLY FAMILY
30'. Shrub to small tree with open, spreading crown. Leaves 2½", oblanceolate to elliptical, toothed. Bark grayish. Flowers tiny, white to yellowish green. Fruit 1/3", berry-like, orange to red. **HABITAT** Floodplains, wet thickets. **RANGE** Panhandle and w coast south to c FL.

GALLBERRY
"Inkberry"
Ilex glabra
HOLLY FAMILY
10'. Shrub. Leaves 2", elliptical to oblanceolate, toothed, leathery, evergreen. Flowers tiny, white; bloom Feb.–May. Fruit tiny, berry-like, purple-black. **HABITAT** Pinelands, thickets, bogs.

AMERICAN HOLLY
Ilex opaca
HOLLY FAMILY
50'. Crown pyramidal; trunk short; branches short, rigid. Leaves 4", oblong to obovate, spiny-toothed, stiff, leathery, evergreen. Bark light gray, warty. Fruit ½", berry-like, bright red. **HABITAT** Moist woods, riversides, towns. **RANGE** n to c FL.

YAUPON HOLLY
Ilex vomitoria
HOLLY FAMILY
25'. Many-branched shrub to small tree with spreading rounded crown; thicket-forming. Leaves 1¼", elliptical, toothed, leathery, evergreen. Bark gray, smooth. Flowers tiny, white to cream, clustered in l[ ] axils; bloom Mar.–Apr. Fruit [ ] berry-like, red. Cultivated a[ ] ornamental, esp. for hedges. **H**[ ] Upland woods, streamsides, [ ] sides, dunes, pine flatwoods [ ] n to sc FL.

ELDERBERRY
Sambucus canadensis
HONEYSUCKLE FAMILY

13'. Shrub to small tree with rounded crown, short trunk, upright branch-es; thicket-forming. Leaves 6", opposite, pinnately or bipinnately compound, with about 5–11 lanceolate to ovate, toothed, 6" leaflets. Bark grayish brown, furrowed. Flowers tiny, white, in flattish 16" clusters; bloom June–Aug. (year-round). Fruit tiny, berry-like, purple-black; used in wine, jam, ripe year-round. **HABITAT** Wet open woods, thickets, disturbed areas.

WALTER VIBURNUM
"Small Viburnum"
Viburnum obovatum
HONEYSUCKLE FAMILY

30'. Shrub to small tree with broad spreading crown. Leaves 2", opposite, obovate to oblanceolate, evergreen. Bark dark brown to black, furrowed into angular blocks. Flowers tiny, white, in flat 2" clusters; bloom Apr.–May. Fruit berry-like, ⅓", red to purple-black. Young stems, leafstalks, and flower stalks covered with rusty scales. **HABITAT** Moist woods, thickets, streamsides.

?ED BUCKEYE
?esculus pavia
?RSE-CHESTNUT FAMILY

Shrub to small tree with open crown, erect branches. Leaves 6", oppo-...n long red stalks; palmately compound, with 5–7 oblanceolate, ...d, 6" leaflets. Bark dark gray or brown, smooth. Flowers 1½", tubular, ...d, in branched clusters; bloom Apr.–May. Fruit 2½", pear-shaped, ...athery capsule; splits to release 1–3 nut-like seeds. **HABITAT** Moist ...mmocks, streamsides, swampsides. **RANGE** n to c FL.

LANCEWOOD
Ocotea (Nectandra) coriacea
LAUREL FAMILY

40′. Trunk narrow, rounded; branches spreading. Leaves 6″, oblong to lanceolate, evergreen. Bark dark reddish brown, rough, warty. Flowers ⅓″, star-shaped, creamy white, fuzzy, in branched clusters; bloom Mar.–Sept. Fruit ½″, berry-like, olive-shaped, green to purple-black, in red cup. HABITAT Hammocks. RANGE nc FL and south (mainly e coast).

CRAPE-MYRTLE
Lagerstroemia indica
LOOSESTRIFE FAMILY

25′. Shrub to small tree; crown irreg.; trunks and branches twisted. Leaves 2½″, elliptical to obovate. Bark light brown, smooth. Flowers 1½″, with 4–7 wrinkled petals; white, pink, lavender, or purple; in branched clusters; bloom June–Aug. Cultivated species that often escapes into wild. HABITAT Disturbed areas, towns. RANGE n and c FL (local).

BUTTONBUSH
Cephalanthus occidentalis
MADDER FAMILY

10′. Shrub to small tree with rounded spreading crown. Leaves 6″, opposite or whorled, elliptical to ovate. Bark dark grayish brown to blackish, fissured in broad ridges. Flowers tiny, white, in fuzzy, pincushion-like heads. Fruit tiny, seedlike, on rough, brown, woody, ¾″ balls. HABITAT Swamps, lakes, ponds, streams, floodplains.

SCARLETBUSH
"Firebush"
Hamelia patens
MADDER FAMILY

13′. Shrub to small tree. Leaves 6″, in whorls of 3–7, elliptical to ovate, red-veined, red-stalked, evergreen. Bark brownish or grayish, smooth. Flowers 1″, tubular, orange-red, in 1-sided clusters; bloom year-round. Berries ½″, red to purple-black, with conspicuous ring on top. HABITAT Hammocks, shell mounds, open disturbed areas. RANGE c FL and south (usu. coastal).

WILD COFFEE
Psychotria nervosa
MADDER FAMILY

7'. Few-branched shrub; stems and branches often hairy. Leaves 6", opposite, elliptical to narrowly obovate, glossy, evergreen. Flowers tiny, white, in flat 2½" clusters; bloom May–Aug. (year-round). Fruit ⅓", berry-like, yellow to red. **HABITAT** Hammocks, thickets. **RANGE** Peninsular FL (usu. coastal).

CHINABERRY
"Umbrella Tree"
Melia azedarach
MAHOGANY FAMILY

50'. Wide-branching tree with rounded crown. Leaves 20", bipinnately compound, with many ovate, toothed, 3" leaflets. Bark dark to reddish brown, furrowed. Flowers ¾", star-shaped, lavender; bloom Apr.–June. Fruit ½", berry-like, pale yellow. **CAUTION** Fruit poisonous. **HABITAT** Thickets, woods, disturbed areas.

MAHOGANY
"West Indian Mahogany"
Swietenia mahagoni
MAHOGANY FAMILY

40'. Crown large, dense, rounded; trunk buttressed. Leaves 7", pinnately compound, with 8–20 ovate, long-pointed, 2½" leaflets. Flowers ⅓", star-shaped, pale yellow to orange-yellow; bloom June–Aug. Fruit 4", pear-shaped, brown. **HABITAT** Towns, hammocks (uncommon in wild). **RANGE** Extreme s FL (mainly coastal).

LOCUST BERRY
"Key Byrsonima"
Byrsonima lucida
MALPIGHIA FAMILY

20'. Multi-trunked shrub to small tree; crown irreg.; branches erect, spindly. Leaves 2", opposite, obovate, leathery, evergreen. Bark pale brown, smooth. Flowers ½", white to pinkish to crimson, with 5 stalked petals around cup-like center; bloom Mar.–June. Fruit ½", berry-like, red. **HABITAT** Pinelands. **RANGE** s tip FL (e coast and Keys).

MARLBERRY
Ardisia escallonioides
MYRSINE FAMILY

25'. Large shrub to small tree; crown narrow, rounded; branches slender, upright. Leaves 6", elliptical to obovate, wavy-edged, leathery, evergreen. Bark light gray, scaly. Flowers ⅓", 5-petaled, white or lavender, in branched clusters; bloom Apr.–May (year-round). Fruit ½", berry-like, purple-black. **HABITAT** Hammocks, pinelands. **RANGE** c FL and south (often coastal).

MYRSINE
"Rapanea"
Myrsine floridana (Rapanea punctata)
MYRSINE FAMILY

20'. Shrub to small tree; crown open, irreg.; branches few, slender. Leaves 4", oblanceolate to elliptical, with rolled-under edges, leathery, often crowded at branch ends, evergreen. Bark light gray, smooth. Flowers tiny, greenish white with reddish streaks, in dense clusters; bloom Oct.–Jan. (year-round). Fruit tiny, berry-like, blue-black. **HABITAT** Hammocks, pinelands. **RANGE** c FL and south (mainly coastal).

MELALEUCA
"Cajeput Tree" "Punk Tree" "Paperbark Tree"
Melaleuca quinquenervia
MYRTLE FAMILY

50'. Trunk irregularly divided into many often drooping branches. Leaves 4", lanceolate, leathery. Bark grayish white, spongy, sheds in thin strips. Flowers tiny, creamy white, in 6" bottlebrush-like spikes; bloom year-round. Fruit ½", hard brown capsules. Introduced; replacing native plants. **HABITAT** Wet pine flatwoods, cypress swamps, low wet areas. **RANGE** c FL and south.

CHRISTMAS BERRY
Lycium carolinianum
NIGHTSHADE FAMILY

10′. Shrub; branches long, curved, bushy, spreading; twigs thorny-tipped. Leaves 1″, linear-oblanceolate, fleshy, often clustered. Flowers ½″, bluish, funnel-shaped; bloom June–Nov. Berries ½″, red. **HABITAT** Salt marshes, salt flats, beaches, shell mounds, mangrove swamp edges. **RANGE** Coastal FL.

POTATO TREE
"Mullein Nightshade"
Solanum erianthum
NIGHTSHADE FAMILY

16′. Shrub or small tree; crown low, flat; branches spreading. Leaves 11¾″, ovate to obovate, often wavy-edged, hairy, evergreen. Bark light green to grayish brown, warty. Flowers ½″, star-shaped, white, in rounded clusters; bloom year-round. Berries ¾″, yellow. **HABITAT** Hammocks, thickets, disturbed areas. **RANGE** Peninsular FL (mainly coastal).

TALLOWWOOD
"Hog-plum"
Ximenia americana
OLAX FAMILY

20′. Sprawling shrub to short tree; crown narrow, irreg.; trunk(s) twisted; branches spreading, crooked, thorny. Leaves 3″, elliptical or oblanceolate, evergreen. Bark red-brown, smooth. Flowers ⅓″, yellowish white; bloom Apr.–Oct. (year-round). Fruit berry-like, 1¼″, yellow. **HABITAT** Hammocks, scrub, pinelands. **RANGE** Peninsular FL.

FLORIDA PRIVET
"Inkberry"
Forestiera segregata
OLIVE FAMILY

10'. Straggly shrub or shrubby tree. Leaves 2", opposite, oblanceolate. Bark gray, smooth. Fruit ½", olive-shaped, purple-black. **HABITAT** Coastal hammocks, thickets, scrub. **RANGE** Coastal peninsular FL.

POP ASH
"Water Ash" "Carolina Ash"
Fraxinus caroliniana
OLIVE FAMILY

40'. Small tree with open rounded crown; usu. multi-trunked. Leaves 12", opposite, pinnately compound, with 5–7 ovate to oblong leaflets, each 6", untoothed to irregularly toothed. Bark light gray, often blotchy, scaly. Flowers minute, greenish yellow; males in dense elongated clusters, females in branched elongated clusters; bloom Mar.–Apr. Fruit 2½", brown, 1-winged key. **HABITAT** Swamps, woods, pondsides.

WILD OLIVE
"Devilwood"
Osmanthus americanus
OLIVE FAMILY

50'. Shrub to small tree with rounded crown, short trunk, slender branches. Leaves 6", opposite, elliptical to ovate, with curled-under edges; leathery, evergreen. Bark dark to reddish gray, rough, with thin scales. Flowers tiny, white, bell-shaped, clustered, bloom Apr.–May. Fruit ½", berry-like, green to bluish black. **HABITAT** Swamps, hammocks, moist woods. **RANGE** n to c FL.

PAPAYA
Carica papaya
PAPAYA FAMILY

10'. Crown narrow; trunk tall, soft. Leaves 24", evergreen, deeply palmately 7-lobed, with main lobes pinnately lobed. Bark green to grayish brown, smooth. Flowers 2", trumpet-shaped, yellow; bloom year-round. Papayas 3½" (larger in cultivated plants), round to pear-shaped, green to orange, clustered near treetop; edible, ripe year-round. Introduced; grows as a weed. **HABITAT** Hammocks, shell mounds, thickets. **RANGE** c FL and south (local; mainly coastal).

SWEET ACACIA
Acacia farnesiana
PEA FAMILY

16'. Shrub to small tree; crown spreading; twigs zigzag, spiny. Leaves 4", feather-like, with many tiny linear leaflets. Bark reddish brown, shaggy. Flowers minute, yellow, fragrant, in ½" pincushion-like heads; bloom Feb.–Apr. **HABITAT** Shell mounds, hammocks, pinelands, disturbed areas, towns. **RANGE** nc FL and south (mainly coastal).

MIMOSA
"Silk Tree"
Albizia julibrissin
PEA FAMILY

50'. Small tree; crown umbrella-like; trunk short. Leaves 12", feather-like, with many linear, curved, ½" leaflets. Bark grayish, smooth. Flowers minute, pink, in 3" pincushion-like heads; bloom Mar.–June. Pods 8", linear-oblong, flat, yellowish green. **HABITAT** Disturbed areas. **RANGE** n to c FL.

EASTERN REDBUD
"Judas Tree"
Cercis canadensis
PEA FAMILY

25'. Shrubby tree; crown low, spreading, flat to rounded. Leaves 5", heart-shaped. Bark brown, scaly, ridged. Flowers ½", magenta, pea-flower-like, in small clusters; bloom Apr.–May (before leaves). Fruit 4", flat, oblong, brown, hanging pods. Popular ornamental. **HABITAT** Moist woods, yards. **RANGE** n to c FL.

CORAL BEAN
Erythrina herbacea
PEA FAMILY

16'. Low shrub to small tree (in s FL); branches brittle, spiny. Leaves yellowish green, 8", divided into 3, arrowhead-shaped, 3" leaflets. Bark smooth, yellowish. Flowers 2", tubular, red, in long clusters; bloom Feb.–June. Pods 4", oblong, black-brown. **CAUTION** Pods contain poisonous, bright red seeds. **HABITAT** Pinelands, hammocks, disturbed areas, thickets.

LEAD TREE
"Jumbie-bean"
Leucaena leucocephala
PEA FAMILY

35'. Broad, multi-stemmed shrub or small tree with spreading crown. Leaves 12", feather-like, with many oblong ⅜" leaflets. Bark dark brown, ridged, scaly. Flowers minute, white to yellowish, in pincushion-like ¾" heads; bloom year-round. Pods 6", flat, brown. **HABITAT** Hammocks, coastal strands, disturbed areas. **RANGE** nc FL and south.

JERUSALEM THORN
"Mexican Palo Verde"
Parkinsonia aculeata
PEA FAMILY

25'. Shrub to small tree; crown open, spreading; branches slender, thorny. Leaves 20", feather-like, bipinnately compound, with many tiny elliptical leaflets that fall off, leaving flat stiff stalks. Bark brown or reddish, smooth. Flowers ½", pea-like, yellow; bloom May–June. Pods 4", leathery, brown. **HABITAT** Disturbed areas, towns. **RANGE** Coastal peninsular FL (local).

FLORIDA FISH POISON TREE
"Jamaica Dogwood"
Piscidia piscipula
PEA FAMILY

50'. Small tree; crown irregularly rounded; branches twisted. Leaves 10", grayish-green, leathery, evergreen, pinnately compound, with 5–11 ovate 2¾" leaflets. Bark gray, mottled, scaly. Flowers ⅓", pea-like, lavender-white, in 4" clusters; bloom Apr.–May. Pods 4", rectangular, light brown, with 4 papery, wavy-edged wings. In W. Indies, powder made from roots, bark, and leaves was used to stun fish. **HABITAT** Shell mounds, coastal hammocks. **RANGE** c FL and south (mainly coastal s FL).

RED MANGROVE
Rhizophora mangle
RED MANGROVE FAMILY

50'. Shrub to small tree supported by interlacing "prop roots" from trunk or large branches. Leaves 6", opposite, elliptical, leathery, evergreen. Bark gray, furrowed, scaly-ridged. Flowers ½", funnel- to star-shaped, white or yellowish, hairy; bloom year-round. Fruit 1", egg-shaped, rusty brown; germinates on tree, with a long, green, torpedo-shaped root. **HABITAT** Tidal swamps. **RANGE** Coastal peninsular FL.

PARSLEY HAW
"Parsley Hawthorn"
Crataegus marshallii
ROSE FAMILY

26'. Small tree with rounded crown; branches often thorny. Leaves 2", ovate to triangular, deeply lobed, toothed. Bark scaly, thin, gray. Flowers ¾", 5-petaled, white to pink, in flat-topped, branched clusters; bloom Mar.–Apr. Fruit tiny, berry-like, bright red. **HABITAT** Moist woods, floodplains, riversides. **RANGE** n to c FL.

ONE-FLOWERED HAWTHORN
"Dwarf-thorn" "One-flowered Haw"
Crataegus uniflora
ROSE FAMILY

10'. Large shrub to small tree; trunk short, stout; branches often zigzag and thorny. Leaves 1¼", oblanceolate, toothed, hairy. Bark gray, furrowed, scaly. Flowers ¾", 5-petaled; bloom Mar.–Apr. Fruit ½", berry-like, reddish to yellowish green. **HABITAT** Sandhills, dry woods. **RANGE** n FL.

GREEN HAWTHORN
"Green Haw"
Crataegus viridis
ROSE FAMILY

35'. Shrub to small tree; crown rounded; branches spreading; often thorny. Leaves 2½", ovate to elliptical, often shallowly lobed, toothed, yellowish green. Bark grayish, sheds in irreg. thin plates. Flowers ¾", 5-petaled, white or pinkish; bloom Mar.–May. Fruit ⅓", berry-like, bright red to orange. **HABITAT** Streamsides, swamps, pondsides, lowland woods. **RANGE** n to nc FL.

RED CHOKEBERRY
Photinia pyrifolia (Aronia arbutifolia)
ROSE FAMILY

10'. Colony-forming shrub with wand-like stems, few branches. Leaves 4", elliptical to obovate, toothed (teeth tipped with red glands). Flowers ½", 5-petaled, white, in flat-topped, branched clusters; bloom Mar.–Apr. Fruit ⅓", berry-like, bright red to dark purple. **HABITAT** Bogs, moist pinelands, flatwoods. **RANGE** n to sc FL.

FLATWOODS PLUM
"Hog Plum"
Prunus umbellata
ROSE FAMILY

20'. Small tree; crown compact; trunk crooked. Leaves 2½", elliptical to oblong, toothed. Bark brown, scaly. Flowers ½", 5-petaled; bloom Mar.–Apr. Fruit ¾", berry-like, purplish; used in pies, jam; ripe June–Sept. **HABITAT** Hammocks, pinewoods, coastal scrub. **RANGE** n to sc FL.

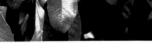

GUM BUMELIA
Sideroxylon (Bumelia) lanuginosum
SAPODILLA FAMILY

16'. Shrub to small tree; crown narrow, rounded; branches thick, spiny, brown-hairy. Leaves 4", oblanceolate, brown-hairy below. Bark reddish brown, fissured in narrow ridges. Flowers tiny, white, bunched in leaf axils; bloom June–Aug. Berries ⅓", purple-black. **HABITAT** Dry woods. **RANGE** n to nc FL.

TOUGH BUMELIA
Sideroxylon tenax
SAPODILLA FAMILY

20'. Shrub to small tree; branches rusty- to brown-hairy, spiny. Leaves 2", oblanceolate to elliptical, brown and densely silky-hairy below. Bark reddish brown, fissured in scaly ridges. Flowers tiny, white, bunched in leaf axils; bloom June–Aug. Berries ⅓", purple-black. **HABITAT** Dry woods, coastal scrub. **RANGE** n to s FL.

VIRGINIA-WILLOW
Itea virginica
SAXIFRAGE FAMILY

6′. Open shrub. Leaves 4″, oblong to oblanceolate, toothed. Flowers ⅓″, star-shaped, white, in long arched clusters; bloom Apr.–May. **HABITAT** Wet woods, swamps, streamsides. **RANGE** All FL, ex. extreme south.

BIGLEAF SNOWBELL
Styrax grandifolius
SNOWBELL FAMILY

40′. Shrub to small tree; crown rounded; branches short, spreading. Leaves 5″, oval to obovate, grayish-hairy below. Bark dark red-brown, smooth. Flowers 1″, bell-shaped, white, fragrant, in drooping clusters; bloom Apr. Fruit ½″, round, green to brown. **HABITAT** Dry bluffs, hammocks, floodplains. **RANGE** Panhandle and ne peninsular FL.

SOAPBERRY
Sapindus saponaria
(incl. *S. marginatus*)
SOAPBERRY FAMILY

50′. Crown dense, broadly rounded; sometimes shrub-like. Leaves 12″, scaly, pale gray, pinnately compound, with usu. 6 lanceolate to oblong, 7″ leaflets. Flowers tiny, creamy white, in large branched clusters; bloom June–Oct. (year-round). Fruit ¾″, berry-like, brownish or yellowish. **HABITAT** Hammocks, shell mounds.

JOEWOOD
Jacquinia keyensis
THEOPHRASTA FAMILY

20′. Shrub to small tree; crown rounded. Leaves 3″, yellow-green, evergreen, elliptical to obovate, with notched tips and rolled-under edges, crowded at branch ends. Bark smooth, thin, blue-gray with pale patches. Flowers ½″, yellowish, fragrant, in long clusters; bloom year-round. Berries ½″, green to orange-red. **HABITAT** Coastal hammocks, scrub; pinelands. **RANGE** s FL.

BEAUTY BUSH
"Beauty Berry"
Callicarpa americana
VERBENA FAMILY

6'. Hairy shrub with many arched branches. Leaves 6", opposite, ovate, toothed, hairy below. Flowers tiny, lavender-pink, in rounded 1½"clusters; bloom Apr.–Oct. Fruit tiny, berry-like, magenta, in 1½" rounded clusters. HABITAT Woods, thickets, hammocks, towns.

BUTTONWOOD
Conocarpus erectus
WHITE MANGROVE FAMILY

50'. Spreading shrub to low-branching tree with narrow rounded crown; thicket-forming. Leaves 4", elliptical to obovate, evergreen. Bark gray to dark brown, rough, ridged. Flowers minute, greenish, in tiny, dense, egg-shaped heads; bloom year-round. Fruit tiny, seed-like, in reddish-green, cone-like 1¼" clusters. HABITAT Swamps, hammocks, towns. RANGE Coastal peninsular FL.

WHITE MANGROVE
Laguncularia racemosa
WHITE MANGROVE FAMILY

50'. Shrub or tree with narrow rounded crown; trunk short, crooked, often with "knees"; thicket-forming. Leaves 3", opposite, oblong to ovate, leathery, evergreen. Bark reddish brown, scaly-ridged. Flowers tiny, greenish, in hairy spikes; bloom Apr.–June (year-round). Fruit ½", leathery, flattish, ribbed, reddish. HABITAT Tidal swamps. RANGE Coastal peninsular FL.

INDIAN ALMOND
"Sea Almond"
Terminalia catappa
WHITE MANGROVE FAMILY

50'. Tree with whorled spreading branches. Leaves 12", obovate, leathery, crowded at twig ends; turn deep red Nov.–Feb. Bark scaly, dark gray. Flowers ⅓", greenish to whitish, in narrow spikes; bloom June–Aug. (year-round). Fruit 2½", almond-shaped, woody, yellowish green; kernel edible, ripe Aug.–Sept. **HABITAT** Mangrove swamps, disturbed hammocks, beaches. **RANGE** Coastal s FL.

COASTAL PLAIN WILLOW
"Carolina Willow"
Salix caroliniana
WILLOW FAMILY

35'. Small slender tree with spreading open crown. Leaves 8", linear-lanceolate, with long pointed tip; toothed, dangling, grayish below, often with conspicuous kidney-shaped structures where leafstalk attaches to branch. Bark gray, scaly-ridged. Flowers tiny, yellowish green; males in pendulous catkins, females in shorter, erect clusters; bloom Apr.–May. Fruit tiny capsules in fuzzy 1½" clusters. **HABITAT** Swamps, ditches, watersides.

WITCH HAZEL
Hamamelis virginiana
WITCH HAZEL FAMILY

25'. Large shrub to small tree with rounded crown, multiple trunks. Leaves 6", obovate to broadly elliptical, scalloped; turn yellow in fall. Bark light brown, smooth to scaly. Flowers ¾", yellow, with ribbon-like petals; bloom Dec.–Jan. (before leaves). Fruit ½", egg-shaped, light brown capsules; eject seeds with force. **HABITAT** Open woods, streamsides. **RANGE** n to c FL.

Leaf Shapes

scales

needles in bundle

needles in cluster

linear

oblong

lanceolate

oblanceolate

obovate

ovate

rounded

heart-shaped

arrowhead-shaped

elliptical

toothed

lobed

palmately lobed

pinnately lobed

palmately compound

pinnately compound

bipinnately compound

Leaf Arrangements

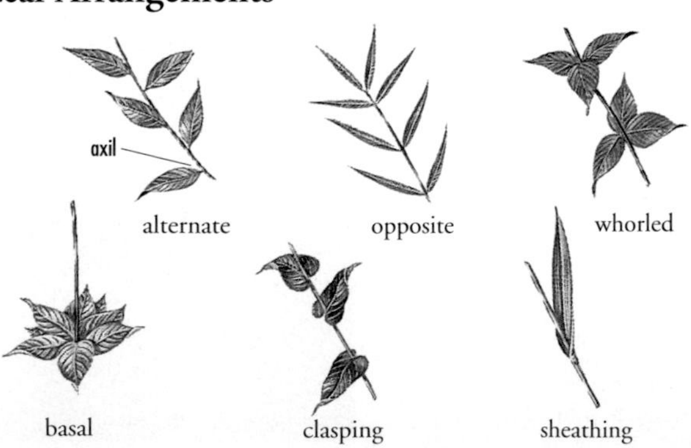

axil

alternate

opposite

whorled

basal

clasping

sheathing

Flower Types

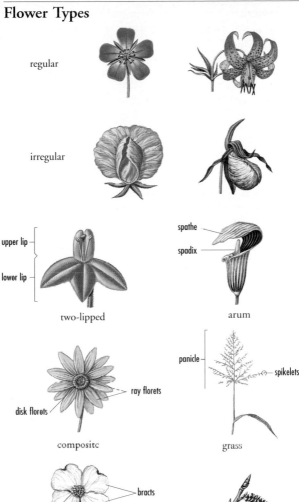

regular

irregular

upper lip
lower lip

two-lipped

spathe
spadix

arum

ray florets
disk florets

composite

panicle
spikelets

grass

bracts
flower cluster

bracts and flower cluster

catkin

Flower Cluster Types

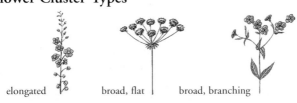

elongated

broad, flat

broad, branching

Wildflowers

Florida has nearly 4,000 species of flowering plants in more than 190 families. This section covers a broad selection of common and interesting wildflowers, including vines, grasses, and water plants.

The term "wildflower" has many connotations: one person's wildflower is another person's weed—a plant growing where it's not wanted. For the purposes of this field guide, wildflowers are defined as relatively small, noncultivated flowering plants that die back after each growing season.

The wildflowers included here are mainly herbaceous (nonwoody); some are woody but too small to be placed with the shrubs; a few have a woody base with herbaceous stems. These plants come in many forms. Many have a single, delicate, unbranched, erect stem terminated by a single flower or a flower cluster. Some have very robust stems; others are many-branched and shrubby. In some, the stems trail along the ground, sometimes spreading by runners. Those known as vines have a long, slender, often flexible stem that either trails on the ground or climbs, sometimes with tendrils to hold it in place. Plants of the grass family have erect, jointed stems and blade-like leaves; some other plants, such as rushes and sedges, are described as grass-like because they have narrow leaves and slender stems. Aquatic plants are adapted to life in or along water.

Wildflowers are most often identified by features of their flowers. The flowers or flower clusters may be borne in the leaf axils along the main stem or on branches off the stem. Modified leaves called *bracts* are often situated at the base of the flower or flower cluster. Flowers are typically composed of four sets of parts. The outermost set in a "complete" flower is the green, leaf-like *sepals* (known collectively as the *calyx*) that protect the often colorful second set—the *petals.* The next set is the *stamens,* the "male" part of the flower, each consisting of pollen sacs *(anthers)* typically on a stalk *(filament).* The innermost set is the "female" part of the flower, with one or more *pistils,* each of which typically has a swollen base, the *ovary* (containing the ovules that after fertilization become the seeds), and a stalk *(style)* topped by the pollen-collecting *stigma.* The fruit develops from the ovary, forming a covering for the seed or seeds. The form of the fruit varies from species to species.

Parts of a Flower

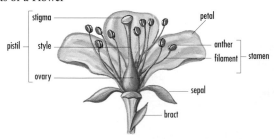

Although many plants have flowers with both stamens and pistils, some species have unisexual flowers that may occur on the same or separate plants. Many wind-pollinated species, such as Common Ragweed, grasses, and cattails, have reduced flowers that often lack petals and/or sepals. These wind-pollinated flowers tend to be inconspicuous, unlike flowers that need to attract insects for pollination.

Seed dispersal is often aided by animals: migrating birds and other animals eat fruit or seeds whole and disperse seeds in their droppings; fruits that are bur-like or covered with various kinds of sticky hairs attach to animals on contact and later fall off or are shed along with fur. Plants such as hawkweeds bear tiny fruits that have parachute-like tops and are carried by the wind far from the parent plant.

Flowers of a few representative types are illustrated on page 137. The buttercup and the lily are *regular* flowers: their parts radiate in a wheel-like (radially symmetrical) fashion. Pea and orchid flowers are commonly encountered flowers of *irregular* shape. Many plants in the lobelia, mint, and snapdragon families have tubular, *two-lipped* flowers. The tiny flowers of the arum family are clustered on a club-like *spadix,* which is usually enfolded by a leaf-like *spathe.* The *composite* "flower" of the daisy or aster is actually a head of many flowers: tiny tubular *disk florets* form a disk in the center, encircled by petal-like *ray florets.* (Hawkweeds have flower heads made up of all ray florets; true thistles have flower heads of all disk florets.) Grasses have tiny, reduced florets enclosed in scale-like bracts; these are organized in overlapping arrangements called *spikelets,* which typically form a larger, often plume-like arrangement called a *panicle.*

Dogwood "flowers" consist of a dense head of tiny flowers encircled by several large, petal-like *bracts.* The tiny unisexual flowers of oaks and many other species of trees and shrubs are clustered into slender pendulous spikes called *catkins.* Many plants bear flowers in clusters along or atop the stems or branches. Flower clusters take many forms, such as small round bunches, elongated spikes, feathery plumes, and broad, flat-topped or branching arrangements.

In the accounts that follow, sizes given are typical heights of mature specimens.

TWIN FLOWER
Dyschoriste oblongifolia
ACANTHUS FAMILY

12″. Trumpet-shaped, 5-lobed, lavender, 1¼″ flowers in leaf axils, with dark purple spots on lowermost lobe. Stems and leaf edges hairy. **BLOOMS** Apr.–Oct. **HABITAT** Pinelands, sandhills. **RANGE** e panhandle south to sc FL.

WILD PETUNIA
Ruellia caroliniensis
ACANTHUS FAMILY

3'. Trumpet-shaped, 5-lobed, lavender, 2" flowers in leaf axils. Stems hairy. Leaves elliptical to oval, hairy to smooth. **BLOOMS** Apr.–Sept. **HABITAT** Dry pinelands, woods. **RANGE** All FL, ex. s tip.

SPANISH BAYONET
"Spanish Dagger"
Yucca aloifolia
AGAVE FAMILY

7'. Stout stem topped by rosette of erect, sword-like leaves around large loose spray of creamy white, bell-shaped, 2½" flowers. **CAUTION** Leaves sharp. **BLOOMS** Apr.–July. **HABITAT** Beaches, saltmarsh banks, shell mounds, dry open woods. **RANGE** Mainly coastal FL.

BEAR GRASS
"Adam's Needle" "Silk-grass"
Yucca filamentosa
AGAVE FAMILY

8'. Basal rosette of stiff, fraying, spine-tipped, evergreen leaves encircles tall stem topped by loose spray of creamy white, bell-shaped, 2" flowers. **BLOOMS** Apr.–Sept. **HABITAT** Sandhills, fields, dry open woods. **RANGE** n to sc FL.

SWAMP LILY
"String Lily"
Crinum americanum
AMARYLLIS FAMILY

3'. Cluster of 2–6 lily-like, 8" flowers with 6 thin white petals, 6 prominent stamens. Strap-like leaves to 5'. **BLOOMS** Year-round. **HABITAT** Marshes, swamps, streamsides, ditches.

SPIDER LILY
Hymenocallis crassifolia
AMARYLLIS FAMILY

24". 2–3 spidery, white, 7" flowers with 6 narrow petals atop tubular base; toothed central cup has 6 radiating stamens. Leaves strap-like. **BLOOMS** Apr.–June. **HABITAT** Marshes, streamsides. **RANGE** n to c FL.

ALLIGATOR LILY
Hymenocallis palmeri
AMARYLLIS FAMILY

18". Spidery, fragrant, white, 8" flowers with 6 narrow petals atop tubular base; toothed, funnel-shaped central cup has 6 radiating stamens. Leaves strap-like. **BLOOMS** July–Sept. **HABITAT** Wet prairies, woods. **RANGE** c FL and south.

ATAMASCO LILY
"Rain Lily"
Zephyranthes atamasco
AMARYLLIS FAMILY

12". Flowers 3", white, sometimes pink-tinged, with 6 curved petals, 6 stamens. Leaves linear, sharp-edged. **BLOOMS** Apr.–June. **HABITAT** Moist pine flatwoods, meadows. **RANGE** n to sc FL.

LANCE-LEAVED ARROWHEAD
Sagittaria lancifolia
ARROWHEAD FAMILY

3′. Flowers 1½″, white, with 3 round petals around cluster of many stamens or pistils; in whorls of 3 on leafless stalk. Leaves linear to ovate, basal. **BLOOMS** Apr.–Dec. **HABITAT** Ponds, rivers, swamps, ditches.

ALLIGATOR FLAG
"Arrowroot" "Fireflag"
Thalia geniculata
ARROWROOT FAMILY

12′. Zigzag drooping branches bear pairs of flowers protruding from bracts; each flower ½″, purple, irregularly shaped, with 7 petal-like stamens. Leaves large. **BLOOMS** June–Nov. **HABITAT** Swamps, streamsides, riversides. **RANGE** e panhandle and south.

JACK-IN-THE-PULPIT
Arisaema triphyllum
ARUM FAMILY

3′. Hood-like 3″ spathe, often maroon striped, curves over fleshy green spadix. 1–2 large, long-stalked, 3-part leaves. Red clustered berries. **CAUTION** Berries cause mouth irritation. **BLOOMS** Apr.–Sept. **HABITAT** Moist woods, swamps, bogs. **RANGE** Mainly n to c FL.

GOLDEN CLUB
"Neverwet"
Orontium aquaticum
ARUM FAMILY

24″. Flowers tiny, golden yellow, atop fleshy 4″ spikes. Leaves ovate to elliptical, bluish, emergent or floating. Berries blue-green, inflated. **BLOOMS** Dec.–June (probably year-round). **HABITAT** Shallow streams, ponds, swamps. **RANGE** n to c FL.

WATER LETTUCE
"Water Bonnets"
Pistia stratoites
ARUM FAMILY

10". Forms dense mats. Flower spikes whitish, 1½". Leaves ovate, fleshy, gray-green, ribbed; form tight, lettuce-head-like rosette. Noxious weed. **BLOOMS** Year-round. **HABITAT** Ponds, streams, canals. **RANGE** Peninsular FL.

ALOE VERA
Aloe vera
ASPHODELUS FAMILY

3'. Flowers 1¼", tubular, nodding; bright yellow, orange, or red; densely clustered atop tall stem encircled at base by large rosette of thick, fleshy, spiny leaves. **BLOOMS** Jan.–June. **HABITAT** Rocky shorelines, dunes. **RANGE** Keys.

Plants That Cause Allergies

An allergy is a sensitivity in certain individuals to ordinarily harmless substances. "Allergy plants" include those that produce airborne pollen, which causes hay fever in susceptible individuals (reportedly at least 10 to 20 percent of the population). The cold-like symptoms include respiratory irritation, sneezing, and eye inflammation, and may lead to more serious conditions such as ear infections and asthma.

Allergy plants typically have inconspicuous flowers that produce copious pollen. They include various grasses and trees (such as pines and oaks), as well as the most common agents of hay fever in the United States: the infamous ragweeds (*Ambrosia* species). The amount of pollen in the air generally peaks at three times during the year, depending on the plant species in bloom: early spring (mainly early-flowering trees), midsummer (mainly grasses, some other herbaceous plants, and a few late-flowering trees), and fall (ragweeds and a few other plants)

Some plants are unfairly blamed for allergies. For example, the conspicuous, insect-pollinated goldenrods (*Solidago* species) are not responsible for late summer–autumn allergies; ragweed is probably the culprit.

COMMON RAGWEED
Ambrosia artemisiifolia
ASTER FAMILY

6′. Coarse, hairy, branched stems bear tiny, greenish, bell-shaped flowers in elongated 6″ clusters. Leaves deeply bipinnately dissected into many lobes. Wind-borne pollen among primary causes of hay fever. **BLOOMS** Apr.–Dec. **HABITAT** Disturbed areas.

CLIMBING ASTER
Aster carolinianus
ASTER FAMILY

L variable. Sprawling shrub or vine. Flowers 1½″, with pink to lavender rays around yellow or reddish-yellow disk. Leaves elliptical, clasping. **BLOOMS** Nov.– Mar. (year-round in s FL). **HABITAT** Swamps, wet hammocks, mangrove thickets, marshes, streamsides. **RANGE** e panhandle to peninsular FL.

WHITE BUSHY ASTER
Aster dumosus
ASTER FAMILY

5′. Flowers 1″, with pale lavender to whitish rays around yellow disk that often turns purplish; line one side of branches. Leaves linear. **BLOOMS** June–Nov. **HABITAT** Pinelands, wet woods, clearings, meadows.

WHITE-TOP ASTER
Aster reticulatus
ASTER FAMILY

3′. Flat-topped clusters of 1½″ flowers with white rays around pale yellow to reddish-purple disk. Leaves hairy, elliptical. **BLOOMS** Apr.–Sept. **HABITAT** Moist pinelands. **RANGE** n to sc FL.

YELLOW BUTTONS
Balduina angustifolia
ASTER FAMILY

3'. Flowers 1½", yellow, with toothed rays around disk. Multibranched. Stems hairy. Leaves linear. Fruit embedded in flower center that hardens and looks honeycomblike. **BLOOMS** Year-round (mainly June–Nov.) **HABITAT** Sandhills, dry pinelands, scrub.

COMMON GREEN-EYES
Berlandiera subacaulis
ASTER FAMILY

18". Flowers 2", with yellow rays around greenish-yellow "eye." Stems rough-hairy. Leaves pinnately lobed, hairy below. **BLOOMS** Year-round (mainly Apr.–Aug.). **HABITAT** Pinelands, disturbed areas. **RANGE** e panhandle and peninsular FL.

COMMON BEGGAR-TICKS
Bidens alba
ASTER FAMILY

3'. Flowers 1", with white rays around yellow disk. Leaves unlobed or divided into 3–5 ovate segments. Seed-like, barbed fruits stick to people and animals. **BLOOMS** Year-round. **HABITAT** Disturbed areas.

SEA DAISY
"Sea Oxeye"
Borrichia frutescens
ASTER FAMILY

3'. Flowers 1½", yellow, with up to 13 rays around disk; spiny bracts below. Stems and leaves grayish-hairy, aromatic. **BLOOMS** Year-round. **HABITAT** Beaches, salt marshes, mangrove swamp edges. **RANGE** Coastal FL.

VANILLA PLANT
"Vanilla Leaf" "Deer's Tongue"
Carphephorus odoratissimus
ASTER FAMILY

6'. Tiny, bell-shaped, lavender-pink flowers in very large, layered, flat-topped clusters. Large, thick, ovate to oblanceolate leaves form rosette at stem base. Exudes vanilla odor, esp. when dried. **BLOOMS** July–Dec. **HABITAT** Moist pinelands. **RANGE** All FL, ex. s tip.

HORRIBLE THISTLE
Cirsium horridulum
ASTER FAMILY

5'. Extremely prickly. Flowers 2½", purple (rarely cream to yellow), urn-shaped, surrounded by spiny bracts. Stems stocky, spiny, cottony-hairy. Leaves pinnately lobed, spiny-toothed and spiny-tipped, clasping. **BLOOMS** Year-round. **HABITAT** Pinelands, meadows, disturbed areas.

COMMON TICKSEED
Coreopsis leavenworthii
ASTER FAMILY

5'. Flowers 1½", with yellow, 3-toothed rays around brown to maroon disk. Stems slender. Leaf shape variable. **BLOOMS** Year-round (mainly Apr.–June). **HABITAT** Wet pinelands, flatwoods, ditches, roadsides.

SOUTHERN FLEABANE
"Oak-leaf Fleabane"
Erigeron quercifolius
ASTER FAMILY

3'. Flowers ¾", with many lavender to white rays around yellow disk. Stems slender, hairy. Leaves oak-like, hairy, clasping. **BLOOMS** Mar.–Sept. (year-round in s FL). **HABITAT** Open woods, disturbed areas.

DOG FENNEL
Eupatorium capillifolium
ASTER FAMILY

10'. Feathery-looking; arching branches covered with tiny, white, fragrant flowers. Stems many-branched. Leaves delicate, unlobed or divided into thread-like segments. **BLOOMS** July–Dec. **HABITAT** Pinelands, disturbed areas.

LATE BONESET
"Late-flowering Throughwort"
Eupatorium serotinum
ASTER FAMILY

10'. Clumps of hairy stems branch into broad, flat-topped clusters of tiny, fuzzy, cup-like, white flowers. Leaves elliptical to ovate, toothed, hairy below. **BLOOMS** Sept.–Dec. **HABITAT** Moist to wet areas.

SWEET EVERLASTING
"Rabbit Tobacco"
Gnaphalium obtusifolium
ASTER FAMILY

3'. Flat-topped clusters of tiny, white to yellowish, cylindrical, fragrant flowers. Stems silvery-white, wooly. Leaves linear to lanceolate, white-wooly below. Common weed throughout N. Amer. **BLOOMS** July–Dec. (probably year-round in s FL). **HABITAT** Dry open areas, esp. disturbed areas.

NARROW-LEAVED SUNFLOWER
Helianthus angustifolius
ASTER FAMILY

6′. Wide-spreading branches bear daisy-like, 2½″ flowers with 10–12 yellow rays around purple-brown disk. Leaves linear to narrowly lanceolate, rough-hairy, with curled-under edges. **BLOOMS** June–Nov. **HABITAT** Wet pinelands, flatwoods, roadsides, ditches, fields. **RANGE** n to sc FL.

FINE-LEAVED BLAZING STAR
Liatris tenuifolia
ASTER FAMILY

4′. Showy elongated clusters of ½″, bell-shaped, rose-purple flowers with protruding style branches; bloom from top downward. Leaves linear to thread-like. **BLOOMS** June–Nov. **HABITAT** Pinelands, dry open woods, sandhills, roadsides.

CLIMBING HEMPWEED
"Climbing Hempvine"
Mikania scandens
ASTER FAMILY

3′ (L variable). Climbing or mat-forming vine with long-stalked, flat-topped clusters of white to pink, cylindrical, ⅓″ flowers. Leaves heart- to arrowhead-shaped. **BLOOMS** Year-round. **HABITAT** Wet woods, thickets, swamp edges, ditches, prairies.

GOLDEN ASTER
"Silkgrass" "Grass-leaved Golden Aster"
Pityopsis (Chrysopsis) graminifolia
ASTER FAMILY

3′. Flowers 1¼″, yellow, with 8–13 rays around disk. Leaves grass-like, linear to lanceolate, silvery-hairy. **BLOOMS** June–Nov. **HABITAT** Dry pinelands, sandhills, scrub.

TALL WHITE FLEABANE
Pluchea longifolia
ASTER FAMILY

8'. Hairy; rank-smelling. Flowers tiny, creamy white, in long-stalked, flat-topped clusters. Leaves oblong to ovate, toothed. **BLOOMS** July–Oct. **HABITAT** Wet areas. **RANGE** se panhandle and c peninsular FL.

SALTMARSH FLEABANE
"Camphorweed"
Pluchea odorata (purpurescens)
ASTER FAMILY

5'. Hairy; camphor-scented. Flowers tiny, pink to lavender, in long-stalked, flat-topped clusters. Leaves ovate to elliptical, toothed. **BLOOMS** June–Nov. (year-round in s FL). **HABITAT** Swamps.

BLACK-EYED SUSAN
Rudbeckia hirta
ASTER FAMILY

3'. Flowers 3", with long, yellow, daisy-like rays around brown central cone; solitary on slender stalks. Stems and leaves very bristly; may irritate skin. **BLOOMS** June–Nov. **HABITAT** Open disturbed areas.

HOLLOW GOLDENROD
Solidago fistulosa
ASTER FAMILY

6'. Plume-like clusters of long arching branches bear yellow, daisy-like, ⅓" flowers on one side. Stems hairy. Leaves oblanceolate, rough-hairy, clasping. **BLOOMS** June–Nov. **HABITAT** Dry pinelands, flatwoods, ditches, roadsides.

SEASIDE GOLDENROD
Solidago sempervirens var.
mexicana
ASTER FAMILY

6'. Flowers ½", yellow, with 7–11 rays around disk; cover one side of arching upper branches. Stems thick. Leaves oblanceolate, tapered at base, thick, fleshy, clasping. **BLOOMS** June–Nov. **HABITAT** Wet pinelands, salt marshes, bay shores. **RANGE** Mainly coastal FL.

SPINY-LEAVED SOW THISTLE
Sonchus asper
ASTER FAMILY

6'. Weedy. Flowers ½", dandelion-like, with many fine yellow rays. Stems smooth, angled. Leaves prickly-edged, lanceolate; with curled lobes at base; clasping. Fruit seed-like, with fluffy parachute-top. **BLOOMS** Mar.–Sept. **HABITAT** Disturbed areas.

TALL IRONWEED
Vernonia gigantea
ASTER FAMILY

12'. Flowers ½", purple, bell-shaped. Leaves lanceolate, toothed. **BLOOMS** May–Nov. (year-round in s FL). **HABITAT** Open wet areas. **RANGE** n to sc FL.

ASIATIC HAWK'S-BEARD
Youngia japonica
ASTER FAMILY

18". Flowers ¾", dandelion-like, yellow, in short-branched clusters atop leafless stems. Leaves oblanceolate, pinnately lobed. Fruit seed-like, with fluffy parachute-top. **BLOOMS** Year-round. **HABITAT** Disturbed areas.

FLORIDA BELLFLOWER
Campanula floridana
BELLFLOWER FAMILY

16″. Flowers ½″, blue-purple, star-like, with 5 spreading lobes. Stems slender, weakly ascending to reclining. Leaves linear to elliptical, finely toothed. **BLOOMS** Year-round. **HABITAT** Wet areas. **RANGE** e panhandle and nc to sc peninsular FL.

CARDINAL FLOWER
Lobelia cardinalis
BELLFLOWER FAMILY

6′. Leafy stems bear spike of red flowers, each 1¾″, tubular, 2-lipped, with upper lip 2-lobed, lower 3-lobed. Leaves lanceolate, toothed. Hummingbird-pollinated. **BLOOMS** July–Oct. **HABITAT** Streamsides, springs, swamps. **RANGE** n to nc FL.

BAY LOBELIA
Lobelia feayana
BELLFLOWER FAMILY

12″. Flowers ⅓″, tubular, 2-lipped, lavender to purple, with white eye; in elongated clusters at stem ends. Leaves lanceolate on stem, ovate to heart-shaped at base. **BLOOMS** Apr.–Oct. **HABITAT** Wet pine flat-woods, roadsides, ditches. **RANGE** Peninsular FL, ex. s tip.

COASTAL PLAIN LOBELIA
"Glades Lobelia"
Lobelia glandulosa
BELLFLOWER FAMILY

3′. Flowers 1¼″, tubular, 2-lipped, lavender-blue to purple, with white eye; in elongated clusters atop unbranched stems. Leaves linear to lanceolate, toothed. **BLOOMS** Year-round. **HABITAT** Wet pine savannas, flatwoods, ditches, bogs, streamsides and pondsides.

TRUMPET VINE
"Trumpet Creeper"
Campsis radicans
BIGNONIA FAMILY

L/H variable. Woody vine; climbs via aerial roots. Hanging clusters of 3″, trumpet-shaped flowers; dull orange-red outside, yellowish and red-streaked inside. Stems have pale shreddy bark. Leaves pinnately compound. **BLOOMS** Apr.–Sept. **HABITAT** Thickets, moist woods. **RANGE** n to c FL.

BLUE BUTTERWORT
"Violet Butterwort"
"Common Butterwort"
Pinguicula caerulea
BLADDERWORT FAMILY

8″. Flowers funnel-shaped, 1¼″, deep violet to pale lavender. Sticky basal leaves trap and digest insects. **BLOOMS** Apr.–June. **HABITAT** Wet pinelands, ditches, roadsides. **RANGE** e panhandle to peninsular FL, ex. s tip.

FLOATING BLADDERWORT
"Swollen Bladderwort"
Utricularia inflata
BLADDERWORT FAMILY

6″. Yellow ¾″ flowers top stems above whorl of inflated leafstalks. Leaves divided into thread-like segments; have tiny air bladders that trap and digest small aquatic creatures. **BLOOMS** Year-round. **HABITAT** Ponds, swamps, drainage ditches, canals.

BLOODWORT
"Bloodroot" "Redroot"
Lachnanthes caroliniana
BLOODWORT FAMILY

4′. Flowers ½″, urn-shaped, yellow, with 3 sepals, 3 petals; packed into broad, wooly 4″ clusters. Stems wooly toward top. Leaves sword-like. Roots red, contain red sap. **BLOOMS** May–Oct. **HABITAT** Wet pinelands, bogs, ditches, swamps.

FLOATING HEARTS
Nymphoides aquatica
BUCKBEAN FAMILY

Water-lily-like; floats flat. Flowers ¾", with 5 white wrinkled petals. Leaves heart- to kidney-shaped, thick, rough, with purple undersides; on long underwater stalks. **BLOOMS** Apr.–Sept. **HABITAT** Ponds, swamps, sluggish streams.

RATTAN VINE
"Supplejack"
Berchemia scandens
BUCKTHORN FAMILY

L variable. Trailing or high-climbing vine with flexible woody stems. Flowers tiny, greenish white, in short clusters. Leaves elliptical to ovate, wavy-edged. Fruit tiny, blue-black, berry-like. **BLOOMS** Apr.–June. **HABITAT** Hammocks, wet woods, swamps.

CORAL VINE
Antigonon leptopus
BUCKWHEAT FAMILY

L variable. Vine; climbs via tendrils at ends of long clusters of ½", cup-like, rose-pink flowers. Leaves ovate to heart-shaped, wavy-edged. **BLOOMS** Year-round. **HABITAT** Hammocks, disturbed areas. **RANGE** e panhandle and nc to s peninsular FL.

MILD WATER-PEPPER
Polygonum hydropiperoides
BUCKWHEAT FAMILY

20". Flowers tiny, funnel-shaped, white to pinkish; in long, narrow, 2½" clusters. Stems jointed. Leaves lanceolate to linear, short-hairy; bases form sheathing tube around stem. **BLOOMS** Apr.–Oct. (year-round in s FL). **HABITAT** Swamps, streams, marshes, wet ditches, canals.

HASTATE-LEAVED DOCK
"Heart-wing Sorrel"
Rumex hastatulus
BUCKWHEAT FAMILY

3'. Colony-forming. Slender stems topped by long, branching, 16" clusters of minute greenish to reddish flowers. Leaves arrowhead-shaped; tubular bases enclose stem. **BLOOMS** Mar.–June. **HABITAT** Disturbed areas. **RANGE** n to sc FL.

YELLOW COLIC ROOT
Aletris lutea
BUNCHFLOWER FAMILY

3'. Flowers ⅓", urn-shaped, yellow, shiny, in long, narrow, spike-like clusters. Stems somewhat sticky, with very reduced leaves. Leaves yellow-green, elliptical, in basal rosette. **BLOOMS** Mar.–Sept. **HABITAT** Pine flatwoods, savannas, bogs.

PINE HYACINTH
Clematis baldwinii
BUTTERCUP FAMILY

24". Flowers 2", bell-shaped, pendulous, lavender to pinkish; with 4 curled, fleshy, petal-like sepals. Leaves variable in shape (lanceolate to elliptical, unlobed to deeply 3- to 5-lobed). Fruit seed-like, with long feathery tail. **BLOOMS** Apr.–Oct. **HABITAT** Pinelands. **RANGE** From nc FL southward.

PRICKLY-PEAR
Opuntia humifusa
CACTUS FAMILY

3'. Forms clumps or mats. Flowers 3", yellow, often with reddish center; has many petals and stamens. Stems segmented into flat, fleshy, bristly and spiny pads. Berries red to purple; edible, ripe Apr.–Sept. **CAUTION** Bristles barbed, difficult to remove from skin. **BLOOMS** Apr.–Aug. **HABITAT** Sandy pinelands, open dry woods, dunes, pastures.

GOLDEN CANNA
Canna flaccida
CANNA FAMILY

4′. Flowers 6″, irregularly shaped, yellow, wrinkled, floppy, fragrant; open at dusk. Leaves 24″, elliptical, sheathing. **BLOOMS** Jan.–Sept. **HABITAT** Swamps, marshes, pond sides, ditches. **RANGE** Mainly peninsular FL.

WATER HEMLOCK
Cicuta maculata (mexicana)
CARROT FAMILY

8′. Flat, loose, 8″ clusters of many tiny white flowers. Stems smooth, sturdy, branched, magenta-streaked. Leaves bi- or tripinnately compound. **CAUTION** All parts deadly poisonous. **BLOOMS** Jan.–Oct. **HABITAT** Swamps, marshes, ditches, streams.

RATTLESNAKE MASTER
"Button Snakeroot"
Eryngium yuccifolium
CARROT FAMILY

3′. Tall, stiff, ridged stems topped with spherical, bristly, greenish-white, 1″ flower clusters. Leaves 3′, linear to lanceolate, bristly, stiff. **BLOOMS** June–Sept. **HABITAT** Pinelands, flatwoods, prairies, ditches.

Poisonous Plants

Poisonous plants are those that contain potentially harmful substances in high enough concentrations to cause injury if touched or swallowed. Determining whether a plant species is "poison" or "food" requires expertise. The information in this guide is not to be used to identify plants for edible or medicinal purposes.

Sensitivity to a toxin varies with a person's age, weight, physical condition, and individual susceptibility. Children are most vulnerable because of their curiosity and small size. Toxicity can vary in a plant according to season, the plant's different parts, and its stage of growth; and plants can absorb toxic substances, such as herbicides, pesticides, and pollutants from the water, air, and soil. Among the potentially deadly plants in Florida are Water Hemlock, Yellow Jessamine, Chinaberry, Castor Bean, and Rosary Pea.

Physical contact with plants that contain irritating resinous compounds causes rashes in many individuals. The main offenders in Florida are well-known members of the cashew family: Poison Ivy, Poison Oak, Poison Sumac, and Poisonwood. All parts of these plants contain the irritating compounds. The sap of many plants, such as Brazilian Pepper, Oleander, and Trumpet Vine can also cause dermatitis. Tread Softly, a common weed in Florida, is covered with needle-like hairs that release stinging substances when touched.

POISON IVY
Toxicodendron radicans
CASHEW FAMILY

L/H variable. Climbing vine or erect or trailing shrub. Flowers tiny, in yellowish-white 1½" clusters in leaf axils. Leaves variable; often palmately compound, with 3 ovate leaflets; dull or shiny; red in fall. Fruit tiny, white, berry-like. **CAUTION** Contact can cause severe skin inflammation. Berries poisonous. **BLOOMS** Apr.– Sept. **HABITAT** Woodlands, beaches, roadsides, other disturbed areas.

SOUTHERN CATTAIL
Typha domingensis
CATTAIL FAMILY

10'. Erect stem ends in club-like, greenish to brownish flower spike densely covered with minute flowers, upper ones (male) separated by naked stem from lower ones (female). Leaves tall, flat, stiff, sheathing. **BLOOMS** Apr.–Oct. **HABITAT** Marshes, shorelines, shallow waters, ditches.

BLUE DOGBANE
"Blue Star"
Amsonia ciliata
DOGBANE FAMILY

4'. Flowers ½", star-like, light blue with white eye, in loose clusters. Stem hairy. Leaves narrowly linear. **BLOOMS** Apr.–Sept. **HABITAT** Dry pinelands, sandhills. **RANGE** n to c FL.

RUBBER VINE
"Devil's Potato"
Echites umbellata
DOGBANE FAMILY

L variable. Twining, tangled vines with loose clusters of pinwheel-like, white to greenish, 2½" flowers. Leaves ovate, thick. Pods 8", greenish to brownish. **BLOOMS** Year-round. **HABITAT** Coastal pinelands. **RANGE** Coastal, from ec FL south.

DUCKWEED
Lemna species
DUCKWEED FAMILY

grain of rice (right) for scale

Whole individual plant tiny, leaf-like, obovate to elliptical; solitary or joined with 2 to several others, each with 1 root. Flowers minute, rare. New plants bud from side pouches; forms stands covering water. **HABITAT** Stagnant water.

LONG-STALKED SEEDBOX
Ludwigia arcuata
EVENING PRIMROSE FAMILY

18″. Flowers ¾″, yellow, with 4 petals on short tube; borne singly on long stalks from leaf axils. Stems creeping, hairy. Leaves oblanceolate to elliptical. **BLOOMS** Apr.–Oct. **HABITAT** Lakesides, swamps, ditches, marshes. **RANGE** n to sc FL.

COMMON PRIMROSE WILLOW
Ludwigia peruviana
EVENING PRIMROSE FAMILY

13′. Shrubby. Flowers 2″, yellow, with 4 or 5 petals. Stems hairy. Leaves ovate to lanceolate, hairy. Weedy; commonly in shallow water. **BLOOMS** Apr.–Nov. (year-round in s FL). **HABITAT** Swamps, pondsides, ditches, canals, marshes.

CUT-LEAVED EVENING PRIMROSE
Oenothera laciniata
EVENING PRIMROSE FAMILY

3′. Sprawling. Flowers 1″, yellow to reddish, with 4 petals, X-shaped stigma; opens at dusk. Stems hairy. Leaves elliptical, irregularly toothed to pinnately lobed; usu. hairy. **BLOOMS** Year-round. **HABITAT** Roadsides, fields, grasslands.

SCORPION-TAIL
Heliotropium angiospermum
FORGET-ME-NOT FAMILY

3′. Hairy, erect to sprawling. Flowers tiny, paired, white with yellow eye; bloom on uppersides of unfurling spikes. Leaves elliptical. **BLOOMS** Year-round. **HABITAT** Hammocks, shell mounds, roadsides. **RANGE** c FL and south (mainly coastal).

BRAZILIAN ELODEA
Egeria densa
FROG'S-BIT FAMILY

Flowers ¾", white, with 3 round petals. Stems floating to slightly submerged, sparingly branched. Leaves linear, toothed, bright green, whorled. **BLOOMS** Mar.–June. **HABITAT** Canals, ponds, streams.

NARROW-LEAVED SABATIA
Sabatia brevifolia
GENTIAN FAMILY

24". Flowers 1¼", star-like, white with yellow-green eye; style split in 2 flat twisted pieces; solitary at branch ends. Leaves linear. **BLOOMS** Apr.–Sept. **HABITAT** Wet pinelands. **RANGE** All FL, ex. extreme s tip.

LARGE-FLOWERED SABATIA
Sabatia grandiflora
GENTIAN FAMILY

3'. Flowers 2", star-like, rose-pink with yellow-green, red-bordered eye; solitary at branch tips. Leaves elliptical to linear, fleshy. **BLOOMS** Year-round. **HABITAT** Wet pinelands, ditches, low areas, pondsides. **RANGE** Mainly peninsular FL.

CRANESBILL
"Carolina Geranium"
Geranium carolinanum
GERANIUM FAMILY

24". Flowers ½", pale pink to lavender, with 5 spine-tipped sepals, 5 petals; in loose clusters. Stems hairy. Leaves deeply palmately 5- to 9-lobed, deeply toothed, hairy. **BLOOMS** Mar.–Aug. **HABITAT** Open disturbed areas.

PERENNIAL GLASSWORT
Salicornia perennis
GOOSEFOOT FAMILY

12″ (branches). Seemingly leafless, jointed, fleshy plant with creeping main stem and erect branches; turns deep red. Flowers minute, sunken into fleshy, greenish to reddish, 4″ spike. Leaves minute, scale-like. **BLOOMS** June–Nov. **HABITAT** Salt flats, beaches, salt marshes. **RANGE** Coastal FL.

CREEPING CUCUMBER
Melothria pendula
GOURD FAMILY

L variable. Climbing, slender-stemmed vine. Flowers tiny, yellow. Leaves heart-shaped, palmately lobed, toothed, rough-hairy. Berries 1″, green to purple-black. **BLOOMS** Mar.–Dec. **HABITAT** Woods, marshes, roadsides, disturbed areas.

WILD BALSAM APPLE
Momordica charantia
GOURD FAMILY

L variable. Climbing vine. Flowers 1¼″, cup-like, yellow, with 5 petal lobes. Leaves deeply palmately 5- to 7-lobed, toothed, often hairy. Fruit 5″, yellow, spiny; splits, exposing bright red seeds. **BLOOMS** Year-round. **HABITAT** Thickets, disturbed areas. **RANGE** nc FL and south.

VIRGINIA CREEPER
Parthenocissus quinquefolia
GRAPE FAMILY
L variable. Woody climbing vine. Flowers tiny, yellowish-green. Leaves palmately compound, with 3–5 toothed pointed leaflets; turn red. Berries tiny, purple-black. **BLOOMS** Apr.–June. **HABITAT** Woodlands, esp. hammocks.

SOUTHERN FOX GRAPE
"Scuppernong" "Bullace Grape"
Vitis rotundifolia
GRAPE FAMILY
L variable. Woody climbing vine. Leaves heart-shaped to round, toothed. Berries ½–1", purplish when ripe; edible, ripe June–Sept., used for jam and wine. **BLOOMS** Apr.–June. **HABITAT** Woodlands, beaches, swamps.

FIELD SANDSPUR
"Coastal Sandspur"
Cenchrus incertus
GRASS FAMILY
20". Often sprawling. Tiny, roundish, greenish to beige burs enclose minute flowers in 4" clusters. Leaves linear, sheathing. **CAUTION** Burs sharp. **BLOOMS** Year-round. **HABITAT** Beaches, pinelands, sandhills, fields, disturbed areas.

MAIDENCANE
Panicum hemitomon
GRASS FAMILY
6'6". Flowers in narrow green 8" clusters. Leaves linear, sheathing. Forms extensive stands. **BLOOMS** May–Oct. **HABITAT** Ponds, streams, swamps, wet disturbed areas.

KNOTGRASS
"Seashore Paspalum" "Thompson Grass"
Paspalum distichum
GRASS FAMILY
8". Mat-forming. Flowers in spreading to downcurved, greenish, 2½" plumes. Leaves linear, sheathing. Troublesome weed in irrigation canals. **BLOOMS** Apr.–Oct. **HABITAT** Beaches, brackish marshes, disturbed areas.

SUGAR CANE
Saccharum officinarum
GRASS FAMILY
12'. Flowers in silvery 24" plumes of many silky-haired spikelets. Stems thick, with sweet juice. Leaves linear, sheathing. Native to Asia; escaped from cultivation. **BLOOMS** Oct.–March. **HABITAT** Disturbed areas. **RANGE** sc FL and south.

SALTMARSH CORDGRASS
"Smooth Cordgrass"
Spartina alternifolia
GRASS FAMILY
6'. Flowers in beige 6" panicles of upright spikelets. Leaves linear, flat, sheathing. Large colonies cover large seaside areas, force out other species. **BLOOMS** June–Oct. **HABITAT** Open, wet, brackish areas; tidal flats. **RANGE** Coastal FL.

SALTMEADOW CORDGRASS
"Marshhay Cordgrass" "Salthay"
Spartina patens
GRASS FAMILY
5'. Flowers in brownish, erect, 2¾" panicles. Leaves linear, sheathing, edges in-rolled. Grows in tufts. **BLOOMS** June–Oct. **HABITAT** Salt marshes, beaches, dunes, tidal flats. **RANGE** Coastal FL.

SEA OATS
Uniola paniculata
GRASS FAMILY

6'. Flowers in greenish to beige, flat, 18" panicles of 10–20 spikelets. Leaves linear, sheathing. Cultivated on beaches to control erosion; protected by state laws (do not pick!). Often grows in clumps. **BLOOMS** Jan.–June. **HABITAT** Beaches with drifting sand. **RANGE** Coastal FL.

WILD BAMBOO
"Catbrier" "Greenbrier"
Smilax auriculata
GREENBRIER FAMILY

L variable. Woody climbing vine. Flowers tiny, star-like, greenish, in roundish clusters. Stems tangled, prickly. Leaves variable, on twisted stalks; evergreen. Berries tiny, reddish purple to black. **BLOOMS** Apr.–July. **HABITAT** Pinelands, sand dunes, open woods, thickets.

TRUMPET HONEYSUCKLE
"Coral Honeysuckle"
Lonicera sempervirens
HONEYSUCKLE FAMILY

L variable. Climbing or trailing woody vine. Flowers 2", tubular, 5-lobed, red outside, yellow inside. Stems slender. Leaves elliptical to obovate, semi-evergreen. Berries tiny, red. Pollinated by hummingbirds. **BLOOMS** Apr.–Sept. **HABITAT** Woodlands, thickets, fences. **RANGE** n to c FL.

SEA PURSLANE
Sesuvium portulacastrum
ICE-PLANT FAMILY

L 6′. Mat-forming, sprawling, profusely branched, fleshy. Flowers ¾″, star-like, with 5 pointed, petal-like sepals; bright pink inside, green outside; arise on stalks from leaf axils. Leaves linear, fleshy; edible, crisp, salty-tasting. **BLOOMS** Year-round. **HABITAT** Beaches, dunes, salt flats. **RANGE** Coastal FL.

ANGLEPOD BLUE FLAG
"Prairie Iris"
Iris hexagona var. *savannarum*
IRIS FAMILY

4′. Flowers 4½″, with 9 spreading, petal-like parts (3 drooping sepals, 3 erect petals, 3 erect styles); purple, sepals with yellow hairy crest. Stems zigzag somewhat. Leaves 3′, stiff, erect, sword-like. **BLOOMS** Mar.–June. **HABITAT** Swamps, prairies, ditches, canals, marshy shores. **RANGE** e panhandle, peninsular FL, ex. southeast.

BLUE-EYED-GRASS
"Pointed Blue-eyed-grass"
Sisyrinchium angustifolium
IRIS FAMILY

24″. Flowers ¾″, purple-blue with yellow eye; star-shaped, with 6 petals, each tipped with long point; clustered atop flat stiff stems. Leaves grass-like; very narrow, linear. **BLOOMS** May–Aug. **HABITAT** Wet woods, fields.

LOVE VINE
Cassytha filiformis
LAUREL FAMILY

L variable. Parasitic vine on herbaceous and woody plants. Flowers tiny, cup-shaped, whitish; on short spikes. Stems slender, leafless, yellow-green; intertwine to form thick mats. Fruit tiny, white, berry-like. **BLOOMS** Year-round. **HABITAT** Pinelands, hammock edges. **RANGE** sc FL and south.

SEA LAVENDER
Limonium carolinianum
LEADWORT FAMILY

3′. Tiny, papery, pale purple flowers along one side of many diffuse, wiry, curved branches that form fan-like array at stem ends. Leaves variably shaped, clasping, mostly basal. **BLOOMS** July–Dec. (year-round in s FL). **HABITAT** Brackish marshes, salt flats, mangrove swamps. **RANGE** Coastal FL.

CATESBY'S LILY
"Pine Lily"
Lilium catesbaei
LILY FAMILY

3′. Flowers 3½″, with 6 stalked petals, 6 stamens surrounding long style; orange-red with yellow, purple-spotted base. Leaves linear to lanceolate. **BLOOMS** June–Nov. **HABITAT** Pine flatwoods, savannas, bogs. **RANGE** All FL, ex. s tip.

LIZARD'S-TAIL
Saururus cernuus
LIZARD'S-TAIL FAMILY

4′. Forms extensive colonies. Zigzag stems topped with many tiny, white, fragrant flowers in 12″ bottlebrush-like clusters tapering to drooping tips. Leaves arrowhead- to heart-shaped, clasping. **BLOOMS** Feb.–Oct. **HABITAT** Swamps, marshes, wet woods, streams.

YELLOW JESSAMINE
"Carolina Jasmine"
Gelsemium sempervirens
LOGANIA FAMILY

L variable. High-climbing, woody vine with 1¼", trumpet-shaped, fragrant, yellow flowers in leaf axils. Leaves lanceolate, leathery, evergreen. **CAUTION** All parts (incl. nectar) poisonous. **BLOOMS** Jan.–Apr. **HABITAT** Woods, thickets, roadsides. **RANGE** n to sc FL.

LANCE-LEAVED LOOSESTRIFE
Lythrum alatum var. lanceolatum
LOOSESTRIFE FAMILY

4'. Wand-like stems topped by small leaves with star-like, lavender, ½" flowers in axils. Leaves linear-lanceolate. **BLOOMS** May–Oct. **HABITAT** Open wet ground, marshes. **RANGE** e panhandle to peninsular FL.

YELLOW LOTUS
"American Lotus" "Lotus-lily"
"Water Chinquapin"
Nelumbo lutea
LOTUS FAMILY

3'. Flowers 10", pale yellow, bowl-shaped, with many petals and stamens surrounding large conical structure. Leaves round. Each flower/leaf on tall stalk. **BLOOMS** May–Sept. **HABITAT** Streams, ponds, estuaries. **RANGE** n to sc FL.

BUTTONWEED
Diodia viginiana
MADDER FAMILY

L variable. Flowers ½", white, with 4 hairy petal lobes on long narrow tube; unstalked, in leaf axils. Stems prostrate. Leaves lanceolate to elliptical. **BLOOMS** Year-round. **HABITAT** Wet pinelands, woods, swamps.

SWAMP HIBISCUS
Hibiscus grandiflorus
MALLOW FAMILY

10'. Flowers 6", hibiscus-like, pink with maroon center, with 5 petals around central tube (fused stamens and style); borne singly or in small clusters in upper leaf axils. Stems hairy. Leaves variably shaped (heart-shaped, unlobed, or 3-lobed), blunt-toothed, velvety. **BLOOMS** Apr.–Sept. **HABITAT** Swamps, marshes, ditches, canals, pondsides, lakesides.

SEASHORE MALLOW
"Saltmarsh Mallow"
Kosteletzkya virginica
MALLOW FAMILY

5'. Flowers 2¾", hibiscus-like, pink with yellow center, with 5 petals around curved tube (fused stamens and style). Leaves heart-shaped to lanceolate, toothed, hairy. **BLOOMS** Apr.–Oct. **HABITAT** Marshes. **RANGE** Mainly coastal FL (occ. inland).

TURK'S CAP
Malvaviscus arboreus
MALLOW FAMILY

10'. Spreading sprawling shrub. Flowers 2¾", red, tubular, with 5 overlapping erect petals around slender protruding tube. Leaves ovate to heart-shaped, toothed, evergreen. **BLOOMS** Apr.–Oct. (probably year-round in s FL). **HABITAT** Disturbed areas. **RANGE** Local; Dade County and Keys.

YELLOW MEADOW BEAUTY
Rhexia lutea
MEADOW BEAUTY FAMILY
24". Flowers 1¼", with 4 yellow petals, each tipped with a hair-like projection. Stems stiff, hairy. Leaves oblanceolate to elliptical, toothed, yellowish-hairy. **BLOOMS** Apr.–July. **HABITAT** Bogs, flatwoods. **RANGE** Panhandle to ne peninsular FL.

PALE MEADOW BEAUTY
"Maryland Meadow Beauty"
Rhexia mariana
MEADOW BEAUTY FAMILY
3'. Flowers 1½", pink to almost white, with 4 lopsided petals, 8 prominent stamens; in broad clusters. Stems square, hairy. Leaves linear to elliptical, toothed, hairy. **BLOOMS** Apr.–Oct. **HABITAT** Wet pinelands, ditches, bogs, flatwoods. **RANGE** All FL, ex. s tip.

RED MILKWEED
"Lance-leaved Milkweed"
Asclepias lanceolata
MILKWEED FAMILY
4'. Flowers ½", with 5 red-orange, folded-back petals around orange elevated crown; in 2" flat-topped clusters. Stems purplish. Leaves 10", lanceolate to linear. **BLOOMS** June–Sept. **HABITAT** Wet meadows and ditches, swamps, bogs, marshes.

BUTTERFLY WEED
"Orange Milkweed"
Asclepias tuberosa
MILKWEED FAMILY
3'. Hairy. Flowers ½", orange, star-like, with 5 folded-back petals around elevated crown; in 2" clusters at branch ends. Leaves oblong, with watery juice. Seedpods 6", greenish to brownish. **BLOOMS** May–Oct. **HABITAT** Pinelands, sandhills, dry roadsides.

CANDY WEED
"Wild Bachelor's Button"
"Orange Milkwort"
Polygala lutea
MILKWORT FAMILY

16". Flowers tiny, bright orange (dry to pale yellow), in dense, cylindrical, 1" heads. Leaves spoon-shaped to obovate. **BLOOMS** Apr.–Sept. **HABITAT** Wet pinelands, savannas, wet ditches, roadsides. **RANGE** All FL, ex. s tip.

WILD BACHELOR'S BUTTON
Polygala nana
MILKWORT FAMILY

6". Flowers tiny, lemon yellow, in compact, clover-like, 2" clusters. Leaves spatula-shaped. **BLOOMS** Apr.–Sept. (probably year-round in s FL). **HABITAT** Moist pinelands, disturbed areas. **RANGE** All FL, ex. s tip.

YELLOW BACHELOR'S BUTTON
Polygala rugelii
MILKWORT FAMILY

3'. Flowers, ⅓", orange-yellow (dry to bluish-green or yellowish-green), in dense, cylindrical, 1¼" heads. Stem leaves linear with rounded tip; basal leaves spoon-shaped, often gone by flowering. **BLOOMS** Apr.–Oct. **HABITAT** Moist pinelands. **RANGE** Peninsular FL.

COMMON BITTER MINT
Hyptis mutabilis
MINT FAMILY

6'. Flowers ⅓", tubular, lavender with white splotches; 2-lipped, with upper lip 2-lobed, lower lip 3-lobed and pouch-like; whorled on spikes at branch tips. Stems square, rough-hairy. Leaves ovate, toothed, short-hairy. Unpleasant odor. **BLOOMS** Year-round. **HABITAT** Open wet areas.

TROPICAL SAGE
"Scarlet Sage"
Salvia coccinea
MINT FAMILY

3'. Flowers 1¼", bright red, tubular; 2-lipped, with upper lip 2-lobed, lower lip 3-lobed; 2 stamens and style protrude; whorled in long clusters. Stems square, hairy. Leaves heart-shaped, scalloped. **BLOOMS** Apr.–Sept. **HABITAT** Hammocks, thickets, roadsides.

COMMON LARGE SKULLCAP
"Rough Skullcap"
Scutellaria integrifolia
MINT FAMILY

24". Flowers 1", curved-tubular, lavender to purple; 2-lipped, with upper lip hood-like, lower lip toothed and white at base; calyx conspicuously crested; in long clusters. Stems square, finely hairy. Leaves ovate to oblong, rough, toothed to untoothed, stalked to unstalked. **BLOOMS** Mar.–Oct. **HABITAT** Pinelands, bogs, meadows, wet thickets. **RANGE** n to c FL.

FLORIDA BETONY
"Hedge Nettle"
Stachys floridana
MINT FAMILY

24". Colony-forming. Flowers ½", tubular, pink to pale lavender; 2 lipped, with upper lip 2-lobed and hood-like, lower lip 3-lobed and purple spotted; in whorls at upper leaf axils. Stems square, hairy. Leaves oblong, scalloped. A common weed. **BLOOMS** Year-round. **HABITAT** Open woods, disturbed areas. **RANGE** Mainly n to sc FL.

BLUE CURLS
"Bastard Pennyroyal"
Trichostema dichotomum
MINT FAMILY

3'. Bushy. Flowers ½", blue to deep blue-purple; 2-lipped, with upper lip 2 lobed, lower lip 3-lobed; lower-most lobe drooping, white with purple spots at base; stamens blue, long-curled; in small branched clusters in upper leaf axils. Stems hairy. Leaves elliptical, hairy. **BLOOMS** June–Oct. **HABITAT** Dry pinelands, hammocks, fields, roadsides.

MISTLETOE
Phoradendron leucarpum
MISTLETOE FAMILY

3'. Ball-shaped parasitic shrub on branches and trunks of various broadleaf trees. Flowers minute, greenish yellow, in 1¼" spikes. Stems jointed, brittle. Leaves roundish, thick, leathery, evergreen. Berries tiny, white to yellowish. **CAUTION** Berries poisonous. **BLOOMS** Oct.–Jan. **HABITAT** Anywhere broadleaf trees grow.

MOON FLOWERS
"Moon Morning Glory"
Ipomoea alba
MORNING GLORY FAMILY

L variable. Twining vine. Flowers 5½", funnel-shaped, white with 5 yellowish-green, radiating stripes, shallowly 5-lobed; fragrant, open at night. Leaves heart-shaped. **BLOOMS** Year-round. **HABITAT** Thickets, edges of hammocks and mangrove swamps. **RANGE** nc FL and south.

BEACH MORNING GLORY
Ipomoea imperati
MORNING GLORY FAMILY

L variable. Very long, trailing, fleshy; attached to sand by roots along stems. Flowers 2½", funnel-shaped, white with yellow center, shallowly 5-lobed. Leaves unlobed or 3- to 7-lobed, thick, leathery. **BLOOMS** Apr.–Nov. **HABITAT** Beaches. **RANGE** Coastal FL, ex. se peninsula.

BLUE MORNING GLORY
Ipomoea indica
MORNING GLORY FAMILY

L variable. Climbing vine. Flowers 3½", funnel-shaped, deep blue-purple with white center, shallowly 5-lobed. Stems often hairy. Leaves heart-shaped. **BLOOMS** Year-round. **HABITAT** Thickets, swamp edges, disturbed areas. **RANGE** Mainly c FL and south.

RAILROAD VINE
Ipomoea pes-caprae
MORNING GLORY FAMILY

L variable. Very long, trailing vine. Flowers 2½", funnel-shaped, magenta with darker center, 5-lobed. Stems fleshy. Leaves ovate or kidney-shaped, tip broadly notched, folded along midvein, thick. **BLOOMS** Mainly June–Oct. **HABITAT** Beaches, dunes. **RANGE** Coastal FL.

GLADES MORNING GLORY
Ipomoea sagittata
MORNING GLORY FAMILY

L variable. Twining woody vine. Flowers 3½", funnel-shaped, rose-pink to rose-purple with darker center, 5-lobed. Leaves arrowhead-shaped, with long, diverging basal lobes. **BLOOMS** June–Oct. **HABITAT** Brackish marshes, prairies. **RANGE** Mainly coastal FL.

SOUTHERN SEA ROCKET
Cakile lanceolata
MUSTARD FAMILY

24". Clump-forming. Fleshy straggling stems with ½", 4-petaled, white or pale lavender flowers clustered at branch tips. Leaves oblong, coarsely toothed to pinnately lobed. Shoots and seedpods peppery-tasting. **BLOOMS** Apr.–Oct. **HABITAT** Beaches, edges of saline ponds, and marshes. **RANGE** Coastal FL.

POOR MAN'S PEPPER
"Pepperweed" "Peppergrass"
Lepidium virginicum
MUSTARD FAMILY

3'. Tiny, white, cross-shaped flowers in 4" clusters. Leaves linear-elliptical, shallowly to very deeply lobed. Common roadside and garden weed. All parts pungent-tasting. **BLOOMS** Year-round. **HABITAT** Disturbed areas.

BOG HEMP
"False Nettle"
Boehmeria cylindrica
NETTLE FAMILY

4′. Minute green flowers clustered into compact 4″ spikes. Stems hairy. Leaves ovate, toothed, short-hairy. Lacks stinging hairs of true nettle. **BLOOMS** Apr.–Nov. **HABITAT** Wet woods, thickets, ditches; marshes, swamps, streamsides, canals.

JIMSON WEED
Datura stramonium
NIGHTSHADE FAMILY

5′. Stout, rank-smelling. Flowers 4″, white to lavender, trumpet-shaped, 5-lobed. Stems often purple. Leaves ovate, coarsely toothed. Fruit 1½″, spiny, green to brown. **CAUTION** All parts extremely poisonous. **BLOOMS** Apr.–Nov. **HABITAT** Disturbed areas. **RANGE** Mainly n FL.

AMERICAN BLACK NIGHTSHADE
"Common Nightshade"
Solanum americanum
NIGHTSHADE FAMILY

3′. Flowers ⅓″, star-like, nodding, with 5 curved-back petals; white with yellow central column of anthers; in pendulous, few-flowered clusters. Leaves ovate, wavy-edged to coarsely toothed. Berries ⅓″, black-purple. **CAUTION** Foliage and fruit poisonous. **BLOOMS** Year-round. **HABITAT** Woods, thickets, disturbed areas.

GRASS PINK
Calopogon tuberosus
ORCHID FAMILY

4'. Flowers 2", butterfly-shaped, bright pink to magenta, with 6 petals, uppermost bearded and splotched with white and yellow; in long loose clusters atop leafless stems. Leaves 18", linear, clasping, basal. **BLOOMS** Mar.–Aug. **HABITAT** Marshes, bogs, wet pine flatwoods and ditches.

BUTTERFLY ORCHID
Encyclia tampensis
ORCHID FAMILY

24". Grows on palms, other trees. Flowers 1½", yellowish green tinged with brown or maroon; lowermost petal 3-lobed, white with magenta spot; in loose arching clusters, fragrant. Leaves linear-elliptical, sheathing, basal. **BLOOMS** June–Aug. (year-round). **HABITAT** Swamps, hammocks. **RANGE** nc FL and south.

GREENFLY ORCHID
Epidendrum conopseum
ORCHID FAMILY

16". Grows on tree branches. Flowers ¾", green, sometimes tinged with purple; with 6 petals, lowermost petal 3-lobed; clustered atop slender stems; fragrant; resemble insects. Leaves elliptical, leathery, unstalked, basal, few. The only FL orchid that is epiphytic (grows on other plants but is not a parasite). Common but inconspicuous. **BLOOMS** June–Sept. **HABITAT** Swamps, hammocks. **RANGE** n to c FL.

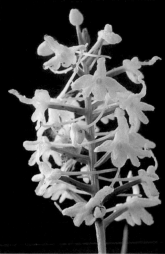

WATER-SPIDER ORCHID
"Floating Orchid"
Habenaria repens
ORCHID FAMILY

3′. Floating (often in mats of vegetation) leafy stems topped by long, erect, dense clusters of spidery, yellowish-green ½″ flowers. Leaves linear to lanceolate, somewhat fleshy, sheathing. **BLOOMS** Year-round. **HABITAT** Swamps, marshes, bogs, streams, ponds, ditches, canals.

SNOWY ORCHID
"Bog Torch"
Platanthera nivea
ORCHID FAMILY

3′. Flowers ½″, white, with 6 unequal petals, uppermost ones curved backward; spur up-curved. Stems slender, rigid. 2–3 linear to lanceolate, folded, basal leaves. **BLOOMS** June–Sept. **HABITAT** Wet pine flatwoods, prairies.

GIANT LADIES'-TRESSES
"Grass-leaved Ladies'-tresses"
Spiranthes praecox
ORCHID FAMILY

2′6″. Flowers ½″, hood-like, greenish white, with 6 unequal petals, lowest one largest, wavy-toothed, green-veined; in spiral or straight rows atop stems. Leaves 10″, grass-like, linear to thread-like. One of at least a dozen species of Ladies'-tresses known in e U.S. **BLOOMS** Apr.–Sept. **HABITAT** Swamps, sandhills, wet pine flatwoods, marshes.

LAWN ORCHID
Zeuxine strateumatica
ORCHID FAMILY
10″. Weedy-looking. Flowers ½″, hood-like, white to greenish, with 6 unequal petals, lowermost fleshy, yellow; in long dense clusters atop fleshy stems hidden by overlapping, linear to lanceolate leaves. **BLOOMS** Dec.–Mar. **HABITAT** Lawns, roadsides.

PASSIONFLOWER
"Maypop" "Apricot-vine"
Passiflora incarnata
PASSIONFLOWER FAMILY
L variable. Climbing or trailing vine with tendrils. Flowers 3″, elaborate, with 10 lavender petals/sepals, concentric rings of purple and white thread-like segments; 5 greenish- and maroon-streaked stamens arched around 3 styles. **BLOOMS** Apr.–Sept. **HABITAT** Dry woods, thickets, disturbed areas.

ROSARY PEA
"Black-eyed Susan" "Crab's-eye"
Abrus precatorius
PEA FAMILY
L variable. Woody vine with dense clusters of tiny, reddish-purple pea-flowers. Leaves pinnately compound, with many leaflets. Pods brown; seeds red with black spot. **CAUTION** Seeds deadly poisonous. **BLOOMS** June–Sept. **HABITAT** Dry thickets, disturbed areas. **RANGE** nc FL and south.

BASTARD INDIGO
"Indigo Bush"
Amorpha fruiticosa
PEA FAMILY
12″. Leafy shrub with dense clusters of hood-like, dark purple flowers, each a ⅓″ petal wrapped around golden-tipped stamens. Leaves pinnately compound, with many leaflets. **BLOOMS** May–Sept. **HABITAT** Wet woods, marshes, streamsides, riversides. **RANGE** All FL, ex. s tip.

CLIMBING BUTTERFLY-PEA
Centrosema virginianum
PEA FAMILY

L variable. Climbing or trailing vine, with 1½″ lavender pea-flowers, with largest petal purple-veined and white-splotched. Leaves divided into 3 leaflets. **BLOOMS** Year-round. **HABITAT** Pinelands, dunes.

PARTRIDGE-PEA
Chamaecrista fasciculata
PEA FAMILY

3′. Flowers 1½″, butterfly-like, with 5 unequal yellow petals with red spots at base. Stems erect to arching. Leaves pinnately compound, with many bristle-tipped leaflets. **BLOOMS** Apr.–Oct. (year-round in s FL). **HABITAT** Pinelands, open woods, disturbed areas.

SHOWY CROTALARIA
"Showy Rattlebox"
Crotalaria spectabilis
PEA FAMILY

5′. Long clusters of numerous 1″, yellow pea-flowers, with uppermost petal finely dark-lined. Stems dark, purplish. Leaves 8″, obovate, short-stalked to unstalked. Fruit inflated black 2″ pods. Seeds rattle in dry pod. **BLOOMS** Year-round. **HABITAT** Disturbed areas.

GLOBE-HEADED PRAIRIE CLOVER
Dalea feayi
PEA FAMILY

3′. Tiny, star-like, bright pink to pink-purple flowers in 1½″ spherical heads. Leaves pinnately compound, with 5–9 linear to thread-like leaflets. **BLOOMS** Apr.–Sept. **HABITAT** Pinelands, scrub. **RANGE** se panhandle, and from nc FL south.

SUMMER FAREWELL
Dalea pinnata
PEA FAMILY

4′. Flowers ⅓″, white, packed into ½″ roundish clusters enclosed at base by reddish-brown bracts. Leaves pinnately compound, with 3–7 thread-like leaflets. **BLOOMS** July–Dec. **HABITAT** Dry pinelands, sandhills, scrub. **RANGE** n to sc FL.

WHITE MILK PEA
Galactia elliottii
PEA FAMILY

L variable. Trailing to climbing, hairy-stemmed vine with ½″ white to pinkish pea-flowers in 6″ clusters. Leaves pinnately compound, with 7–9 leaflets. **BLOOMS** Apr.–Oct. **HABITAT** Dry pinelands, thickets, scrub. **RANGE** Peninsular FL.

ROUND-HEADED BUSH-CLOVER
Lespedeza hirta
PEA FAMILY

5′. Erect leafy stems, with dense roundish ½″ clusters of tiny, creamy white pea-flowers, each with reddish splotch on upper petal. Leaves divided into 3 ovate to obovate leaflets. **BLOOMS** Aug.–Nov. **HABITAT** Pinelands, dry woods. **RANGE** n to sc FL.

SKY-BLUE LUPINE
Lupinus diffusus
PEA FAMILY

3′. Silky-hairy, stout. Erect to sprawling, clustered stems end in long clusters of whorled, blue-purple ½″ pea-flowers. Leaves oblong to elliptical. **BLOOMS** Mar.–June (year-round in s FL). **HABITAT** Sandhills, pine scrub. **RANGE** w panhandle and peninsular FL.

WHITE SWEET CLOVER
Melilotus alba
PEA FAMILY

8′. Tiny, white, fragrant pea-flowers in slender, cylindrical, 5″ clusters. Leaves divided into 3 obovate to lanceolate leaflets. **BLOOMS** Year-round. **HABITAT** Disturbed areas.

SMOOTH-LEAVED SENSITIVE BRIER
Mimosa quadrivalvis (Schrankia microphylla)
PEA FAMILY

L variable. Trailing, prickly. Flowers tiny, bright pink, in ¾" fuzzy spherical heads on long stalks. Leaves bipinnately compound, with many leaflets; fold up when touched. **BLOOMS** Year-round. **HABITAT** Pine lands, grasslands, roadsides. **RANGE** All FL, ex. southeast.

SPANISH GOLD
"Daubentonia"
Sesbania punicea
PEA FAMILY

10'. Leafy shrub with drooping clusters of 1", bright orange red pea-flowers. Leaves pinnately compound, with many leaflets. **BLOOMS** Apr.–Oct. **HABITAT** Thickets, marshy shorelines, disturbed areas. **RANGE** n to sc FL.

WHITE CLOVER
Trifolium repens
PEA FAMILY

L 16". Turf-forming. Flowers ½", tubular, in 1¼" roundish clusters; age from white to pinkish to brownish. Stems creeping. Common on lawns. Leaves 3-parted. **BLOOMS** Year-round. **HABITAT** Lawns, fields, roadsides.

FLORIDA VETCH
Vicia floridana
PEA FAMILY

L variable. Slender-stemmed, reclining or sprawling vine with 1-sided clusters of ⅓", lavender and white pea-flowers. Leaves pinnately compound, tendril-tipped, with 2–6 elliptical leaflets. **BLOOMS** Apr.–Aug. **HABITAT** Wet woods, pondsides and riversides, ditches, roadsides. **RANGE** Mainly n to c FL.

YELLOW VIGNA
"Cowpea"
Vigna luteola
PEA FAMILY

L variable. Trailing or twining, often tangled vine with ¾″ yellow pea-flowers. Leaves pinnately compound, with 3 ovate to linear-lanceolate leaflets. **BLOOMS** Year-round. **HABITAT** Thickets, tidal flats, tidal marshes, flatwoods, ditches, roadsides. **RANGE** Mainly peninsular and coastal FL.

ANNUAL GARDEN PHLOX
Phlox drummondii
PHLOX FAMILY

24″. Flowers 1″, trumpet-shaped, 5-lobed; white, pink, red, lavender, or combination, often with contrasting eye. Stems sticky-haired. Leaves elliptical, with gland-tipped hairs. Forms masses along roadsides. **BLOOMS** Mar.–June. **HABITAT** Disturbed areas. **RANGE** Mainly n to sc FL.

WATER HYACINTH
Eichhornia crassipes
PICKERELWEED FAMILY

4′. Usu. floating, occ. rooted in mud. Flowers 4″, funnel-shaped, lavender, with yellow spot on uppermost petal; in dense spikes. Leaves round, on spongy inflated stalks. Spreads via runners, clog waterways. **BLOOMS** Apr.–Sept. **HABITAT** Streams, ditches, marshes, lakes.

PICKERELWEED
Pontederia cordata
PICKERELWEED FAMILY

3′. Each tall stalk bears 1 large leaf or flower spike. Flowers ½″, 2-lipped, blue-purple, uppermost petal with yellow and white splotch. Leaves heart-shaped or lanceolate, on fleshy stalks. **BLOOMS** Year-round. **HABITAT** Streams, marshes, ponds, ditches.

QUILL-LEAF
"Wild Pine"
Tillandsia fasciculata
PINEAPPLE FAMILY

24". Grows on cypress and pine trees. Flowers in 6", purple-and-red or purple-and-yellow spikes. Leaves linear, tapering at tip, curved-back, sheathing, grayish green; evergreen. **BLOOMS** Oct.–Jan. **HABITAT** Hammocks, cypress swamps. **RANGE** c FL and south.

BALL MOSS
Tillandsia recurvata
PINEAPPLE FAMILY

10". Grows on various trees. Ball-shaped cluster of curved, tangled, silvery-scaled stems and leaves; evergreen. Flowers in purple, scaly, 1¼" spikes. **BLOOMS** Apr.–Oct. **HABITAT** Hammocks, pinelands, scrub. **RANGE** Peninsular FL.

AIR PLANT
"Wild Pine"
Tillandsia setacea
PINEAPPLE FAMILY

6". Grows on magnolias and oaks. Stiff tufts of clustered, silvery-scaled leaves; evergreen. Flowers in reddish spikes. **BLOOMS** June–Sept. **HABITAT** Hammocks, swamps. **RANGE** c FL and south.

SPANISH MOSS
Tillandsia usneoides
PINEAPPLE FAMILY

6'. Grows on oaks and other trees. Pendulous bundles of wiry, curly, silvery-scaled stems and leaves. Rootless; absorbs water and nutrients via scales. **BLOOMS** Apr.–June. **HABITAT** Hammocks, pinelands, scrub.

COMMON CHICKWEED
Stellaria media
PINK FAMILY

12″. Flowers tiny, star-like, white, with 5 petals deeply cut to look like 10, and 5 long sepals (longer than petals). Stems prostrate, with lines of hairs. Leaves ovate. Common lawn and garden weed. **BLOOMS** Year-round. **HABITAT** Lawns, disturbed areas.

PIPEWORT
"Hard-head Pipewort"
Eriocaulon decangulare
PIPEWORT FAMILY

3′. Leafless stalk topped with grayish-white, knob-like ¾″ head of tiny feathery flowers; rises from tuft of 16″, tapering, grass-like leaves. Stems twisted, ridged. **BLOOMS** May–Oct. **HABITAT** Wet pine flatwoods, pondsides, ditches.

HOODED PITCHER-PLANT
Sarracenia minor
PITCHER-PLANT FAMILY

24″ (leaves). Flowers 3″, yellow, with 5 drooping petals and umbrella-like center. Leaves pitcher-like, with overarching hood; white patches and reddish veins near top; semi-evergreen. Insects attracted by secretions inside hood are trapped and digested by plant. **BLOOMS** Apr.–June. **HABITAT** Bogs, pinelands, marshes. **RANGE** e panhandle to c FL.

POKEWEED
Phytolacca americana var. *rigida*
POKEWEED FAMILY

10′. Flowers somewhat cup-like, white to pinkish, with 5 petals, 10 stamens, and button-like pistil; in clusters. Stems fleshy, age to bright pink. Leaves 6″, elliptical to ovate. Berries tiny, purple-black. **CAUTION** Berries and leaves usu. poisonous. **BLOOMS** Year-round. **HABITAT** Hammocks, floodplain forests, disturbed areas.

CAROLINA POPPY
"White Prickly Poppy"
Argemone albiflora
POPPY FAMILY

3'. Prickly. Flowers 4", white, cup-like, with 5–6 wrinkled petals, numerous yellow stamens, maroon stigma. Leaves 8", whitish, obovate, spiny-toothed, clasping; coarsely, irregularly lobed. Sap yellow. **BLOOMS** Apr.–Oct. **HABITAT** Roadsides, fields, vacant lots. **RANGE** All FL, ex. extreme south.

MEXICAN POPPY
"Yellow Prickly Poppy"
Argemone mexicana
POPPY FAMILY

3'. Flowers 2¾", yellow, cup-like, with 6 wrinkled petals, many stamens. Leaves 10", whitish green, obovate, spiny-toothed, clasping; coarsely, irregularly lobed. Sap bright yellow. **BLOOMS** May–Sept. **HABITAT** Disturbed areas.

PINK PURSLANE
"Rose Moss"
Portulaca pilosa
PURSLANE FAMILY

8". Prostrate to erect, fleshy. Flowers ½", pinkish purple, with 5 petals, numerous yellow stamens; in clusters at stem ends. Leaves linear to lanceolate; axils hairy-tufted. **BLOOMS** Apr.–Oct. **HABITAT** Pinelands, sandy disturbed areas.

CLUSTERED ROCK-ROSE
"Frostweed"
Helianthemum corymbosum
ROCK-ROSE FAMILY

12". Flowers ¾", with 5 yellow petals, numerous orange stamens; in dense clusters mainly of buds that never open. Stems hairy, grayish. Leaves elliptical, hairy, silvery below. **BLOOMS** Mar.–Sept. (year-round in s FL). **HABITAT** Pinelands, dunes, open woods.

SWAMP ROSE
Rosa palustris
ROSE FAMILY

6′. Prickly shrub. Flowers 2½″, with 5 pink crinkled petals around yellow center with many stamens and pistils. Leaves pinnately compound, with 3–9 elliptical toothed leaflets. Fruit reddish rose hips. **BLOOMS** Mar.–June. **HABITAT** Marshes, streamsides, ditches, pondsides, lakesides. **RANGE** e panhandle to c peninsular FL.

SAND BLACKBERRY
Rubus cuneifolius
ROSE FAMILY

5′. Flowers 1½″, with 5 white petals, numerous stamens and pistils clustered at center. Stems woody, barbed, tangled, erect to arching. Leaves palmately compound, prickly-stalked. Blackberries 1″, purple-black; edible, ripe June–Oct. **BLOOMS** Apr.–Oct. **HABITAT** Sandy thickets, woodland edges, fields.

SOUTHERN DEWBERRY
Rubus trivialis
ROSE FAMILY

L variable. Sprawling. Flowers 1½″, white to pinkish, 5-petaled. Stems woody, tangled, barbed, hairy. Leaves palmately compound, prickly, toothed; age to red. Fruit 1¼″, purple-black, blackberry like; edible, ripe June–July. **BLOOMS** Mar.–June. **HABITAT** Roadsides, thickets, woodland edges, disturbed areas. **RANGE** All FL, ex. extreme south.

CLUSTER-LEAF ST.-JOHN'S-WORT
Hypericum cistifolium
ST.-JOHN'S-WORT FAMILY

3′. Flowers tiny, yellow, with 5 petals, many stamens. Stems ridged, with successive pairs of branches at right angles. Leaves lanceolate, leathery, clasping. **BLOOMS** Apr.–Sept. **HABITAT** Wet pinelands, streamsides and pondsides.

HEART-LEAVED ST.-PETER'S-WORT
Hypericum tetrapetalum
ST.-JOHN'S-WORT FAMILY

3′. Few-branched shrub. Flowers 1¼″, yellow, with 4 unequal sepals, numerous stamens; borne singly on branch ends. Stems slender, woody, reddish. Leaves heart-shaped, clasping. **BLOOMS** Apr.–Nov. **HABITAT** Wet pinelands, hammocks, prairies.

SAWGRASS
Cladium jamaicense
SEDGE FAMILY

10′. Forms huge colonies. Flowers in 8′, brownish plumes. Stems 3-angled. Leaves linear, stiff, toothed. Main component of Everglades' "sea of grass." **CAUTION** Leaves have saw-toothed edges. **BLOOMS** July–Oct. **HABITAT** Swamps, brackish marshes.

FINE-LEAVED WHITE-TOP SEDGE
"Star-rush" "White-tops"
Rhynchospora (Dichromena) colorata
SEDGE FAMILY

24″. Flowers minute, enclosed by cluster of tiny whitish scales, surrounded by whorl of 4–6 white-based, petal-like leaves. Stems 3-angled. Leaves linear. **BLOOMS** Mar.–Nov. **HABITAT** Prairies, wet pinelands, ditches.

WATER HYSSOP
Bacopa monnieri
SNAPDRAGON FAMILY

10″. Forms extensive mats. Flowers ⅓″, pale lavender-pink to white, 5-lobed, in leaf axils. Stems creeping, succulent. Leaves oblanceolate to obovate, thick. **BLOOMS** Nearly year-round. **HABITAT** Open wet ground, shallow water.

COMMON BLUE HEARTS
Buchnera americana
SNAPDRAGON FAMILY

24″. Rough stems topped by loose spikes of ½″, purple or white, 5-lobed flowers. Leaves lanceolate, irregularly toothed. **BLOOMS** Apr.–Nov. **HABITAT** Pinelands, meadows, bogs, disturbed areas.

OLD FIELD TOADFLAX
"Blue Toadflax"
Linaria canadensis
SNAPDRAGON FAMILY

24″. Flowers ½″, lavender, short-tubular; 2-lipped, with upper lip 2-lobed, lower lip 3-lobed and with raised white area at base; conspicuously spurred. Stems slender, with basal rosette of branches. Leaves linear. **BLOOMS** Feb.–June. **HABITAT** Open disturbed areas.

SLENDER BEARD-TONGUE
"Southern Beard-tongue"
Penstemon australis
SNAPDRAGON FAMILY

3'. Flowers 1", tubular, hairy; 2-lipped, with upper lip rose-pink and erect, lower lip horizontal, white with pink veins. Stems smooth or with gland-tipped hairs. Leaves mostly obovate, untoothed to slightly toothed. **BLOOMS** Apr.–June. **HABITAT** Dry pinelands. **RANGE** n to c FL.

ERECT DAYFLOWER
Commelina erecta
SPIDERWORT FAMILY

3'. Erect to prostrate, jointed stems tipped with delicate blue flowers, each protruding from a ¾", heart-shaped, folded bract; bloom for 1 day. Leaves elliptical to ovate, sheathing. **BLOOMS** Apr.–Oct. **HABITAT** Pinelands, scrub, dry woods.

COMMON SPIDERWORT
"Ohio Spiderwort"
"Reflexed Spiderwort"
Tradescantia ohiensis
SPIDERWORT FAMILY

3'. Flowers purple-blue, with 3 petals, 6 stamens with beaded hairs on filaments; bloom for 1 day. Leaves 16", grass-like, linear to lanceolate, folded lengthwise, sheathing. **BLOOMS** Apr.–July. **HABITAT** Open woods and disturbed areas. **RANGE** n to sc FL.

TREAD SOFTLY
Cnidoscolus stimulosus
SPURGE FAMILY

3'. Flowers 1", white, trumpet-shaped, 5-lobed, in branched clusters atop stems. Leaves variable; usu. 8", palmately 3- to 5-lobed. **CAUTION** Do not touch; covered with stinging hairs; can cause severe reactions. **BLOOMS** Mar.–Oct. (probably year-round in s FL). **HABITAT** Dry woods, fields.

PAINTED-LEAF
Poinsettia cyathophora
SPURGE FAMILY

5'. Erect stems topped by flower-like whorls of red-based leaves surrounding tiny green flower clusters. Leaves vary in shape from linear to ovate to fiddle-shaped. **CAUTION** Milky sap poisonous. **BLOOMS** Year-round. **HABITAT** Sand dunes, hammocks, disturbed areas.

CASTOR BEAN
Ricinus communis
SPURGE FAMILY

16'. Shrub-like. Flowers in reddish or greenish clusters. Leaves large, umbrella-like, green to red. **CAUTION** Seeds deadly poisonous if chewed. **BLOOMS** June–Oct. (year-round in s FL). **HABITAT** Thickets, disturbed areas. **RANGE** Mainly peninsular FL.

COMMON STAR GRASS
Hypoxis juncea
STAR-GRASS FAMILY

12". Flowers ¾", star-like, with 6 yellow petals. Stems slender, hairy, shorter than leaves. Leaves 12", grass-like, hairy, basal. **BLOOMS** Apr.–Sept. **HABITAT** Pine flatwoods, wet ditches. **RANGE** All FL, ex. s tip.

POOR MAN'S PATCH
"Stickleaf"
Mentzelia floridana
STICK-LEAF FAMILY
3'. Flowers ¾", yellow, with 5 petals, many stamens. Stems brittle, rough-hairy, often sprawling. Leaves ovate, often 3-lobed, toothed; minutely barbed, stick to animals and people. **BLOOMS** Year-round. **HABITAT** Hammocks, dunes. **RANGE** Coastal peninsular FL.

PINK SUNDEW
Drosera capillaris
SUNDEW FAMILY
12". Curved leafless stems topped with 1-sided cluster of ½", pink, 5-petaled flowers. Leaves spoon-shaped, reddish, sticky; covered with long, gland-tipped hairs whereby plant traps and digests insects. **BLOOMS** Apr.–Aug. **HABITAT** Pinelands, bogs, wet ditches.

MOSS VERBENA
Glandularia pulchella
(Verbena tenuisecta)
VERBENA FAMILY
12". Mat-forming, hairy. Flowers ⅜", with 5 notched petal lobes; all-white, or pink or purple with white eye; in spikes atop upright branches. Leaves deeply dissected into narrow segments. **BLOOMS** June–Oct. **HABITAT** Open disturbed areas. **RANGE** Mainly n to sc FL.

LANTANA
"Shrub Verbena"
Lantana camara
VERBENA FAMILY
5'. Flowers ½", with 4 unequal lobes, cream, yellow, or pink, usu. age to orange or red; clustered into multicolored heads. Leaves ovate, toothed, rough-hairy. Fruit ⅓", berry-like, metallic blue. **BLOOMS** Year-round. **HABITAT** Open woods, disturbed areas.

FLORIDA VIOLET
Viola sororia (V. affinis, V. floridana)
VIOLET FAMILY
12″. Flowers 1½″, pansy-like, with 5 purple to lavender petals, white at base, upper 2 curved-back, lower 3 purple-veined; on separate long stalks from heart-shaped, scalloped leaves. **BLOOMS** Mar.–June. **HABITAT** Open wet woods. **RANGE** All FL, ex. s tip.

TALL HYDROLEA
"Sky-flower"
Hydrolea corymbosa
WATER-LEAF FAMILY
24″. Flowers ¾″ with 5 blue petals, in loose clusters. Stems smooth below, short-hairy above. Leaves lanceolate, finely toothed. **BLOOMS** June–Oct. **HABITAT** Swamps, marshes, ditches. **RANGE** Mainly peninsular FL.

SPATTERDOCK
"Yellow Pond Lily" "Yellow Cow-lily"
Nuphar luteum
WATER-LILY FAMILY
Floats flat. Flowers 1½″, cup-like, yellow, with cylindrical pistil. Leaves round or heart-shaped, wrinkled, on long underwater stalks. **BLOOMS** Mar.–July. **HABITAT** Ponds, marshes, sluggish streams, canals.

YELLOW WATER LILY
"Banana Water Lily"
Nymphaea mexicana
WATER-LILY FAMILY

Floats flat. Flowers 4″, with many bright yellow petals and stamens. Leaves round to ovate, notched to center; brownish-blotched above, purple below. **BLOOMS** Apr.–Dec. **HABITAT** Ponds, sluggish streams, ditches, canals. **RANGE** Peninsular FL.

FRAGRANT WATER LILY
"White Water Lily"
Nymphaea odorata
WATER-LILY FAMILY

Floats flat. Flowers 4¾″, with numerous white petals intergrading with many yellow stamens at center; fragrant. Leaves round, notched to center. **BLOOMS** Apr.–Sept. **HABITAT** Ponds, lakes, sluggish streams.

YELLOW WOOD SORREL
Oxalis stricta
WOOD-SORREL FAMILY

10″. Flowers ½″, shallowly funnel-shaped, yellow, 5-petaled. Stems hairy. Leaves clover-like, palmately compound, with 3 heart-shaped leaflets; edible, sour-tasting. **BLOOMS** Apr.–Oct. **HABITAT** Open woods, fields, disturbed areas.

BROAD-SCALE YELLOW-EYED-GRASS
Xyris platylepis
YELLOW-EYED-GRASS FAMILY

3′3″. Flowers ⅜″, yellow or white, with 3 wrinkled petals around feathery center; in groups on brown, cone-like base; each lasts 1 day. Stems twisted. Leaves 16″, grass-like, twisted, with pinkish bases. **BLOOMS** June–Sept. **HABITAT** Pineland ponds, ditches. **RANGE** All FL, ex. s tip.

Invertebrates

Biologists divide the animal kingdom into two broad groupings—vertebrates, animals with a backbone, and invertebrates, those without. While this distinction seems apt, perhaps because we are vertebrates ourselves, it is really one of mere convenience. Vertebrates are but a small subphylum of the animal kingdom, and invertebrates comprise the vast majority of animal life forms that inhabit water, air, and land. Invertebrates have thrived on earth for more than a billion years, with species evolving and disappearing through the eons; they include a fascinating spectrum of phyla with extraordinarily diverse lifestyles and evolutionary developments. This guide describes selected species from six phyla found in marine, terrestrial, and freshwater environments:

Phylum Porifera	Sponges
Phylum Cnidaria	Hydrozoans, jellyfishes, sea anemones, and corals
Phylum Annelida	Marine worms and earthworms
Phylum Mollusca	Chitons, gastropods, bivalves, and cephalopods
Phylum Arthropoda	Crustaceans, centipedes, millipedes, horseshoe crabs, arachnids, and insects
Phylum Echinodermata	Sea stars, sea urchins, and sea cucumbers

There are two basic invertebrate body structures. *Radially symmetrical* invertebrates, such as cnidarians and echinoderms, have a circular body plan with a central mouth cavity and a nervous system that encircles the mouth. *Bilateral* invertebrates have virtually identical left and right sides like vertebrates, with paired nerve cords that run along the belly, not the back, and a brain (in species with a head). All invertebrates are cold-blooded, and either become dormant or die when temperatures become too high or low.

In this guide, marine invertebrates are covered first, followed by freshwater and land invertebrates. Many of the groups covered below are described in more detail in separate introductions.

Plant or Animal?

Some marine invertebrates, such as sponges and sea anemones, are often mistaken for plants, but several key features place them in the animal kingdom. Plant cell walls, made of cellulose, are thick and strong, while those of animals are thin and weak. Plants have no nervous system, and therefore react slowly; almost all animals have a nervous system and can react quickly. Through the process called photosynthesis, most plants manufacture their own food from inorganic raw materials, while animals obtain energy by ingesting and metabolizing plants and/or other animals. Plants grow throughout their lives, while most animals stop growing at maturity (a few types, such as fish and snakes, keep growing but at a very slow rate). Finally, most plants are sedentary, while most animals move about. A sponge, coral, or sea anemone may be as immobile as a seaweed, but it qualifies as an animal on the basis of the above and other characteristics, such as the nature of its reproductive organs and its developmental pattern.

Marine Invertebrates

Florida marine environments are home to a wide variety of clinging, digging, swimming, and scuttling invertebrates. This text covers representatives from six invertebrate phyla. Members of other invertebrate marine phyla are generally small or difficult to see.

Sponges of the phylum Porifera are the simplest of multicellular creatures, lacking body organs and a mouth; they filter food and oxygen from the water. Mainly sedentary, sponges vary from tiny cups to wide encrustations. In the phylum Cnidaria are the hydrozoans, jellyfishes, sea anemones, and corals. All are radially symmetrical, and most have tentacles armed with stinging cells that ensnare and paralyze tiny animals. Hydrozoans can be either sedentary filter-feeders or free-floating bell-shaped medusas with downward-facing mouths. Sea anemones are nearly always sedentary, attached at their bases to hard objects, although a few species can swim to new locations. Corals can be either soft and flexible with retractable feeding polyps, or stony, with a calcium carbonate skeleton on which tiny polyps live. Many Florida cnidarians cause painful stings, burns, or rashes if touched, and a few are extremely dangerous to humans. The phylum Annelida, segmented worms, is represented in Florida by the bristle worms (class Polychaeta), which are mobile or live in a tube. Their visible external segments are covered with bundles of bristles that aid them in swimming, crawling, or digging. The phylum Mollusca, including many of the most familiar marine invertebrates, is discussed on page 199. Species of the phylum Arthropoda usually are identified by their rigid exoskeleton and jointed legs. Of the five marine arthropod classes, we cover two: horseshoe crabs (class Merostomata) and crustaceans (class Crustacea). Crabs in name only, horseshoe crabs have more in common with spiders. Crustaceans, such as barnacles, crabs, and lobsters, live primarily in sunlit waters. Their forms are so diverse that their single common characteristic is paired antennae. Crabs and lobsters are discussed on page 206. The phylum Echinodermata, discussed on page 209, includes sea stars, brittle stars, sea urchins, and sea cucumbers.

The following accounts give typical adult lengths or heights unless otherwise noted. Many species can survive in a wide range of water depths, which are noted in the accounts; the term *intertidal zone* refers to the area between the high- and low-tide lines.

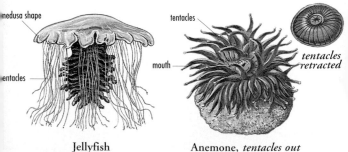

Jellyfish

Anemone, *tentacles out*

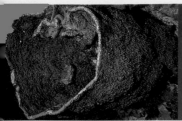

VASE SPONGE
Ircinia campana
SILICEOUS AND HORNY SPONGE CLASS
3′. Body vase- or basket-shaped, with deep central cavity; reddish brown, reddish, or gray. Outer surface spongy, with coarse vertical ridges; inside covered with pores. Usu. solitary. **HABITAT** Low-tide line to 50′ deep; on rocks.

FIRE SPONGE
Tedania ignis
SILICEOUS AND HORNY SPONGE CLASS
8″. Body smooth, soft, with wide irregular lobes, few large pores; bright red or orange. Colonial; encrusts on rocks, corals, mangrove roots. **CAUTION** Causes severe rashes and blisters. **HABITAT** Low-tide line to 50′ deep; bays, lagoons.

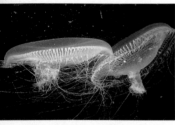

MANY-RIBBED HYDROMEDUSA
Aequorea aequorea
HYDROZOAN CLASS
W 5″. Body saucer-shaped; thick, jelly-like, transparent; luminescent at night. 25–100 radial canals, blue (male) or rosy (female). Short tentacles fringe outer edge. Often washes ashore. **HABITAT** Floats at or below surface of open ocean and along coasts.

CRENELATED FIRE CORAL
Millepora alcicornis
HYDROZOAN CLASS
12″. Resembles a coral. Body upright, branched; brown to creamy yellow. Covered with tiny white polyps with retractable, hair-like tentacles. **CAUTION** Highly toxic; causes severe burning rash if touched. **HABITAT** Coral reefs, cement pilings, rocky bottoms. **RANGE** s FL.

PORTUGUESE MAN-OF-WAR
Physalia physalis
HYDROZOAN CLASS
10″. Body balloon-like, gas-filled; translucent, with iridescent blue or pink tinge. Tentacles blue, to 60′ long. Pink ridged crest; blue tubular digestive area. Changes shape to catch wind and alter course. **CAUTION** Stinging tentacles cause severe burns and blisters, even when dead. **HABITAT** Ocean surface.

LION'S MANE
Cyanea capillata
JELLYFISH CLASS
W 18". Body a smooth, saucer-shaped, yellowish-orange to reddish-brown, nearly translucent bell. 150 yellowish stinging tentacles to 5' long. **CAUTION** Highly toxic; causes severe burns, blisters; sometimes fatal. **HABITAT** Ocean surface; in winter, chiefly ne FL.

MOON JELLYFISH
Aurelia aurita
JELLYFISH CLASS
W 12". Body saucer-shaped, translucent. Many short, fringe-like, white tentacles. 4 round or horseshoe-shaped gonads near center; yellow, pink, or bluish in adults; white when imm. **CAUTION** Causes mild rashes, burns. **HABITAT** Inshore ocean surface; often washes ashore.

UPSIDE-DOWN JELLYFISH
Cassiopeia xamachana
JELLYFISH CLASS
W 10". Body saucer-shaped, with rounded edges; pale brown. 8 fleshy branched feeding arms covered with clusters of symbiotic algae. Thousands lie together upside-down on ocean floor waving arms. **CAUTION** Sting causes mild rash. **HABITAT** Shallow stagnant bays.

COMMON SEA FAN
Gorgonia ventalina
CORAL AND SEA ANEMONE CLASS
24". Body an upright flexible fan of interlocking lacy branches on one compressed plane extending from short trunk. Yellow, purple, rarely whitish. Covered with small pores that hold tiny, tentacled, retractable polyps. **HABITAT** Coral reefs, rocks. **RANGE** Keys.

PALMER'S SEA ROD
Eunicea palmeri
CORAL AND SEA ANEMONE CLASS
24". Body upright, branched; purplish gray or brown. Branches knobby, slender, flexible; tipped with pores. Adult bushy, imm. in one plane. Branches wave in water. **HABITAT** Coral reefs, rocks. **RANGE** se FL, Keys.

PINK-TIPPED ANEMONE
Condylactis gigantea
CORAL AND SEA ANEMONE CLASS
5″. Body columnar; pale blue, green, whitish, orange, or red. 100 retractable tentacles with colorful tips. Anchors to objects; swims to new location. **CAUTION** Stings. **HABITAT** Sea-grass beds, coral reefs, rocks. **RANGE** s FL.

STAGHORN CORAL
Acropora cervicornis
CORAL AND SEA ANEMONE CLASS
H 4′; W 6′. Body sprawling; yellowish or purplish brown. Branches cylindrical, slender, with pointed whitish tips. Surface covered with tiny cups facing tips. Overharvested. **HABITAT** Coral reefs. **RANGE** Keys.

ELKHORN CORAL
Acropora palmata
CORAL AND SEA ANEMONE CLASS
H 6′; W 4′. Body sprawling; yellow-green, cream, or brown. Branches wide, flattened, with whitish tips. Covered with tiny cups facing edges. **CAUTION** Cuts from this heal slowly. **HABITAT** Coral reefs. **RANGE** Keys.

CLUBBED FINGER CORAL
Porites porites
CORAL AND SEA ANEMONE CLASS
H 12″; W 12″. Body upright; pale yellow, brown, or purple. Branches low, thick, with clubbed tips about 1″ wide. Surface covered with tiny cups. A stony coral. **HABITAT** Shallow coral reefs, rocks. **RANGE** se FL.

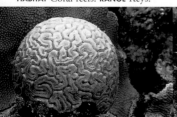

LABYRINTHINE BRAIN CORAL
Diploria labyrinthiformis
CORAL AND SEA ANEMONE CLASS
H 5′; W 5′. Body a convex "boulder"; pale orange, green, or brown. Surface hard, with winding narrow valleys ¼″ deep; covered with tiny, greenish, retractable tentacles. Resembles a human brain. **HABITAT** Shallow coral reefs. **RANGE** se FL.

ORANGE FIRE WORM
Eurythoe complanata
POLYCHAETE WORM CLASS
4″. Body long, flattened; pale orange-yellow. Side appendages have reddish gills, white bristles. 4 eyes, 5 tentacles. **CAUTION** Bristles break off in skin; cause burning, itching. **HABITAT** Low-tide line to 50′ deep; coral reefs, flat bottoms. **RANGE** s FL.

Marine Mollusks

Mollusks, of the phylum Mollusca, are amazingly numerous and diverse, with Florida species ranging in size from near-microscopic to conchs several feet long. Worldwide, seven classes of mollusks inhabit land, freshwater, and marine environments; four are commonly found in inshore Florida marine waters.

Chitons have eight-valved shells held together by a tough outer membrane (the girdle); they crawl about on rocks and pilings, scraping up algae and microscopic animals. Gastropods, including snails and their relatives, usually have a single calcium carbonate shell, whorled to the right, although nudibranchs are shell-less; they feed on marine plants and animals, scraping food with their tiny teeth as they crawl or swim about. Bivalves, which include clams and oysters, have two separate shells called valves, from which protrude two siphons and a muscular foot; they filter-feed on microscopic plant and animal life. Normally, bivalves attach to a hard substrate or burrow into sand, mud, or wood, although some species, such as scallops, can swim. Cephalopods, the most advanced mollusks, include the squids, which have a thin internal shell-like structure, and octopuses, which are shell-less; all have highly developed eyes and long tentacled arms; they move by swimming and water propulsion and feed by grabbing and eating crabs, fish, and other mollusks.

Gastropods and bivalves can be easily observed at most coastal locations. Chitons can sometimes be found under rocks and inside empty whelk shells. Cephalopods generally live in subtidal waters. Florida's inshore molluscan habitats include sand- and mudflats, salt marshes, coral reefs, mangrove swamps, sea-grass beds, piers, and pilings. Shell-collecting is popular on Florida's beaches. Storms often wash up common and unusual deepwater shells; the best places to look for shells are mudflats and quiet beaches. Recreational shellfishing is less common in Florida than in waters farther north. Environmental conditions, such as seasonal blooms of toxic "red-tide" algae, sometimes make local shellfish populations unsafe to eat, so always check with local authorities before harvesting.

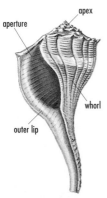

Gastropod Shell

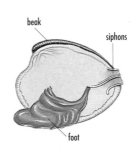

Bivalve Shell

ROUGH-GIRDLED CHITON
Ceratozona squalida
CHITON CLASS

1½". Body oval; pale green. Shells mottled, rough. Girdle brownish, covered with short, thick, yellowish hairs. Rolls into ball if disturbed. HABITAT Intertidal zone, shallow waters; on coral reefs, rocks. RANGE se FL.

CAYENNE KEYHOLE LIMPET
Diodora cayenensis
GASTROPOD CLASS

1½". Shell oval, conical, widest at rear; rough surface has vertical and concentric ridges. Whitish, pink, gray, or buff. Keyhole-shaped opening at apex. Often covered with algae. HABITAT Intertidal zone to 90' deep; rocks, jetties.

BLEEDING TOOTH
Nerita peloronta
GASTROPOD CLASS

1¼". Shell globular, thick; spire flattened. Whitish or yellowish, with black, brown, and reddish zigzag markings. Outer lip lined with fine teeth; inner lip reddish, with 1 large and 1 small tooth. HABITAT Rocky shores, shallows. RANGE s FL.

PINK CONCH
"Queen Conch"
Strombus gigas
GASTROPOD CLASS

10". Shell spindle-shaped; spire short, conical, with rounded knobs on shoulder. "Skin" yellowish or pale brown. Opening long, narrow; outer lip flared, pinkish. Edible; overfished. HABITAT 5–15' deep; sand, rubble, sea-grass beds. RANGE s FL.

FLORIDA FIGHTING CONCH
Strombus alatus
GASTROPOD CLASS

3½". Shell oval, thick; spire high, with short spines on shoulder. Brownish gray or purple, sometimes with brown mottling. Lip of opening wide; sharp-edged plate snaps closed for protection. HABITAT Shallow sandbars, sea-grass beds.

TRUE TULIP SNAIL
Fasciolaria tulipa
GASTROPOD CLASS

7″. Shell spindle-shaped, smooth, with weak spiral threading; spire high, sharp. Pink, olive, gray, or (in Keys) orange-red; mottled and finely banded with dark brown. Opening wide. **HABITAT** Low-tide line to 30′ deep; sand, grass bottoms.

LIGHTNING WHELK
Busycon contrarium
GASTROPOD CLASS

10″. Shell wide at top, narrows toward bottom; spirals to left; spire low, knobbed. White or buffy, with dark brown vertical lines. Opening wide, long. **HABITAT** Low-tide line to 10′ deep; sand, mud, shell bottoms.

LETTERED OLIVE
Oliva sayana
GASTROPOD CLASS

2″. Shell glossy, cylindrical, spire short, pointed. White or pale buff, with brown zigzag lines. Opening long, narrow; outer lip thin, light purple inside. Digs mole-like tunnels under surface. **HABITAT** Shallow waters; mud, sand bottoms.

FLORIDA HORSE CONCH
Pleuroploca gigantea
GASTROPOD CLASS

10″ (to 24″). Shell heavy, spindle-shaped; spire high; whorls knobbed, with irreg. ridges. White or orange, with darker bands. Often encrusted with tiny barnacles. Opening rounded; orange inside. **HABITAT** Low-tide line to 20′ deep; sand, mud bottoms.

STIFF PEN SHELL
Atrina rigida
BIVALVE CLASS

7″. Shell thick, wedge-shaped, with low radiating ridges; straight where valves join; one end rounded, other pointed. Brown or dark purple. Burrows into sand or wedges itself into coral, round edge up. Produces black pearls. **HABITAT** Low-tide line to 90′ deep; sand, mud bottoms.

ATLANTIC BAY SCALLOP
"Blue-eyed Scallop"
Argopecten (Aequipecten) irradians
BIVALVE CLASS

2½″. Shell nearly round, convex, with 18 radiating ribs. Gray, brownish, or reddish; imm. brightly colored. Many blue eyes along margin. Pumps valves to swim. Edible. **HABITAT** Low-tide line to 60′ deep; sand, mud, grass bottoms.

COMMON JINGLE SHELL
Anomia simplex
BIVALVE CLASS

1½″. Shell thin, roundish, smooth, with wavy edge. Translucent gold or silver; inside shiny. Attachment muscle uses hole on lower valve. Several strung shells jingle in breeze. **HABITAT** Low-tide line to 30′ deep; on rocks, shells, wood.

EASTERN OYSTER
Crassostrea virginica
BIVALVE CLASS

4″ (to 10″). Shell thick, irregularly oval to elongated; coarsely ridged; upper shell flattened, lower deeper. Grayish white. Free-swimming larvae settle on hard surfaces. Edible. **HABITAT** Intertidal zone to 40′ deep; brackish bays, estuaries.

FLORIDA SPINY JEWEL BOX
Arcinella cornuta
BIVALVE CLASS
1¼". Shell roundish, irreg., plump; 7–9 heavy radiating ridges with curving pointed spines. White; inside pinkish, smooth. Valves nearly equal. When washed ashore, spines are quickly worn off. **HABITAT** Shallow waters; rubble bottoms.

COQUINA
Donax variabilis
BIVALVE CLASS
¾". Shell an elongated triangle, with rounded edges. Whitish with vertical and/or horizontal bands of purple, pink, orange, yellow, brown, or blue. Digs quickly into sand when wave retreats. Edible. **HABITAT** Intertidal zone; sandy beaches.

SUNRAY VENUS
Macrocallista nimbosa
BIVALVE CLASS
4". Shell a flat, glossy, elongated oval with low concentric ridges. Pale brown, pink, or gray, with broken radiating brown lines; inside white. Often washed ashore by storms. **HABITAT** 3–25' deep; mud, sand bottoms; most common on panhandle.

ANGEL WING
Cyrtopleura costata
BIVALVE CLASS
6". Shell elongated, oval, narrows toward rear; scaly radial ridges. White or light pink. Spoon-like projection under beak. When open, shape suggests an angel's wings. Edible. **HABITAT** Intertidal zone to 60' deep; sand, mud, clay bottoms.

ATLANTIC LONG-FINNED SQUID
Loligo pealei
CEPHALOPOD CLASS
15". Body cylindrical, tapers toward rear; milky white with tiny, reddish-purple spots. Head has 2 large eyes, 8 arms with suction cups, 2 tentacles. Triangular fin on each side at rear. Edible. **HABITAT** Ocean surface to 600' deep.

COMMON ATLANTIC OCTOPUS
Octopus vulgaris
CEPHALOPOD CLASS
6′. Body globe-shaped, smooth; pink, brown, or gray. 8 thick arms with suckers. Head broad with 2 high eyes; tubular siphon below; tough, parrot-like beak. Hides by day in crevices, under rocks. **HABITAT** Coral reefs, shallow rocky areas.

LONG-ARMED OCTOPUS
Octopus macropus
CEPHALOPOD CLASS
24″. Body globe-shaped; tan to reddish brown with small whitish spots, small warts. 8 long, thick arms with suckers. Head broad with 2 high eyes; tubular siphon below; tough, parrot-like beak. Hides by day in crevices, under rocks. **HABITAT** Coral reefs, rocks. **RANGE** Keys.

ATLANTIC HORSESHOE CRAB
Limulus polyphemus
HORSESHOE CRAB CLASS
Female 18″; male 12″. Carapace horseshoe-shaped, turtle-like, dull greenish brown or brown; abdomen triangular; tail long, spiked. Eyes bulbous, unstalked, on forepart of midline. Mouth surrounded by 5 pairs of walking legs, with 2 pincers in front. Lays eggs on beaches at high-tide line in early spring. **HABITAT** Mud and sand bottoms to 75′ deep.

IVORY BARNACLE
Balanus eburneus
CRUSTACEAN CLASS

1″. Body conical; white. 4 smooth side plates, 2 grooved plates open at top. Feathery retractable feeding appendages extend from gape. Limy, root-like attachment tubes below. **CAUTION** Plate edges extremely sharp. **HABITAT** Shallow waters, estuaries; on rocks, pilings.

BIG-EYED BEACH-FLEA
Talorchestia megalophthalma
CRUSTACEAN CLASS

¾″. Body shrimp-like; pale gray to pink. Head has 4 antennae, round black eyes. Back arched; legs tiny. Leaps 12″ or more. Feeds on organic debris; does not bite. **HABITAT** Clean sandy beaches; under debris at high-tide line.

RED-LINED CLEANING SHRIMP
"Peppermint Shrimp"
Lysmata wurdemanni
CRUSTACEAN CLASS

2″. Exoskeleton translucent; pale pink with red stripes. Beak long; antennae and legs long, thin; tail fan-shaped. Removes parasites and organic debris from fish, corals, anemones. **HABITAT** Low-tide line to 100′ deep; rocks, jetties, coral reefs.

COMMON MANTIS SHRIMP
Squilla empusa
CRUSTACEAN CLASS

6″. Exoskeleton centipede-like, with 5 low ridges; greenish, blue-green, or brownish. Forward slashing appendage has 6 sharp spines on claw. Edible. **CAUTION** Can give deep lacerations. **HABITAT** Low-tide line to 500′ deep; burrows into sand.

BANDED CORAL SHRIMP
Stenopus hispidus
CRUSTACEAN CLASS

1½″. Exoskeleton spiny; banded red, white, and purple. Antennae and legs very long, narrow; 1st pair of legs have long pincers. A cleaning shrimp; attracts fish by waving antennae. **HABITAT** Coral reefs. **RANGE** se FL, Keys.

Crabs and Lobsters

Crabs and lobsters, of the order Decapoda, fall into two categories: short-tailed decapods, or true crabs, and long-tailed decapods. As the name implies, all have ten legs. True crabs have a large cephalothorax, or fore-body, and a small abdomen tucked beneath their shells. They can move well in all directions, but usually walk sideways. Some, like Blue Crabs, have paddle-like hindlegs for swimming. Others, like male fiddler crabs, have a greatly enlarged pincer. Most species are scavengers, although some feed on living animals; fiddlers are generally plant-eaters. Long-tailed decapods, such as lobsters and hermit crabs, have elongated abdomens, or "tails." Hermit crabs protect their soft abdomens by hiding in empty gastropod shells. They are fascinating to observe as they carry their homes about, switching shells as they grow. Take care when handling crabs and lobsters; some are aggressive, and all can pinch. Measurements in accounts refer to the carapace, the shell part that extends over the head and thorax, but not the abdomen.

Parts of a Crab

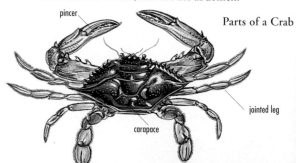

pincer

jointed leg

carapace

LONG-CLAWED HERMIT CRAB
Pagurus longicarpus
CRUSTACEAN CLASS

½". Lives in gastropod shell. Body oblong, with long soft abdomen; gray, green, or buff. Right pincer larger than left; 5th pair of walking legs turned up. **HABITAT** Beaches and ocean bottoms to 150' deep.

WEST INDIES SPINY LOBSTER
Panulirus argus
CRUSTACEAN CLASS

10" (to 24"). Body spiny; "tail" has flexible plates above; pale gray, tan, green, or reddish brown; often spotted yellow. 2 thick, forward-pointing spines above eyes. 1st pair antennae black, thin; 2nd pair pale blue, thick, longer than body. Walking legs lack pincers. Edible; overharvested. **HABITAT** Low-tide line to 300' deep; coral reefs, rocks, sponges.

BLUE CRAB
Callinectes (Cancer) sapidus
CRUSTACEAN CLASS

W 6″. Carapace wide, bluish green, edged with red spines; long spine at each side. Pincers large, blue (male) or red (female); legs blue, 5th pair paddle-shaped. Fast swimmer. Edible; commercially important. **HABITAT** Low-tide line to 120′ deep; shallows, brackish creeks.

STONE CRAB
Menippe mercenaria
CRUSTACEAN CLASS

W 3½″. Carapace oval, smooth; above reddish brown with gray dots; below pale brown. Pincers heavy, unequal, tipped black. Walking legs stout. Eyes recessed. Edible; harvesting strictly regulated. **HABITAT** Low-tide line to 20′ deep; shellfish beds, mud bottoms.

COMMON SPIDER CRAB
Libinia emarginata
CRUSTACEAN CLASS

3″. Carapace round, with spines on edges and midline; grayish yellow to dark brown. Beak pointed. Legs stout, male's much longer (to 12″); pincers equal, with white fingers. Moves slowly. **HABITAT** Low-tide line to 400′ deep; among seaweeds.

ARROW CRAB
Stenorhynchus seticornis
CRUSTACEAN CLASS

2″. Carapace arrowhead-shaped; gray or tan with brown or cream stripes. Eyes bulging, red. Legs spider-like, pale red with darker joints; pincers thin, blue. Walks elegantly with body raised. **HABITAT** Low-tide line to 5,000′ deep; ocean bottoms, coral reefs, wharves.

LAND HERMIT CRAB
Coenobita clypeatus
CRUSTACEAN CLASS

1¼″. Lives in gastropod shell. Body cylindrical, reddish or purplish brown; "tail" long, soft. 3 pairs red legs; pincers wide, purple, unequal. Eyestalks long; 4 retractable antennae. **HABITAT** Among plants near shore; sometimes well inland.

ATLANTIC MOLE CRAB
Emerita talpoida
CRUSTACEAN CLASS

1½″. Carapace oval, convex; sandy yellow to white. Abdomen and legs tightly clasped below carapace. 4 antennae; 1 pair feathery, strains seawater for plankton. Burrows in sand. **HABITAT** Intertidal zone; open sandy beaches.

GHOST CRAB
Ocypode quadrata
CRUSTACEAN CLASS

W 1½″. Carapace square, covered with fine bumps; yellow, white, or gray (blends with sand). Eyestalks large, club-like; eyes black. Pincers unequal, saw-toothed, white. Stands on tips of claws; runs swiftly sideways. **HABITAT** Sandy beaches.

GREAT LAND CRAB
Cardisoma guanhumi
CRUSTACEAN CLASS

W 5″. Carapace globe-shaped, smooth; ridged along sides; blue or gray, imm. purple. Eyestalks have shallow sockets. Legs long, stocky, slightly hairy; pincers unequal, white. Edible. **HABITAT** Beaches, muddy areas, mangroves, inland waterways. **RANGE** s FL.

SAND FIDDLER
Uca pugilator
CRUSTACEAN CLASS

W 1¼″. Carapace square; male purplish with blackish markings; female darker. Male has 1 pincer greatly enlarged; female has 2 short pincers. Eats detritus at low tide. **HABITAT** Salt marshes, mudflats, calm beaches. **RANGE** ne and nw FL.

Echinoderms

In Florida, the phylum Echinodermata is represented by sea stars, sea urchins, and sea cucumbers. All species in this phylum are covered with spines or bumps (*echinoderm* means "spiny skin"), are radially symmetrical, and have a unique water vascular system consisting of internal canals that pump fluids through the body. These canals end in hundreds of tube feet, slender appendages that expand and contract to allow the animal to move and feed. Sea stars have varying numbers of arms radiating from a central disk; they feed mainly on mollusks and other echinoderms. Sea urchins, including sand dollars, feed on plankton, algae, and tiny organic particles in sand. The spines of the elongated sea cucumbers are actually embedded in the skin, which is outwardly smooth; these animals feed almost exclusively on plankton. Measurements in the accounts are of diameters, including arms and spines, unless otherwise noted.

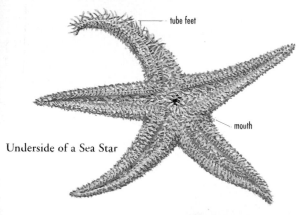

Underside of a Sea Star

CUSHION STAR
Oreaster reticulatus
SEA STAR CLASS
10″. Disk large, arched; 5 thick arms. Red, orange, or yellow; imm. olive or purplish brown. Raised network of yellow knobby squares and triangles. Largest sea star in FL (to 20″). **HABITAT** Shallow waters; sand, coral, sea-grass bottoms.

THORNY/SPINY SEA STARS
Echinaster species
SEA STAR CLASS
4″. Disk small; 5 blunt-tipped arms. Red, orange, or dark purple. Covered with rows of small, widely spaced spines. **HABITAT** Shallow waters; rock, reef, sea-grass bottoms; most common in s FL.

COMMON SEA STAR
"Forbes' Sea Star"
Asterias forbesi
SEA STAR CLASS

7". Disk large; 5 long, blunt-tipped arms. Tan, brown, olive, or pink. Covered with spines. Pulls open bivalves, everts stomach into shell. **HABITAT** Low-tide line to 160′ deep; rock, gravel, sand bottoms.

SPINY BRITTLE STAR
Ophiocoma echinata
SEA STAR CLASS

10". Disk small, round, flat, with scalloped border; arms long, sinuous, spiny. Dark brown or black. Feeds on larval fish; sifts sand for microorganisms. **HABITAT** Shallow waters; coral reefs, seagrass beds, under rocks. **RANGE** s FL.

LONG-SPINED URCHIN
Diadema antillarum
SEA URCHIN CLASS

3". Body oval. Covered with sharp, barbed, black or dark purple spines, banded white on young. Spines longest on top, to 16". Roe edible. **CAUTION** Spines penetrate footwear; cause painful stings. **HABITAT** Shallow waters; coral reefs, rocks, tidepools.

ATLANTIC PURPLE SEA URCHIN
"Brown Rock Urchin"
Arbacia punctulata
SEA URCHIN CLASS

1½". Body oval; blackish. Covered with thick, grooved, blunt-tipped, purplish-brown, reddish-gray, or tan spines to 1" long. **HABITAT** Intertidal zone to 750′ deep; rock, shell, sea-grass bottoms.

VARIEGATED URCHIN
Lytechinus variegatus
SEA URCHIN CLASS

2½". Body oval; light green. Covered with short, stout, red, pink, brown, purple, or white spines. Usu. camouflaged with debris. **HABITAT** Low-tide line to 180′ deep; sand and sea-grass bottoms; among mangroves.

FIVE-HOLED KEYHOLE URCHIN
Mellita quinquiesperforata
SEA URCHIN CLASS

4". Resembles a sand dollar. Flattened, sharp-edged disk covered with fine spines; light brown or gray. 5-pointed star-shaped pattern in center, surrounded by 5 keyhole-shaped slots. White, spineless when washed ashore. **HABITAT** Shallow waters; sand bottoms.

LONG-SPINED SEA BISCUIT
"Great Red-footed Urchin"
Plagiobrissus grandis
SEA URCHIN CLASS

L 7". Body oval, thick, irregularly lobed; yellow, tan, or reddish. Covered with short furry spines; several dozen long slender spines on top. Below flat, pale yellow. **HABITAT** 5–50′ deep; sand areas in coral reefs.

FLORIDA SEA CUCUMBER
Holothuria floridana
SEA CUCUMBER CLASS

L 7". Body long, cylindrical, cucumber-shaped; dark brown, slaty, or reddish. Covered with short pointed bumps. Head has dense cluster of short yellowish tentacles. Exudes sticky threads from anus if disturbed. Edible. **HABITAT** Shallow waters; sea-grass beds.

Freshwater and Land Invertebrates

Tens of thousands of invertebrate species thrive in Florida's freshwater and terrestrial environments. Ponds and meadows are home to literally billions of invertebrates per acre, and even tree trunks and acidic bogs support a varied assortment. The most commonly seen Florida invertebrates belong to three phyla. Land and freshwater members of the phylum Mollusca are the generally small, drab species of slugs, snails, and clams. They are both aquatic, living amid vegetation or in bottom sediment, and terrestrial, found under leaves, boards, and rocks. Earthworms, of the phylum Annelida, can occur at an average of 1,000 pounds per acre; they help fertilize and oxygenate soil by pulling vegetation underground. The phylum Arthropoda comprises the largest number of freshwater and land invertebrates, with five classes covered here: crustaceans, millipedes, centipedes, arachnids, and insects. Crustaceans include freshwater crayfish. Terrestrial millipedes and centipedes look like worms with legs—two per segment for vegetarian millipedes and one per segment for predatory centipedes. Arachnids—spiders, scorpions, daddy-long-legs (harvestmen), ticks, chiggers, and vinegarones—are discussed on page 214. Insects, introduced on page 218, are comprised of many well-known invertebrate orders, including dragonflies, grasshoppers, beetles, flies, butterflies, and ants, wasps, and bees (see their separate introductions within the section). The seasonal activity of freshwater and terrestrial invertebrates varies widely, depending on location and weather. In southern Florida such creatures are active year-round, while in northern and central Florida they are active from spring to fall (although in central Florida this varies with the severity of the weather). In the accounts that follow specific seasonal information is given when possible.

EARTHWORMS
"Night Crawlers"
Lumbricus species
EARTHWORM CLASS

L 5". Body soft, cylindrical, with dozens of segments; purplish orange. Legless; moves via tiny bristles. Aerates moist soil; common on surface after heavy rains. **HABITAT** Woods, meadows, lawns.

FLORIDA TREE SNAIL
Liguus fasciatus
GASTROPOD CLASS

L 1½". Shell elongated; 4–5 whorls with slightly raised ridges; apex pointed. White, buff, or yellow; occ. banded or mottled brown. Opening rounded. Head has 2 clubbed, antennae-like tentacles. **HABITAT** Hardwood hammocks; lichens, mosses, algae. **RANGE** s FL, Keys.

FLORIDA APPLE SNAIL
Pomacea paludosa
GASTROPOD CLASS
L 2". Shell globular, smooth; apex blunt; olive-brown with brown bands. Opening large, round. Head has 2 long, antennae-like tentacles. Breathes with gills in water or primitive lungs on land. Main prey of Limpkin and Snail Kite. **HABITAT** Marsh vegetation. **RANGE** Peninsular FL.

POND CRAYFISH
Procambarus fallax
CRUSTACEAN CLASS
L 4". Body like a lobster's, but smaller, with thinner pincers; often grayish brown with dark specks. 2 long antennae; 4 pairs of walking legs. Feeds on vegetation, small animals. Edible. **HABITAT** Small streams, floodplain pools.

MILLIPEDES
Narceus species
MILLIPEDE CLASS
L 4". Body worm-like; gray, brown, or black. 20–50 segments, each with 2 pairs of short legs; antennae short. Slow-moving; rolls into ball when threatened, releasing foul-smelling secretion. Many FL species. **HABITAT** Woods; under leaves, stones, logs.

CENTIPEDES
Scolopendra species
CENTIPEDE CLASS
L 3". Body flattened; black or reddish brown, with pale red or orange sides. 12–20 segments. Legs and antennae long; 2 rear-facing legs at rear. Fast-moving; venom paralyzes insects, spiders. **HABITAT** Woods; under bark, logs, trash.

Spiders and Kin

The class Arachnida includes spiders, ticks, mites, harvestmen, scorpions, and pseudoscorpions. These generally dreaded invertebrates are much maligned; in fact, most species are harmless to humans, many are beneficial to the environment, and all have habits worthy of the naturalist's attention.

Spiders have two body parts and eight legs. Most also have eight simple eyes, the arrangement of which differs from genus to genus. On jumping spiders, which hunt without benefit of a web, two eyes are tremendously enlarged, a trait that enables them to judge accurately distances to their prey. All spiders extrude three or four types of silk from spinnerets on their undersides:

8 eyes

A spider's face

one to make cocoons for their eggs; another, much finer, for lowering themselves; sturdy strands to construct radial web lines; and finally, the sticky silk they use to entrap prey.

Spiders hunt by stalking, ambushing, or ensnaring their victims, then subduing or killing them with a poisonous bite. Their venom acts as a powerful digestive fluid, which liquefies their prey so they can suck it up. All spiders are venomous, but most are harmless to humans, and indeed retreat quickly when we arrive on the scene. Spiders are not parasitic on humans or domesticated animals, nor do they transmit any diseases to humans. They can be incredibly abundant, especially in meadows, where hundreds of thousands can inhabit a single acre. Their hearty appetites help to control the insect population.

In addition to spiders, there are many other arachnids among us. Harvestmen, also called daddy-long-legs, are nonvenomous and have one body part and very long, fragile legs. They are normally solitary, but in winter they may huddle together in masses. Ticks are parasites with little foreclaws that grasp onto passing animals. To feed, they bury their heads under the skin and draw blood. Some species are carriers of serious diseases, including Lyme disease (see box, page 217). Scorpions and vinegarones are large and distinctive.

The accounts below give typical lengths of females, not including legs; the rarely seen males are often much smaller.

BLACK WIDOW SPIDER
Latrodectus mactans
ARACHNID CLASS

⅜″. Body black, glossy. Female abdomen bulbous, with red hourglass pattern below; male much smaller, with red and white sides. Builds irregular web with funnel-like exit. **CAUTION** Poisonous (mainly female bites). **HABITAT** Woodpiles, debris, crawl spaces.

SILVER ARGIOPE
Argiope argentata
ARACHNID CLASS

½". Body black to brownish; abdomen egg-shaped, with silvery bands and spots. Legs banded blackish brown and yellow. Web large (up to 30" wide), with conspicuous X-shaped cross strands in center. **HABITAT** Fields, gardens. **RANGE** s FL.

BLACK-AND-YELLOW GARDEN SPIDER
Argiope aurantia
ARACHNID CLASS

1". Head/thorax has short silvery hair. Abdomen large, egg-shaped; black with bold yellow or orange markings. Legs long, hairy; banded yellow or reddish and black. Web large (12" or more wide), with thick vertical zigzag pattern in center; placed among plants in sunny sheltered area. **HABITAT** Gardens, bushy meadows.

CRAB-LIKE SPINY ORB WEAVER
Gasteracantha cancriformis (elipsoides)
ARACHNID CLASS

⅜". Head/thorax tiny. Abdomen disk-shaped; whitish or yellow, with black spots and 6 prominent reddish spines on sides and rear. Web a vertical orb with few central spiral strands. **HABITAT** Woodland edges, shrubby gardens.

ARROW-SHAPED MICRATHENA
Micrathena sagittata
ARACHNID CLASS

⅜". Head/thorax tiny; dark reddish brown. Abdomen triangular; yellowish with brown spots, 2 dark red diverging spines at rear. Builds vertical web with central hole where it rests. **HABITAT** Woodland edges, fields, and gardens.

GOLDEN-SILK SPIDER
Nephila clavipes
ARACHNID CLASS

1". Head/thorax pale gray with black spots. Abdomen cylindrical; orange, yellow, or greenish, with white spots. Legs banded yellow-orange and black; tufts of black hair on first and last pairs. Web large (24–36") with strong thick strands. **HABITAT** Woods, swamps.

VENUSTA ORCHARD SPIDER
Leucauge venusta
ARACHNID CLASS

¼″. Head/thorax greenish brown. Abdomen bulbous; silvery white with black and yellow stripes; red spots below and near tip. Powerful jaws. Hides under horizontal web or on vegetation nearby. **HABITAT** Woodland edges, shrubby meadows.

CAROLINA WOLF SPIDER
Lycosa carolinensis
ARACHNID CLASS

1¼″. Body like a tarantula's, but less hairy; gray-brown. Legs hairy. Eyes dark, in 3 rows of 2, 2, and 4; top 2 very large. Active hunter; scurries by night over leaves, rocks, grass. **HABITAT** Fields.

HENTZ'S STRIPED SCORPION
Centruroides hentzi
ARACHNID CLASS

2½″. Body yellowish brown with darker markings. Abdomen segmented, narrow; stinger at tip curves up strongly. Pincers crayfish-like. Nocturnal; hides by day under logs and debris. **CAUTION** Sting is painful but not lethal. **HABITAT** Fields, woodland edges.

DADDY-LONG-LEGS
Leiobunum species
ARACHNID CLASS

⅜″. Head/thorax and abdomen joined in single body; yellowish-brown with dark stripes. Legs long, thin, arching; 2nd pair longest, used like antennae. Body held near surface. Feeds on spiders, insects, plant juices. **HABITAT** Tree trunks, buildings.

WOOD TICKS
"Dog Ticks"
Dermacentor species
ARACHNID CLASS

⅛″. Body oval. Female reddish brown, with silvery shield near small orange head. Male gray with reddish-brown spots. **CAUTION** If bitten, remove tick head to prevent infection. **HABITAT** Brush, tall grass.

DEER TICK
"Blacklegged Tick"
Ixodes scapularis
ARACHNID CLASS

¹/₁₆″. Body oval, minute; light brown (larva, nymph) to reddish brown (adult). **CAUTION** Can transmit Lyme disease, a serious illness (see box below). **HABITAT** Brushy fields, open woods.

Deer Ticks and Lyme Disease

Ticks of the genus *Ixodes* are carriers of Lyme disease, a dangerous illness that can be difficult to treat. In Florida, the Deer Tick carries the responsible spirochete (spiral-shaped bacterium), *Borrelia burgdorferi*. Both nymphs and adults can be infectious. Deer Ticks are tiny and the nymphs are almost microscopic. They inhabit woods and fields, especially where deer are numerous. To avoid infection, it helps to wear light-colored pants tucked into socks, and carefully check clothing and skin after outings. Initial symptoms of Lyme disease vary, but about 75 to 80 percent of all victims develop a circular, expanding red rash around the tick bite, which can appear up to 35 days after the bite. Other symptoms include stiff neck, headache, dizziness, fever, sore throat, muscle aches, joint pain, and general weakness. Should these symptoms develop, consult a physician promptly, as antibiotics are most effective in early stages of infection. Untreated Lyme disease can be difficult to cure, and may cause chronic arthritis, memory loss, and severe headaches.

CHIGGERS
"Red Bugs"
Trombicula species
ARACHNID CLASS

¹/₁₆″. Body minute, round; reddish or orangish. Larva bites under close-fitting clothing (esp. at ankles and waist), causing welts and itching. **HABITAT** Tall grass in meadows, woods. **SEASON** Chiefly Apr.–Nov.

GIANT VINEGARONE
Mastigoproctus giganteus
ARACHNID CLASS

3″. Body disk-shaped; brown or black. Large pincers held forward; Long "tail" at abdomen tip curved over back. Releases vinegary secretion when disturbed. Nocturnal. **HABITAT** Under logs, wood, debris, and in houses.

Insects

Insects (class Insecta) fascinate children with their forms and colors, bewilder naturalists with their ecological intricacies, and cause rational adults to cringe at their mere presence. Their vast repertory of environmental adaptations is overwhelming, as are their sheer numbers and staying power. Try as we might (and we have tried mightily), we have not succeeded in exterminating any Florida insect pests. Perhaps instead we should spend more time observing their beauty and variety. It is impossible to underestimate the importance of insects to the ecological health of the planet. In Florida insects pollinate approximately 80 percent of the flowering plants. They are a vital link in every ecosystem.

All insects have three main body parts—head, thorax, and abdomen—to which various other organs are attached. The head has a pair of antennae, which may be narrow, feathery, pointed, short, or long (sometimes much longer than the body). The eyes are compound and the mouthparts are adapted to chewing, biting, piercing, sucking, and/or licking. Insect wings (usually four) and legs (six) attach at the thorax. The abdomen, usually the largest section, houses the reproductive and other internal organs.

A remarkable aspect of invertebrate life is the transformation from egg to adult, known as metamorphosis. In complete metamorphosis, which includes a pupal stage and is unique to insects, the adults lay eggs from which the larvae are hatched. The larva feeds and grows, molting its skin several times, until it prepares for its immobile pupal state by hiding or camouflaging itself. Within the pupa, larval organs dissolve and adult organs develop. In incomplete metamorphosis, there is no pupal stage, and insects such as mayflies, dragonflies, grasshoppers, and bugs gradually develop from hatched nymphs into adults.

This book introduces representative species or genera of insects from many orders in a taxonomic sequence from primitive to more advanced. We have placed the butterflies and moths last, although traditionally they precede ants, bees, and wasps. For many insects, there is no commonly accepted English name at the species level. Descriptions and seasonal information refer to adult forms unless otherwise noted. Measurements are of typical adult body lengths; in the butterfly accounts wingspan measurements are given.

MAYFLIES
Ephemera species
MAYFLY ORDER

¾". Looks like giant brownish mosquito. Forelegs and tail appendages long; wings translucent, veined, with dark mottling. Adult short-lived. Aquatic nymph (½") caterpillar-like, with biting mouth. **HABITAT** Rivers, streams, ponds. **SEASON** Apr.–Sept. **RANGE** n FL.

Dragonflies

Dragonflies are large predatory insects, many of which specialize in killing mosquitoes. The order is 300 million years old and comprises two major groups—dragonflies and damselflies. Both have movable heads and large compound eyes that in dragonflies nearly cover the head and in damselflies bulge out from the sides. Their legs are attached to the thorax just behind their heads, a feature that makes walking all but impossible but greatly facilitates their ability to grasp and hold prey while tearing into it with sharp mouthparts. They have four powerful wings that move independently, allowing for both forward and backward flight. At rest, the wings are held horizontally by dragonflies, and together over the abdomen by damselflies. Nymphs, called naiads, live among the vegetation and muck in ponds and streams and feed on mosquito larvae, other insects, tadpoles, and small fish. Many of Florida's 150 or so colorful species have captured the interest of bird and butterfly enthusiasts. In the accounts that follow, all species not noted as damselflies are dragonflies. The size given for dragonflies is the typical adult body length (not the wingspread).

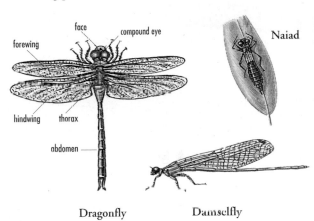

Dragonfly · Damselfly · Naiad

EBONY JEWELWING
"Black-winged Damselfly"
Calopteryx maculata
DRAGONFLY ORDER
1¾". Damselfly. Male metallic green; wings black. Female brown; wings smoky with glistening white spot near tip. Naiad pale brown with darker markings. **HABITAT** Wooded streams, rivers. **SEASON** Feb.–Nov. **RANGE** n and c FL.

COMMON SPREADWING
Lestes disjunctus
DRAGONFLY ORDER

1⅝". Damselfly. Abdomen long, blackish, with bluish-white tip. Eyes and face blue; pale green shoulder stripe. Wings transparent, short; held half open (unlike most damselflies). **HABITAT** Ponds, marshes. **RANGE** n and c FL.

VARIABLE DANCER
Argia fumipennis
DRAGONFLY ORDER

1¼". Damselfly. Head and top of thorax violet; abdomen dark violet with blue tip. Female duller. Wings dark brown. **HABITAT** Streams, rivers, ponds. **RANGE** n and c FL.

ATLANTIC BLUET
Enallagma doubledayi
DRAGONFLY ORDER

1⅓". Damselfly. Male thorax black with blue stripes; abdomen mostly blue, with black rings becoming wider toward tip. Female blue above, with black stripes. Eyes blue. Wings clear. **HABITAT** Ponds, lakes. **RANGE** South to Ft. Lauderdale.

ORANGE BLUET
Enallagma signatum
DRAGONFLY ORDER

1⅓". Damselfly. Male black; thorax sides and shoulders striped orange; abdomen orange-tipped. Female duller, sometimes bluish; lacks orange tip. Wings clear. **HABITAT** Lakes, ponds, slow-moving streams. **RANGE** South to Lake Okeechobee.

RAMBUR'S FORKTAIL
Ischnura ramburii
DRAGONFLY ORDER

1¼". Damselfly. Thorax black with pale green sides; abdomen blue-tipped. Small blue spots on head; pale green shoulder stripes. Wings transparent. **HABITAT** Wetlands, pond edges.

COMMON GREEN DARNER
Anax junius
DRAGONFLY ORDER

3". Thorax green. Abdomen blue (male) or reddish brown (female). Wings clear, female's tinged with amber. Flies with hindwings flat, forewings slightly raised. **HABITAT** Ponds, lakes, fields. **RANGE** All FL, ex. Keys. Active all year in s FL; many migrate south from n FL in fall.

COMET DARNER
Anax longipes
DRAGONFLY ORDER

3¼". Thorax green; male has bright red abdomen, green eyes; female has red-brown abdomen, blue eyes. Wings transparent. Uncommon and beautiful. **HABITAT** Shallow grassy ponds. **SEASON** Mar.–Nov. **RANGE** All FL, ex. Keys.

REGAL DARNER
Coryphaeschna ingens
DRAGONFLY ORDER

3½". Thorax green with brown stripes; abdomen brown with narrow green rings above. Eyes green (male, imm.) or blue (female). Wings transparent. **HABITAT** Lakes, slow-moving streams, woods. **SEASON** Feb.–Oct.

DRAGONHUNTER
Hagenius brevistylus
DRAGONFLY ORDER

3¼". Thorax and abdomen black with bold yellow stripes. Head green, small, contrasts with swollen thorax; eyes green. Wings transparent. Preys on other dragonflies. **HABITAT** Streams, rivers. **SEASON** Apr.–Oct. **RANGE** South to Lake Okeechobee.

HALLOWEEN PENNANT
"Brown-spotted Yellow-wing"
Celithemis eponina
DRAGONFLY ORDER

1½". Body blackish with dull yellow or orange markings above. Eyes brown. Wings yellow-orange with large dark brown bands and spots. Often perches atop prominent vegetation. **HABITAT** Fields, marshes, ponds.

SCARLET SKIMMER
Crocothemis servilia
DRAGONFLY ORDER

1⅝". Male entirely bright red. Female and imm. mostly yellowish; abdomen has black stripe above; white shoulder stripes. Wings transparent, with amber spot at hindwings base. Introduced from Asia. **HABITAT** Wetlands, fields. **RANGE** Orlando and south.

EASTERN PONDHAWK
Erythemis simplicicollis
DRAGONFLY ORDER

1¾". Male pale blue with green face. Female, called Green Jacket, and imm. bright green with dark markings on abdomen. Wings clear. Often rests on ground. **HABITAT** Ponds, nearby fields.

GREAT PONDHAWK
Erythemis vesiculosa
DRAGONFLY ORDER

2½". Head and thorax bright green; abdomen slender, green, with black bands. Eyes brownish. Wings transparent. **HABITAT** Ponds, still waters. **RANGE** s FL.

GOLDEN-WINGED SKIMMER
Libellula auripennis
DRAGONFLY ORDER

2". Male bright orange; abdomen has black stripe above. Female and imm. pale orange; thorax sides have yellow stripe; abdomen yellow. Wings transparent, male's with orange veins. **HABITAT** Grassy ponds, lakes. **RANGE** South to Lake Okeechobee.

BLUE CORPORAL
Libellula deplanata
DRAGONFLY ORDER

1⅓". Male thorax and abdomen bright blue; head black. Female and imm. reddish brown; thorax has 2 creamy stripes. Wings transparent, with dark markings at base. **HABITAT** Ponds, still waters. **SEASON** Jan.–May. **RANGE** South to Naples.

GREAT BLUE SKIMMER
Libellula vibrans
DRAGONFLY ORDER

2¼". Male thorax and abdomen pale blue. Female brown. Both sexes: eyes greenish blue, face white. Wings transparent with dusky tips. **HABITAT** Woodland ponds, streams. **SEASON** Mar.–Oct. **RANGE** South to Naples.

ROSEATE SKIMMER
Orthemis ferruginea
DRAGONFLY ORDER

2". Male thorax pale blue; abdomen pink; occ. all red in Keys. Female and imm. thorax brown; abdomen reddish brown. Both sexes: head and eyes dark brown. Wings transparent. **HABITAT** Lakes, ponds, fields.

BLUE DASHER
Pachydiplax longipennis
DRAGONFLY ORDER

1⅓". Thorax striped black and greenish yellow; abdomen pale blue with black tip, female's with 2 broken yellow lines. Face creamy; eyes green. Female duller. Wings mostly clear. **HABITAT** Ponds, marshes, sluggish streams.

WANDERING GLIDER
"Globetrotter"
Pantala flavescens
DRAGONFLY ORDER

2". Thorax light brown; abdomen mostly golden yellow; eyes chestnut. Wings clear, with broad base on hindwings. Flies almost constantly. Widespread; only dragonfly found worldwide. **HABITAT** Ponds, fields.

EASTERN AMBERWING
Perithemis tenera
DRAGONFLY ORDER

1". Stocky. Body yellow-brown, with 2 greenish stripes on thorax. Wings amber, female's with dark spots. Flies over water; perches on plants. **HABITAT** Ponds. **RANGE** All FL, ex. Keys.

CAROLINA SADDLEBAGS
Tramea carolina
DRAGONFLY ORDER

2". Thorax brown; abdomen red with black tip. Face violet (male); blue and orange (female). Wings clear; large red-brown band covers basal ¼ of broad hindwings. **HABITAT** Ponds.

AMERICAN COCKROACH
"Waterbug"
Periplaneta americana
COCKROACH ORDER
2″. Body reddish brown; large, pale yellow head shield; antennae longer than body. Yellow stripe on front margin of forewings. Legs dark. **HABITAT** Vegetation, buildings.

GERMAN COCKROACH
Blattella germanica
COCKROACH ORDER
⅝″. Body brown; 2 blackish stripes on pale yellow-brown shield behind head. With adhesive pads on pale legs, can climb vertical smooth surfaces. Introduced from Eurasia; pest in all N. Amer. cities. **HABITAT** Buildings.

EASTERN SUBTERRANEAN TERMITE
Reticulitermes flavipes
TERMITE ORDER
⅜″ (worker). Reproductive: body elongated, black or brown; 4 long membranous wings held flat over abdomen. Worker and soldier smaller; lack eyes, wings; whitish or pale yellowish. Feeds on rotting, moist wood; causes severe structural damage to buildings. **HABITAT** Rotting trees, wood.

CAROLINA MANTID
Stagmomantis carolina
MANTID ORDER
2⅜″. Body elongated; pale green or brownish gray. Long front pair of legs held bent, as if in prayer. Flexible neck can turn in all directions. Wings shorter than abdomen. **HABITAT** On shrubs in fields, gardens. **Praying Mantis** *(Mantis religiosa)* has black spot on inside of forelegs near body; wings extend beyond abdomen tip.

PALMETTO WALKINGSTICK
Anismorpha buprestoides
WALKINGSTICK ORDER
Female 3″; male 2″. Body greatly elongated; stick-like; dark brown with buff markings. Legs long, slender. Male much smaller than female. Resembles a dead twig. Feeds on foliage; active mainly at night. **HABITAT** Palmetto scrub, woods.

Grasshoppers and Kin

Members of the order Orthoptera are beloved for their musical abilities and despised for their voracious appetites. All species have mouthparts designed to bite and chew, and straight membranous wings. Grasshoppers and crickets have greatly developed hindlegs for jumping. Females have long ovipositors, straight in most species but sickle-shaped in katydids; they lay eggs in soil or tree vegetation. While no insects have true voices, orthopterans manage to make themselves heard in a variety of distinctive ways; most melodies are produced by males trying to attract mates. Crickets and katydids raise their wings and rub together specialized parts to produce their well-known calls. Most crickets are "right-winged," rubbing their right wings over their left, while katydids are "left-winged." Grasshoppers rub their hindlegs and wings together, and also make rattling, in-flight sounds by vibrating their forewings against their hindwings.

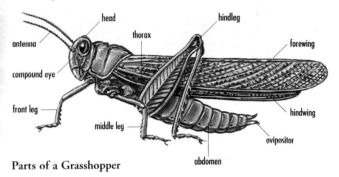

Parts of a Grasshopper

CAROLINA LOCUST
Dissosteira carolina
GRASSHOPPER ORDER
1¾". Body elongated; cinnamon brown, incl. eyes. Hindwings black with broad, light yellow border (visible in flight). Flies with purring, fluttering sound. **HABITAT** Roadsides, meadows. **SEASON** Apr.–Nov.

RED-LEGGED LOCUST
Melanoplus femur-rubrum
GRASSHOPPER ORDER
1". Body elongated; dark brown, sometimes greenish. Hind femur herringbone-patterned; hind tibia red with black spines. Wings dusky; male wings at rest project beyond abdomen tip. Eats grasses, weeds, field crops. **HABITAT** Fields.

SOUTHEASTERN LUBBER GRASSHOPPER
Romalea microptera
GRASSHOPPER ORDER

2½". Body stout; yellow with black markings. Wings short, stubby; forewings have reddish stripe; hindwings red with black border. Flightless; slow-moving. Emits foul-smelling secretion when disturbed. **HABITAT** Roadsides, field edges, salt marshes.

AMERICAN BIRD GRASSHOPPER
Schistocerca americana
GRASSHOPPER ORDER

2". Body elongated; brown and beige above, with black markings and pale midline stripe; yellow below. Legs reddish brown. Wings clear. Flies readily when disturbed. **HABITAT** Meadows, woodland edges.

BROAD-WINGED KATYDID
Microcentrum rhombifolium
GRASSHOPPER ORDER

2¼". Body robust; gray-green; ovipositor curves sharply upward; antennae long, thin. Wings dark green, veined, tapering almost to points. Call a loud *katy-DID-katy-DIDN'T,* made by rubbing serrations at base of forewings. **HABITAT** Woods, shrubby fields. **RANGE** n FL.

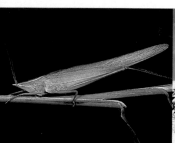

CONE-HEADED GRASSHOPPERS
Neoconocephalus species
GRASSHOPPER ORDER

1¼". Body long, slender; green, sometimes light brown. Head cone-shaped. Wings green; long and narrow. Can fly considerable distances. Makes both a monotonous buzzing sound and a loud *tsip-tsip.* **HABITAT** Moist grassy meadows.

HOUSE CRICKET
Acheta domestica
GRASSHOPPER ORDER

¾". Body stout, cylindrical; yellowish brown. Wings extend well beyond abdomen tip. Often hides in houses; gives monotonous triple chirps, sometimes for hours, day or night. Eats crumbs, vegetable scraps. **HABITAT** Buildings.

FIELD CRICKET
Gryllus pennsylvanicus
GRASSHOPPER ORDER

1". Body black, with spiky abdominal appendages. Antennae long; hindlegs strong, spiny. Wings short, dusky. Gives ½-second triple chirps. **HABITAT** Fields, occ. houses; hides under stones, in undergrowth.

NORTHERN MOLE CRICKET
Gryllotalpa hexadactyla
GRASSHOPPER ORDER

1¼". Body stout, elongated; brown. Forelegs spade-like, used to burrow through soil. Wings narrow. Lives underground, emerging to mate. Eats plant roots; can be pest. **HABITAT** Moist woods, meadows, gardens.

CICADAS
Tibicen species
CICADA ORDER

1½". Body stout; blackish with green markings. Head wide; eyes bulbous. Wings long, membranous; clear, with green front edges. Male gives rapid, saw-like clicking call on hot summer days. **HABITAT** Woods, adjacent meadows. **RANGE** n FL.

MEADOW SPITTLEBUG
"Froghopper"
Philaenus spumarius
CICADA ORDER

⅜". Body pear-shaped; gray, green, yellow, or brown. Antennae, wings short. Nymph oval, pale yellowish; emits protective froth on vegetation. Adults hop about on leaves. **HABITAT** Brushy meadows, roadsides.

EASTERN DOBSONFLY
Corydalus cornutus
NERVEWING ORDER

2". Body elongated; head round. Wings long, grayish, veined. Male mandibles long, forceps-like. Larva an aquatic predator. **HABITAT** Larva lives in fast-flowing streams, rivers; adult aerial over flowing water. **RANGE** n FL.

GREEN LACEWINGS
Chrysopa species
NERVEWING ORDER

⅝". Body long, pale green. Head narrow; eyes large, coppery; antennae long. Wings clear, veined, at least ¼ longer than body. Larva eats destructive aphids. **HABITAT** Meadows, gardens, woodland edges.

ANTLIONS
Myrmeleon species
NERVEWING ORDER

1½". Body soft; abdomen long; light gray-green. Antennae knobbed. Wings clear, narrow. A poor flier. Larva (⅝") builds funnel in sand, seizes sliding ants with powerful jaws. **HABITAT** Adult: woodland edges; larva: sandy areas.

Adult (top left), funnel in sand (top right), larva (bottom right)

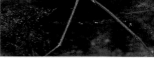

WATER BOATMEN
Arctocorixa and *Corixa* species
TRUE BUG ORDER

½". Body oval; gray-brown. Wings gray-brown, veined. Forelegs short, scoop-like; other legs paddle-shaped, used for rowing. Aquatic; can fly. Feeds on algae in birdbaths. **HABITAT** Ponds, puddles.

COMMON WATER STRIDER
Gerris remigis
TRUE BUG ORDER

⅝". Body black, slender. Middle and hindlegs very long, slender. Skates over water using surface tension. Feeds on mosquito larvae and insects that fall in water. **HABITAT** Still, fresh water.

SMALL MILKWEED BUG
Lygaeus kalmii
TRUE BUG ORDER

½". Body oval, black; red band behind head. Forewings have large, bright red X shape. Toxic to predators. Lays eggs on milkweeds; immune to plant's toxins. **HABITAT** Meadows with milkweeds.

FLORIDA LEAF-FOOTED BUG
Acanthocephala femorata
TRUE BUG ORDER

⅞". Body broad, with high ridge on thorax; black. Antennae long, red-tipped. Legs long, with red markings; hindleg femora flattened. Sucks plant juices. Releases foul-smelling secretion when disturbed. **HABITAT** Fields, meadows.

Beetles

There are more species of beetles (order Coleoptera) than any other animals on earth. Not all are called beetles: weevils and fireflies are included in this order. Beetles' forewings are hardened dense sheaths known as *elytra,* which meet in a straight line down the back. Their hindwings underneath function as the organs of flight. Beetle legs and antennae vary from long and straight to stout and angled. Both adults and larvae (known as grubs) have mouthparts adapted for biting and chewing. They are vegetarians, predators, scavengers, and in a few instances parasites. Some, like lady beetles, are highly prized by gardeners because they eat aphids and other garden pests, while others are major nuisances at best. They range in size from microscopic organisms to some of the largest insects in the world.

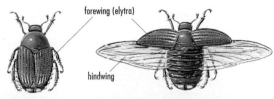

forewing (elytra)

hindwing

TIGER BEETLE
Cicindela scutellaris
BEETLE ORDER
⅝". Body elongated. Head, thorax, and wings metallic green; abdomen blackish. Legs long. A fast runner; captures insects with powerful jaws. **HABITAT** Open sandy areas.

FIERY SEARCHERS
"Caterpillar Hunters"
Calosoma species
BEETLE ORDER
1¼". Body long. Head and thorax black, with greenish gold on sides. Forewings metallic greenish blue. Nocturnal; forages on ground for caterpillars. **HABITAT** Open woods, gardens.

GREEN JUNE BEETLE
Cotinus nitida
BEETLE ORDER
⅞". Body robust, elongated. Head small, black; antennae short. Forewings metallic green, with pale, rusty gold edges. Active day and night; produces buzzing in-flight sounds. Feeds on fruit and flower pollen. **HABITAT** Gardens, open woods, orchards.

EASTERN HERCULES BEETLE
"Unicorn Beetle"
Dynastes tityus
BEETLE ORDER
2¼". Body robust; grayish green or brown; black spots on forewings. Large horn on male projects forward from thorax over head. Eats leaves, fruit. **HABITAT** Open woods. **RANGE** n FL.

RHINOCEROS/OX BEETLES
Strategus species
BEETLE ORDER
1". Body robust; head, thorax, and forewings dark brown or black. Male has 3 prominent, forward-facing horns. Feeds on leaves, fruit. **HABITAT** Open woods, brushy fields.

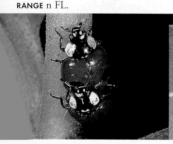

TWO-SPOTTED LADY BEETLE
Adalia bipunctata
BEETLE ORDER
¼". Body oval, rounded. Forewings reddish orange, with 1 black spot on each. Adult and larva feed on aphids. Overwinters in houses and under bark. **HABITAT** Fields, gardens.

PYRALIS FIREFLY
"Lightning Bug"
Photinus pyralis
BEETLE ORDER
½". Body long. Head/thorax shield has black spot ringed with orange. Forewings blackish; yellow lines down edges and center. Flashes yellow-green light from abdomen every 2–3 seconds when courting. Eggs, larvae, pupae also luminous. **HABITAT** Meadows, woodland edges. **SEASON** May–Sept.

CAROLINA SAWYER
Monochamus carolinensis
BEETLE ORDER
1". Body narrow, elongated; grayish brown. Forewings have whitish markings. Antennae much longer than body. Larva feeds on roots, trunks of dying trees; adult feeds on twig bark, conifer needles. **CAUTION** Bites. **HABITAT** Woods.

PALM WEEVIL
Rhynchophorus cruentatus
BEETLE ORDER

1¼". Body elongated; shiny dark brown to blackish. Long, conspicuous, down-curving snout; mouthparts at tip. Adult eats palm sap; larva eats bud and leaf sheaths. **HABITAT** Palms (esp. Florida Royal, Cabbage Palmetto). **RANGE** s FL.

Flies and Mosquitoes

Flies and mosquitoes, some of humankind's least favorite insects, are nonetheless worthy of a second glance. All species have only two wings and mouthparts formed for sucking, or piercing and sucking combined. The legless and wingless larvae undergo complete metamorphosis. Terrestrial larvae, called maggots, are almost always whitish or grayish in color. Aquatic larvae have various names; those of mosquitoes are called wrigglers. Adults fly with a wingbeat frequency often in the range of 300 beats per second, and in tiny species this can be many times faster. This incredible speed produces the familiar in-flight buzzing sounds. Flies feed on decomposing matter, nectar, and, in the case of biting flies, blood. Mosquitoes' lower lips form a proboscis with six knife-sharp organs, some smooth and some saw-toothed, that cut into skin.

CRANE FLIES
Tipula species
FLY ORDER

2½". Body long, delicate, gray to yellow-brown; legs very long, slender. Wings clear, veined; held at 60-degree angle from body. **HABITAT** Watersides; often enters houses.

SUMMER MOSQUITOES
Aedes species
FLY ORDER

¼". Body slender, delicate. Thorax brown, with pale mid-dorsal stripe; abdomen dark brown. Wings transparent, tinged pale brown. **HABITAT** Near stagnant water, puddles.

HOUSE MOSQUITO
Culex pipiens
FLY ORDER

¼". Body long. Thorax light brown; abdomen banded white and brown, often raised parallel to ground at rest. Wings dusky, transparent. Female sucks blood; male drinks plant juices. Common at night. **HABITAT** Watersides, swamps, houses.

DEER FLIES
Chrysops species
FLY ORDER

½". Body flattish; head small. Thorax black; abdomen striped golden. Wings veined, with black patches. **CAUTION** Circles targets silently, giving quick nasty bite on landing. **HABITAT** Woods and roadsides near water.

BLACK HORSE FLY
Tabanus atratus
FLY ORDER

1". Body large; black. Abdomen has bluish sheen. Fine hairs on thorax. Wings dark. Eyes large, black. Male sips nectar, female sucks blood, esp. of livestock. **CAUTION** Bites. **HABITAT** Meadows and pastures near streams.

AMERICAN HOVER FLY
"Flower Fly"
Metasyrphus americanus
FLY ORDER

⅜". Body stout; black to metallic green; abdomen has 3 yellow crossbands. Wings clear. Coloring mimics a bee, but does not sting or bite. Hovers above flowers; drinks nectar. **HABITAT** Fields, open woods.

HOUSE FLY
Musca domestica
FLY ORDER

¼". Body rotund; gray with black stripes. Wings clear. Eyes large, red-brown; legs hairy. Egg hatches in 10–24 hours; matures in 10 days; lives 15 (male) to 26 (female) days. Sucks liquid sugars from garbage; spreads disease. **HABITAT** Buildings, esp. restaurants; farms.

GREEN BOTTLE FLIES
Phaenicia species
FLY ORDER

½". Body stout; metallic blue-green with gold highlights, black markings. Black hairs cover thorax. Wings clear, with brown veins. Eats carrion and decaying organic matter. **HABITAT** Near manure and garbage.

LOVE BUG
Plecia nearctica
FLY ORDER

⅓". Body elongated; head and wings velvety black; thorax orange above. A recent immigrant from the south-central states. Often seen mating in air, over highways. Feeds on nectar, pollen. **HABITAT** Fields, roadsides.

Ants, Wasps, and Bees

The insects of the order Hymenoptera include primarily the narrow-waisted bees, wasps, and ants. Hymenopterans have two pairs of membranous, transparent wings, mouthparts modified to chew and lick, and, in adult females, an ovipositor. All species undergo complete metamorphosis.

The narrow-waists are divided into two broad groupings. The first, parasitic wasps, include the large and varied assemblage of nonstinging ichneumon wasps, who live as parasites during their larval stage. Some ichneumons are greatly feared by humans for their astonishingly long ovipositors, which are used not for stinging but to probe about in woody vegetation for suitable insects to lay eggs on. The second group of narrow-waists are the stinging insects, with ovipositors that have been modified into stinging organs. Included here are vespid wasps (such as yellow jackets), bees, and many ants.

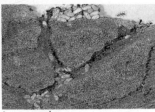

Carpenter ant colony   Paper wasp nest

Ants and some wasps and bees are highly social creatures, but some species in this order live solitary lives. The nests constructed by ants, wasps, and bees vary in complexity from a single-cell hole in the ground to the Honey Bee's elaborate comb structures. Many ant species excavate in soil or wood, building multichambered homes mostly hidden from sight. Bumble bees and yellow jackets build similar homes. Unlike ants, though, they build separate six-sided chambers for each of their young, made of a papery material that consists of wood or bark and adult saliva. Paper wasps often construct their nests in open situations, while Honey Bees utilize man-made hives or hollow trees or logs. The Honey Bees' two-sided, vertically hanging beeswax combs can contain more than 50,000 cells.

Our bees and flowering plants have developed a great many interdependencies over the eons as they have evolved together. We would lose too many of our flowers and fruits were we to let our bees be poisoned out of existence. We would also lose some of the greatest known examples of animal industry.

COW KILLER
"Velvet Ant"
Dasymutilla occidentalis
ANT, WASP, AND BEE ORDER

⅞". Wasp. Body covered with short hairs; above red with narrow black band; below black. Male wings brownish. Female wingless. **CAUTION** Female stings. **HABITAT** Sandy areas in meadows, woodland edges.

ALLEGHENY MOUND ANT
Formica exsectoides
ANT, WASP, AND BEE ORDER

⅜". Narrow neck and waist; head and thorax rusty; abdomen large, blackish. Builds flattened sand and gravel mounds, about 12" wide, with central entrance. **CAUTION** Gives painful but harmless bite. **HABITAT** Woodland clearings, edges.

RED FIRE ANT
Solenopsis invicta
ANT, WASP, AND BEE ORDER

¼". Narrow neck and waist; head and thorax dull red; abdomen dark. Builds underground nest, leaving soil piled above. Feeds on young plants, insects; denudes foliage. **CAUTION** Stings, bites. **HABITAT** Fields, open woods.

SHORT-TAILED ICHNEUMONS
Ophion species
ANT, WASP, AND BEE ORDER

⅝". Body elongated; light yellowish to reddish brown. Abdomen long, compressed; legs and antennae long, pale. Wings clear. Feeds on flower nectar. Female ovipositor short; deposits egg into living caterpillar; larva pupates inside cocoon. **HABITAT** Woods, brushy fields.

PAPER WASPS
Polistes species
ANT, WASP, AND BEE ORDER

1". Body slender, with narrow waist; reddish brown with black and yellow bands. Wings reddish brown. Female builds globular hanging nest with narrow stem below overhanging rock, eave, or porch. **CAUTION** Stings but is not aggressive. **HABITAT** Fields, gardens.

EASTERN YELLOW JACKET
Vespula maculifrons
ANT, WASP, AND BEE ORDER
⅝″. Wasp. Body stout; black, with yellow bands on thorax and abdomen. Wings dusky. Nests under log, stone, or in crevice. Raids picnic food, trash cans. **CAUTION** Stings repeatedly if bothered. **HABITAT** Fields, woods, gardens.

BLACK-AND-YELLOW MUD DAUBER
Sceliphron caementarium
ANT, WASP, AND BEE ORDER
1″. Wasp. Body slender, with long, narrow waist; black with yellow markings on thorax and beginning of abdomen. Legs yellow. Builds tubular mud nest under eaves, overhangs. **CAUTION** Stings but is not aggressive. **HABITAT** Fields, gardens.

HONEY BEE
Apis mellifera
ANT, WASP, AND BEE ORDER
⅝″. Body rotund. Thorax hairy, brown; abdomen banded black and golden. Wings dusky. Builds honeycomb hive in tree hollows or beekeepers' boxes, each with complex social system of drones, queens, workers. **CAUTION** Stings but is not aggressive; if stung, remove stinger immediately. **HABITAT** Fields and orchards.

AMERICAN BUMBLE BEE
Bombus pennsylvanicus
ANT, WASP, AND BEE ORDER
⅞″. Body robust, hairy; mainly yellow, with black accents. Wings smoky. Gathers nectar; pollinates flowers. Queen and imm. overwinter to start next year's colony. Nests underground. **CAUTION** Stings but is not aggressive. **HABITAT** Open areas, woods.

Butterflies and Moths

The order Lepidoptera comprises the familiar groups of butterflies (including skippers) and moths. *Lepidoptera* means "scale-winged," and refers to the minute wing scales on all butterflies and moths. Lepidopterans undergo complete metamorphosis. Eggs are laid singly, or in rows, stacks, or masses, depending on the species. The emergent larva, usually referred to as a caterpillar, feeds on plant life, and grows through several stages, or instars, shedding its skin each time. When fully grown, the caterpillar prepares to pupate by spinning a silken cocoon (moth) or finding a secure hiding place (butterfly). Then the caterpillar sheds its last larval skin, revealing the pupa, an outer shell with no head or feet, within which the wings and other adult features develop. The time required for this process is different for each species. Many have only one emergence of adults per year; others have two or three. Most Florida lepidopterans live out their entire lives within the state, although a few species, like the world-famous Monarch, migrate long distances. Most species pass the winter as eggs, larvae, or pupae; others, especially in south Florida, are active all year.

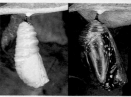

Metamorphosis of a Monarc

Several key differences distinguish moths and butterflies. Moths' antennae are either feather-like or wiry, and lack the clubbed tip of butterflies' antennae. Moths rest with their wings outstretched or at an angle above the body; butterflies rest with their wings outstretched or held together vertically, like a sail. Moths fly day and night, while butterflies fly only by day. Color and size are poor general distinguishing features between the two groups.

When trying to identify a species, pay special attention to the wing colors, shape, and pattern. Most of the characteristic wing markings on moths are found on the uppersides. In butterflies, look for distinguishing markings on the uppersides of those species that rest with outstretched wings and on the undersides of those that rest with their wings folded up.

Butterflies drink nectar from many species of wildflowers and shrubs. Among the many wild nectar plants in Florida are Buttonbush, milkweeds, asters, mustards, mints, and peas. Many garden flowers also attract butterflies and moths, including Shrimp Plant, Butterfly Bush, yarrows, lantanas, snapdragons, phlox, and salvias. Nocturnal moths are also drawn to lights.

Each larva, or caterpillar, species has its own select food plants, and the accounts that follow list many of these. Measurements are of typical wingspans for adult forms, from tip to tip.

PIPEVINE SWALLOWTAIL
Battus philenor
SWALLOWTAIL FAMILY

3⅛". Mostly black above, with creamy spots along borders; iridescent blue on hindwings. Below, hindwings blue, with large orange spots. Female duller. Caterpillar black to dark red with red tubercules. **HABITAT** Fields, open woods, gardens. **FOOD PLANTS** Pipevines, incl. Virginia Snakeroot. **SEASON** Feb.–Nov. **RANGE** n and c FL.

ZEBRA SWALLOWTAIL
Eurytides marcellus
SWALLOWTAIL FAMILY

3". Black above, with white or pale greenish stripes; hindwings have large red spot near body, blue spots near very long tail. Below, hindwings have red stripe. Caterpillar pea green with black and yellow bands. **HABITAT** Woodland streams. **FOOD PLANTS** Pawpaw trees. **SEASON** Mar.–Dec.

BLACK SWALLOWTAIL
Papilio polyxenes
SWALLOWTAIL FAMILY

3". Black above, with median yellow band (larger on male), yellow spots on rear edges; hindwings have tail, blue spots (larger on female). Below, hindwings have orange spots. Caterpillar pale green with black bands. **HABITAT** Fields, gardens. **FOOD PLANTS** Carrot family, incl. Queen Anne's Lace.

GIANT SWALLOWTAIL
Papilio cresphontes
SWALLOWTAIL FAMILY

4½". Brownish black above, with broad yellow diagonal band across forewings and yellow band along margins. Spatulate tail has yellow spot at end. Below, mostly yellow with black veins. Caterpillar brown with large white patches, red horns. **HABITAT** Open woods, citrus groves. **FOOD PLANTS** Citruses, Torchwood.

EASTERN TIGER SWALLOWTAIL
Papilio glaucus
SWALLOWTAIL FAMILY

4½". Mainly yellow above; forewings have 4 black "tiger" stripes; trailing edge black with small yellow spots, mixed in hindwings with several orange and blue spots. Below, mostly pale yellow, with narrow black lines; row of orange spots along outer margins. Caterpillar green with

black and orange eyespots. **HABITAT** Meadows, open woods, gardens. **FOOD PLANTS** Tulip and cherry trees. **SEASON** Mar.–Nov. **RANGE** All FL, ex. Keys.

PALAMEDES SWALLOWTAIL
Papilio palamedes
SWALLOWTAIL FAMILY

4½″. Blackish above, with yellow marginal spots; yellow band, broken on forewings; blue spots on hindwings. Below, orange, yellow, blue spots; yellow line near base of hindwings. Caterpillar green with orange and black eyespots. **HABITAT** Wooded swamps, borders. **FOOD PLANTS** Red Bay, Sassafras. **SEASON** Mar.–Dec. **RANGE** All FL, ex. Keys.

FLORIDA WHITE
"Tropical White"
Appias drusilla
WHITE AND SULPHUR FAMILY

2″. Male all white above and below, with dusky markings along slightly pointed forewing margins. Female forewings have dark smudges; hindwings yellowish. **HABITAT** Hardwood hammocks. **FOOD PLANTS** Capers. **RANGE** s FL.

GREAT SOUTHERN WHITE
Ascia monuste
WHITE AND SULPHUR FAMILY

2″. All white above; forewings have black triangular markings along veins on outer edge; female forewings have isolated blackish dot in middle. Below, creamy yellow. **HABITAT** Coastal areas, gardens. **FOOD PLANTS** Southern Sea Rocket, Saltwort. **RANGE** All FL, ex. panhandle.

SOUTHERN DOGFACE
Colias cesonia
WHITE AND SULPHUR FAMILY

2¼″. Yellow above, with black markings on forewings in poodle-head shape, complete with black "eye"; hindwings have scalloped black edges. Below, mostly yellow. **HABITAT** Open woods, scrub oaks. **FOOD PLANTS** Indigo Bush, Alfalfa, clovers. **RANGE** All FL, ex. Keys.

CLOUDLESS SULPHUR
"Cloudless Giant Sulphur"
Phoebis sennae
WHITE AND SULPHUR FAMILY

2½″. Broad-winged. Male clear yellow above; below, yellow with tiny brown dots. Female yellow or white above and below, with black spots along margins. **HABITAT** Open areas, gardens, beaches. **FOOD PLANTS** Sennas, clovers. **SEASON** n FL: Mar.–Nov.; s FL: year-round.

ORANGE-BARRED SULPHUR
"Orange-barred Giant Sulphur"
Phoebis philea
WHITE AND SULPHUR FAMILY

3¼". Broad-winged. Male yellow above; wide orange wash at middle of forewings, outer edge of hindwings; female pale yellow; brownish marginal spots. Both sexes golden yellow below. **HABITAT** Open areas, gardens. **FOOD PLANTS** Sennas, Royal Poinciana. **RANGE** s FL; sometimes strays north.

LARGE ORANGE SULPHUR
"Giant Orange Sulphur"
Phoebis agarithe
WHITE AND SULPHUR FAMILY

2⅜". Male bright, clear, orange-yellow above; below, pale orange, with diagonal brown line on forewings, numerous reddish-brown specks on hindwings. Female paler, with faint diagonal line above and below. **HABITAT** Meadows, scrubland. **FOOD PLANTS** Blackbead, Cat's Claw. **SEASON** Mar.–Dec. **RANGE** s FL.

BARRED YELLOW
"Barred Sulphur"
Eurema daira
WHITE AND SULPHUR FAMILY

1¼". Yellow above; forewings have wide black border, heavy black bar along lower edge; hindwings have broad black border on outer margin. Below, dusky white in summer, rusty brown in winter. **HABITAT** Brushy fields, dunes. **FOOD PLANTS** Pea family.

LITTLE YELLOW
Eurema lisa
WHITE AND SULPHUR FAMILY

1¼". Yellow above, with black on tips and along margins. Below, yellowish with brownish specks. **HABITAT** Open areas, roadsides. **FOOD PLANTS** Pea family.

DAINTY SULPHUR
"Dwarf Yellow"
Nathalis iole
WHITE AND SULPHUR FAMILY
1". Yellow above; forewings broadly tipped black; black bar along rear of forewings, front of hindwings. Below, yellowish or olive, with orange on forewing margins. Smallest N. Amer. Sulphur. **HABITAT** Fields, roadsides, dunes. **FOOD PLANTS** Asters. **RANGE** All FL, ex. panhandle.

ATALA
Eumaeus atala
GOSSAMER-WING FAMILY
1¾". Black above; forewings have central iridescent blue patch; hindwings have blue spots along margins. Below, hindwings have 3 rows of iridescent bluish spots and red-orange patch near base. Abdomen bright red-orange. A threatened species. **HABITAT** Bushy woodland edges. **FOOD PLANTS** Coontie. **RANGE** se FL.

GREAT PURPLE HAIRSTREAK
Atlides halesus
GOSSAMER-WING FAMILY
1⅜". Iridescent blue above, with black borders, 2 black tails. Below, grayish or brownish, with 3 reddish spots at base and patch of blue. Body red-orange below. **HABITAT** Woods with Mistletoe. **FOOD PLANTS** Mistletoe. **RANGE** South to Tampa.

GRAY HAIRSTREAK
Strymon melinus
GOSSAMER-WING FAMILY
1¼". Dark gray above, with orange and black eyespots near 2 narrow tails. Below, gray with black, orange, and rust median line crossing hindwings; orange and blue to black patch near tail. **HABITAT** Fields, woodland edges. **FOOD PLANTS** Pea family. **SEASON** Apr.–Oct.

BARTRAM'S SCRUB-HAIRSTREAK
Strymon acis
GOSSAMER-WING FAMILY

1". Dark brown above; red spot near 2 pairs of tails: one short, one long, narrow. Below, gray with bold white vertical lines: 1 on each forewing, 2 on each hindwing; hindwings have large, red-orange patch. **HABITAT** Woods. **FOOD PLANTS** Croton. **RANGE** s FL.

MALLOW SCRUB-HAIRSTREAK
Strymon columella
GOSSAMER-WING FAMILY

1". Gray-brown above; trailing edge of hindwings tinged blue. Below, grayish crossed with broken dark spots; orange and black eyespot near tail. **HABITAT** Fields. **FOOD PLANTS** Mallows, Bay Cedar. **RANGE** Coastal s FL.

RED-BANDED HAIRSTREAK
Calycopis cecrops
GOSSAMER-WING FAMILY

1". Brownish black above; hindwings have faint blue iridescence. Below, gray-brown crossed with conspicuous red, white-edged line; black eyespots near tail. **HABITAT** Brushy fields, woodland edges. **FOOD PLANTS** Oaks, Croton, Wax Myrtle.

EASTERN PYGMY-BLUE
Brephidium isophthalma
GOSSAMER-WING FAMILY

⅝". Brown above. Below, brown with many fine white lines; hindwings have row of black spots along outer margin. One of N. Amer.'s smallest butterflies. **HABITAT** Salt marshes. **FOOD PLANTS** Glasswort. **RANGE** All coasts, ex. se FL.

CASSIUS BLUE
Leptotes cassius
GOSSAMER-WING FAMILY

⅝". Male light purplish blue above. Female white above, with blue wash at margins. Both sexes below: white with brown spots and stripes; 2 prominent black, yellow-ringed eyespots. **HABITAT** Fields, woodland edges, residential areas. **FOOD PLANTS** Leadwort. **RANGE** c and s FL.

CERAUNUS BLUE
Hemiargus ceraunus
GOSSAMER-WING FAMILY

⅞". Blue (male) or brown (female) above, with narrow black border and white fringe. Below, grayish with dark spots and bars outlined in white; large dark eyespots, sometimes ringed with orange. **HABITAT** Open areas, open woods with pines. **FOOD PLANTS** Pea family.

LITTLE METALMARK
Calephelis virginiensis
GOSSAMER-WING FAMILY

¾". Metallic brownish orange above, with many irregular rows of black dots and bands of silvery spots. Below, slightly paler. **HABITAT** Moist grassy areas; pine savannas. **FOOD PLANTS** Yellow Thistle.

GULF FRITILLARY
Agraulis vanillae
BRUSHFOOT FAMILY

2¾". Forewings long, fairly narrow. Orange above, with black spots and lines; forewings have 3 silvery spots at front edge, visible above and below. Below, pale brownish orange, with many large silvery markings. **HABITAT** Fields, gardens. **FOOD PLANTS** Passionflower.

JULIA
Dryas iulia
BRUSHFOOT FAMILY

3⅜". Forewings long, narrow. Male bright orange above, with narrow black borders, black spots or bar near forewing margins; female similar, but with light brown bands on forewings. Below, light brown with darker markings; white streak on leading edge of hindwings. **HABITAT** Hardwood hammocks, fields. **FOOD PLANTS** Passionflower. **RANGE** s FL.

ZEBRA LONGWING
Heliconius charitonius
BRUSHFOOT FAMILY

3¼". Forewings long, narrow. Jet black above; forewings have 3 yellow bands; hindwings have 1 yellow band, row of yellow spots. Below, paler with red spots at base. Caterpillar black and white with black spines. Florida's state butterfly. **HABITAT** Hardwood hammocks, deep woods, gardens. **FOOD PLANTS** Passionflower.

PHAON CRESCENT
"Phaon Crescentspot"
Phyciodes phaon
BRUSHFOOT FAMILY

1". Brown above, with orange checkerspots, irregular whitish and black bands. Below, hindwings mostly yellowish cream, with pale tan crescents in dark margins. **HABITAT** Moist open areas; fields. **FOOD PLANTS** Verbena family. **SEASON** Mar–Dec.

AMERICAN LADY
"American Painted Lady"
Vanessa virginiensis
BRUSHFOOT FAMILY

2". Orange above; outer forewings black with white line, white spots near tip; outer hindwings have black-rimmed blue spots. Below, lacy brown, black, and pink; 2 large eyespots. Caterpillar banded yellow and black; 2 rows of white spots on back. **HABITAT** Open areas, gardens. **FOOD PLANTS** Asters.

RED ADMIRAL
Vanessa atalanta
BRUSHFOOT FAMILY

2″. Brownish black above, with wide orange band across middle of forewings and on outer edge of hindwings; forewings have white spots near tip. Below, heavily mottled brown and black; forewings have several red, white, and blue marks. Migratory; population erratic. **HABITAT** Fields, woodland edges, gardens. **FOOD PLANTS** Nettles.

COMMON BUCKEYE
Junonia (Precis) coenia
BRUSHFOOT FAMILY

2¼″. Tawny brown or dark brown above, with orange near margins; forewings have 2 orange bars, whitish band with bold eyespots; hindwings have 2 bold eyespots, orange band. Below, plain brown. **HABITAT** Fields, shores. **FOOD PLANTS** Plantain and verbena families.

WHITE PEACOCK
Anartia jatrophae
BRUSHFOOT FAMILY

2¼″. Whitish above and below, with fine dark lines, blending to pale brownish and orange along outer margins; small black eyespots: 1 on each forewing, 2 on each hindwing. **HABITAT** Moist or swampy areas. **FOOD PLANTS** Water Hyssop, Ruellia. **RANGE** All FL, ex. Keys.

VICEROY
Limenitis archippus
BRUSHFOOT FAMILY

2¾″. Two FL forms. One mimics Monarch: Orange above and below, with thick black veins, white-spotted black borders, transverse black line on mid-hindwing (lacking in Monarch). One mimics Queen: Bronzy orange above (no black veins), with white spots on forewings. Glides with wings held horizontal. **HABITAT** Marshy fields, meadows. **FOOD PLANTS** Willows. **SEASON** Apr.–Sept. **RANGE** All FL, ex. Keys.

RUDDY DAGGERWING
Marpesia petreus
BRUSHFOOT FAMILY

2¾″. Orange above, with thin lengthwise brown lines, long brown tail; forewings have curving hooked tip. Below, orange-brown with thin brown lines. **HABITAT** Hardwood hammocks, wooded swamps. **FOOD PLANTS** Fig trees. **RANGE** c and s FL.

FLORIDA LEAFWING
Anaea floridalis
BRUSHFOOT FAMILY

2⅞″. Reddish orange above, with brown margins and dark lines near outer borders; short tail. Below, grayish with dark striations, resembling a dead leaf. **HABITAT** Pines (esp. Slash Pine), palmetto scrub. **FOOD PLANTS** Woolly Croton. **RANGE** Endemic to s FL, Keys.

CAROLINA SATYR
Hermeuptychia sosybius
BRUSHFOOT FAMILY

1½″. Uniformly dull brown above. Below, brown with white dusting and 2 dark midwing lines; 2 large and several small yellow-ringed eyespots near outer hindwing margin. **HABITAT** Shaded grassy areas. **FOOD PLANTS** Grasses. **RANGE** South to Key Largo.

SOUTHERN PEARLY-EYE
Enodia portlandia
BRUSHFOOT FAMILY

1⅞″. Chocolate brown above, with row of large dark spots near borders. Below, violet-brown; yellow-ringed eyespots on paler margins. **HABITAT** Woods. **FOOD PLANTS** Grasses, canes. **SEASON** Apr.–Nov. **RANGE** n and c FL.

GEORGIA SATYR
Neonympha areolata
BRUSHFOOT FAMILY

1⅝″. Uniformly dull brown above. Below, hindwings dull brown with 3 tiny eyespots; rear of hindwings have 4 red-orange lines and row of 5 large, yellow-ringed eyespots. **HABITAT** Open, moist grassy areas. **FOOD PLANTS** Grasses.

MONARCH
Danaus plexippus
BRUSHFOOT FAMILY

3½". Orange above, with black veins, orange- and white-spotted blackish margins; male has black spot on vein of mid-hindwing. Below, duller yellow-orange; similarly patterned. Glides with wings held at an angle. Caterpillar banded black, white, and yellow. Adult and caterpillar poisonous to predators. Most common in fall when migrants arrive from north, en route to Mexico. **HABITAT** Open areas. **FOOD PLANTS** Milkweeds.

QUEEN
Danaus gilippus
BRUSHFOOT FAMILY

3¼". Rich brownish orange above; black border dotted with fine white spots, larger on forewings. Below, hindwings have prominent black veins. Caterpillar brownish white with yellow and brown bands and yellow-green lateral stripes. Adult and caterpillar toxic to predators. **HABITAT** Open areas. **FOOD PLANTS** Milkweeds, Oleander.

MANGROVE SKIPPER
Phocides pigmalion
SKIPPER FAMILY

2¼". Brown above; forewings have blue lines; hindwings have iridescent blue spots. Below, hindwings have blue lines. **HABITAT** Mangrove swamps. **FOOD PLANTS** Red Mangrove. **RANGE** c and s FL.

SILVER-SPOTTED SKIPPER
Epargyreus clarus
SKIPPER FAMILY

2". Rusty brown above; rectangular gold patches on forewings. Below, large silver patch on hindwings. **HABITAT** Woodland edges, brushy fields, gardens. **FOOD PLANTS** Locusts, Wisteria. **RANGE** All FL, ex. Keys.

LONG-TAILED SKIPPER
Urbanus proteus
SKIPPER FAMILY

1¾". Brown above; row of white squares on forewings; blue sheen on body and hindwings; long rounded tail. Below, gray-brown with 2 black bands on hindwings. **HABITAT** Open areas. **FOOD PLANTS** Pea and mustard families.

TROPICAL CHECKERED-SKIPPER
Pyrgus oileus
SKIPPER FAMILY

1¼″. Slaty brown above, with numerous creamy spots; male has conspicuous bluish-gray hair-like scales. Below, tan with dark brown and gray spots outlined in black. Wings spread at rest. **HABITAT** Open areas. **FOOD PLANTS** Mallows, Hollyhock.

FIERY SKIPPER
Hylephila phyleus
SKIPPER FAMILY

1¼″. Male yellow-orange above, with irregular black border, dark stripes on mid-forewing; female dark brown with many orange markings. Below, hindwings dull yellow with few indistinct dark spots. Wings folded at rest. **HABITAT** Weedy grassy areas. **FOOD PLANTS** Grasses.

MONK SKIPPER
Asbolis capucinus
SKIPPER FAMILY

1⅞″. Wings pointed; male uniformly dark brown above and below. Female, above, has diffuse light patch on forewings. Body robust. Wings folded at rest. **HABITAT** Settled areas near palm trees. **FOOD PLANTS** Palm and palmetto trees. **RANGE** c and s FL.

LUNA MOTH
Actias luna
GIANT SILKWORM MOTH FAMILY

4″. Wings pale green, eyespot on each; leading edge of forewings purple, others edged in purple and white; hindwings with very long tail. Body yellow-green. Nocturnal. Caterpillar green; yellow side stripe; red, orange, and yellow tubercles. **HABITAT** Broadleaf woods. **FOOD PLANTS** Hickories, birches. **SEASON** Mar.–Sept. **RANGE** Mainly n FL.

POLYPHEMUS MOTH
Antheraea polyphemus
GIANT SILKWORM MOTH FAMILY

5″. Wings pale orange-brown, with eyespots: yellow on forewings, yellow and black on hindwings; narrow black and white line near trailing edges. Body orange-brown. Nocturnal. Caterpillar green with thin yellow bands and small red, orange, and yellow bumps. **HABITAT** Broadleaf woods. **FOOD PLANTS** Many broadleaf trees. **SEASON** Feb.–July, Oct.–Dec.

IO MOTH
Automeris io
GIANT SILKWORM MOTH FAMILY

2½". Forewings yellow-orange (male) or reddish brown (female); hindwings yellow with prominent black eyespot; narrow black and rusty bands near outer edge. Body yellow-brown, robust, cylindrical. Nocturnal. Caterpillar green with reddish and white stripes on sides and branching black spines; stings. **HABITAT** Open woods. **FOOD PLANTS** Azaleas, palmettos, dogwoods. **SEASON** Mar.–Nov.

IMPERIAL MOTH
Eacles imperialis
GIANT SILKWORM MOTH FAMILY

5". Wings yellow with large purplish-brown patches and fine dark flecks. Body checkered yellow and purplish brown. Nocturnal. Caterpillar green, orange, or brown, with yellowish head and sparse white hairs. **HABITAT** Mixed and broadleaf woods. **FOOD PLANTS** Oaks, pines, walnuts, and many other trees. **SEASON** Apr.–Oct.

NESSUS SPHINX MOTH
Amphion floridensis
SPHINX MOTH FAMILY

2". Wings narrow; chocolate brown, with dark orange band on hindwings. Body stout, dark brown, with 2 yellow bands. Feeds on flowers by day; hovers like a hummingbird. **HABITAT** Gardens, woodland edges. **FOOD PLANTS** Grape vines, Cayenne Pepper. **SEASON** Mar.–Oct.

RUSTIC SPHINX MOTH
Manduca rustica
SPHINX MOTH FAMILY

4½". Wings blackish brown, with intricate white marks, resembling lichen. Body blackish brown with 3 pairs of yellow spots on sides of abdomen. **HABITAT** Open woods, gardens. **FOOD PLANTS** Crossvine, jasmines, Fringetree. **SEASON** May–Nov.

PINK-SPOTTED HAWK MOTH
Agrius cingulatus
SPHINX MOTH FAMILY

4". Forewings narrow; brown and gray pattern resembles bark; hindwings gray-brown with black and pink to orange bands, small pink patch at base. Body brown with pink bands; black bands on abdomen. **HABITAT** Open areas. **FOOD PLANTS** Jimsonweed, Sweet Potato. **SEASON** May–Oct.

RATTLEBOX MOTH
"Bella Moth"
Utetheisa bella
TIGER MOTH FAMILY

1⅜". Forewings red, orange, or yellow, with rows of white-ringed black spots; hindwings bright pink with irregular black borders; conspicuous in flight. **HABITAT** Open areas, woodland edges. **FOOD PLANTS** Pea family, esp. Rattlebox.

GIANT LEOPARD MOTH
Ecpantheria scribonia
TIGER MOTH FAMILY

3½". Forewings white with bluish-black circles; hindwings white with dark streaks. Body white with black spots; legs banded black and white. Caterpillar black, hairy; a garden pest. **HABITAT** Gardens, shrubby areas. **FOOD PLANTS** Leaves of banana and orange trees, cabbages **SEASON** Apr.–Sept.

UNDERWINGS
Catocala species
OWLET MOTH FAMILY

1¾". Forewings mottled grayish brown; provide excellent camouflage when at rest on tree trunk; hindwings red with 2 black bands; conspicuous in flight. Body plump, gray-brown. Nocturnal. **HABITAT** Open woods, fields, gardens. **FOOD PLANTS** Oaks.

Vertebrates

There are approximately 43,000 vertebrate species on earth. The evolution of a variety of anatomical structures has made them extraordinarily successful for half a billion years. Today vertebrates are one of the most widespread groups of animals, inhabiting every corner of the globe, from ocean depths to mountaintops, deserts, and polar regions.

Vertebrata is one of three subphyla of the phylum Chordata. All members of Chordata possess an internal stiffening rod called a notochord during their embryonic development. The sac-like, marine sea squirts, salps, and their relatives (members of the subphylum Urochordata, the most primitive of the Chordata) lose their notochord completely as they develop, and in the file-shaped, marine lancelets (of the subphylum Cephalochordata) the notochord remains an unsegmented rod. In vertebrates the notochord is replaced during the animal's development by a series of cartilaginous or bony disks, known as vertebrae, that run along the back.

The evolution of the vertebrates stemmed from an invertebrate sea squirt–like animal, passed through a "missing link" invertebrate-to-vertebrate stage with the lancelets, and reached the beginnings of the vertebrate stage some 500 million years ago (mya) with the appearance of the first jawless fishes. During the following 350 million years, the various classes of vertebrates evolved. The ancestors of modern fishes developed from their jawless ancestors about 400 mya; 100 million years further into vertebrate development, amphibians evolved from fishes crawling about in search of water during the droughts of the Devonian period. Reptiles first appeared about 250 mya and flourished because of their ability to reproduce on land. Mammals and birds, warm-blooded and able to successfully live in places too cold for fishes, amphibians, and reptiles, spread across the world's environments, mammals beginning about 170 mya and birds about 150 mya.

Today's vertebrates share a number of characteristics that separate them from the estimated 50 million or so invertebrate species with which they share the earth. Virtually all vertebrates are bilaterally symmetrical; that is, their left and right sides are essentially mirror images of one another. Their strong but flexible backbone, composed of vertebrae, protects the spinal cord and serves as the main structural component of the internal skeletal frame and the segmented muscles that attach to it. Vertebrates are well-coordinated runners, jumpers, swimmers, and/or fliers because of this unique combination of skeletal and muscular development. Other shared characteristics of nearly all vertebrates include one pair of bony jaws (with or without teeth), one or two pairs of appendages, a ventrally located heart (protected by a ribcage), and blood contained in vessels.

The subphylum Vertebrata includes several classes: three classes of living fishes, the amphibians, the reptiles, the birds, and the mammals.

Fishes

Living fishes fall into three major groups: the primitive hagfishes and lampreys (several lampreys occur in Florida but are not covered in this book), the cartilaginous fishes (sharks, skates, and rays), and the bony fishes. Aquatic, mostly cold-blooded vertebrates with fins and internal gills, fish are typically streamlined and have a muscular tail. Most move through the water by weaving movements of their bodies and tail fins, using their other fins to control their direction. The skin of a fish is coated with a slimy secretion that decreases friction with the water; this secretion, along with the scales that cover most fish, provides their bodies with a nearly waterproof covering. The gills are located in passages that lead from the throat usually to a pair of openings on the side, just behind the head. With rare exceptions, fish breathe by taking water in through the mouth and forcing it past the gills and out through the gill openings; the thin-walled gills capture oxygen from the water and emit carbon dioxide.

The body shapes of fishes vary from cylindrical eels and elongated, spindle-shaped mackerels (rounded in the middle, with tapered ends) to vertically compressed (flattened) sunfishes to horizontally compressed skates and rays. Body colors can vary within a species due to season, sex, age, individual variation, and water temperature, and the color normally fades or otherwise changes after death. Most fishes have one or more dorsal (back) fins that may be spiny or soft (a few fishes, such as trout and salmon, have an additional fleshy fin behind the dorsal fins, called an adipose fin); a tail (caudal) fin, usually with an upper and a lower lobe; and an anal fin, just in front of the tail along the edge of the ventral (belly) side. They also have a pair of pectoral fins, usually on the sides behind the head, and a pair of pelvic fins, generally under the middle of the body. Some fishes lack one or more of these fins.

The mouths and snouts of fishes may be disk-shaped, pointed, tubular, or sword-like; depending on the species, the upper jaw (the snout) projects beyond the lower, the two parts of the jaw are of equal length, or the lower jaw projects beyond the upper. Some species have sensory barbels, whisker-like projections of the skin, usually on the lower jaw, that detect objects, especially in muddy or murky water. Most fish are covered with scales, but some species lack scales altogether, and some lack scales on the head or other areas; in other species, scales have been modified into bony plates. Some fishes have a conspicuous lateral line, a sensory organ beneath the skin that responds to vibrations in the water and often looks like a thin stripe along the side.

Some fish species are solitary, some live in small groups, and others are found mainly in enormous schools, in which members respond as a unit to stimuli while feeding or migrating.

Lengths given (from tip of snout to tip of tail) are for typical adults, although, as fish grow throughout their lives, larger individuals may be seen. The term "open seas" includes the Atlantic Ocean and the Gulf of Mexico. The icon ![icon] denotes fishes that can be found in both salt and fresh water.

Cartilaginous Fishes

The cartilaginous fishes have skeletons of somewhat flexible cartilage and several (usually five) pairs of conspicuous external gill slits. This group includes, in waters off Florida, sharks, skates, rays, and saw-fishes. Sharks typically have an elongated shape that tapers toward each end; one or two triangular dorsal fins, sometimes with a fin spine on the leading edge; two large pectoral fins; two smaller pelvic fins; a tail fin of which the upper lobe is usually larger than the lower; and sometimes an anal fin and a pair of horizontal keels at the base of the tail. The skates and rays have flattened bodies, usually round or dia-mond-shaped, with greatly enlarged pectoral fins that are attached to the side of the head, forming "wings" with which they "fly" through the water. The mouth is located on the underside of the head. Sharks have several rows of sharply pointed teeth; when a tooth breaks off or is worn down, a new tooth takes its place. The skin is rough and sand-papery, studded with tiny, tooth-like scales called denticles. Because cartilaginous fishes lack the swim bladder that keeps the bony fishes buoyant, and the efficient "gill pump" of bony fishes that keeps water

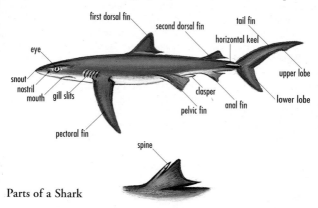

Parts of a Shark

moving over their gills, many sharks must swim constantly. Most live in ocean waters, though a few may enter large rivers. The male has a pair of external copulatory organs called claspers, modifications of the pelvic fins that are used to internally fertilize the female. Depending on the species, the female lays eggs enclosed in a horny case, retains the eggs internally until they hatch, or gives birth to live young.

Shark attacks are not common in Florida, and only a few fatali-ties have been recorded. Attacks that do occur are often not directed at humans but are the result of ill-advised human activity. To avoid attack, refrain from swimming in murky water, avoid wearing shiny or silvery objects that mimic the reflections of small fish, and avoid holding fish (especially wounded or bleeding fish) or lobsters un-derwater. These cautions are especially important when snorkeling, scuba diving, or spear-fishing offshore or in quiet waters.

WHALE SHARK
Rhincodon typus
WHALE SHARK FAMILY

20–30′. World's largest fish. Elongated, with hump on back before 1st dorsal fin. Head blunt; snout short; mouth very broad; teeth small, nonfunctional. Dark gray or dark brown on back and sides, all heavily spotted with white; white crossbars on back and sides; underside clear white or yellowish. 7 lengthwise ridges from nape to base of tail. 1st dorsal fin very large, triangular, rounded at tip; 2nd dorsal fin similar but much smaller; pectoral fins large; tail fin has tall upper lobe; all fins white-spotted. Strains plankton from seawater with sieve-like gill rakers; also feeds on small crustaceans and fish; does not attack humans or large vertebrates. **HABITAT** Near surface in open seas.

SHORTFIN MAKO
Isurus oxyrinchus
MACKEREL SHARK FAMILY

6–10′. Long, slender, with pointed snout. Blue-gray to deep blue above; white on lower sides and below. 1st dorsal fin large, rounded; upper lobe of tail fin slightly longer than lower. Teeth large, smooth-edged, pointed backward. Feeds on schooling fishes, esp. mackerel. **CAUTION** Will attack humans, small boats. **HABITAT** Offshore to 500′ deep.

TIGER SHARK
Galeocerdo cuvier
REQUIEM SHARK FAMILY

7–12′. Elongated, heavy-bodied; snout very short, broadly rounded from above or below. Dark blue-gray or brownish gray above; paler on sides; white below. Young and adults up to 6′ long have conspicuous dark brown blotches and striking pattern of wide, dark gray vertical bands on back, sides, and upper half of fins. 1st dorsal fin triangular; pectoral fins narrow, dark; upper lobe of tail fin very long, notched. Teeth broad, coarsely serrated, uppers and lowers alike. Usu. solitary. **CAUTION** Dangerous; has attacked humans. **HABITAT** Open seas to 460′ deep; will enter shallow bays, esp. at night.

SCALLOPED HAMMERHEAD
Sphyrna lewini
HAMMERHEAD SHARK FAMILY

6–9'. Elongated, laterally compressed. Head laterally expanded: from above looks like a mallet, with large eye at each end of lateral expansion; tapered in side view; front edge arched. Back and sides gray; white below. 1st dorsal fin long, pointed; upper lobe of tail fin long, narrow, swept-back. Mouth on underside of head. Swift predator capable of quick maneuvers. **CAUTION** Known to attack humans. **HABITAT** Inshore and offshore waters to 900' deep; enters estuaries.

 SMALLTOOTH SAWFISH
Pristis pectinata
SAWFISH FAMILY

9–13'. Shape between a shark and a ray: body and sloping head flattened in side view; snout extended with saw-like blade one-quarter body length, lined with 24 or more pairs of teeth. Gray above; paler along margins of fins; whitish below. 1st dorsal fin rounded at tip, set far back, above pelvic fins; pectoral fins triangular, placed forward. Tail fin fairly small: upper lobe larger, triangular; lower lobe tiny. Gill slits on underside of body. Slashes saw from side to side as it charges through schools of fish; returns to seize the injured. **CAUTION** Causes serious injuries if handled. **HABITAT** Shallow coastal waters, estuaries, lower parts of rivers.

SOUTHERN STINGRAY
Dasyatis americana
STINGRAY FAMILY

L 4'–5'6"; W 2'6"–3'. Flattened, kite-shaped; leading edge between snout and point of enlarged pectoral fin "wings" straight. Back color matches local sea bottom: light brown, gray, or olive; whitish below. Lacks dorsal fin, but has irreg. row of short spines along midback ridge. Tail very long, whip-like, with poisonous, rigid, barbed and grooved spine near base. Mouth on underside; teeth flat, powerful for crunching mollusks, crustaceans. Undulates "wings" when swimming. Often rests half-buried in sand in shallow water. **CAUTION** Tail spine causes serious wounds if stepped on. **HABITAT** Inshore; shallow sand and mud bottoms.

SPOTTED EAGLE RAY
Aetobatus narinari
EAGLE RAY FAMILY

L 3′6″–5′; W 4′6″–6′. Flattened, diamond-shaped; enlarged, wing-like pectoral fins broad with pointed tip. Back brown, with many white to yellowish spots; white below. 1 small dorsal fin just before tail. Tail very long, black, whip-like, with 2 poisonous, rigid, barbed spines at base. Snout shovel-shaped, with duck-like bill for probing mud. "Flies" through water slowly, gracefully with steady "wingbeats." Gathers in large schools; often seen from bridges and boats. When pursued, gives loud croak, leaps into air. **CAUTION** Nonaggressive, but jabs with spine if speared. **HABITAT** Shallow coastal waters, bays, estuaries.

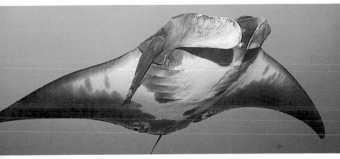

MANTA
Manta birostris
MANTA FAMILY

L 8–14′, W 14–18′. Flattened, diamond-shaped. Head has large eyes at outer edge of U-shaped head fin flaps. Black or olive-brown above, white below. 1 small triangular dorsal fin far back near tail. Pectoral fins form broad pointed "wings." Tail black, narrow, pointed; lacks spines. Uses head fins to funnel plankton, shrimp, small fish into its wide mouth. Rests and splashes about on surface alone, in pairs, or in groups. Young develops within mother's body. **HABITAT** Sea surface; may visit coasts, inlets.

Bony Fishes

Bony fishes normally have harder, less flexible bony skeletons than cartilaginous fishes, as well as a gas- or fat-filled swim bladder that keeps them buoyant. Most bony fishes have overlapping scales embedded in flexible connective tissue, though some lack scales entirely. There is a single gill opening on each side protected by a hard gill cover.

More than 99 percent of all living fishes are ray-finned bony fishes; a few bony fishes (none of which occur in Florida waters) are classified as lobe-finned fishes. The fins of ray-finned bony fishes consist of a web of skin supported by bony rays (either segmented soft rays or stiffer spines), each moved by a set of muscles, which makes the fins very flexible. The tail fin is typically symmetrical.

Most bony fishes reproduce by spawning: males directly fertilize eggs after the females release them from their bodies into the water. The eggs may float at mid-levels, rise to the surface, or sink to the bottom. A few fish guard nests or incubate eggs in a pouch or the mouth. Newborn fish are called larvae; within a few weeks or months, a larva develops to resemble a miniature adult, and is called a juvenile or fry.

This section is presented as two categories—saltwater fishes (starting on page 257) and freshwater fishes (starting on page 272). Most fishes live strictly in either salt water or fresh water. Other species are frequently found in brackish water, where fresh and salt water become mixed, and some primarily saltwater species breed in fresh water, but return to spend most of their lives at sea. The icon 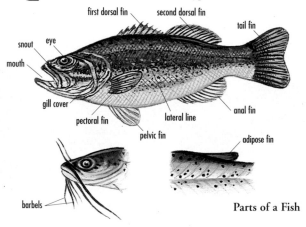 denotes those that live in both types of water.

Parts of a Fish

The Importance of Estuaries for Marine Fishes

Estuaries are defined generally as semi-enclosed bodies of water that have a free connection with the sea and that receive freshwater inflow through streams and runoff. Because large amounts of organic matter are carried downstream and into them, estuaries are more than simply a transition zone between land and ocean; they provide nutrients necessary for the growth of the early life stages of many species of marine fishes and invertebrates, such as oysters and clams, making them, along with adjacent salt marshes, among the most productive biological systems in the world. For example, some 97 percent of the commercial marine fishes in the Gulf of Mexico are dependent upon estuaries during some phase of their life cycle. Until recently, these bodies of water were regarded as of no particular value, and many estuarine and saltmarsh areas along the Florida coasts have been destroyed or permanently altered by dredge-and-fill operations. Streams that carry nutrients into estuaries may carry large quantities of pesticides and other poisons, which can kill fishes in their early life stages or cause serious problems to fishes later in their life cycles. Absorption of such substances into the body tissues of fishes people eat can cause serious human health problems. Thus the protection of estuaries from pollution has far-reaching benefits, for humans and for biological systems in general.

LADYFISH
"Tenpounder"
Elops saurus
TARPON FAMILY

16–20″. Elongated, slightly compressed; scales small. Back blue-gray; sides silvery; belly yellowish. Fins dusky, with yellowish tinge; single dorsal fin triangular; tail fin narrow, deeply forked. Head small; eyes large; jaws equal in length, down-slanted. **HABITAT** Shallow marine and brackish waters; enters river mouths rarely.

TARPON
Megalops atlanticus
TARPON FAMILY

4–6′. Elongated, robust, compressed; scales very large, smooth. Mouth huge, down-slanted; lower jaw extends well beyond upper. Back olive-gray; sides and belly silvery. Fins dusky, single dorsal fin short, triangular, last ray long and thread-like; tail fin deeply forked, lobes equal in size. Strong fast swimmer; at times rests on sea surface. **HABITAT** Open seas, shallow coastal waters, estuaries as adults; brackish marsh pools, rivers, canals from larvae to 2 years. **RANGE** More common in s FL and in s Gulf waters from Boca Grande to Keys.

BONEFISH
Albula vulpes
BONEFISH FAMILY

18–27″. Elongated, slender, slightly compressed. Snout long, conical; upper jaw protrudes. Back bluish, often with 7–9 thick, faint to dark, saddle-like bars; sides silvery with thin, dark, horizontal lines; belly whitish. Single dorsal fin short, triangular; tail fin deeply forked. Tail often shows as fish up-ends while feeding on mollusks and hermit crabs on incoming tide. **HABITAT** Shallow coastal waters over sand and mud bottoms; mangroves. **RANGE** All FL; most common off Keys.

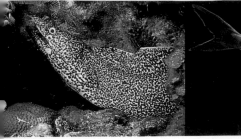

SPOTTED MORAY
Gymnothorax moringa
MORAY FAMILY

18–32″. Snake-like; robust in front, compressed to rear; skin thick, leathery. White or yellowish, densely spotted with dark purple blotches. Fringing dorsal fin continuous with fringing anal fin; both may be edged in black or white; lacks pectoral and pelvic fins. Head swollen behind large white eyes; jaws large; teeth canine-like, sharp. **CAUTION** Bites in or out of water. **HABITAT** Coral reefs, shallow rocky and grassy areas.

GAFFTOPSAIL CATFISH
Bagre marinus
SEA CATFISH FAMILY

12–18″. Elongated; scale-less; top of head flattened from snout to 1st dorsal fin. Mucous film on skin. Dark blue-gray above fading to silvery on sides; belly white. Long filaments extend from top of 1st dorsal and pectoral fins; small rounded adipose fin; tail fin deeply forked. Upper jaw protrudes; pair of short barbels below lower jaw; very long barbel from gape of mouth backward. **HABITAT** Shallow coastal waters, estuaries; offshore in deeper water in winter.

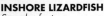

INSHORE LIZARDFISH
Synodus foetens
LIZARDFISH FAMILY

8–18″. Elongated, cigar-shaped. Head scaly; snout pointed; teeth conspicuous; mouth large, extends well past eye. Pale olive-brown above, many with dark brown, diamond-shaped blotches; pale yellow below. 1 dorsal fin; tiny adipose fin; tail fin small, forked; pelvic fins pointed, used for balancing on sand. Voracious predator; eats smaller fish and bait. **HABITAT** Shallow sand and mud bottoms.

ATLANTIC FLYINGFISH
Cypselurus melanurus
FLYINGFISH FAMILY

8–10″. Cigar-shaped. Dark blue-green above, silvery below. 1 low dorsal fin set far back; tail fin dusky, forked, lower lobe much longer. Pectoral fins greatly enlarged, wing-like, dusky, with pale central area and trailing edge; pelvic fins smaller, also wing-like. Glides on outstretched pectoral fins up to 4′ high in air for 300′ or more; becomes airborne by rapid skittering of tail on water surface. **HABITAT** Open seas; enters bays; remains near surface.

TRUMPETFISH
Aulostomus maculatus
TRUMPETFISH FAMILY

20–30″. Elongated, compressed. Snout long, tubular with large eyes at base and small upturned mouth at tip; tiny chin barbel. Pale orange-brown with fine white lines, tiny black dots. Single dorsal and anal fins far back, opposite each other; tiny spines along entire back. Tail fin fan-shaped, often square. Feeds vertically on sea bottom. **HABITAT** Sea-grass beds and coral reefs. **RANGE** s FL, Gulf of Mexico.

LINED SEAHORSE
Hippocampus erectus
PIPEFISH FAMILY

3–4″. Elongated; swims upright with head above body, tail dangles below; armored with lines and ridges. Head and tubular snout angle downward. Color variable: gray, brown, or dull red. Dorsal fin fan-shaped; tail prehensile, finless, curls around vegetation. Swims (weakly) by rapid vibration of dorsal fin. When mating, pair makes musical sounds; female lays eggs in male's pouch; young hatch and are expelled by male one at a time several weeks later. **HABITAT** Sea grasses and man-made structures in shallow water.

SPOTTED SCORPIONFISH
Scorpaena plumieri
SCORPIONFISH FAMILY

6–9″. Robust, high-backed. Head large, with 3 spines, many forked fleshy tabs. Pattern variegated: back and sides pale brown with several large, darker brown blotches; belly whitish. 1st dorsal fin long, with spiny rays; 2nd dorsal fin rounded; tail fin fan-like, with 3 dark bands separated by white; pectoral fins wide, fan-like. Rests camouflaged among rocks; feeds on fish that swim too close. **CAUTION** Spines can release pain-causing venom. **HABITAT** Coral reefs; rocky areas to 180′ deep.

LEOPARD SEAROBIN
Prionotus scitulus
SEAROBIN FAMILY

5–8″. Elongated, slender. Snout broad, flat, appears rounded from above; eyes large, yellow. Back, sides, fins pale yellow-brown with many reddish-brown spots. 1st dorsal fin triangular, with 2 blackish spots; tail fin short, fan-shaped. Pectoral fins large, wing-like; 1st 3 rays unwebbed, used as "legs." Creeps along bottom; feeds on bait, invertebrates. **HABITAT** Open seas, bays; over sand to 150′ deep.

COMMON SNOOK
"Robalo"
Centropomus undecimalis
SNOOK FAMILY

18–26″. Slender, elongated; tapers gradually from high point at 1st dorsal fin. Yellowish brown above; yellowish white below; distinct black lateral line extends onto tail fin. 2 separated triangular dorsal fins; tail fin forked. Snout pointed; lower jaw protrudes; mouth large, well-toothed. **HABITAT** Shallow coastal seas, bays, rivers, some lakes, incl. Okeechobee. **RANGE** Year-round: s FL. Summer: n FL.

SAND PERCH
Diplectrum formosum
SEA BASS FAMILY

5–8″. Body slender, elongated. Buffy orange; thick blackish bands above; thin blue horizontal lines on sides. Dorsal fin continuous; tail fin slightly forked. Head, eyes, and mouth large; wavy blue lines on cheeks; 2 radiating clusters of spines between eyes and gill cover. **HABITAT** Bays, sea-grass beds, reefs, shallow banks, coarse sand bottoms.

JEWFISH
Epinephelus itajara
SEA BASS FAMILY

4–5′. Very robust, cylindrical. Gray-brown; back and sides have irreg. wide black bars and many black dots; belly yellowish white. 1st dorsal fin long, low, spiny; 2nd dorsal, tail, and anal fins rounded. Head large, flattened; eyes small; mouth and lips down-slanted, very wide. Feeds mainly on crustaceans; sluggish. **HABITAT** Shallow coastal waters at and near rocks, reefs, pilings, wrecks, mangroves. Some young enter fresh water.

RED GROUPER
Epinephelus morio
SEA BASS FAMILY

20–28″. Robust, somewhat compressed. Color and pattern variable: all dull gray, or reddish brown with wide pale saddles on back, smaller pale spots on sides. 1st dorsal fin spiny, 2nd continuous with 1st; tail fin slightly concave or squared. Head and eyes large; mouth very wide, down-slanted; lower jaw protrudes. Most common in Gulf of Mexico. **HABITAT** Open seas, reefs, deepwater channels; hard bottoms to 360′ deep.

BLUEFISH
Pomatomus saltatrix
BLUEFISH FAMILY

20″. Elongated, compressed schooling fish. Blue-green above, shading to silvery below. 1st dorsal fin short, with 7 projecting spines; 2nd dorsal and anal fins similar, with long bases; tail fin deeply forked. Mouth wide; teeth prominent. Voraciously eats smaller fish and squid, leaving trail of carnage. **CAUTION** When caught, will try to bite. When feeding, may bite swimmers. **HABITAT** Oct.–May: inshore and offshore waters. **RANGE** All FL coasts. Summer: most adults migrate north as far as Cape Cod.

COBIA
Rachycentron canadum
COBIA FAMILY

24–36″. Elongated, cylindrical. Dark brown above; sides silvery white; appears to have 2 pale stripes with thick blackish line between them from snout through eye to base of tail fin; belly whitish. All fins blackish; 1st dorsal fin is series of 8 very short, unconnected spines; 2nd dorsal fin long, higher in front; tail fin crescent-shaped. Head broad, flattened on top, pointed in profile; lower jaw protrudes. **HABITAT** Open seas, channels, reefs. **RANGE** All FL, coasts. Winter: mainly s FL.

CREVALLE JACK
Caranx hippos
JACK FAMILY

18–30″. Robust, somewhat compressed. Dark blue-green above; sides and belly yellowish silver; lateral line curves high over pectoral fin; black spot on gill cover. 1st dorsal fin short, spiny; dusky 2nd dorsal and yellow anal fin long, higher at front edges; pectoral fins long, black at base; tail fin long, narrow, deeply forked. Head large, with rounded forehead, blunt snout; lower jaw protrudes; eyes large. Fast powerful swimmer. **HABITAT** Inshore bays to deep waters; enters coastal rivers.

BAR JACK
"Runner" "Skipjack"
Caranx ruber
JACK FAMILY

16–20″. Elongated, somewhat compressed. Bright blue or blue-gray above; sides silvery; belly washed yellowish; black stripe flanks dorsal fins and continues through lower lobe of tail fin. 1st dorsal fin spiny, triangular; 2nd dorsal and anal fins long, higher at front edges; pectoral fins thin, elongated; tail fin narrow, deeply forked. Head large; snout pointed. Often jumps above surface. **HABITAT** Clear shallow waters, reefs. **RANGE** Mainly s and e FL.

LOOKDOWN
Selene vomer
JACK FAMILY

6–8″. Very compressed, deep; head profile nearly vertical. Head and body silvery; scales smooth, tiny. 1st dorsal fin is row of short spines; 2nd dorsal and anal fins low, continuous to base of tail; front lobes of both very elongated. Tail fin deeply forked. Lower jaw protrudes; mouth small. Occurs in schools. **HABITAT** Shallow coastal waters with sand or mud bottoms. **RANGE** All FL; most common in se FL and Keys.

FLORIDA POMPANO
Trachinotus carolinus
JACK FAMILY

10–16". Compressed, deep. Head profile rounded; snout blunt; mouth small. Back blue-gray; sides silvery; belly yellowish; scales small, smooth. 1st dorsal fin is row of short spines; dusky 2nd dorsal and yellow anal fins short, continuous to base of tail, front lobes of both longer; tail fin deeply forked. Often leaps and slaps across wave tops. HABITAT Surf, bays; inlets to 120' deep. RANGE All FL. Summer: many migrate north as far as Cape Cod.

GREATER AMBERJACK
Seriola dumerili
JACK FAMILY

32–40". Elongated, somewhat compressed. Olive-brown or bluish above, shading to whitish below; diffuse wide amber stripe on side; may have dark stripe from snout through eye to 1st dorsal fin. 1st dorsal fin small; 2nd dorsal fin low, continuous on rear half of body, 1st rays highest. Mouth wide, up-turned. Schools often inspect boats. HABITAT Inshore waters, reefs; open seas to 1,200' deep. RANGE All FL. Winter: mainly s FL.

DOLPHINFISH
"Dolphin" "Dorado"
Coryphaena hippurus
DOLPHINFISH FAMILY

30–50". Elongated, compressed, tapering, deepest at nape. Male's forehead high, female's low, sloping. Head, upper body, and single long, continuous dorsal fin iridescent blue-green; yellow below; blue spots over body. Tail fin deeply forked, green or yellow. Fast surface swimmer; follows shadows of airborne flying-fish. Colors fade quickly at death. HABITAT Sea surface over deep water, rarer near shore.

RED SNAPPER
Lutjanus campechanus
SNAPPER FAMILY

23–27". Fairly deep, moderately compressed. Head large, sloping; snout fairly long; eyes red, well above and behind rear of down-slanted mouth. Head and body red, darkest on back, shading to pink on sides, white on belly. Fins reddish, sometimes edged in black; 1st and 2nd dorsal fins long, continuous; tail fin notched. Occurs in vast schools. HABITAT Over rocks and reefs 30–400' deep. RANGE Most common off Gulf Coast, esp. panhandle.

YELLOWTAIL SNAPPER
Ocyurus chrysurus
SNAPPER FAMILY

13–18". Oblong schooling fish; dorsal and ventral profiles evenly rounded. Back light blue, with yellow and reddish spots; sides and belly silvery; long, wide, yellow stripe along side from snout to tail. Dorsal fin long, continuous, yellow; tail fin deeply forked, bright yellow. Jaws up-slanted, of equal length; eyes large, yellow. HABITAT Coastal waters over reefs and rocks to 60' deep. RANGE Most common in s FL.

SPOTFIN MOJARRA
Eucinostomus argenteus
MOJARRA FAMILY

4–5″. Oblong, compressed. Snout pointed; protrusible mouth envelops invertebrates in sand; eyes conspicuous, with black pupil. Color varies with background: silvery in open water, striped greenish brown near sea-grass beds. Dorsal fin short, continuous, with notch; may have black spots; usu. folded into sheath. Tail fin deeply forked. "Hovers" in water near divers. **HABITAT** Over shallow mud and sand bottoms.

PORKFISH
Anisotremus virginicus
GRUNT FAMILY

10–13″. Deep, compressed schooling fish. Forehead and snout steep, blunt; mouth small. Adult golden or greenish with 7–10 blue stripes; 2 wide, black, vertical bands: one from top of head through eye to base of mouth, other encircling rear of head. Dorsal fin continuous, short; tail fin forked; all fins yellow. Gleans parasites from other fish. **HABITAT** Shallow water over reefs and rocks. **RANGE** Mainly s FL.

WHITE GRUNT
Haemulon plumieri
GRUNT FAMILY

11–16″. Fairly deep, compressed; dorsal profile arched. Snout long; mouth wide. Yellowish bronze; body scales whitish with pale blue centers; head covered with narrow, wavy blue lines. Dorsal fin continuous; tail fin forked. Exhibits "kissing" behavior: two fish face each other, push with mouths open. **HABITAT** Reefs, sand- and grass-bottom bays, harbors; to 115′ deep.

SHEEPSHEAD PORGY
Archosargus probatocephalus
PORGY FAMILY

24–36″. Deep, compressed. Head profile very steep; broad incisor teeth protrude from small mouth. Iridescent silvery with 5–7 thick, black, vertical bars, first on nape. Dorsal fin continuous; rays of 1st dorsal and anal fins have stout sharp spines; tail fin forked. Usu. a solitary, suspicious bottom dweller. **HABITAT** Mainland coasts in muddy shallows, under piers; some enter fresh water.

JOLTHEAD PORGY
Calamus bajonado
PORGY FAMILY

15–22″. Deep, compressed. Forehead steep; back strongly arched, tapered to rear. Color varies: scales have blue centers, brassy margins; can appear blue in open water or orangy with brown blotches near bottom. Dorsal fin low, continuous; tail fin forked. Large eyes high on head; blue line below eye; corner of mouth orange; front teeth conical. **HABITAT** Reefs, sand and sea-grass bottoms to 150′ deep.

PINFISH
Lagodon rhomboides
PORGY FAMILY

6–9″. Compressed; dorsal profile arched. Head somewhat pointed, concave between eyes. Back olive; sides mix of thin horizontal blue, green, and yellow stripes often crossed by 5–7 faint, dusky greenish bars; large dark spot at start of yellow lateral line. Dorsal fin continuous; tail fin forked. Mouth small; front teeth incisor-like. **HABITAT** Shallow grassy flats of bays, inlets, below piers; some enter rivers.

ATLANTIC CROAKER
Micropogonias undulatus
DRUM FAMILY

10–15″. Moderately elongated, compressed. Snout conical; mouth small; upper jaw projects; minute chin barbels. Grayish above, with obscure rows of brown dots; pale orange or silvery below. Fins transparent; dorsal fin continuous, with notch; tail fin squared. **HABITAT** Shallow coastal waters, estuaries. **RANGE** Year-round: Tampa and Cape Canaveral. Winter: s FL.

BLACK DRUM
Pogonias cromis
DRUM FAMILY

20–32″. Deep, somewhat compressed; profile rounded above, flat below. Forehead sloping; jaws of equal length; mouth low, horizontal; many medium-length barbels on chin. Older fish all blackish; young dark gray or silvery, with 4–5 wide black bands on back and sides. All fins slaty; dorsal fin continuous; tail fin squared. Stony teeth in throat for crushing shellfish. **HABITAT** Shallow bays, lagoons, estuaries, under piers.

RED DRUM
"Redfish" "Channel Bass"
Sciaenops ocellatus
DRUM FAMILY

26–34″. Elongated, slightly compressed; profile somewhat rounded above, straight below. Snout conical, extends over mouth; no chin barbels. Color iridescent, variable: reddish, yellowish brown, or gray; paler below; dark centers of large scales form rows of spots. Dorsal fin continuous; large black spot on tail before squarish tail fin. **HABITAT** Surf zone, piers, to open sea; sometimes in fresh water.

SPOTFIN BUTTERFLYFISH
Chaetodon ocellatus
BUTTERFLYFISH FAMILY

3–6". Deep, compressed; profile round. Forehead steep, concave near eyes; snout pointed. Body white; fins yellow; 1 wide, vertical, black band through eye; 2nd dorsal fin has large, black, oval spot at base, smaller black spot on tip (male). Young pale brown; dark brown bar through eye and at rear of body. 1st dorsal fin spiny, continuous with 2nd; tail fin fan-shaped. **HABITAT** Inshore rocky areas, coral reefs, jetties.

FOUREYE BUTTERFLYFISH
Chaetodon capistratus
BUTTERFLYFISH FAMILY

2–5". Deep, compressed; profile round, with short, pointed, yellow snout; mouth very small. Whitish or pale silvery yellow; thin black diagonal lines form chevrons at lateral line; 1 large, black, eye-like spot at base of tail; 1 wide, black, vertical band through eye. Lightly banded, continuous dorsal and anal fins appear continuous with tail fin; pelvic fins pale yellow. Occurs singly or in pairs. **HABITAT** Inshore rocky areas, coral reefs, seawalls.

QUEEN ANGELFISH
Holacanthus ciliaris
ANGELFISH FAMILY

9–12". Deep, compressed. Forehead steep, concave, with large, blue-ringed black spot at top. Blue or blue-green; orange spot on each scale gives speckled effect; large, blue-ringed black spot at base of yellow pectoral fins. Continuous dorsal and anal fins sweep back to wispy points often well past end of small, yellowish-green, fan-shaped tail fin. Mouth small. **HABITAT** Coral reefs. **RANGE** s FL.

ROCK BEAUTY
Holacanthus tricolor
ANGELFISH FAMILY

9–12". Deep, compressed. Head, front of body, tail fin yellow; rest of body covered with black, horseshoe-shaped patch; lips black. Continuous black dorsal and anal fins sweep back to wispy points with yellow-edged streamers; tail fin fan-shaped, with short streamers at top and bottom. Young all yellow ex. for single blue-ringed black spot on side. **HABITAT** Shallow rocky areas, coral reefs.

ATLANTIC SPADEFISH
Chaetodipterus faber
SPADEFISH FAMILY

12–18″. Very deep, compressed; profile round, with steep rounded forehead. Silvery white with a few thick and thin vertical black bands that fade in older fish. 1st dorsal fin tiny, spiny, rarely raised; 2nd dorsal and anal fins black-edged; lead rays of both very long, rear-facing; tail fin concave. Mouth small. Occurs in large schools. **HABITAT** Shallow waters over reefs, rocks, wrecks; under piers; mangroves.

SERGEANT MAJOR
Abudefduf saxatilis
DAMSELFISH FAMILY

4–7″. Oblong, deep, compressed. Back yellow; pale bluish white on sides and belly; forehead greenish; body crossed by 5 wide, black, vertical bars. Dorsal fins continuous; 1st low, even; 2nd triangular, swept-back (like anal fin); tail fin deeply forked. Mouth small. Swims with pectoral fins. Male guards eggs. **HABITAT** Reefs, rocks, sea-grass beds, pilings.

YELLOWTAIL DAMSELFISH
Microspathodon chrysurus
DAMSELFISH FAMILY

4–7″. Fairly deep, compressed; forehead steep. Body, head, and most fins dark brown; few blue spots above; tail fin forked, bright yellow. Continuous dorsal fin and anal fin lobed to rear. Mouth small; eyes high on head. Young mainly black, with about 20 blue spots all over; tail fin yellow. Solitary, territorial; feeds on algae as adult. **HABITAT** Reefs, rocky areas inshore or offshore; to 30′ deep.

STRIPED MULLET
Mugil cephalus
MULLET FAMILY

10–20″. Rather stout, elongated. In cross section, rounded in front, compressed to rear. Head small, flat between eyes. Back olive green; sides silvery with 6–7 thin, faint, darker, horizontal stripes; belly whitish; scales large, spiny. Dorsal fins small, triangular, well separated; tail fin large, forked. Mouth small, wide. Feeds on algae on muddy bottoms; occurs in large schools. **HABITAT** Shallow bays; enters rivers.

GREAT BARRACUDA
Sphyraena barracuda
BARRACUDA FAMILY

27–32". Elongated, robust; round in cross section. Head large pointed; top of head flat or concave; jaws massive, lower jaw longer, with large, pointed canine and shearing teeth. Green, purplish, or dark gray above, with wide blackish bars; sides silvery with a few random large black spots; belly whitish; lateral line thin, black; scales small. Dorsal fins small, triangular, widely separated; pelvic and anal fins mirror dorsal fins; tail fin large, forked. Curious; approaches divers and swimmers. Smaller ones occur in schools near shore; larger ones often solitary, live well offshore. **CAUTION** Attracted to shiny objects in silty water and to speared fish. Jaws and teeth capable of serious bites, but rarely attacks humans intentionally. **HABITAT** Over sandy bottoms; mangroves; open seas.

SPANISH HOGFISH
Bodianus rufus
WRASSE FAMILY

8–14". Moderately deep. Snout pointed; forehead slopes at 45-degree angle. Back and top half of head purplish red; sides, belly, base of broad tail, and lower jaw yellow. Dorsal fin continuous: purplish at front, yellow at rear; tail fin yellow; all fins have several elongated rays. Adult from deep water all reddish purple. Strong teeth at tips of jaws. Occurs alone or in small groups. **HABITAT** Coral and rocky reefs to 200' deep.

SLIPPERY DICK
Halichoeres bivittatus
WRASSE FAMILY

5–8". Elongated, slender; snout pointed. Pale green above. Sides silvery white, crossed by 2 horizontal stripes: upper blackish, starts on snout near eye; lower black or yellowish, thinner, starts at tiny pectoral fin. Adult male flecked with pink and blue. Dorsal fin low, continuous, with black dot at base of last ray; tail fin fan-shaped. Mouth small; teeth protrude. **HABITAT** Coral and rocky reefs, over nearby sand bottoms, pilings.

QUEEN PARROTFISH
Scarus vetula
PARROTFISH FAMILY

12–20″. Moderately deep. Head large; mouth tiny; upper jaw overhangs lower; teeth fused into small, beak-like plates. Adult male green with large reddish-edged scales and diagonal yellow and blue stripes on face. Continuous low dorsal fin and anal fin green with yellow band at bases; tail fin blue, concave. Adult female all purplish brown with 1 wide white stripe on side. Scrapes algae and bits of coral from reef. **HABITAT** Coral reefs. **RANGE** s FL.

male

female

STOPLIGHT PARROTFISH
Sparisoma viride
PARROTFISH FAMILY

10–16″. Moderately deep. Head large; mouth small; teeth fused into small, beak-like plates. Older adult male green; head blue or green with several paler blue stripes on face. Dorsal fin low, continuous, pink; tail fin concave, blue with yellow base and crescent. Adult female silvery with black-edged scales; belly orange-red; tail fin red with white base; head gray-brown with wavy black lines. **HABITAT** Coral reefs. **RANGE** s FL.

BLUE TANG
Acanthurus coeruleus
SURGEONFISH FAMILY

7–12″. Deep, compressed; profile almost round. Adult blue or light purple. Young yellow, with blue edging on dorsal and anal fins, blue eye ring. Single dorsal fin smooth-edged (not spiny), mirrors anal fin; tail fin concave; sharp yellow spine on side of tail folds forward. Eyes high on head; mouth small; lips puckered. Occurs in large schools. **CAUTION** Flesh toxic; spine causes painful wound. **HABITAT** Coral reefs, inshore grassy and rocky areas.

ATLANTIC CUTLASSFISH
Trichiurus lepturus
SNAKE MACKEREL FAMILY
24–48″. Very elongated, compressed, ribbon-like; tail tapers to a point. Lower jaw protrudes; mouth large; teeth large, fang-like. Silvery blue; lateral line low on body. Dorsal fin low, continuous; lacks pelvic fins. Voracious predator of other fish; large schools periodically invade areas. Swims with snake-like undulations. **HABITAT** Shallow bays to open seas to 1,150′ deep.

WAHOO
Acanthocybium solandri
MACKEREL FAMILY

3′8″–5′. Elongated, slender, somewhat compressed. Snout pointed; jaws elongated, beak-like, strongly toothed. Dark greenish blue above, silvery below; sides have slaty, wavy, vertical bars. Long, low 1st dorsal fin almost meets triangular 2nd dorsal fin. Tail fin large, concave, rigid; 9 dorsal and anal finlets. Often solitary; fast swimmer; feeds on other fish, squid. **HABITAT** Surface of open seas and over reefs; some inshore in clear water.

LITTLE TUNNY
"Little Tuna" "Bonito"
Euthynnus alletteratus
MACKEREL FAMILY
18–30′. Robust, slightly compressed. Snout short; lower jaw protrudes. Blue-gray above, with slaty wavy lines on midback; silvery below, with 5–10 slaty spots. Dorsal fins small, triangular, separated; 8 dorsal and 7 anal finlets; tail fin concave. Fast swimmer; most common tuna off FL; occurs in large schools. **HABITAT** Open seas; some inshore in clear water.

ATLANTIC BONITO
Sarda sarda
MACKEREL FAMILY

23–29″. Elongated, somewhat compressed. Head large; snout pointed; jaws long, heavily toothed. Steel blue above; 7–11 slanted blackish stripes on sides; silvery below. Dorsal fins triangular: 1st long, with straight profile; 2nd short; 8 dorsal and 7 anal finlets; large median keel at base of tail; tail fin crescent-like. Lateral line wavy. Large schools prey on smaller fish. **HABITAT** Surface of open seas, usually well offshore.

SPANISH MACKEREL
Scomberomorus maculatus
MACKEREL FAMILY
18–24″. Elongated, compressed. Snout short; teeth small. Iridescent dark blue-green above; 15–25 large yellowish-bronze spots on sides; silvery below; lateral line slopes evenly downward. Front of 1st dorsal fin black, rear whitish; 8–9 dorsal and anal finlets; tail fin deeply forked. Travels in large schools. **HABITAT** Surface of open coastal waters, inshore reefs, bays.

SAILFISH
Istiophorus platypterus
BILLFISH FAMILY

6–8'. Elongated, moderately compressed; tapers to rear. Nape humped; jaws rounded in cross section, end in point; upper jaw much longer, toothless. Dark blue above, silvery below; adult speckled golden on sides. 1st dorsal fin very high, sail-like, spiny-tipped, wavy in outline; dark blue with black spots. 2nd dorsal fin tiny, set far back; pectoral fins long, thick at base; pelvic fins long, slender; 2 small anal fins; tail fin black, crescent-shaped. Sail can be folded into groove on back; raised underwater when group of sailfish corral schooling fish for feeding. Very fast swimmer. **HABITAT** Open sea surface and mid-depths.

BLUE MARLIN
Makaira nigricans
BILLFISH FAMILY

5–10'. Elongated, moderately compressed, deep; tapers to rear. Head profile fairly steep; jaws rounded in cross section, end in point; upper jaw much longer. Dark blue or brown above, silvery below; 12–16 vertical, cerulean blue bars on sides. Fins dark blue; lead rays of 1st dorsal and anal fins long, pointed; 1st dorsal fin abruptly shorter rearward, covers most of back; 2nd dorsal tiny, set far back; pelvic fins long, slender; tail fin black, crescent-shaped. Very fast swimmer; feeds on tuna, bonito, squid. **HABITAT** Open sea surface and mid-depths. **RANGE** Off all coasts (uncommon). Spring: mainly east of Gulf Stream off e FL. Highly nomadic; some migrate northward in summer, others cross Atlantic to African waters.

SOUTHERN FLOUNDER
Paralichthys lethostigma
LEFTEYE FLOUNDER FAMILY

14–24". Flat, oval, with long, wedge-shaped tail fin. Head small, pointed; lower jaw protrudes; eyes on left side of head. Dorsal color matches background: olive or sandy with diffuse, dark brown blotches and spots; white below. Dorsal and anal fin bases long, continuous. Larval fish swims upright, adult on side; right eye "migrates" to upper (left) side. **HABITAT** Inshore and fresh waters over muddy bottoms. **RANGE** Mainly n and c FL.

HOGCHOKER
Trinectes maculatus
SOLE FAMILY

2½–4". Flat; a rounded rectangle. Head blunt; eyes small, close together, on right side; mouth small, wavy, with few or no teeth. Gray-brown. Adult has 7–8 thin black bars; white below; scales small, spiny. Juv. black-spotted above. Continuous dorsal and anal fins fringe body edge; tail fin stubby, rounded; lacks pectoral fins. **HABITAT** Mud, silt, and sand bottoms in shallow bays, estuaries; juv. enters rivers, often far inland.

SCRAWLED FILEFISH
Aluterus scriptus
LEATHERJACKET FAMILY

18–24″. Elongated, compressed; back concave. Head very large; snout concave; lower jaw protrudes; mouth tiny. Body and head olive-brown with diffuse darker brown patches, many cerulean blue streaks, black dots; scales tiny, sandpaper-like. 1st dorsal fin a single long white spine above high-placed eyes; 2nd dorsal and anal fins very low, long; tail fin very long, fan-shaped; lacks pelvic fins. Often swims with head down. **HABITAT** Sea-grass beds, reefs, under wharves.

QUEEN TRIGGERFISH
Balistes vetula
LEATHERJACKET FAMILY

10–20″. Compressed; oval in profile. Head large, eyes placed high; mouth small. Color varies with light and background: pale blue-green, yellowish gray, or blackish blue; chin and chest yellow-orange; bright blue band at base of tail; blue or golden streaks radiate from eye; 2 bright blue stripes run from snout to pectoral fin. Spine on 1st dorsal fin can be locked in upright position by 2nd spine; 2nd dorsal and anal fins long, 1st rays elongated; tail fin concave, with filamentous rays at top and bottom. **HABITAT** Coral and rocky reefs, pilings, jetties.

SPOTTED TRUNKFISH
Lactophrys bicaudalis
BOXFISH FAMILY

10–16″. Deep; profile rounded above, flat below; abruptly tapered at rear; triangular in cross section; encased in solid rigid carapace that allows movement of only eyes, mouth, fins, tail, rear-facing spine below. Forehead sloping; eyes large, bulbous, high on head; mouth small. Body, head, tail fin pale greenish tan, covered with round brown spots. Small single dorsal and anal fins just before tail; lacks pelvic fins; tail fin long, rounded. Slow-moving bottom feeder. **HABITAT** Shallow sea-grass beds, coral reefs.

PORCUPINEFISH
Diodon hystrix
PUFFER FAMILY

10–26″. Cylindrical; covered with spike-like spines erected when body is inflated defensively. Olive-brown above, with many black spots; whitish below. Single dorsal and anal fins small, far back on body; pectoral fins larger; tail fin rounded; all fins black-spotted. Eyes large; mouth small with parrot-like beak. Crushes hard-shelled invertebrates. **HABITAT** Shallow bays and reefs to 50′ deep.

LONGNOSE GAR
Lepisosteus osseus
GAR FAMILY

24–32″. Cylindrical. Head slender; snout very long, spear-like; teeth needle-like. Olive-brown above; black spots on sides, heaviest toward rear; white below; scales thick. Single dorsal and anal fins small, rounded, close to rounded tail fin. Floats near surface. **HABITAT** Fresh and brackish rivers, marshy saltwater channels, swamps, lakes. **RANGE** Panhandle; peninsular FL south to Sebring area. **Florida Gar** *(L. platyrhincus)* has larger black spots; peninsular FL south through Everglades.

BOWFIN
Amia calva
BOWFIN FAMILY

15–25″. Cylindrical, robust. Head large; jaws heavily toothed; bony plates on head and lower jaw; nostrils tubular. Olive green above; dark and light brown net-like pattern on sides; creamy below. Single dorsal fin low, very long, wavy-edged; tail fin rounded, banded; male has gold-ringed, eye-like black spot at upper base of tail. Skeleton is of bone and cartilage; has gills and lungs, can breathe air. **HABITAT** Clear quiet ponds, swamps, rivers with vegetation.

AMERICAN EEL
Anguilla rostrata
FRESHWATER EEL FAMILY

20–32″. Long, snake-like; in cross section, round in front, flattened to rear; scales tiny, deeply embedded in skin. Gray-brown or yellowish brown above and on sides; paler below. Dorsal fin begins before anal fin; both low, continuous with tail fin; pectoral fins small. Male prefers brackish waters; female swims far up rivers for 8–20 years before trip back to spawn and die. **HABITAT** Rivers, estuaries, open seas.

GOLDFISH
Carassius auratus
CARP AND MINNOW FAMILY

4–16″. Fairly deep, robust. Color varies: olive, gold, orange, or white. Single dorsal fin and anal fin each have a heavy lead spine that tapers to rear; tail fin forked. Mouth small; no barbels on lower jaw. Native to China; common in home aquariums; often released. **HABITAT** Heavily vegetated artificial pools and natural ponds.

GRASS CARP
Ctenopharyngodon idella
CARP AND MINNOW FAMILY

24–32″. Elongated, robust. Head smooth, blunt, broad; snout short; jaws short, oblique. Back olive-brown; sides silvery; belly whitish; scales black-edged, patterned like a fish net. Single dorsal fin short-based, on midback; tail fin has 2 large rounded lobes. Eats own weight daily. Introduced from Asia as weed controller and food fish; destroys habitat for other organisms. **HABITAT** Rivers, ponds, reservoirs. **RANGE** Mainly near developed areas (local).

YELLOW BULLHEAD
Ameiurus natalis
BULLHEAD CATFISH FAMILY

8–12″. Robust, heavy-looking. Back dark olive-brown; sides yellowish tan; belly pale yellow. Single dorsal fin rounded; fleshy adipose fin; anal fin long, rounded; tail fin straight, not forked, with rounded corners. Head long; eyes small; 4 pairs of barbels, upper 2 black, lower 2 white or yellow. Searches muddy bottoms at night for prey. **HABITAT** Slow, well-vegetated river bottoms, ponds, lakes.

BROWN BULLHEAD
"Speckled Catfish"
Ameiurus nebulosus
BULLHEAD CATFISH FAMILY

8–12″. Elongated, robust. Back and sides brown, heavily mottled, with darker brown blotches; belly whitish. Fins dusky; single dorsal fin narrow, high, rounded; adipose fin; anal fin long, low; tail fin square to slightly notched. 4 pairs of dark barbels flank mouth. **HABITAT** Mud-bottomed lakes, streams.

CHANNEL CATFISH
Ictalurus punctatus
BULLHEAD CATFISH FAMILY

18–30″. Elongated, slender. Back blue-gray; sides tan or silvery blue with few scattered blackish spots; belly white; lateral line straight. Single dorsal fin short, high, rounded; adipose fin; anal fin long, with rounded outer edge; tail fin forked. Head long; upper jaw overhangs lower; 4 pairs of barbels, upper 2 black, lower ones white. **HABITAT** Flowing rivers with clear bottoms; lakes and ponds. **RANGE** South to Ft. Myers and Palm Beach.

WALKING CATFISH
Clarias batrachus
LABYRINTH CATFISH FAMILY

10–14″. Elongated; in cross section, round in front, compressed to rear. Olive-brown, darker above; pinkish white in albino morph. Continuous long dorsal fin (male's has black spots); anal fin long, low; tail fin small, fan-shaped. Head small, pointed; 4 pairs of barbels. Can breathe air in lung-like sacs; enters new waters via wriggling "walk" overland on stiffened pectoral fins for several days. Introduced from se Asia in 1968; threatens native fish food supply; spreading rapidly. **HABITAT** Lakes, swamps, canals. **RANGE** s peninsular FL.

CHAIN PICKEREL
Esox niger
PIKE FAMILY

12–25". Elongated, moderately compressed; snout long, concave above; mouth wide. Olive to yellowish brown; sides covered with darker brown markings resembling interlocking chains; dark vertical bar under yellow eye. Single dorsal fin and anal fin both placed far back; tail fin deeply forked; all fins plain dusky. **HABITAT** Weedy lakes, swamps, and stream pools.

MOSQUITOFISH
Gambusia holbrooki
LIVEBEARER FAMILY

¾–1½". Male pencil-shaped, shorter than robust female; both compressed. Pale olive-brown above; sides silvery; pale yellow below; scales dark-edged in net-like pattern. 1–3 rows of black spots on single dorsal fin and rounded tail fin. Snout high on flat forehead; mouth up-slanted; distinct black "tear-drop" below eye. Female gives birth to 3–4 annual broods of 200 or more fully formed young. **HABITAT** Ponds, lakes, drainage ditches, sluggish streams, brackish waters.

REDBREAST SUNFISH
Lepomis auritus
SUNFISH FAMILY

7–9". Oblong, compressed. Dark olive green above; sides pale yellow with small red dots; belly reddish, especially forward; lateral line complete, arched. 1st dorsal fin spiny, adjacent to rounded 2nd dorsal fin; tail fin long, forked. Head olive with thin wavy blue lines; eyes large, red; mouth small; gill cover long, narrow, black. **HABITAT** Flowing streams with open bottoms, ponds, lakes. **RANGE** n FL.

REDEAR SUNFISH
"Shellcracker"
Lepomis microlophus
SUNFISH FAMILY

6–14". Oblong, compressed. Back dark olive green with brown specks; sides pale green; belly white or yellow-orange; lateral line complete, arched. 1st dorsal fin spiny, adjacent to rounded 2nd dorsal fin; pectoral fins long, pointed; tail fin forked, lobes rounded. Eyes large, red; mouth small; gill cover flap round, black and red. Crushes snails with molar-like teeth. **HABITAT** Warm springs, stream pools, vegetated lakes and ponds.

LARGEMOUTH BASS
Micropterus salmoides
SUNFISH FAMILY

13–20″. Elongated, with large head; mouth extends to point below rear of eye. Dark green above; sides olive green with brownish mottling; belly whitish. Dark mid-lateral band disappears with age. 1st dorsal fin spiny; 2nd dorsal fin rounded; tail fin slightly forked. **HABITAT** Warm shallow waters with vegetation.

BLUEGILL
Lepomis macrochirus
SUNFISH FAMILY

7–10″. Oval, extremely compressed. Olive above, with 5–9 vertical dusky green bands; male orange below, with blue gills; female whitish below. Dark spot on rear of single dorsal fin; tail fin slightly forked. Gill cover deep blue with black edge. **HABITAT** Shallow vegetated lakeshores, stream pools.

BLACK CRAPPIE
Pomoxis nigromaculatus
SUNFISH FAMILY

7–10″. Oval, extremely compressed; forehead concave; lower jaw protrudes. Pale brown or sooty green, heavily mottled with dark brown spots. Single dorsal fin and anal fin large, rounded, begin with 6–8 spines; tail fin forked; most fins distinctly spotted. **HABITAT** Ponds, warm streams.

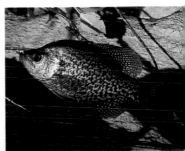

MOZAMBIQUE TILAPIA
Tilapia mossambica
CICHLID FAMILY

10–15″. Deep, compressed. Forehead concave, sloping; mouth small. Back and sides dark olive fading to yellowish on belly. Continuous dorsal fin and anal fin long, pointed toward rear, speckled green and black; tail fin ends in straight line. Breeding male: blacker; mouth swollen, blue; lower jaw white; tail fin edged in red. Accidentally introduced from se Africa; now competes with native fish for prey. **HABITAT** Slow vegetated streams, canals, ponds. **RANGE** Peninsular FL; most common in south.

Amphibians

The ancestors of today's amphibians began evolving from fish about 300 million years ago. Members of the class Amphibia typically start life in fresh water and later live on land. Most undergo metamorphosis (a series of developmental stages) from aquatic, water-breathing larvae to terrestrial or partly terrestrial, air-breathing adults. The most primitive of terrestrial vertebrates, amphibians lack claws and external ear openings. They have thin, moist, scaleless skin and are cold-blooded; their body temperature varies with that of their surroundings. In colder months, they burrow deep into leaf litter, soft soils, and the mud of ponds, and maintain an inactive state. Unlike reptiles, amphibians can become dehydrated in dry environments and must live near water at least part of the year and for breeding. Their eggs lack shells, and most are laid in water. Florida has more amphibian and reptilian species (139 native, 27 introduced) than any other state in the country.

Salamanders

Salamanders, members of the order Caudata, have blunt rounded heads, long slender bodies, short legs, and long tails. Most lay eggs in fresh water that hatch into four-legged larvae with tufted external gills; after several months or years, the larvae typically lose their gills and go ashore. Members of the siren family, however, retain their gills and are aquatic their entire lives, while most lungless salamanders lay eggs on land and skip the gilled larval stage; adults breathe through their skin. During all life stages, salamanders eat small animal life. Most are voiceless and generally hard to see, as they feed under wet leaves and logs. Salamanders differ from lizards, which are reptiles, in having thin moist skin (lizards have scales) and four toes on the front feet (lizards have five), and in their lack of claws and external ear openings. Salamanders, like frogs, are fast declining in number worldwide, due to habitat destruction and perhaps acid rain, pesticides, and increasing ultraviolet light.

The size given for salamanders is the typical length from the tip of the nose to the end of the tail.

GREATER SIREN
Siren lacertina
SIREN FAMILY
20″. Stout, eel-like; head rounded from above, pointed in side view; eyes tiny; gills external; legs tiny, behind gills; hindlimbs absent; tail compressed, fringed by fin, tip rounded. Olive-gray to brown, flecked with greenish yellow. Eats snails, insects, small fish, bait. **HABITAT** Shallow fresh waters with weeds, muddy bottoms. **ACTIVITY** Nocturnal.

DWARF SALAMANDER
Eurycea quadridigitata
LUNGLESS SALAMANDER FAMILY

3″. Slender; head small, blackish; eyes bulbous; snout blunt; tail very long, thin; 4 toes on each foot (most salamanders have 5 on hindfeet). Body and tail pale orange-brown or olive above, black on sides. Usu. hidden. **HABITAT** Beds of pine needles; under moist logs, sphagnum mats; pond margins. **ACTIVITY** Day and night. **RANGE** c and s FL.

SLIMY SALAMANDER
Plethodon glutinosus
LUNGLESS SALAMANDER FAMILY

6″. Slender; head blunt, black; eyes bulbous; tail medium length. Body and tail shiny black, with tiny silvery flecks above, large yellow spots on sides. Excretes glue-like slime, deterring predators and handlers. Eats earthworms, slugs. **HABITAT** Woods: moist rotting logs, burrows, leaf litter. **ACTIVITY** Mainly nocturnal. **RANGE** n FL south to Tampa area.

Frogs

Adult frogs and toads (order Anura) have large heads and eyes, and wide, usually toothless mouths; they appear neckless, and most lack tails. Many can rapidly extend a long tongue for capturing insects. They have two long muscular hindlegs and two smaller front legs. All must keep their skin moist and avoid drying out in the sun. In colder parts of Florida, frogs hibernate in winter in the mud at the bottom of ponds or under tree bark, while in the extreme south many remain active all year. The male vocalizes to attract the larger female, and clings to her while fertilizing eggs as she lays them, usually in water. The eggs hatch into round-bodied, long-tailed aquatic larvae called tadpoles or pollywogs, which begin life with external gills that are soon covered with skin. The tadpole later transforms into a tail-less ground, tree, or marsh dweller with air-breathing lungs. Members of the spadefoot family (Pelobatidae) have a hard spade on their hindfeet to facilitate burrowing; they breed in fish-free puddles after very heavy rains, and develop from egg to tadpole to frog in only two weeks. Coquis (Leptodactylidae) lay eggs on land that hatch directly into miniature frogs. Members of the toad family (Bufonidae) have shorter legs for hopping and warty skin that secretes poisons that cause irritations. On each side of the neck or behind the eyes, toads have large glandular structures, called parotoid glands, that produce mucus. In the treefrog family (Hylidae), tadpoles live in water and adults live in trees; treefrogs have suction pads on their toes for clinging to vertical surfaces. The true frogs (Ranidae) are large, with slim waists, long legs, pointed toes, and webs on their hindfeet; most live in or near water and are good jumpers. Like salamanders, frogs are fast declining in number worldwide.

Frogs and toads have excellent hearing and vocal capabilities. Their well-developed ears feature a conspicuous external eardrum, a round disk located behind the eye. In warmer months, most male frogs and toads announce their presence with loud vocalizations that vary from species to species. When calling, the animals rapidly inflate and deflate balloon-like vocal sacs on the throat that amplify the sound. Calls are primarily used during the breeding season to attract mates; some species, like the Bronze Frog, give calls to defend feeding territories long after breeding. On warm nights, one can often hear a chorus of sounds made by several species of frogs.

The size given for frogs is the typical length from the tip of the nose to the end of the body.

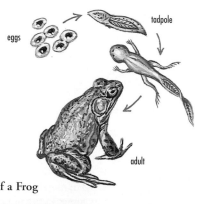

Life Cycle of a Frog

EASTERN SPADEFOOT
Scaphiopus holbrookii
SPADEFOOT FAMILY

2″. Face blunt, rounded; eyes large, bulbous, brassy, vertically oriented; fine teeth on upper jaw; ridges behind eyes. Hindfeet have black, sickle-shaped spade at heels. Skin smooth; olive or brown above, with small orange-tipped warts; whitish below. **CAUTION** Skin secretions can irritate eyes, skin. **VOICE** Low explosive *quonnks*. **HABITAT** Loose sand or loam in open woods. **ACTIVITY** Nocturnal. **RANGE** All FL, ex. Keys.

GREENHOUSE FROG
Eleutherodactylus planirostris
COQUI FAMILY

1″. Tiny. Skin rough; reddish to sandy brown overall; back and sides striped or spotted dark brown. Attracted to lawns with sprinklers. Introduced from West Indies; now most common frog in many areas. **VOICE** 1–6 bird-like chirps. **HABITAT** Woods, farms, gardens. **ACTIVITY** Nocturnal. **RANGE** All FL, ex. panhandle.

GIANT TOAD
"Marine Toad"
Bufo marinus
TOAD FAMILY

5". Snout blunt; ridge between eyes; parotoid glands large, swollen, extend from behind eyes onto sides. Skin rough; brown to yellow-brown; large, irreg., dark brown spots and small creamy spots on spiny warts above and on legs. Introduced from S. Amer. to eat insects; now a nuisance. **CAUTION** Toxic if eaten by animals; skin secretions can inflame human eyes, skin. **VOICE** Low trill, like idling engine. **HABITAT** Fields, farms, watersides, towns. **ACTIVITY** Mainly nocturnal. **RANGE** se FL.

OAK TOAD
Bufo quercicus
TOAD FAMILY

1". Skin rough; light brown to blackish overall; paired large, dark brown splotches and small rusty warts above; yellow-orange line from snout to rump. Snout blunt; parotoid gland swollen, oval. **VOICE** Loud, high-pitched *cheep*s from water. **HABITAT** Sandy oak scrub and pine flatlands. **ACTIVITY** By day.

SOUTHERN TOAD
Bufo terrestris
TOAD FAMILY

3". Skin rough; usu. brown overall; darker brown blotches and rusty warts above; some have creamy or reddish stripe on back. 2 swept-back ridges between eyes; parotoid glands swollen, kidney-shaped. **VOICE** Loud, long, high-pitched trill. **HABITAT** Mostly in sandy pine and oak woods. **ACTIVITY** Nocturnal.

SOUTHERN CRICKET FROG
Acris gryllus dorsalis
TREEFROG FAMILY

1". Snout pointed; legs long; feet partly webbed; toes have large pads. Skin rough; solid or mottled brown, gray, or olive above; many have bright green or orangy stripe on back, dark arrowhead on nape; white below. **VOICE** Continual *click-click-click*. **HABITAT** Swamps, watersides, woods, fields. **ACTIVITY** By day.

GREEN TREEFROG
Hyla cinerea
TREEFROG FAMILY

2". Legs long, slender. Skin smooth, usu. bright green above, some with long white stripe on side; yellowish below. Feeds along branches, on windows; great leaper. **VOICE** Continual cowbell-like *quaink*, often in chorus, with frogs singing at different pitches. **HABITAT** Waterside vegetation, towns. **ACTIVITY** Nocturnal.

PINE WOODS TREEFROG
Hyla femoralis
TREEFROG FAMILY

1½". Skin granular; rich or pale brown or gray, with dark brown blotches; may show blackish line from nostril through eye and on side; whitish below; underside of thighs black with golden spots. Toe pads large. **VOICE** Low raspy notes in early evening. **HABITAT** Pinewoods near water. **ACTIVITY** Nocturnal.

BARKING TREEFROG
Hyla gratiosa
TREEFROG FAMILY

2½". Skin granular; green, greenish brown, or yellowish green with brown spots; whitish line from upper lip onto side. Snout rounded; toe pads large. **VOICE** Bell-like mating call from watersides; 10 loud barks from treetops in rain. **HABITAT** Treetops most of year. **ACTIVITY** Nocturnal; burrows in cold weather.

SQUIRREL TREEFROG
Hyla squirella
TREEFROG FAMILY

1½". Skin smooth, shiny; color can change rapidly: green or brown, plain or with few small dark spots; may have yellow upper lip stripe. Nose blunt; toe pads large. **VOICE** Nasal trill near water when mating; rapid chatter in trees in rain. **HABITAT** Woods, thickets, gardens. **ACTIVITY** Nocturnal.

CUBAN TREEFROG
Osteopilus septentrionalis
TREEFROG FAMILY

5". Skin warty; gray, brown, or dull green; may have dark brown splotches. Nostrils raised; toe pads large. Attracted to lights on billboards, buildings. Introduced from Cuba in 1800s. **VOICE** Snore of varying pitch. **HABITAT** Woods, gardens. **ACTIVITY** Nocturnal. **RANGE** Sarasota and Melbourne south to Keys.

GOPHER FROG
Rana capito aesopus
TRUE FROG FAMILY

4". Skin granular. FL race (Florida Gopher Frog) dusky gray to creamy brown above, with sides and legs silvery white; all covered with large oval brown spots; lips, ridges on sides of back peppered yellow; chin white with brown spots. Snout rounded; legs shortish. **VOICE** Deep snore; choruses sound like surf. **HABITAT** Open woods or scrub with well-drained soils. **ACTIVITY** Nocturnal. By day, rests near or in burrow of Gopher Tortoise or large mammal. **RANGE** c and s FL.

BULLFROG
Rana catesbeiana
TRUE FROG FAMILY

6". Head large, rounded; ridge from eye to eardrum; midback bulge. Yellowish green above, with dark mottling; pale yellow below. Legs dark-banded; feet mainly webbed. **VOICE** Deep resonant *jug-o-rum.* **HABITAT** Marshes, ponds, rivers. **ACTIVITY** Day and night. **RANGE** South to Ft. Myers, Melbourne.

BRONZE FROG
"Green Frog"
Rana clamitans
TRUE FROG FAMILY

2¾". Bulging ridges down to midback. Solid brown above, few brown spots on sides; belly pale yellow. Legs long, banded dark brown. Hindfeet partly webbed. **VOICE** 1–2 notes, like a plucked banjo string. **HABITAT** Streamsides, swamps, wet woods. **ACTIVITY** Mainly nocturnal. **RANGE** n half of FL.

PIG FROG
Rana grylio
TRUE FROG FAMILY

4". Snout pointed. Skin granular; olive to greenish brown, some with small spots; lower jaw and undersides yellow with light brown netting; legs mottled brown. Hindfeet webbed, ex. tip of longest toe. **VOICE** Pig-like grunt; chorus like low roar. **HABITAT** Marshes, lily pads, shorelines. **ACTIVITY** Mainly nocturnal.

SOUTHERN LEOPARD FROG
Rana utricularia
TRUE FROG FAMILY

3". Head narrow; snout pointed. Skin granular; green to brown, with few brown spots; whitish ridges along sides; white line below eyes. Legs long; toes of hindfeet free of webbing. **VOICE** Guttural trill. **HABITAT** Freshwater shores, brackish marshes, woods, grasslands. **ACTIVITY** Mainly nocturnal.

Reptiles

Members of the class Reptilia are cold-blooded, like amphibians. Their body temperature varies with that of their surroundings; reptilian activities come to a halt in cold weather, when they hibernate alone or in communal dens. Florida has members of three reptile orders: turtles, snakes and lizards, and crocodiles. The reptilian body is low-slung and has a long tail and, except for the snakes and a few lizards, four short legs. Unlike the thin-skinned amphibians, reptiles are covered with protective scales (some of which are modified into plates in turtles) that waterproof their bodies and also help keep them from becoming dehydrated. They breathe via lungs. All breed on land and mate via internal fertilization. Their eggs have brittle or leathery shells; some give birth to live young.

Turtles

Members of the order Testudines, turtles are the oldest living group of reptiles, dating back to the time of the earliest dinosaurs. The upper part of their characteristic bony shell is the carapace, the lower part the plastron; both parts are covered with hard plates called scutes. Some species have ridges, called keels, on the carapace and tail. Most can withdraw the head and legs inside the shell for protection. Turtles are the only toothless reptiles, but their horny beaks have sharp biting edges. Aquatic species have flipper-like legs. The exposed skin of turtles is scaly and dry. Most, especially aquatic turtles, spend hours basking in the sun. From November to February, some northern Florida turtles hibernate. All turtles lay eggs; most dig a hollow, lay the eggs, cover them up, and leave them alone. When the eggs hatch, the young claw their way to the surface and fend for themselves. The size given for turtles is the length of the carapace of a typical adult.

Parts of a Turtle

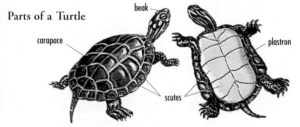

COMMON MUD TURTLE
Kinosternon subrubrum
MUSK AND MUD TURTLE FAMILY

4″. Carapace oval, highly domed, smooth, smooth-edged, keel-less; solid blackish brown. Plastron has 2 hinges that close shell to protect soft parts. Head blackish, with 2 thin yellow lines. Aquatic, but wanders away from water. Secretes foul fluid from glands under carapace. **HABITAT** Salt and fresh marshes, ponds, islets. **ACTIVITY** Mainly by day.

COMMON MUSK TURTLE
"Stinkpot"
Sternothaerus odoratus
MUSK AND MUD TURTLE FAMILY

5″. Carapace highly domed; brown, with large scutes. Plastron small, buffy. Head large, pointed, black, with yellow stripes; neck long. Tail short, fat. Has offensive musky smell. **CAUTION** Male aggressive; will bite. **HABITAT** Sluggish streams and ponds. **ACTIVITY** Mainly by day; basks on logs and low trees.

SNAPPING TURTLE
Chelydra serpentina
SNAPPING TURTLE FAMILY

15". Carapace oval, somewhat domed; smooth or with 3 rows of keels, with central keel heavier; trailing edge jagged; black or dark brown. Plastron cross-shaped, yellowish. Head massive, neck long. Tail as long as carapace, with sawtoothed keels. FL race has small pointed knobs on neck. Excellent swimmer; rarely leaves water except for nesting. **CAUTION** Powerful jaws can give a serious bite. **HABITAT** Fresh waters with mucky bottoms. **ACTIVITY** Day and night. **Alligator Snapping Turtle** (*Macroclemys temmincki*) one of world's largest freshwater turtles (22"); occurs in panhandle; has bumpier carapace keels and heavier beak; lacks tail keels.

CHICKEN TURTLE
Deirochelys reticularia
POND AND BOX TURTLE FAMILY

6". Carapace oval, domed; olive-brown, with net-like orange, yellow, or greenish lines; edged in orange. Plastron yellow or orange. Yellow stripes on legs, long brown neck. **HABITAT** Shallow, fresh waters. **ACTIVITY** Mainly by day; basks on logs.

DIAMONDBACK TERRAPIN
Malaclemys terrapin
POND AND BOX TURTLE FAMILY

Female 8"; male 5". Carapace oval; central keel. Plastron creamy yellow. FL east coast race: carapace blackish. Gulf coast race (pictured): carapace scutes dark brown with orange centers. **HABITAT** Salt marshes, tidal flats, lagoons. **ACTIVITY** Mainly by day.

RIVER COOTER
Pseudemys (Chrysemys) concinna
POND AND BOX TURTLE FAMILY

10". Carapace oval, domed; black, brown, or olive; fine yellowish rings on scutes. Plastron yellow or orange. Head and legs blackish, with yellow stripes. **HABITAT** Springs, rivers, turtle-grass beds. **ACTIVITY** Mainly by day; basks on logs. **RANGE** Panhandle and Gulf coast south to Tampa Bay.

COMMON COOTER
Pseudemys (Chrysemys) floridana
POND AND BOX TURTLE FAMILY

12". Carapace oval, domed; brownish, with fine yellowish markings. Plastron yellow, with dark smudges where it joins carapace. Head blackish with yellow stripes. **HABITAT** Springs, vegetated fresh waters. **ACTIVITY** Mainly by day; basks. **RANGE** South to n edge of Everglades.

FLORIDA REDBELLY TURTLE
Pseudemys (Chrysemys) nelsoni
POND AND BOX TURTLE FAMILY

10″. Carapace round, domed; black with few light reddish-brown bars; edge yellowish. Plastron reddish. Head blackish with narrow yellow stripes, 1 arrow-shaped on snout. Feet, tail black with yellow stripes. **HABITAT** Fresh waters, mangrove-lined creeks. **ACTIVITY** Mainly by day; basks. **RANGE** c and s FL.

SLIDER
Trachemys scripta
POND AND BOX TURTLE FAMILY

8″. Carapace round, domed. FL race black, with vertical yellow band on each side scute. Plastron yellow with dark smudges. Head black, with yellow stripes below and yellow ear patch. Legs, tail black with yellow stripes. **HABITAT** Fresh waters with soft bottoms, vegetation. **ACTIVITY** Mainly by day; basks. **RANGE** n FL.

FLORIDA SOFTSHELL TURTLE
Trionyx ferox
SOFTSHELL TURTLE FAMILY

Female 16″; male 8″. Carapace fairly flat, nearly round, knobbed in front; has leathery, dark brown skin with olive-brown rings; edge pale yellow-orange. Plastron smooth, flat, gray. Head brown with orange streaks; snout narrow, tubular. Feet webbed. **HABITAT** Lakes, ponds, canals. **ACTIVITY** By day; floats on water; basks.

GOPHER TORTOISE
Gopherus polyphemus
TORTOISE FAMILY

12″. Carapace oval, domed, sides nearly vertical; gray, brown, or tan; scutes grooved in rings. Plastron yellowish. Forelegs flattened for digging; hindlegs round; claws strong. Terrestrial; excavates burrows in sandy soils. **HABITAT** Open woods, scrub, grasslands. **ACTIVITY** By day. **RANGE** Most of FL; very local in s FL.

Marine Turtles

Marine turtles are large turtles with low tapered shells and limbs modified into powerful flippers. Two families are represented in Florida: the sea turtles and the leatherbacks. Members of both families mate in shallow water off nesting beaches (though not all species covered below nest in Florida). From April through September, females come ashore at night to lay eggs. They dig nest holes above the high-tide line with their hind flippers, deposit a clump of between 50 and 175 eggs, depending on the species, then cover them with sand. Several weeks later, the young emerge all at once, at night, and march across the sand to the ocean with no parental ontact. Some are lost on the beach to predators, such as crabs and raccoons; others are drawn inland by lights. Survivors spend their lives at sea, feeding underwater day and night, and surfacing for air. They return many years later to their ancestral beach to breed. All species are declining in number and are now protected.

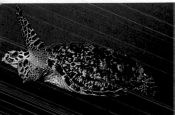

LOGGERHEAD
Caretta caretta
SEA TURTLE FAMILY

3′. Carapace elongated, heart-shaped, with 3 lines of knobby keels, 1 knob per scute; older individuals smoother, with central keel only; dark reddish brown. Plastron creamy yellow. Head large, with dark brown scales on top; beak pointed. Skin light yellow. Scales of flippers dark brown, edged with yellow skin. Most common sea turtle in FL. **HABITAT** Oceans, bays, estuaries.

GREEN TURTLE
Chelonia mydas
SEA TURTLE FAMILY

4′. Carapace broad, oval, unkeeled; light or dark brown, plain or lightly mottled (species named for its green fat). Plastron creamy yellow. Head large, with olive-brown scales on top; beak pointed. Skin white or light yellow. Scales of flippers dark brown, edged with yellow skin. **HABITAT** Shallow ocean waters rich in marine plants. **RANGE** Nests mainly on c Atlantic coast between Cape Canaveral and Palm Beach.

ATLANTIC RIDLEY
"Kemp's Ridley"
Lepidochelys kempii
SEA TURTLE FAMILY

26″. Carapace rounded, with jagged rear; smooth, with very reduced keel; pale olive green. Plastron double-keeled, yellowish white. Head rounded; skin olive. Tail of male extends beyond shell. Eats crabs, mollusks, fish. Endangered by shrimp boat nets. Nests in Mexico and Texas. **HABITAT** Shallow coastal waters. **RANGE** Most common off Gulf coast.

LEATHERBACK
Dermochelys coriacea
LEATHERBACK SEA TURTLE FAMILY

7′. World's largest turtle. Carapace elongated, oblong to teardrop-shaped, with 7 high keels; covered with smooth, leathery, slate to blue-black skin. Plastron white, with 5 keels. Flippers very long. Male has concave plastron; tail longer than hindlegs. Backward-pointing spine line mouth and esophagus to aid holding and swallowing its m food, slippery jellyfish. Endang **HABITAT** Oceans, bays, estu **RANGE** Off both coasts (rare)

Lizards

Lizards (suborder Sauria of the scaled reptile order, Squamata) generally have long tails; most species have legs and are capable of running, climbing, and clinging, although in some the legs are tiny or lacking. Geckos have myriad microscopic bristles and tiny suction cups on their toe pads, which enable them to cling to walls, glass, and ceilings. Typical lizards resemble salamanders but can be distinguished from them by their dry scaly skin, clawed feet, and external ear openings. Lizard species vary greatly in size, shape, and color; in many, colors and patterns differ among adult males, adult females, and young. Most lizards are active by day (though most geckos are nocturnal), and many are particularly active in the midday heat. Most do not swim in water. None in Florida are poisonous. Fertilization is internal; most lay eggs rather than give birth to live young. The size given for lizards is the typical length from the tip of the snout to the end of the tail.

GREEN ANOLE
Anolis carolinensis
IGUANID FAMILY

7″. Anoles: slender; snout long, wedge-shaped; change color in response to light, temperature, emotions; brown or brown and green, occ. spotted. This species: body, head, sides green; white below. Male has pink throat fan. Toes padded; tail long, thin. FL's most common anole. **HABITAT** Trees, shrubs, vines, fences, walls. **ACTIVITY** By day.

BROWN ANOLE
Anolis sagrei
IGUANID FAMILY

7″. Slender; snout short, pointed. Changes from light to dark brown. Male back has dark stripe, rows of yellow dots, pale ridge from nape to top of tail; yellow or reddish-orange throat fan with white edge (shows as white streak when not extended). Female back has yellow stripe. **HABITAT** Below trees, shrubs. **ACTIVITY** By day. **RANGE** Tampa Bay and Palm Beach south.

GREEN IGUANA
Iguana iguana
IGUANID FAMILY

5′. Stout; head large; snout blunt; low crest along back. All green (young) or green with wide brown or blue-green bands; large black-edged scale below ear; extensible throat fan. Tail long, tapering. Can run upright on hindlegs. Looks frightening but is docile vegetarian. Introduced from Cen. Amer. **HABITAT** Large trees, grassy areas, towns. **ACTIVITY** By day. **RANGE** Miami, Boca Grande, other areas.

CARINATE CURLY-TAILED LIZARD
Leiocephalus carinatus
IGUANID FAMILY

9". Slender. Grayish brown with stripes of darker spots; yellow line from upper jaw down side of back. Tail narrow, banded dark brown. Scampers across ground or up trees with tail curled over back like a scorpion. Introduced from Bahamas. **HABITAT** Open woods, beaches, gardens. **ACTIVITY** By day. **RANGE** se FL.

EASTERN FENCE LIZARD
Sceloporus undulatus
IGUANID FAMILY

6". Slender; head blunt; scales rough. Gray, with dark brown side stripe. Male has bright blue patches on sides of belly and throat. Female has wavy dark crossbars on back, bluish wash below. Feeds mainly in trees. **HABITAT** Fences, stumps, trees, open pinewoods, fields. **ACTIVITY** By day. **RANGE** South to Tampa Bay.

FLORIDA SCRUB LIZARD
Sceloporus woodi
IGUANID FAMILY

5". Slender; scales spiny. Male gray above; blackish stripe on side, bright blue patches on side of belly; throat black with median white stripe and blue spots. Female gray above, with 7–10 wavy chevrons, wider blackish side stripe, bluish wash below. Feeds mainly on ground. **HABITAT** Sandy, scrubby pine-oak areas, sand dunes. **ACTIVITY** By day. **RANGE** Peninsular FL (local).

MEDITERRANEAN GECKO
Hemidactylus turcicus
GECKO FAMILY

5". Slender. Snout short, rounded; eyes large, lack eyelids. Translucent grayish or buffy with light pink and dark brown spots; belly pale yellow; raised white spots on sides. Tail long; toes unwebbed. Introduced from Mediterranean area; spreading. **VOICE** High-pitched, mouse-like squeak. **HABITAT** Building walls, lights. **ACTIVITY** Nocturnal. **RANGE** Gainesville to Key West.

REEF GECKO
Sphaerodactylus notatus
GECKO FAMILY

2". Chubby, elongated. Snout pointed, flattened. Back scales keeled, rough. Male brown, flecked with tiny black dots; female simila but with darker brown stripes. T round; toes round-tipped. Scur out of leaf litter to hide when turbed. Smallest N. Amer. ? **HABITAT** Leaf litter, palm grov dens. **ACTIVITY** Mainly daw **RANGE** Ft. Lauderdale to K

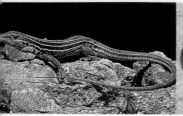

SIX-LINED RACERUNNER
Cnemidophorus sexlineatus
WHIPTAIL AND RACERUNNER FAMILY

8″. Slender; snout wedge-shaped, pointed; tail long, thin, whip-like. Head, body, and sides of tail dark brown, with 6–7 thin golden stripes; belly scales large, rectangular. Throat and belly blue-green in male, white in female. Tail mainly brown in adult, blue in young. Very fast in fleeing danger. **HABITAT** Open woods, grasslands. **ACTIVITY** By day; basks often.

BROADHEAD SKINK
Eumeces laticeps
SKINK FAMILY

11″. Stocky. Male plain olive-brown; head broad, triangular, turns reddish in breeding season. Female dark brown with 2 bold yellow stripes on side, thin yellow stripe down back; head smaller. Young black, with yellow stripes and blue tail. Feeds low or high in trees. **HABITAT** Woods, rubble piles. **ACTIVITY** By day. **RANGE** South to Orlando.

SOUTHEASTERN FIVE-LINED SKINK
Eumeces inexpectatus
SKINK FAMILY

7″. Long, cylindrical; scales smooth, sleek; legs small. Adult uniformly brown or with 4–5 thin golden stripes above, middle one narrower. Breeding male has red face, throat. Young (pictured) blacker; golden stripes merge into blue on tail. Feeds on ground or in trees; coils up inside wet log in cold spells. **CAUTION** Can sicken cats if eaten. **HABITAT** Woods, grassy areas, barrier islands. **ACTIVITY** By day. **RANGE** All FL, incl. Dry Tortugas.

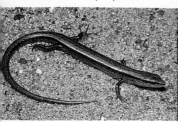

GROUND SKINK
Scincella lateralis
SKINK FAMILY

5″. Very slender; head small; legs very small; tail very long and thin. Adult reddish brown above; black stripe on side; belly washed bluish with yellow under. Young has blue-gray tail. window in movable lower eyelet light in, keeps dirt out. Avoids quirms like a snake when flee **AT** Leaf litter of woods, gar **ITY** By day.

EASTERN GLASS LIZARD
Ophisaurus ventralis
ANGUID LIZARD FAMILY

3′. Slender, legless, snake-like, but has eyelids, external ear openings. All ages look white-speckled. Adult black with greenish wash; yellow below. Young brown above, black on sides, buffy below. Tail breaks off in predator's grasp; can be regrown. Feeds in grass, often near roads. **HABITAT** Moist meadows, pine and broadleaf woods. **ACTIVITY** By day.

Snakes

Snakes (suborder Serpentes of the scaled reptile order, Squamata) have elongated scaly bodies without limbs, eyelids, or external ear openings. They grow throughout their lives, shedding their skin from snout to tail several times each year. Carnivorous, snakes swallow their prey whole. The flicking, forked tongue serves as an organ of smell, collecting information on potential prey and dangers. Florida's snakes often mate in the fall, laying eggs from April to July that hatch from July to September; a few give birth to live young. During the cool winter months, most snakes from northern Florida to central Florida become dormant. Aquatic snakes often bask in the sun to raise their body temperatures. Florida is home to several poisonous species; see the box on snakebite (page 294) and the accounts that follow. However, many snakes are harmless to humans and in fact help keep rodent populations in check. The size given for snakes is the length, from tip of snout to tip of tail, of a typical adult.

RACER
Coluber constrictor
COLUBRID SNAKE FAMILY

4'. Medium girth; scales large, smooth. Southern Black Racer race plain satiny black or slate gray; nose brownish; chin and forward part of underside white, rest of underside gray. Holds head high while moving swiftly over ground; climbs trees to escape danger. Bites prey and holds on; does not constrict or poison. **CAUTION** Aggressive; will bite. **HABITAT** Most habitats, esp. brushy areas.

RING-NECKED SNAKE
Diadophis punctatus
COLUBRID SNAKE FAMILY

13". Very slender; scales smooth. Southern race slate gray above; buffy neck ring interrupted by thin black line; lines of black dots along center and edges of buffy undersides; undertail reddish in panhandle, Keys. Rarely bites when handled, but may void its cloaca. Constricts earthworms, salamanders, frogs, skinks. **HABITAT** Leaf litter of swamps, damp woods.

SCARLET SNAKE
Cemophora coccinea
COLUBRID SNAKE FAMILY

20". Slender; snout pointed, red. Sequence of color bands as follows: black over eye, orange on nape, narrow black, wide red, narrow black-white (or pale yellow)-black, wide red. Bands do not encircle body; underside white or yellow. Scales smooth. Mimics poisonous Eastern Coral Snake, which has blunt black snout, equally wide black and red bands with thin yellow band between each. Seen on roads. Constricts rodents, lizards, small snakes; also eats snake eggs. **HABITAT** Open woods with sand or loam soils.

INDIGO SNAKE
Drymarchon corais
COLUBRID SNAKE FAMILY

7′. Heavy-bodied. Blue-black above and below; red or white patches on lips, throat. Scales large, smooth. Immobilizes small animals with jaws. Threatened due to pet trade and gassing of Gopher Tortoise burrows (a favorite retreat for various snakes). **HABITAT** Woods, palmettos near water, orange groves.

CORN SNAKE
Elaphe guttata
COLUBRID SNAKE FAMILY

3′6″. Slender; head larger than neck; scales large. Eastern race orange or gray, with reddish-brown spots ringed in black; stripe through eye; spear-point pattern on crown. Eats mice, rats, bats, birds. **CAUTION** Coils like rattler when cornered; will bite. **HABITAT** Woods, open areas, farms, old buildings, trash piles.

RAT SNAKE
Elaphe obsoleta
COLUBRID SNAKE FAMILY

5′. Long, slender; head wider than body. Yellow race (pictured), common in most of peninsula, yellowish with 4 blackish stripes. Everglades race orangish; stripes faint. Gray race of panhandle is gray; lacks stripes; brown, white-edged blotches. Swims well; climbs trees; constricts birds, rodents. **HABITAT** Woodland edges, buildings, roadsides.

EASTERN HOGNOSE SNAKE
"Puff Adder"
Heterodon platyrhinos
COLUBRID SNAKE FAMILY

24″. Thick; snout upturned; head and neck swollen, flat. Most yellowish, with dark and pale brown splotches on back; underside of tail whiter than belly. When confronted, puffs up body, hisses, flattens foreparts, lunges at intruder; may play dead. **HABITAT** Sandy areas, open pinewoods, fields.

COMMON KINGSNAKE
Lampropeltis getulus
COLUBRID SNAKE FAMILY

3′4″. Long; medium girth; scales smooth, shiny. Eastern race (pictured) of n and c FL: black or dark brown with bold, white, chain-like pattern. FL race of c and s FL: wide brown bands with white spots, narrower white bands with brown spots. Constricts other snakes, incl. poisonous ones. **HABITAT** Woods, fields, wetlands.

MILK SNAKE
Lampropeltis triangulum
COLUBRID SNAKE FAMILY

24". Small, medium-girth; snout pointed, red. Scarlet Kingsnake race similar to Scarlet Snake; sequence of bands: narrow black-yellow-black, wide red; bands encircle belly. Mimics poisonous Eastern Coral Snake, which has blunt black snout. Constricts. **HABITAT** Pinewoods, scrub.

COACHWHIP
Masticophis flagellum
COLUBRID SNAKE FAMILY

4'6". Large, slender; tail whip-like; scales large, smooth. Eastern race black in front, fades to pale brown. Some in n FL pale brown with foreparts narrowly brown-banded; others all black. Excellent climber; catches fast lizards, birds. **CAUTION** Nervous; bites if cornered. **HABITAT** Swamps, dry flatwoods.

FLORIDA GREEN WATER SNAKE
Nerodia floridana
COLUBRID SNAKE FAMILY

4'. Heavy-bodied; eyes far forward on short face; scales keeled, divided. Olive green above (reddish in s FL); finely speckled with dark brown wavy barring; belly unmarked pale yellow. Swims or dives for crayfish, fish, salamanders, frogs. **CAUTION** Bites. **HABITAT** Swamps, fresh and brackish marshes, ponds, ditches.

Florida race (left), Mangrove race (right)

SOUTHERN WATER SNAKE
Nerodia fasciata
COLUBRID SNAKE FAMILY

3'. Stout; scales keeled. Most have dark stripe from eye to rear of mouth. Fl race of inland FL yellow-brown with darker brown bands; belly tan wi dark wavy bands. Mangrove race of coastal s FL and Keys varies in co usu. has light stripe on side of neck. Color darkens with age. **HABITAT** low fresh and brackish waters. **Salt Marsh Snake** (*N. clarkii*) of salt m smaller (25"). Races vary greatly. Coastal nw FL: yellow-tan with black stripes, belly black with yellow dots; Daytona to Ft. Pierce: thin buffy anterior stripes, buffy blotches on rear two-thirds. Palm Beach south through Keys: olive-brown with buff stripes o

BROWN WATER SNAKE
Nerodia taxispilota
COLUBRID SNAKE FAMILY

4'. Stout; head large, unmarked. Light brown with 3 rows of large, rectangular, dark brown, often light-edged patches; belly yellow with irreg. black spots; scales keeled. Bears live young. Arboreal; often in brush beside water. **CAUTION** Bites readily. **HABITAT** Lakes, rivers, marshes.

ROUGH GREEN SNAKE
Opheodrys aestivus
COLUBRID SNAKE FAMILY

3'. Very slender; head small; tail long, tapering. Bright pea green above and on sides; yellow below. Scales keeled. Young grayish green. Graceful, mild-tempered; weaves through branches and weeds; swims well. Feeds on grasshoppers, crickets, caterpillars, spiders. **HABITAT** Bushes, trees, and vines near water.

PINE SNAKE
Pituophis melanoleucus
COLUBRID SNAKE FAMILY

5'. Stout; head small, pointed; scales keeled. FL race rusty gray in front, rusty brown to rear, with muted darker blotches. Constrictor. Eats small mammals, birds, lizards. **CAUTION** When cornered, hisses, vibrates tail, strikes. **HABITAT** Dry sandy pine-oak areas, weedy fields. **RANGE** South to Lake Okeechobee.

PINE WOODS SNAKE
Rhadinaea flavilata
COLUBRID SNAKE FAMILY

12". Slender; head small, narrow. ...ddish or yellowish-brown above; ... yellowish white; head darker ...; dark line through eye, thin ...sh line above. Scales smooth. ... rotten logs, under boards and ...iva toxic to salamanders, ...ds, harmless to humans; ... flatwoods. **RANGE** South ...chobee.

BROWN SNAKE
Storeria dekayi
COLUBRID SNAKE FAMILY

15". Medium girth; head small; scales keeled. FL race brownish; silvery back stripe flanked by dark spots; belly tan or pink, flecked with black; head has wide brown band and wide light yellow band. Seen in roads on rainy nights. Bears live young. **HABITAT** In, near marshes; pine flatwoods; homes. **RANGE** Peninsular FL.

EASTERN RIBBON SNAKE
Thamnophis sauritus
COLUBRID SNAKE FAMILY

24". Slender; scales keeled. Peninsula race (pictured) brown with tan back stripe, yellow side stripe. Blue-striped race of Big Bend area of nw peninsular FL brown with thin, bluish-white side stripe. Eastern race of panhandle has 3 yellowish stripes. Found in or near water, where swims on surface; climbs bushes. Bears live young. **HABITAT** Swamps, marshes, pine flatwoods.

COMMON GARTER SNAKE
Thamnophis sirtalis
COLUBRID SNAKE FAMILY

24". Slender; scales keeled; head wider than in Ribbon Snake. Variable in color and pattern: always striped, sometimes also blotched or spotted. Eastern race (pictured): 3 yellowish stripes on base of dark brown, or light gray-brown with blackish spots; underside blue-gray with black dots. Blue-striped race of Big Bend area of nw peninsula has light blue stripes. Bears live young. **HABITAT** Woods, fields, watersides, towns.

EASTERN CORAL SNAKE
Micrurus fulvius
CORAL SNAKE FAMILY

24". Slender, shiny, round in cross section; scales smooth, shiny. Head small, blunt, with black snout (best feature for identification); wide yellow band and wide black band on head. Sequence of bands on body: narrow yellow, wide red, narrow yellow, wide black (red and yellow rings touch). Bands encircle body. Similar harmless Scarlet Snake and Scarlet Kingsnake race of Milk Snake have black bands next to red and yellow ones. **CAUTION** Poisonous. Usu. nonaggressive, but bite often fatal if antivenin not applied within few hours. **HABITAT** Woods near lakes, streams; wood piles.

Poisonous Snakes and Snakebite

Florida has six poisonous snake species, four of which are treated on pages 293–295. The Copperhead *(Agkistrodon contortrix)*, which occurs very locally in the panhandle, is pale brown with reddish-brown hourglass-shaped bands above. The Timber Rattlesnake *(Crotalus horridus)*, which occurs in a few counties in the northern peninsula, is pale gray-brown with a dark brown chevron pattern. Most of Florida's poisonous snakes are pit vipers, with long hollow fangs that fold back against the roof of the mouth when not in use; pit viper venom attacks blood vessels and red blood cells. The Eastern Coral Snake is in the same family as cobras and mambas; these snakes have fixed fangs, and their venom affects the nervous and respiratory systems. Most of these snakes will flee from footsteps. If you encounter one of these species, freeze to let it withdraw, then step away. While bites sting, they are rarely fatal. However, for any poisonous snakebite the best course of action is to get to medical care as soon as possible, with the dead snake or a positive identification so that the proper antivenin can be administered. Meanwhile, the victim should avoid moving, as movement helps the venom spread through the system, and keep the injured body part motionless and just below heart level. The victim should be kept warm, calm, and at rest while on the way to medical care. If you are alone and on foot, start walking slowly toward help, exerting the injured area as little as possible. If you run or if the bite has delivered a large amount of venom, you may collapse, but a snakebite seldom results in death.

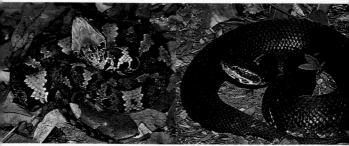

young (left), adult (right)

COTTONMOUTH
Agkistrodon piscivorus
PIT VIPER FAMILY

4'. Heavy-bodied; head much wider than neck; mouth white inside; eyes on sides of head; deep pit between nostril and eye; scales keeled. Dark brown with broad yellow-brown bands; belly creamy with dark blotches. Top of head and line on lower jaw blackish; line behind eye blackish (best feature for identification); yellowish-white line above and below eye, around jaws. Older adults appear mainly blackish. Bears live young. Swims with head well out of water. **CAUTION** Poisonous. Usu. nonaggressive, but bite can be fatal. **HABITAT** Freshwater habitats, esp. pine flatwoods, marshes.

EASTERN DIAMONDBACK RATTLESNAKE
Crotalus adamanteus
PIT VIPER FAMILY

4'6". Heavy-bodied; head broad, triangular, with many tiny scales between eyes; scales keeled; horny interlocking rattles at end of tail. Smoky gray; dark brown diamonds edged in black and pale yellow on back; dark and light diagonal lines on sides of face. Feeds on rodents, rabbits, birds. Disposition varies: some rattle when dogs or people are 30' away; others quiet until you are too near. Bears live young. **CAUTION** Poisonous; coils before striking; if you hear rattles, remain motionless and let snake move on; even rattlers dead a few hours can bite as reflex. **HABITAT** Pine and oak woods, palmetto stands, fields.

PYGMY RATTLESNAKE
"Ground Rattler"
Sistrurus miliarius
PIT VIPER FAMILY

24". Body triangular in cross section; head broad, triangular; scales keeled; horny interlocking rattles at end of slender tail. Dusky Fl. race dusty gray with 3 rows of pale-edged black spots; back may also have row of red spots; belly light gray with few dark blotches. Rattle sounds like an insect. Bears live young. **CAUTION** Poisonous; venom potent, but fangs smaller; can be quick to strike. **HABITAT** Prairies, marshes, watersides, pine flatwoods.

Crocodilians

Florida has two native and one introduced species in the order Crocodylia. Enormous lizard-shaped reptiles with well-armored, heavy bodies, crocodilians have elongated heads with protruding eyes and nostrils, massive jaws with long grasping teeth, ears covered with movable flaps, and a thick, flattened, well-muscled tail. Their five-toed front feet are unwebbed; their four-toed hindfeet are webbed. The sexes are alike. Aquatic carnivores that feed on fish and other large water animals, crocodilians also stalk prey onshore near water. All should be considered dangerous, even those basking in the sun. Females lay between 20 and 80 long white eggs; crocodiles lay eggs in a cavity dug in a sandbank, alligators in a nest mound of vegetation rising above a marsh. Florida's native crocodilians are the American Alligator and the American Crocodile. The introduced species, from Latin America, is the Spectacled Caiman *(Caiman crocodilus),* which is 3 to 6 feet long and distinguished by a bony ridge between its bulbous eyes. Not a threat to people, it resides in canals in southeastern Florida.

AMERICAN ALLIGATOR
Alligator mississippiensis
ALLIGATOR FAMILY

6–12'. Stout, elongated; snout broad, rounded; head wide, flattened; eyes slightly raised on top of head; only downward-pointing teeth of upper jaws visible when jaws closed; legs shortish; claws heavy; tail square in cross section, vertically compressed toward tip; 6 raised ridges on back merge into 2 atop tail. Black to slate gray; throat and chest yellowish white. Young black with bold yellowish-white bands. During droughts, deepens a pool in marsh that benefits other aquatic life. Hibernates in muddy wallows in cooler months in n FL. **CAUTION** Usu. docile; dangerous if surprised or closely approached, esp. near nest. **VOICE** Adult male: bellowing roar. Adult female: softer roar; pig-like grunts. Young: high-pitched *yunk*. **HABITAT** Ponds, swamps, rivers, freshwater and brackish marshes, mangroves, canals; ocean (rare).

AMERICAN CROCODILE
Crocodylus acutus
CROCODILE FAMILY

7–12'. Stout, elongated; snout long, narrow; head flattened; eyes slightly raised on top of head; downward-pointing teeth of upper jaw and large, upward-pointing 4th tooth of bottom jaw visible when mouth closed; legs shortish; claws heavy; tail square in cross section, vertically compressed toward tip; 4 raised ridges on back merge into 2 atop tail. Gray or olive-gray; throat, chest yellowish white. Young gray or greenish. Endangered; about 500 remain in FL. **CAUTION** Dangerous if surprised or closely approached, esp. near nest. **VOICE** Adult male: low growl, weaker than Alligator. Adult female: usu. silent. Young: high-pitched grunt. **HABITAT** Fresh- and saltwater ponds, bays, salt marshes, brackish creeks, open ocean. **RANGE** s tip of Everglades, Florida Bay, Upper Keys.

Birds

Members of the class Aves, birds are the only animals that have feathers; most species are capable of flight. Like their reptile ancestors, they lay eggs; like mammals, they are warm-blooded. They generally have excellent sight and hearing, but few have a good sense of smell. The bird skeleton is adapted for flight: The bones are lightweight, with a sponge-like interior. The forelimbs have become wings, with strong pectoral muscles attached to a keeled breastbone, and the hindlimbs are modified for running, grasping, or perching. Wing shapes vary among types of birds, ranging, for example, from the long, broad wings of the soaring raptors to the narrow, fast-moving wings of hummingbirds.

While all Blue Jays look the same regardless of their sex or the time of year, this is not the case for most birds. Plumages may vary from immature to adult, from male to female, and from breeding to nonbreeding seasons (summer and winter, respectively). We often give the summer or breeding plumages for wintering species since that plumage is often attained in late winter or spring before departure. (If both sexes have a summer plumage distinct from nonbreeding plumage, we note this as "summer adult." If only the male has such a summer plumage, we note "summer male.") In some species, groups living in different geographic areas (subspecies, or races) have slightly or distinctly different plumages. Some birds within a given species have different colorations (called morphs or phases) that have nothing to do with where they live. Some birds have ornamental plumes, often developed in the breeding season. This guide describes the plumages most often seen in Florida. The photograph shows the male or the adult (if adults look alike) unless otherwise noted.

Flight allows birds to migrate great distances, though some are year-round residents in one region. A few birds that spend the winter in warmer tropical climes migrate north to Florida to breed, taking advantage of the more abundant animal life in summertime Florida. Other birds breed in the northern United States and Canada and pass through Florida during migration or spend the winter here. Still others reside in Florida year-round. Most individuals return to the same breeding and wintering grounds throughout their lives.

Northbound migration occurs from February to May, southbound from July to early December, depending on the species. Bird migration in Florida is relatively evenly spaced and steady compared to the major pulses in more northern climes, where southerly spring winds and northerly autumn winds boost the numbers of migrants. Migration to and through the West Indies is orderly island-hopping. Major songbird flights can occur in spring when birds crossing the Gulf of Mexico from Yucatán to the U.S. Gulf coast encounter sudden headwinds from the north. This forces tired migrants to land in large numbers on islands off western Florida, including the Dry Tortugas. For more about bird migration, see the essay on birdwatching on page 300.

In bird species that do not nest in colonies, a male who is ready to breed stakes out and defends a nesting territory from other males. The female chooses a male in part on the quality and size of his territory, the presence of a secure nest site, and the quality of his plumage and song. The avian life cycle typically starts with the female laying one or more eggs in a nest, which, depending on the species, may be a scrape in the sand, a cup of rootlets and fibers, a woven basket, a stick platform, or another type of structure. After an incubation period of roughly two to four weeks, the young are hatched and fed by their parents for a period varying from a few days (shorebirds) to a few weeks (most species) to many months (raptors). Smaller birds tend to breed the year following their birth,

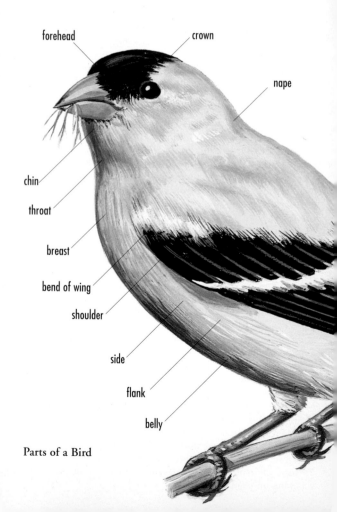

Parts of a Bird

while many larger birds remain immature for several years before breeding. During the breeding season, many male birds exhibit more colorful and elaborate plumages and courtship displays and rituals in order to attract a mate. Most species mate in solitary pairs, the males competing for breeding territories; other species nest colonially. In this section of the guide, assume a bird is a solitary nester unless the description notes that it nests in colonies. Space limitations prevent us from giving descriptions of nests.

Birds use their voices in many ways. In many species, contact and alarm call notes are given year-round by both sexes. The more musical songs, usually given only in spring and summer by the male, attract mates and define territory. Once the young are born, many birds stop singing.

This section's descriptions give the length of the bird from the tip of the beak to the end of the tail. For some large species, both length and wingspan are given.

For suggestions on attracting birds to your yard, see page 344. In this section, the icon 🐦 denotes species that will come into a yard to a feeder. The icon 🏠 indicates species that might use a nest box in a yard.

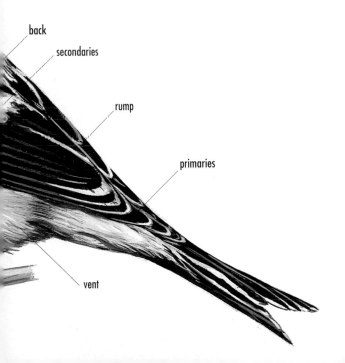

back

secondaries

rump

primaries

vent

Bird-watching

Bird-watching, or birding, as it is often termed, can be a casual activity, develop into a hobby, or become a passion. Some observers enjoy generally keeping track of birds they come across in their daily activities or while hiking, driving, or boating, while others become intent on seeing as many different types of birds as possible. It's possible to see 200 to 300 species a year in Florida.

During the breeding season, many birds tend to live in only one habitat and are active at particular times of day. Freshwater marsh birds (rails, bitterns, and marsh songbirds) are most often calling and active at dawn and dusk. Until mid-morning on hot days, songbirds busily search woodlands, fields, and thickets for food; from mid-morning to late afternoon, they tend to be quiet, and forage again late in the day. Birds that live near beaches, lakes, and other aquatic habitats (herons, cormorants, ducks, and sandpipers) may be active all day. Make an after-dark visit to a forest or swamp to find owls, which may respond to taped or imitated calls, and can be viewed with spotlights.

Unlike much of the United States and all of Canada, there is a greater variety of birds present in Florida in winter than in summer. Southbound migration begins with the shorebirds, with adults returning by July and August, and immatures pass through Florida from August into November. Songbirds pass through from August into December, waterfowl and raptors from late September into December. Major cold snaps sometimes force some wintering birds into southern Florida or beyond. Northbound migration begins in February and March with waterfowl, Tree Swallows, and American Robins. Shorebirds and most songbirds pass through or leave from late March to early May. The volume of migrating birds, especially raptors, is much higher on the Texas coast than in Florida. A few species, such as the Gray Kingbird and the Black-whiskered Vireo, breed in Florida but winter to the south.

For the serious birder, at least one good field guide is essential; many excellent ones are available, including the *National Audubon Society Field Guide to North American Birds (Eastern Region)*. Binoculars (7-, 8-, 9-, or 10-power) are a must; a close-focusing pair is especially helpful. A 15-, 20-, or 30-power telescope with a wide field of view, mounted on a sturdy, collapsible tripod, is invaluable for viewing waterfowl, shorebirds, and raptors.

While many species are rather tame, others are shy or secretive. Learn to move slowly and quietly, and avoid wearing brightly colored or patterned clothing and making loud noises. Please respect local laws, do not unduly frighten birds, and take great care not to disrupt nesting or resting birds.

COMMON LOON
Gavia immer
LOON FAMILY

32". Body stout, duck-like. Bill heavy, pointed. Summer: back black with large white spots; head, neck, and bill black; white bands on neck; eyes red. Winter: slaty above, white below; bill slaty. In flight, legs extend beyond tail. **VOICE** Silent in winter. **HABITAT** Lakes, coastal bays, ocean. **RANGE** Nov.–Apr.: all FL; fewer in s FL.

PIED-BILLED GREBE
Podilymbus podiceps
GREBE FAMILY

13". Body duck-like. Bill short, conical. Summer: body brown; chin black; black ring on silver bill. Winter: body brown; chin white; bill dull yellow, lacks ring. Dives frequently for small fish. **VOICE** Series of 8 *cow* notes (summer only). **HABITAT** Summer: freshwater marshes with open water. Migration and winter: ponds, rivers, brackish lagoons, **RANGE** Resident in FL. May–Sept.: local. Oct.–Apr.: widespread.

NORTHERN GANNET
Morus bassanus
BOOBY AND GANNET FAMILY

3'2". Gull-like. Bill silver, pointed; neck longish; tail wedge-shaped. Adult mostly white; primaries pointed, black; yellow wash on head. 1st-year bird brown above, speckled white; belly white. Dives for fish from on high; in migration, flies in lines low to water. **VOICE** Quiet at sea. **HABITAT** Open seas, sometimes close to shore. **RANGE** Nov.–Apr.: off all coasts.

MAGNIFICENT FRIGATEBIRD
Fregata magnificens
FRIGATEBIRD FAMILY

L 3'4"; WS 7'6". Back and long pointed wings black. Bill longish, silver, hooked at tip. Legs very short; feet tiny, lack webbing (unusual for seabird). Tail long, deeply forked, black. Adult male head and breast black. Adult female head black, breast white. Gifted flier that glides for hours. Very agile when chasing flying fish or forcing seabirds to disgorge their catch; picks up floating dead fish with bill. Rests in trees or tall rocks, never on water or sand. Nests in Keys west of Key West, in colonies on mangrove islands; male has inflatable, balloon-like, red pouch he inflates only at or near nest. **VOICE** Guttural calls at nest. **HABITAT** Open ocean, coastal lagoons; soars over beaches. **RANGE** Resident in s FL; scarcer in n FL. Apr.–Nov.: nonbreeders cruise all coasts.

AMERICAN WHITE PELICAN
Pelecanus erythrorhynchos
PELICAN FAMILY

L 5'2"; WS 8'. Adult all white at rest; bill long, flat, with orange-yellow pouch. Neck long; tail short. Legs short; feet wide, webbed; both orange yellow. Flight reveals black primaries. Imm. (to 4 years) grayish white; bill and pouch gray. Feeds in groups from water surface; dips bill and pouch into water for small schooling fish. Rests on sandbars, not trees. Often flies in V formation or wheels high in sky on midday thermals; does not dive from air like Brown Pelican. **VOICE** Usu. silent. **HABITAT** Coastal lagoons, large inland lakes. **RANGE** Sept.–Apr.: peninsular FL (locally common). Oct.–Dec., Mar.–Apr.: panhandle.

BROWN PELICAN
summer adult (left), winter adult (right)
Pelecanus occidentalis
PELICAN FAMILY

L 4'2"; WS 7'6". Adult body and wings grayish brown; head white, with yellowish wash on crown. Neck long, mainly chestnut brown in summer, all white in winter; bill long, flat, gray (tipped red in summer); pouch black. Legs short; feet wide, webbed, slaty. Tail short. Imm. (to 4 years) brown with white belly; bill and pouch gray. Feeds on fish, alone or in groups; makes spectacular dives, bill-first, into water. Often rests in trees. Flies with slow, regular wingbeats in V formation or glides long distances in lines, skimming tops of waves. Nests in colonies in trees on mangrove islands. **VOICE** Usu. silent; low grunts at nest. **HABITAT** Ocean, bays, estuaries; few wander inland. **RANGE** Resident in coastal FL; very common.

DOUBLE-CRESTED CORMORANT
Phalacrocorax auritus
CORMORANT FAMILY

33". Adult black with greenish cast; breeding crest (2 small tufts) hard to see. Bill narrow, hooked; orange skin on throat. Imm. brownish, whitish from throat to breast. Swims with bill angled upward; flocks often fly in V; spreads wings to dry while resting. Nests in colonies in cypress trees or mangroves. **VOICE** Usu. silent; croaks at nest. **HABITAT** Coasts, large bodies of inland water. **RANGE** Resident breeding population. Oct.–Apr.: numerous migrants from n U.S.

immature (left), adult (above)

male (left), female (right)

ANHINGA
Anhinga anhinga
ANHINGA FAMILY

34". Adult male black with greenish gloss; upper surface of inner wing has long white patch. Adult female head, neck, and chest buffy; back and belly black. Wings and bill long, pointed; neck slender. Legs short; feet webbed, pink; tail very long, fan-shaped. Soars often; resembles flying cross. Rests in trees or sticks over water; holds wings out to dry; lacks oil glands for waterproofing. Called "snakebird" for habit of swimming with just neck and head showing. Stabs fish in the side, then flips it up to swallow headfirst. Nests in small colonies, often with cormorants and herons. **VOICE** Low grunts. **HABITAT** Freshwater marshes, swamps, rivers. **RANGE** Resident in FL.

Herons

Members of the heron family (Ardeidae)—herons, egrets, and bitterns—are large, long-legged, long-necked birds up to 4′ long. They wade in shallows and marshes, where they use their longish, daggerlike bills to seize slippery fish and aquatic frogs, snakes, and invertebrates. While storks, ibises, spoonbills, and cranes fly with outstretched necks, herons normally fold theirs in an S shape when airborne. During courtship (two to four weeks a year), adults of many of these species have ornamental plumes and bright facial colors. Their nests are usually large platforms of sticks, often in large colonies that may include several species of herons and other large waders. Predominantly white heron species are called egrets. Bitterns are shy denizens of marshes with distinct voices.

AMERICAN BITTERN
Botaurus lentiginosus
HERON FAMILY
28″. Adult light brown, with thin white eyebrow and dark streaks on pale neck; black stripe partway down neck. Neck thick; legs greenish. Imm. lacks black neck stripe. Shy; points bill skyward if disturbed. **VOICE** Pumping *uunk-KA-lunk*. **HABITAT** Marshes. **RANGE** Oct.–Mar.: all FL; rare nester.

LEAST BITTERN
Ixobrychus exilis
HERON FAMILY
13″. Adult male back, flight feathers, and short tail black; belly, wings, neck, and head buffy; crown black. Neck long when extended; bill pointed, yellow; legs yellow. Female and imm. back and crown brown. Secretive; walks steadily through cat-tails; usu. noted only in flight low over marsh. **VOICE** Male: soft *coo coo coo*. Female: weak *tick tick*. **HABITAT** Freshwater cat-tail and reed marshes. **RANGE** Resident in FL.

Great Blue (left), Great White race (right)

GREAT BLUE HERON
Ardea herodias
HERON FAMILY

L 4'2"; WS 6'. Adult back and wings blue-gray; shoulder black; crown black with white center; short black plumes from back of head; face white; most of neck buffy; foreneck striped black and white; belly blackish. Legs very long, dull yellow or blackish; thighs rusty. Bill yellow. Imm. crown all black. Great White Heron race: all white; bill yellow; legs and feet yellow (black in Great Egret); resident in Keys and Everglades, some dispersing to c FL. Intermediate color morph, Wurdemann's Heron of far s FL: head and neck white; body bluish; legs yellow. Many Great Blue Herons have lost fear of humans in FL, walking on lawns and expecting castoffs from fishermen. Nests in small to large single-species colonies. **VOICE** Harsh squawk. **HABITAT** All salt and fresh waters, beaches, towns. **RANGE** Resident in FL; most common Nov.–Apr.

GREAT EGRET
Ardea alba
HERON FAMILY

L 3'3"; WS 4'3". All white. Neck long, thin. Bill long, yellow; feet and long legs black. During breeding, long, lacy, white plumes on back; facial skin green. Nests in colonies, with other species. Common in roadside ditches. **VOICE** Deep croak. **HABITAT** Salt- and freshwater marshes, sandbars, watersides. **RANGE** Resident in FL.

breeding (left),
nonbreeding (right)

SNOWY EGRET
Egretta thula
HERON FAMILY

24″. All white. Neck long; bill slender, black; lores (area between eye and bill) yellow. Legs long, black; feet yellow. During courtship, long, lacy, white plumes on back, chest, and crown. Imm. legs dark green. Nests in colonies. **VOICE** Harsh *aah*. **HABITAT** Coastal beaches, marshes, inland waterways. **RANGE** Resident in FL.

adult (left), immature (right)

LITTLE BLUE HERON
Egretta caerulea
HERON FAMILY

27″. Adult body and wings slate-blue; head and neck dull dark purple. Imm. all white; legs and feet dull slaty olive. Neck and legs long; bill gray at base, black-tipped. During courtship, long purplish back and head plumes. Feeds on fish in shallow waters; also feeds on large insects and frogs in meadows. Nests in colonies. **VOICE** Harsh squawk; usu. silent. **HABITAT** Salt- and freshwater mudflats and marshes; swamps; meadows. **RANGE** Resident in FL.

TRICOLORED HERON
"Louisiana Heron"
Egretta tricolor
HERON FAMILY

26″. Adult back, wings, neck, and head slaty blue; belly and underwings white. White line down entire foreneck; base of neck purplish. Neck and legs long; bill very long, thin, gray, black-tipped. During courtship, long, buffy plumes on back. Imm. neck and shoulders rusty. Fishes by slow stalking and wild running pursuit in shallow water. Nests in colonies, with other species. **VOICE** Guttural squawks; usu. silent. **HABITAT** Salt and freshwater mudflats and marshes; swamps; meadows. **RANGE** Resident in FL.

REDDISH EGRET
Egretta rufescens
HERON FAMILY

white morph (left), dark morph (right)

30". Neck long, with long shaggy feathers; bill long, fairly thick, pink, black-tipped; legs long, slaty. Dark morph (more common): body and wings slaty gray; head and neck reddish brown. White morph: body and wings white; bill pink at base, black at tip. Imm: white with black bill. Rushes awkwardly about shallow water, chasing fish; creates canopy with wings to lure fish into shade. **VOICE** Guttural croaks. **HABITAT** Shallow open waters, salt and brackish; mudflats; inland (rare). **RANGE** Resident in FL; uncommon, mostly on sw Gulf coast. Breeds from Keys north to Tampa Bay and Merritt Is.

CATTLE EGRET
Bubulcus ibis
HERON FAMILY

20". All white; bill, legs, feet yellow. Legs shortish for a heron. During courtship, buffy plumes on back, chest, crown; bill, legs, feet orange. Social; small flocks feed together, return to massive communal roosts each night; nests in very large colonies, sometimes with other species. Chases large insects and frogs disturbed by feeding cattle, horses. Self-introduced from Africa via S. Amer. **VOICE** Hoarse croaks; usu. silent. **HABITAT** Meadows, lawns, crop fields. **RANGE** Resident in peninsular FL. In panhandle Apr.–Oct.

GREEN HERON
Butorides virescens
HERON FAMILY

19". Adult back and wings slaty dark green; cap black; neck chestnut; legs dull yellow (breeding male has bright orange legs), shortish; bill dark. Imm. brownish; neck pale with heavy dark brown streaks; legs yellow-green. Often feeds by leaning over water from logs, rocks; also wades. **VOICE** Harsh *keyow*. **HABITAT** Ponds, streams, marshes, mangroves. **RANGE** Resident in FL.

immature (left), adult (right)

BLACK-CROWNED NIGHT-HERON
Nycticorax nycticorax
HERON FAMILY

26". Adult crown and back black; wings gray; lores and underparts white; eyes red. Thick-necked; legs shortish, yellow. Imm. brown, with heavy white streaks and spots. Nests in mixed-species colonies. **VOICE** Low *kwock.* **HABITAT** Ponds, riversides, marshes. **RANGE** Resident in FL; more common inland.

YELLOW-CROWNED NIGHT-HERON
Nyctanassa violacea
HERON FAMILY

26". Adult body and wings slate-gray; head black; cheek and crown white; eyes red; legs yellow. May appear short-necked; legs longer than Black-crowned Night-heron. During breeding, forecrown yellow; 2 long white plumes on nape; legs orange. Imm. grayish brown, speckled white above. Feeds on crabs and crayfish. **VOICE** Loud *quark,* higher and softer than Black-crown. **HABITAT** Salt marshes, mangroves, swamps. **RANGE** Resident in FL; more common along coast.

immature (left), breeding adult (right)

WHITE IBIS
Eudocimus albus
IBIS FAMILY

26". Adult all white, ex. tip of rounded wings black; bill, bare facial skin, and legs brilliant red. Imm. brown, with white belly. Neck and legs long; bill extremely long, downcurved. Probes mud for crustaceans and frogs. Flies with neck out; alternates rapid wingbeats and glides. Nests in large colonies. **VOICE** Nasal *hunk;* usu. quiet. **HABITAT** Tidal mudflats and beaches; marshes, swamps, watersides. **RANGE** Resident in FL; less common in panhandle.

immature (left), adult (right)

GLOSSY IBIS
Plegadis falcinellus
IBIS FAMILY

L 23"; WS 3'1". Neck and legs long; bill extremely long and down-curved. Summer adult: body rusty bronze; wings glossy green; appears black in poor light. Winter adult: body and wings dark green; head and neck brownish. Imm. dull brown. Nests in colonies with herons. **VOICE** Guttural *ka-onk.* **HABITAT** Coastal and freshwater marshes. **RANGE** Resident in FL; most common in c and s FL.

ROSEATE SPOONBILL
Ajaia ajaja
IBIS FAMILY

32". Lower back, wings, belly pink; upper back and neck white; head bare, gray-green; bill slaty; legs red; tail short, orange. Neck and legs long; bill long, narrow in middle, with flat, spoon shaped tip. Sweeps bill from side to side, feeling mud for aquatic invertebrates. Flies with neck out. Nests in colonies with herons. A main attraction at J.N. "Ding" Darling N.W.R. on Sanibel and Flamingo in Everglades N.P. **VOICE** Low grunt. **HABITAT** Coastal flats, lagoons, marshes; inland (rare). **RANGE** Resident in FL; breeds from Keys north to Tampa Bay and Merritt Is.; disperses along coast July–Oct.

WOOD STORK
Mycteria americana
STORK FAMILY

L 3'4"; WS 5'6". Appears all white at rest; bill blackish in adult, yellowish in imm. Slaty scales cover bare head and neck; bill long, sturdy, outer third drooping to a point; legs long, black. Flight reveals black flight feathers and tail. Flies with neck and legs extended; flocks circle high on thermals. Wades slowly in shallow waters, groping for fish,

frogs, snakes, baby alligators. Perches in dead trees. Nests in colonies; skips breeding in very wet years. The only N. Amer. stork. **VOICE** Low croak; usu. silent. **HABITAT** Tidal flats, marshes, flooded pastures. **RANGE** Resident in FL.

immature (left), adult (right)

Waterfowl

The waterfowl family (Anatidae) contains the huge white swans, the medium-size geese, and a wide variety of smaller ducks. All have webbed feet, and thick bills designed for filtering small organisms in the water or for grasping underwater vegetation and invertebrates. Most waterfowl undergo lengthy migrations between northern or inland breeding areas and southern and/or coastal wintering waters. Their nests, made of grasses and lined with feathers, are usually on the ground, hidden in tall grass or reeds. Swans and geese upend like dabbling ducks, rather than dive for food; most patter across the water to get airborne. Ducks may be split into two main groups. Dabblings ducks upend on the surface of fresh and brackish waters, and can jump up and take flight straight out of the water. Diving ducks dive well under the surface of fresh and salt waters; in taking flight, they run and flap horizontally over the water's surface before gaining altitude, like swans and most geese. Waterfowl males are in breeding plumage all winter and spring, and in late summer, develop a drab nonbreeding eclipse plumage similar to that of females.

Mallard dabbling

Mallard taking off, straight up, from surface of water

Canada Goose taking off by running across water

CANADA GOOSE
Branta canadensis
WATERFOWL FAMILY

L 3'4"; WS 6'. Adult back and wings dark brown; head and long neck black; large white chinstrap; breast pale brown; vent and rump white. Neck long; tail short, black. Young downy, yellow. Often flies in V formation. **VOICE** Honking *car-uunk.* **HABITAT** Marshes, ponds, golf courses. **RANGE** Oct.–Mar.: all FL. Introduced populations are resident, mainly in n and c FL.

WOOD DUCK
Aix sponsa
WATERFOWL FAMILY

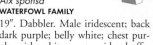

19". Dabbler. Male iridescent; back dark purple; belly white; chest purple with white spots; sides buffy; head green with laid-back crest; throat and 2-pronged chinstrap white; eye ring and base of bill red. Female brown, with elongated white eye ring. FL's most colorful duck. **VOICE** Male: usu. quiet; high whistle when courting. Female: *oo-eek.* **HABITAT** Swamps, marshes. **RANGE** Resident in FL; rare in Keys. Oct.–Mar.: many migrants from n U.S. and s Canada.

GREEN-WINGED TEAL
Anas crecca
WATERFOWL FAMILY
14″. Dabbler. Male body gray, with vertical white stripe behind chest; head chestnut; green eye patch extends to fluffy nape; yellow vent patch; bill small, black. Female brown. Flight reveals green wing patch on secondaries. FL's smallest duck. **VOICE** Male: whistled *crick-et.* **HABITAT** Marshes, ponds. **RANGE** Oct.–Apr.: all FL; much more common in n FL.

MOTTLED DUCK
Anas fulvigula
WATERFOWL FAMILY
22″. Dabbler. Body mottled rusty brown; head and neck paler buffy brown; throat and foreneck plain tawny; bill all yellow; tail blackish. Flight reveals 1 white band below blue-green speculum, white underwing linings. Female Mallard paler, with dark saddle on bill, 2 white bands on speculum, whiter tail. **VOICE** Female: quack; male: high calls. **HABITAT** Fresh and salt marshes; moist meadows. **RANGE** Resident in FL; most common inland from Gainesville to Lake Okeechobee.

MALLARD
Anas platyrhynchos
WATERFOWL FAMILY
24″. Dabbler. Male body and wings gray; head and neck green, with white ring above purplish chest; rump black; tail white; bill yellow. Female buffy brown; bill pale orange with dark saddle. Legs orange. Flight reveals purple wing patch, bordered with white, on secondaries. Domestic Mallards flightless, much heavier toward rear; some all white. **VOICE** Male: quiet; gives *reeb* call when fighting. Female: quack. **HABITAT** Ponds, rivers, marshes. **RANGE** Nov.–Mar: all FL. Semi-domesticated and domestic populations resident in urban FL.

BLUE-WINGED TEAL
Anas discors
WATERFOWL FAMILY
15″. Dabbler. Male body brown, with black dots; head dull blue-gray, with white crescent before eye; crown black. Female mottled brown. Bill heavier, longer than Green-winged Teal. Flight reveals pale cerulean blue shoulder. **VOICE** Male: peep-like notes. Female: high quack. **HABITAT** Marshes, weedy ponds. **RANGE** Sept.–Apr.: all FL .

NORTHERN SHOVELER
Anas clypeata
WATERFOWL FAMILY

18″. Dabbler. Male head green; chest white; sides rusty; eyes yellow; bill black. Female brown, speckled; bill often orange. Neck short; bill long, wide, held close to water. Flight reveals pale blue shoulder. **VOICE** Male: low *took*. Female: quack. **HABITAT** Marshes, ponds, saltwater bays. **RANGE** Oct.–Apr.: all FL.

AMERICAN WIGEON
Anas americana
WATERFOWL FAMILY

21″. Dabbler. Both sexes brownish, with speckled head, dull orange sides. Male forehead white; green patch behind eye; black and white vent. Flight reveals white shoulder patch. **VOICE** Male: whistled *whee whee whew*. Female: quack. **HABITAT** Shallow lakes, esp. near coast. **RANGE** Oct.–Apr.: all FL.

female (left), male (right)

LESSER SCAUP
Aythya affinis
WATERFOWL FAMILY

17″. Diver. Male back gray; head dark purple; sides pale gray; chest and tail area black. Female dark brown, with distinct white face. Bill blue-gray; eyes yellow. Flight reveals white stripe on secondaries of gray wings. Often in flocks of many hundreds. **VOICE** Usu. silent. **HABITAT** Bays, estuaries, lakes. **RANGE** Oct.–Apr.: all FL. **Greater Scaup** *(A. marila)* winters in FL; white wing stripe extends onto primaries; male has dark green head.

RING-NECKED DUCK
Aythya collaris
WATERFOWL FAMILY

17″. Diver. Male chest, back, and tail black; sides gray; shoulder stripe white; head dark purple; crown peaked. Female brown, with pale buffy wash on face, pale eye ring. Bill patterned. Flight reveals black shoulder and gray wing stripe. **VOICE** Usu. silent. **HABITAT** Freshwater lakes, rivers, coastal bays. **RANGE** Nov.–Mar.: all FL.

HOODED MERGANSER
Lophodytes (Mergus) cucullatus
WATERFOWL FAMILY

female (left), male (right)

18″. Diver. Adult male back, head, and neck black; sides rufous; head patch and chest white; eyes yellow. Female gray-brown, with fluffy brown nape. Crest expandable, fan-like; bill black. Imm. male similar to female, with white spot on crest. **VOICE** Low grunts; usu. silent. **HABITAT** Tree-fringed ponds, rivers. **RANGE** Nov.–Apr: all FL.

RED-BREASTED MERGANSER
Mergus serrator
WATERFOWL FAMILY

female (left), male (right)

23″. Diver. Male back black; chest buffy; sides gray; neck and belly white; head dark green. Female gray; head rusty; throat and foreneck white. Bill long, slender, red; nape crest shaggy. Female more common than male in FL. **VOICE** Usu. silent. **HABITAT** Mainly coastal; a few on inland lakes. **RANGE** Nov.–Apr.: all FL.

RUDDY DUCK
Oxyura jamaicensis
WATERFOWL FAMILY

16″. Diver. Breeding male: body ruddy brown; top half of head black, lower half white; bill thick, bright blue. Winter male: head as above; body slaty brown; bill gray. Female body and cap brown, with dark line on pale buff cheeks. Tail black, stiff, fan-shaped, often raised. Gathers in small "rafts" (flocks). Dives for aquatic plants. **VOICE** Usu. silent. **HABITAT** bays, lakes, ponds. **RANGE** Nov.–Apr.: all FL.

Raptors

The word "raptor" is usually used for birds of prey that are active in the daytime (some experts also use the name for the nocturnal owls, described on page 334). Families found in Florida include the American vultures (Carthartidae), the hawks and eagles (Accipitridae), and the falcons (Falconidae). The bills of raptors are strong for tearing flesh, while the feet (usually yellow) are generally powerful (except in vultures), with curved talons for grasping prey. Some raptors are present in Florida only in migration or in winter. The carrion-feeding vultures are black, with broad wings and bare heads. Members of the hawk and eagle family are the very large eagles, with feathered legs; the Osprey, an eagle-sized "fish hawk"; harriers, which fly low over open areas and use their superb hearing as an aid in hunting; and the hawks: the accipiters, whose shorter wings allow them to achieve rapid twisting flight, and the broad-winged, soaring buteos. The pointed-winged falcons are fast fliers. Immature raptors, often striped below, take a year or more to reach adulthood. Females are 10 to 20 percent larger than males in most species. Raptors migrate during the day (unlike most songbirds). When feeding and during migration, they save energy by riding rising columns of air (thermals). While Broad-winged Hawks can be seen in migration along the Florida coast, most raptors that breed in eastern North America and winter in Central and South America migrate via the Texas coast and do not island-hop.

Flight silhouettes of raptors (*illustrations not to relative scale*)

Turkey Vulture

Osprey

Bald Eagle

Northern Harrier

Sharp-shinned Hawk (Accipiter)

Red-tailed Hawk (Buteo)

American Kestrel (Falcon)

~~B~~LACK VULTURE
~~Co~~ragyps atratus
~~A~~MERICAN VULTURE FAMILY

L 24″; WS 4′6″. Adult all black; head naked, scaly, silvery; bill pale gray. Imm. similar; head black, smooth, covered with fine down. Flight reveals short tail, rounded wings, solid black below; whitish patch on outer, "fingered" primaries. Soars often; accelerates with 3–5 quick flaps, glides on horizontal wings. Patrols skies over all habitats; spots dead or dying fish, birds, mammals; flocks to carcasses. Roosts conspicuously on dead trees. **VOICE** Hisses and grunts. **HABITAT** Fields, scrub, watersides, dumps, towns, farms. **RANGE** Resident in FL.

TURKEY VULTURE
Cathartes aura
AMERICAN VULTURE FAMILY

L 28″; WS 6′. Adult all black; head small, naked, red; bill yellow. Imm. head naked, gray. Soars with wings held up at 20 degrees above horizontal; seldom flaps wings. Long rounded tail and pale silver flight feathers can be seen from below. Finds carcasses by sight and smell. Gathers at nightly communal roosts in tall trees or towers. **VOICE** Grunts and hisses; usu. silent. **HABITAT** Woods, fields. **RANGE** Resident in FL.

adult (left), immatures and adult (right)

OSPREY
Pandion haliaetus
HAWK AND EAGLE FAMILY

L 23″; WS 5′6″. Adult brown above with white crown and dark line through eye; white below. Feet gray; eyes yellow. Imm. similar, but crown buffy; pa~~le~~ feather edges on wings and back produce scaly effect. Flies with wings b~~ent~~ at "wrist" like a flattened M; flight feathers and tail finely banded. H~~overs~~ frequently; often flies grasping a fish in its talons. Nest is mass of stick~~s top~~ping dead tree, platform on osprey pole, or navigational buoy. **VOI~~CE~~** ~~em~~phatic *kee-uk* and *cheep*. **HABITAT** Coastal estuaries, rivers, lakes~~.~~ ~~RANGE~~ Resident in FL; most common along coastal waterways.

SWALLOW-TAILED KITE
Elanoides forficatus
HAWK AND EAGLE FAMILY

L 24"; WS 4'2". Shaped like a giant swallow. Adult back and wings black; underparts and head white; bill small, black; tail very long, deeply forked, black. Flight reveals very pointed wings, white wing linings. Graceful flier that swoops down and snatches snakes, lizards, birds from trees, large insects from air. Often eats on the wing. **VOICE** Shrill *clee clee clee*. **HABITAT** Swamps, bottomlands. **RANGE** Mar.–Aug.: all FL.

male (left), female (right)

SNAIL KITE
"Everglade Kite"
Rostrhamus sociabilis
HAWK AND EAGLE FAMILY

17". Adult male body and head slaty black. Female and imm. brown above, heavily streaked brown below; base of bill and legs orange in female, yellow in imm. Bill thin, hooked; bare lores and base of bill red. Legs and feet red. Rump and tail white; black band near tail tip. Flies low and slowly on arched rounded wings, looking for Apple Snails. Endangered species in U.S.; population centered in Loxahatchee N.W.R., Lake Okeechobee, and n Everglades N.P. areas where water levels are favorable to snails. **VOICE** Low cackles; usu. silent. **HABITAT** Freshwater marshes. **RANGE** Resident in s peninsular FL.

NORTHERN HARRIER
Circus cyaneus
HAWK AND EAGLE FAMILY

L 22"; WS 4'. Adult male pearly gray; whiter below. Adult female brown above, dirty white with brown stripes below. Imm. (pictured) brown above; solid rusty orange below. Wings and tail long, narrow; rump white; head and bill small; owl-like facial disks. Flies low over open areas, wings raised at an angle, listening and watching for rodents, frogs, baby birds; often hovers and drops. Generally perches on ground. **VOICE** Weak *pee*. **HABITAT** Marshes, fields. **RANGE** Sept.–Apr.: all FL.

BALD EAGLE
Haliaeetus leucocephalus
HAWK AND EAGLE FAMILY

L 32"; WS 7'6". Adult body, wings, and thighs dark chocolate brown (may appear black); massive head white; bill yellow, strongly hooked; massive legs, feet, and eyes yellow; tail white, somewhat rounded. Imm. appears all dark brown or black when perched; flight reveals diffuse whitish wing linings and base of tail. Flies with slow deliberate wingbeats, wings held flat, straight out, with primaries spread. Sits on tall trees. Numbers increasing, with DDT ban and protection. **VOICE** Piercing scream. **HABITAT** Coasts, inland waterways. **RANGE** Resident in FL; in summer many disperse northward out of state.

adult (left), immature (above)

adult

RED-SHOULDERED HAWK
Buteo lineatus
HAWK AND EAGLE FAMILY

L 20"; WS 3'4". Adult head and back pale brown; underparts barred orange on buff; wings barred black and white above; shoulder rufous; tail black, with 5 thin white bands. Imm. streaked below, like most buteos. Seen from below, all ages have white crescent at base of primaries. Smaller, very pale, washed-out race inhabits s FL. **VOICE** Screaming *kee yarr.* **HABITAT** Wooded wetlands, swamps. **RANGE** Resident in FL.

pale race

immature (left), adult (right)

BROAD-WINGED HAWK
Buteo platypterus
HAWK AND EAGLE FAMILY

L 15"; WS 34". Adult head, back, and wings plain brown; underparts barred reddish brown on white. Flight reveals very white underwing, with narrow black borders; adult tail black with 2–3 wide white bands; in imm., bands less distinct. **VOICE** High whistled *pee-teee*. **HABITAT** Summer: broadleaf woods. Migration and winter: woods, towns. **RANGE** Apr.–Oct.: n FL. Oct.–Mar.: s FL. Migration: all FL. Flocks common along coast in Oct.

SHORT-TAILED HAWK
Buteo brachyurus
HAWK AND EAGLE FAMILY

16". Light morph: back, upperwing, crown, and cheeks slaty gray; underparts, underwing, and throat white. Dark-morph: entire body, head, upperwing, and wing linings black; white on flight feathers below. Short tail has many black and white bands; bill small, with yellow area around nostrils; legs yellow. Soars very high, often above vultures; power dives through them to ground for prey. **VOICE** High-pitched *kleeea*; usu. silent. **HABITAT** Savannas, woods, mangroves. **RANGE** Resident in s and c FL.

RED-TAILED HAWK
Buteo jamaicensis
HAWK AND EAGLE FAMILY

adult (left), immature (right)

L 22"; WS 4'2". Head, back, and wings dark brown; upper chest white; lower chest has band of heavy brown streaks contrasting with white thighs; tail pale orange below, dark rufous above. Seen from below, underwing mainly white, with dark leading edge under shoulder and black crescent beyond wrist. Imm. duller, more streaked; tail not rusty. Perches in trees. Often mobbed by crows, redwings, grackles, kingbirds. **VOICE** Downslurred squeal: *keee-rrr*. **HABITAT** Woodland edges, isolated trees in fields. **RANGE** Resident in mainland FL. In Keys Oct.–Apr. only.

CRESTED CARACARA
Caracara plancus
FALCON FAMILY

23". Body, crown, and crest black; rest of head and neck white; chest finely barred black and white; flight reveals white patch on primaries. Wings long, rounded; face bare, pink; bill heavy, silver; legs long; tail long, finely banded black and white, with black end band. Perches on posts; walks and runs on ground. Feeds on carrion, small animals. Threatened in FL. **VOICE** Harsh cackle. **HABITAT** Savannas, palm groves. **RANGE** Resident in sc peninsular FL, mainly north and west of Lake Okeechobee.

AMERICAN KESTREL
Falco sparverius
FALCON FAMILY

male (left), female (right)

L 11"; WS 23". Male back rufous; wings blue-gray; chest pale buffy; tail rufous, with black terminal band. Female rufous above, with fine black bars. 2 thin, black sideburns on white face. In flight, pointed wings obvious; often hovers. **VOICE** Shrill *killy killy.* **HABITAT** Prairies, farms, towns. **RANGE** Resident in n FL. Sept.–May: c and s FL.

PEREGRINE FALCON
Falco peregrinus
FALCON FAMILY

L 18"; WS 3'4". Upperparts and tail dark slaty gray; underparts and underwing finely gray-barred; head black above, white below, with 1 thick black sideburn. Feet heavy, powerful. Flight reveals pointed wings, broad at base; tail tapers to squared end. Flies low and high, often surveying bird flocks to spot slow-flying, injured individuals. Dives from sky. Numbers plummeted with DDT; now recovering. **VOICE** Harsh *kak kak.* **HABITAT** Coasts, marshes, towns. **RANGE** Sept.–Apr.: all FL.

WILD TURKEY
Meleagris gallopavo
PARTRIDGE FAMILY

Male 4′; female 3′. Male body dark brown, looks iridescent coppery-green; flight feathers black, banded white; tail rufous with black bands; head bare, warty, red and/or blue; black "beard" hangs from chest. Female similar, with smaller, duller head. Legs red. Feeds on ground; visits rural birdfeeders; roosts in trees at night. **VOICE** Male: repeated gobble. **HABITAT** Broadleaf woods, esp. oaks; farms. **RANGE** Resident in n and c FL south to Lake Okeechobee and Naples area.

NORTHERN BOBWHITE
Colinus virginianus
PARTRIDGE FAMILY

10″. Male chest and upperparts rusty; belly speckled black and white; chestnut crown and face patch contrast with white eyebrow and throat. Female similar, with buffy eyebrow and throat. Lives in family groups (coveys). Tail short. **VOICE** Male: whistled *bob white.* **HABITAT** Brushy fields. **RANGE** Resident in mainland FL; not in Keys.

SORA
"Sora Crake"
Porzana carolina
RAIL FAMILY

9″. Plump; bill short, thick, yellow. Adult blackish brown above; sides of neck and chest slaty; belly barred blackish; face and foreneck black; legs olive green. Imm. chest brown; throat white. Usually secretive. **VOICE** Whistled *ker-wee;* descending whinny. **HABITAT** Freshwater marshes. **RANGE** Sept.–Apr.: all FL.

VIRGINIA RAIL
Rallus limicola
RAIL FAMILY

10″. Adult brown above; chest and wings rufous; sides barred black and white; cheeks gray; eyes red; bill long, thin, drooping, red with black tip. Legs dull red; toes long. Tail short. Usu. secretive. **VOICE** Repeated *kid ick;* grunting *oink* notes. **HABITAT** Freshwater marshes. **RANGE** Oct.–Mar.: all FL.

CLAPPER RAIL
Rallus longirostris
RAIL FAMILY

14″. Gray above; belly dark gray with paler bars; chest and head buffy; bill long, stout, yellowish, droops at tip. Legs buffy gray; toes long. Tail short. Often secretive; seen running across roads and low-tide mud near cover, on high ground during very high tides. **VOICE** Harsh *kek kek kek kek kek*. **HABITAT** Saltwater and brackish marshes. **RANGE** Resident in FL. **King Rail** (*R. elegans*) of freshwater marshes (all FL) has brown back, rusty orange face and chest.

PURPLE GALLINULE
Porphyrula martinica
RAIL FAMILY

13″. Green above; head, neck, and underparts dark purplish blue; forehead shield pale blue; bill red, yellow-tipped. Legs bright yellow; white vent under short tail. Feet unwebbed. Imm. pale buffy brown with bluish wings. Cocks tail when walking over floating vegetation. **VOICE** Hen-like, cackling *kek kek kek*; grunts. **HABITAT** Freshwater marshes with water lilies and pickerelweeds. **RANGE** Resident in c and s FL. Apr.–Sept.: n FL and Keys.

COMMON MOORHEN
"Common Gallinule"
Gallinula chloropus
RAIL FAMILY

14″. Back brown; underparts, sides, neck dark slaty; white stripe along sides and vent; head black; frontal shield and bill bright red (duller in winter); bill has yellow tip. Legs red above knee, green below. Feet unwebbed. Imm. slaty brown; white stripe on side. **VOICE** Clucks and grating notes. **HABITAT** Freshwater marshes, watersides. **RANGE** Resident in FL.

AMERICAN COOT
Fulica americana
RAIL FAMILY

15″. Adult sooty gray; head and neck black; bill thick, white, black near tip; sides of undertail white. Feet not webbed, but toes lobed. Imm. paler gray below; bill silvery. Dives and skitters over surface to become airborne like a diving duck, swims like a duck—but not a duck. Often in rafts (flocks). **VOICE** Grating *kuk* notes. **HABITAT** Marshes, ponds. **RANGE** Resident in s FL. Oct.–Apr.: all FL.

LIMPKIN
Aramus guarauna
LIMPKIN FAMILY

26". Body dark brown; head, neck, and back heavily spotted white; bill long, arches downward, pinkish. Neck and legs long; tail short. Jerky flight with rapid upstrokes. Often solitary; feeds heavily on Apple Snail, plus marsh insects and frogs. **VOICE** Piercing wail: *kurr-ur-ee-oww.* **HABITAT** Swamps, freshwater marshes. **RANGE** Resident in FL; most common in inland peninsula.

SANDHILL CRANE
Grus canadensis
CRANE FAMILY

L 3'4"; WS 6'. Mostly gray, often stained rusty; forecrown red; cheeks white. Imm. head and neck brown. Neck long, thin; bill shortish, thin, straight, black. Legs long, black. Flies with neck outstretched; often calls in air. Feeds mainly on seeds, tubers. **VOICE** Loud rattling *kar-r-r-r-o-o-o,* often in flight. **HABITAT** Large freshwater marshes, pastures, open woods. **RANGE** Resident in peninsular FL. Nov.–Apr.: all mainland FL. **Whooping Crane** *(G. americana)* larger (L 4'7"); recently introduced to FL; adult white; cheeks and crown red; primaries black.

Shorebirds

The term "shorebird" is used for certain members of the order Charadriiformes: plovers, oystercatchers, avocets and stilts, and sandpipers, including godwits, dowitchers, yellowlegs, curlews, and small sandpipers informally known as "peeps." Most shorebirds frequent open muddy, sandy, or rocky shores on the coast and around open inland wetlands. On the coast they tend to roost in moderate to enormous mixed-species flocks at high tide; at low tide they spread out to feed on small invertebrates. Most American shorebirds have a distinct breeding plumage in late spring and early summer. Varying numbers of nonbreeding sandpipers spend the summer in Florida, and some breeders return by mid-July from Arctic breeding grounds. Months given in the accounts denote when the largest populations are in the state. In identifying shorebirds, general proportion and shape, as well as behavior and voice, are frequently more important than plumage color.

BLACK-BELLIED PLOVER
Pluvialis squatarola
PLOVER FAMILY

12″. Breeding: back and wings speckled black and white; crown, hindneck, and sides of chest white; face, foreneck, and chest black. Nonbreeding: grayish; back speckled. Bill short, straight; eyes large, black; legs black. **VOICE** Whistled *pee-a-wee*. **HABITAT** Ocean beaches and mudflats. **RANGE** Aug.–May: all FL coasts; inland (rare).

SNOWY PLOVER
Charadrius alexandrinus
PLOVER FAMILY

6″. Pale brown above; white below; bill short, thin, black; legs dark gray. Breeding: forecrown, patch behind eye, and partial neck ring black. Nonbreeding: eye patch and partial neck ring dark brown; no black on forecrown. **VOICE** Musical *chu-wee*. **HABITAT** Coastal beaches. **RANGE** Resident on Gulf coast south to Naples; breeds along panhandle.

WILSON'S PLOVER
Charadrius wilsonia
PLOVER FAMILY

8″. Dark brown above; white below; black bill longer and heavier than other small plovers. Adult male: thick breast band and forecrown line between eye and bill black. Female: thick brown breast band; no black on head. Feigns broken wing near nest. **VOICE** Single or double *wheet*. **HABITAT** Coastal beaches, mudflats. **RANGE** Resident along all coasts; rarer in panhandle, w FL.

SEMIPALMATED PLOVER
Charadrius semipalmatus
PLOVER FAMILY

7½″. Upperparts dark brown; white below. Breeding: base of bill and legs yellow; black breast band. Nonbreeding and imm.: bill short, black; breast band brown. Appears neckless. **VOICE** Whistled *tu-wheet*. **HABITAT** Coastal beaches, mudflats. **RANGE** Aug.–Apr.: all coastal FL; inland (rare).

PIPING PLOVER
Charadrius melodus
PLOVER FAMILY

7″. Upperparts very pale gray; white below; legs yellow. Breeding: partial black collar; base of bill yellow. Nonbreeding and imm.: bill black; lacks collar. Appears neckless; bill short. Threatened. **VOICE** Whistled *peep-lo*. **HABITAT** Coastal beaches, sandy flats. **RANGE** Aug.–Apr.: mainly Gulf coast.

KILLDEER
Charadrius vociferus
PLOVER FAMILY

10″. Adult brown above, white below, with 2 black chest bands; pied face with red eye ring; legs pale yellow, pink, or gray. Flight reveals wing stripe, orange rump and upper tail. Common inland plover in open habitats. Parent feigns broken wing to attract interlopers away from nest or chicks. **VOICE** Strident *killdee*. **HABITAT** Farms, fields, playgrounds, golf courses. **RANGE** Resident south to c FL. Aug.–Apr.: all FL; common.

AMERICAN OYSTERCATCHER
Haematopus palliatus
OYSTERCATCHER FAMILY

19″. Adult dark brown above, with bold white wing stripe; underparts white; head, neck, and tail black; bill stout, long, straight, orange; legs pinkish. Imm. head and bill brown. Flight reveals white wing stripe. **VOICE** Loud *kleep*. **HABITAT** Coastal beaches, mudflats. **RANGE** Resident in FL; most common on coasts of n and c FL.

BLACK-NECKED STILT
Himantopus mexicanus
AVOCET AND STILT FAMILY

15″. Body dark above (male black, female dark brownish black), white below; head mainly dark, with large white spot over eye; bill long, thin, black. Legs very long, red; rump and tail white. Flight reveals wings uniformly blackish above. Wades up to belly, eating aquatic insects and other invertebrates. **VOICE** Sharp *yip yip yip*. **HABITAT** Flooded fields, marsh pools, mudflats. **RANGE** Resident in FL; more common Apr.–Sept.

nonbreeding (left), breeding (right)

AMERICAN AVOCET
Recurvirostra americana
AVOCET AND STILT FAMILY

18″. Back and wings pied black and white; white below; neck long; bill long, slender, upturned, black; legs long, silvery; rump and tail white. Nonbreeding: head and neck gray. Breeding: head and neck pale rusty orange. Feeds in flocks; sweeps bill from side to side in water when feeding. **VOICE** Loud *wheep*. **HABITAT** Flooded fields, open shallow ponds. **RANGE** Sept.–Apr.: c and s FL.

GREATER YELLOWLEGS
Tringa melanoleuca
SANDPIPER FAMILY

14″. Breeding: back brown-black with white dots; head, neck, and sides speckled dark brown. Nonbreeding: paler; faint brown dots on chest. Neck long; bill 1½ times longer than head, has relatively thick gray base and thin, black, slightly upcurved tip. Legs long, bright yellow; rump white. Often nods head. **VOICE** Excited *tew tew tew*. **HABITAT** Coastal and inland mudflats and marshes. **RANGE** Aug.–May: all FL.

LESSER YELLOWLEGS
Tringa flavipes
SANDPIPER FAMILY

11″. Smaller version of Greater Yellowlegs (see previous species): plumages similar; legs also bright yellow; bill shorter (equal to length of head), straight, all black. **VOICE** 1 or 2 mellow *tew* notes. **HABITAT** Coastal and inland mudflats. **RANGE** Aug.–May: all FL.

SPOTTED SANDPIPER
Actitis macularia
SANDPIPER FAMILY

8″. Breeding: brown above; black spots on white un
Nonbreeding: unspotted on sides of chest. O° rump. Flies on stiff k **VOICE** *Pee-weet-weet*. of rivers, lakes, an on coast. **RANGE** ᵀ

WILLET
Catoptrophorus semipalmatus
SANDPIPER FAMILY

15″. Breeding: speckled brownish gray. Nonbreeding: plain gray. Bill thick-based, long, straight; legs blue-gray; tail gray. Flight reveals black wings with broad white central stripe. VOICE Loud *pill-will-willet.* HABITAT Beaches, mudflats. RANGE Resident on all FL coasts.

RUDDY TURNSTONE
Arenaria interpres
SANDPIPER FAMILY

9″. Breeding: back orange and black; head and chest pied black and white. Nonbreeding: somber; brown chest patch. Bill short, upturned. legs orange. Flight reveals harlequin wing pattern. VOICE Rattling *tuk-e-tuk.* HABITAT Beaches, mudflats. RANGE Aug.–May: coastal FL.

WHIMBREL
Numenius phaeopus
SANDPIPER FAMILY

18″. Adult and imm. neck, chest, and back speckled brown; belly dirty white; head has dark brown stripes through eye and bordering pale mid-crown stripe; legs bluish. Neck thin; bill very long, thin, downcurved. In flight appears uniformly brown. VOICE 5–7 whistled *ti* notes. HABITAT Salt marshes, mudflats, beaches. RANGE Aug.–Apr.: coastal FL.

RED KNOT
Calidris canutus
SANDPIPER FAMILY

11″. Breeding: back scaled with black; face and underparts orange. Nonbreeding: uniformly gray. Legs short; bill straight, with thick base. Flight reveals thin white wing stripe, barred rump. Congregates in large flocks at a few sites. VOICE Soft *knut.* HABITAT Seaside rocks, beaches, mudflats. RANGE Sept.–Apr.: coastal FL. Most common Aug.–Oct., Apr.–May.

SANDERLING
Calidris alba
SANDPIPER FAMILY

8″. Breeding: head and upperparts rusty; belly white. Nonbreeding: gray above, white below; bend of wing black. Bill short; legs black. Imm. crown and back heavily black-spotted. Runs ahead of incoming waves. Usu. in parties of 10–20. VOICE Sharp *plic.* HABITAT Sand beaches. RANGE Aug.–Apr.: coastal FL.

WESTERN SANDPIPER
Calidris mauri
SANDPIPER FAMILY

6½". Breeding: rusty above; fine black dots on foreparts. Nonbreeding: gray above, white below. Bill fairly long, black, droops at tip; legs black. Fall imm. rusty on back. **VOICE** High *cheep*. **HABITAT** Coastal and inland mudflats. **RANGE** Aug.–Apr.: all FL. **Semipalmated Sandpiper** *(C. pusilla)* very similar; bill shorter, straight, blunt at tip; common migrant (Apr.–May, Aug.–Oct.).

LEAST SANDPIPER
Calidris minutilla
SANDPIPER FAMILY

6". Breeding: reddish brown above; chest buffy brown, lightly spotted. Nonbreeding: browner than other small sandpipers. Bill short, thin, slightly drooping, black; legs yellow or green. **VOICE** High *kreet*. **HABITAT** Fresh and salt marsh edges and mudflats. **RANGE** Aug.–Apr.: all FL.

PECTORAL SANDPIPER
Calidris melanotos
SANDPIPER FAMILY

9". Scaly dark brown above; foreneck and chest buff with fine black streaks, sharply demarcated from clear white belly. Bill slightly curved. **VOICE** *Krrip*. **HABITAT** Wet meadows, salt marshes. **RANGE** Aug.–Sept.: all FL.

DUNLIN
Calidris alpina
SANDPIPER FAMILY

8". Breeding: reddish brown above, white below with fine black dots; black midbelly patch. Nonbreeding: gray; belly white. Bill long, drooping. Legs black. **VOICE** Soft *krrit*. **HABITAT** Coastal mudflats, beaches; a few inland. **RANGE** Sept.–May: mainly coastal FL.

COMMON SNIPE
Gallinago gallinago
SANDPIPER FAMILY

11". Adult and imm. dark brown above, with several white stripes; sides striped; midbelly white; head has 4 bold blackish stripes; tail rusty. Legs short; bill very long, straight. Flies in erratic zigzag. **VOICE** Hoarse *skaip*. **HABITAT** Wet meadows, marshes. **RANGE** Oct.–Mar.: all FL.

SHORT-BILLED DOWITCHER
Limnodromus griseus
SANDPIPER FAMILY

12″. Breeding: speckled brown above; neck, chest, and sides orange, dotted black; midbelly white. Nonbreeding: gray above, white below. Bill very long, straight. Flight reveals white rump extending up back in wedge. Feeds with rapid sewing-machine motion. **VOICE** Musical *tu tu tu.* **HABITAT** Mudflats, shallow pools. **RANGE** Aug.–Apr.: mainly coastal FL.

AMERICAN WOODCOCK
Scolopax minor
SANDPIPER FAMILY

11″. Mostly clear buff; back darker, speckled. Head massive, with no apparent neck; crown has 3 rectangular black patches; eyes large; bill very long, straight, brownish yellow. Legs very short. Male noisy in high aerial courtship flights in early spring. **VOICE** Buzzy *peeent;* usu. silent most of year. **HABITAT** Swampy areas in woods, thickets. **RANGE** Resident in n FL. Oct.–Feb.: c and s FL.

Gulls and Terns

All members of the gull and tern family (Laridae)—gulls, jaegers, terns, and skimmers—have webbed feet and breed in the open, in colonies, on islands free of land predators. Their nests are usually mere depressions in the ground. Many people erroneously call gulls "seagulls." However, while gulls are common near the sea, few are found far at sea; in fact, many breed far inland near fresh water. Superb fliers, most gulls have wings with white trailing edges, and fairly long, strong bills that are slightly hooked at the tip. These generalist feeders and scavengers eat living and dead animal life, and many have adapted to feed on human refuse. Gulls go through a confusing array of plumages and molts until they reach adulthood in two years (small species), three years (medium), or four years (large). For many gull species, this guide describes selected life-stage categories, including juvenile (the bird's birth summer), first winter, first summer (bird is one year old), second winter, summer adult, and winter adult. Jaegers are quite large, dark brown seabirds that attack other seabirds and steal their fish; they are rare migrants off Florida coasts. The small to medium-size terns, sleek and slender-billed, fly in a buoyant or hovering manner, diving headfirst for small fish; most have black caps (in summer) and elegant, forked tails. Most terns nest in small to enormous colonies on beaches and islands. Skimmers are large, black-and-white shoreline birds with short legs and extra-long lower bills that they use to skim fish from the water.

LAUGHING GULL
Larus atricilla
GULL AND TERN FAMILY

winter adult (left), summer adult (right)

17″. Summer adult: back and wings slaty gray; head black; neck, underparts and tail white; no white on wingtips; eye ring white; bill red. Winter adult: head white; bill black. Bill droops downward; legs black. Juv.: upperparts and chest band unspotted gray-brown; bill black. Nests in colonies on islands. Abundant on beaches in winter. **VOICE** High *haah* notes. **HABITAT** Coastal beaches, mudflats; some on inland waters. **RANGE** Resident in FL.

RING-BILLED GULL
Larus delawarensis
GULL AND TERN FAMILY

winter adult (left), 1st winter (right)

L 19″; WS 4′. Winter adult: head and underparts white, with fine brown spots; back silvery; wings silvery; wingtips black with white spots; bill yellow with black ring near tip; legs greenish yellow. 1st winter: back gray; wing coverts speckled brown; tail white, with black terminal band; bill pink with black tip. **VOICE** High-pitched *high-er.* **HABITAT** Inland lakes, towns, coasts. **RANGE** Sept.–Apr.: all FL. Summer: many nonbreeders remain.

HERRING GULL
Larus argentatus
GULL AND TERN FAMILY

winter adult (left), 1st winter (right)

L 25″; WS 4′10″. Legs and feet pink in all ages. Winter adult: back and wings silvery; wingtips black with white spots; head and underparts white, with fine brown spots; bill yellow with black and red dot near tip. 2nd winter: pale brown with brown spots; flight feathers and tail black; bill pink with black tip. 1st winter: darker brown, with speckled back; bill black. **VOICE** Varied, incl. loud series of *kee-yow* and *gah* notes. **HABITAT** Coastal beaches and waterways; inland waters (local). **RANGE** Sept.–Apr.: all FL. Summer: many nonbreeders remain.

GULL-BILLED TERN
Sterna nilotica
GULL AND TERN FAMILY

15″. Pale silvery above, white below; primaries tipped dark gray; bill black, short, thick for a tern; tail notched, short; legs short, black. Summer adult: crown black. Winter adult: eye ring black; crown white. Feeds on large insects as it courses over grass or water. Rarely dives into water; plucks items at surface. Nests in colonies on small open islands in or near marsh. **VOICE** Raspy *katy-did*. **HABITAT** Marshes, fields, coastal beaches and waters. **RANGE** Apr.–Nov.: all FL, mainly Gulf coast.

CASPIAN TERN
Sterna caspia
GULL AND TERN FAMILY

21″. Pale silvery above, white below; flight reveals black underside of primaries; bill red, thick for a tern; legs short, black; tail notched, short. Summer adult: cap black. Winter adult: cap blackish, streaked white. Flies low when feeding; dives for fish. May nest in colonies. **VOICE** Harsh *kra-haa*. **HABITAT** Mainly coastal waters; fewer inland. **RANGE** Apr.–Sept.: breeds mainly on Gulf coast. Oct.–Apr.: s FL. Apr., Sept.–Oct.: all coasts.

ROYAL TERN
Sterna maxima
GULL AND TERN FAMILY

20″. Pale silvery above, white below; primaries tipped dark gray; bill orange, fairly thick; legs short, black; tail long. Summer adult: cap black, crested. Winter adult: forecrown white, rear crown black-crested. Flies high when feeding; dives for fish. Nests in colonies of up to 10,000 birds on sandy islets. **VOICE** High harsh *keeeeerr*. **HABITAT** Coastal beaches and waters; inland (rare). **RANGE** Resident on all FL coasts; breeds mainly on c Gulf coast.

FORSTER'S TERN
Sterna forsteri
GULL AND TERN FAMILY

summer adult (left), winter adult (right)

15″. Pale silvery above, white below; primaries white; bill slender; tail forked, long. Summer adult: cap black; bill red orange with black tip; legs red. Winter adult: crown white; long black eye mask; bill black. Feeds on aerial insects; dives for fish. **VOICE** Grating *kay-r-r-r;* a repeated *kip*. **HABITAT** Beaches, marshes, lakes. **RANGE** Aug.–Apr.: all FL. Some (nonbreeders) oversummer.

SANDWICH TERN
Sterna sandvicensis
GULL AND TERN FAMILY
20″. Pale silvery above, white below; primaries tipped dark gray; bill slender, black with yellow tip (adult); legs short, black; tail long. Summer adult: cap black, crested. Winter adult: forecrown white, rear crown black. Flies high when feeding; feeds well out to sea. Nests in colonies of other terns on sandy islets. **VOICE** Grating *kerr-ick.* **HABITAT** Coastal beaches, waters. **RANGE** Apr.–Aug.: n FL. Oct.–Mar.: peninsular FL, Keys.

LEAST TERN
Sterna antillarum
GULL AND TERN FAMILY
9″. Summer adult: back and wings silvery; neck and underparts white; crown black, with white forehead; bill yellow with black tip; legs yellow; tail forked. Juv.: pale scaly brown above. Nests in small colonies, in scrapes in sand. FL's smallest tern. Very vulnerable to disturbance by humans and animals. **VOICE** Repeated *kip;* harsh *chee-eek.* **HABITAT** Ocean beaches, coastal waters. **RANGE** Apr.–Sept.: all FL.

SOOTY TERN
Sterna fuscata
GULL AND TERN FAMILY
16″. Adult black above, white below; crown and line through eye black; forehead white; bill thin, black; legs short, black; tail black, with white outer streamers. Plucks small fish and squid from sea's surface. Nests in colonies in sand or on ledges. Dry Tortugas host about 40,000 pairs. **VOICE** Harsh *wide-a-wake.* **HABITAT** Feeds and sleeps far out to sea; nests on remote islet beaches. **RANGE** Feb.–Aug.: Dry Tortugas only; not on mainland.

BROWN NODDY
Anous stolidus
GULL AND TERN FAMILY
15″. Adult uniformly dark brown ex. for white crown that blends into brown neck; bill longish, black; legs short, black; tail wedge-shaped, with tiny notch at tip. Plucks small fish from sea's surface. Dry Tortugas host about 2,000 pairs. **VOICE** Low, crow-like *caarrk.* **HABITAT** Open ocean; nests on remote islets. **RANGE** Mar.–Oct.: Dry Tortugas only; not on mainland.

BLACK SKIMMER
Rynchops niger
GULL AND TERN FAMILY

18″. Adult black above; forehead and underparts white; legs red, short; tail mainly white, short, notched. Imm. brown above, with white scaly feather edges. Bill long, black-tipped, red at base, with lower mandible much longer. Creates ripple in calm waters with lower bill; circles back for fish. VOICE Short barks. HABITAT Coastal lagoons and waterways; inland (rare). RANGE Resident in coastal FL.

ROCK DOVE
Columba livia
PIGEON AND DOVE FAMILY

13″. Typical: head dark gray; coppery sheen on neck; body and tail pale gray; white on upper rump; 2 black bars on secondaries; tail tipped black. Variations: black to pale brown and white. Bill short, black; legs short, red. Powerful flier; wings pointed. Common town pigeon. VOICE Gurgling *coo-cuk-crooo*. HABITAT Towns, parks, farms. RANGE Resident in settled FL.

WHITE-CROWNED PIGEON
Columba leucocephala
PIGEON AND DOVE FAMILY

13″. Adult purplish black, incl. underwing; crown white; eyes yellow; bill small, red, with yellow tip; legs red. Head and legs small; tail fan-shaped. Seen mainly in small flocks on wing; feeds on fruits in tall trees. Nests in colonies. VOICE Owl-like *coo-coo-co-woo*. HABITAT Tropical broadleaf woods, mangroves. RANGE Resident in Keys and on s tip of peninsula; most common Mar.–Sept.

EURASIAN COLLARED-DOVE
Streptopelia decaocto
PIGEON AND DOVE FAMILY

11½″. Body and head pale buffy gray; wings light gray with primaries dark gray above; black half-collar edged in white; bill short, black; legs reddish. Tail fan-shaped; white corners above, white with black base below. Introduced to Bahamas; recently spread to Florida. VOICE Repeated flat *ca-COO-kuk*. HABITAT Towns, parks, fields, farms. RANGE Resident in se FL; expanding range.

MOURNING DOVE
Zenaida macroura
PIGEON AND DOVE FAMILY

12″. Head small; tail long. Back, wings, and tail dull brown; head and underparts pale buffy; black spot below eye; bill short, black; legs short, red; black and white edges on wedge-shaped, pointed tail. Male cap and nape blue-gray. Wings whistle when taking flight. **VOICE** Mournful *coo WHO-O coo, coo, coo.* **HABITAT** Fields, gardens, sandy scrub. **RANGE** Resident in FL.

COMMON GROUND-DOVE
Columbina passerina
PIGEON AND DOVE FAMILY

7″. Sparrow-sized; short-tailed. Body pale brown; black spots on wing coverts; primaries bright rufous; head and chest pinkish gray, scaled black; legs pinkish; white sides to black tail. Pairs walk sandy paths together; fairly approachable. **VOICE** Soft, rising, repeated *coo-ah.* **HABITAT** Open scrubby areas, beaches, open woods. **RANGE** Resident in FL.

YELLOW-BILLED CUCKOO
Coccyzus americanus
CUCKOO FAMILY

12″. Upperparts, crown, and cheeks brown; bright rufous on primaries; clear white below; bill black above, yellow below, slightly downcurved; eye ring yellow; tail long and narrow, brown above, black below, with 6 large white spots. Forages for caterpillars and cicadas in heavy foliage. Shy. **VOICE** 20 guttural notes in descending, slowing sequence. **HABITAT** Hardwood and pinewoods, garden trees, thickets. **RANGE** Apr.–Oct.: all FL.

MANGROVE CUCKOO
Coccyzus minor
CUCKOO FAMILY

12″. Upperparts brown; white below, washed buffy on belly; bill black above, yellow below, slightly downcurved; eye ring yellow; long black patch behind eye; tail long, narrow, brown above, black below with 6 large white spots. Very secretive; best located by call. **VOICE** Series of soft scolding *gaw* notes. **HABITAT** Tall mangrove forests, thickets. **RANGE** Resident in Keys and s FL. Apr.–Oct.: Gulf coast n to Tampa Bay; se Atlantic coast.

SMOOTH-BILLED ANI
Crotophaga ani
CUCKOO FAMILY

14". All plumage, eyes, legs, and bill black; bill smooth-sided, flattened vertically, puffin-like; tail long, flat, narrow, rounded at end. Small parties flop awkwardly around bushes. Flight slow and low. VOICE 2-note, rising *too weak?* HABITAT Farms, town edges, scrublands, fields. RANGE Resident in c and s peninsular FL.

Owls

Owls are nocturnal birds of prey that range in size in Florida from 9 to 23 inches long. They have large heads, with large, forward-facing eyes (yellow in most species). Their eyesight and hearing are acute. Distinct facial disks conceal large ear openings that provide them with keen hearing, which can pinpoint a squeak or a rustle in the grass in total darkness. The ears are asymmetrically placed on either side of the head, providing greater range of sound and better triangulation for pinpointing sources of sounds. Some owls have tufts of feathers at the corners of the head that look like ears or horns and are called ear tufts. Owls' bodies are cryptically colored and patterned to blend with the background of their daytime nest or roost. They are most readily seen in winter in open areas and leafless woodlands. Their bills are short, but strongly hooked. The legs are typically short, and the feet have sharp, curved talons. Owls fly silently;

ear tuft

facial disk

Parts of an Owl

their feathers are delicately fringed and very soft. Imitations and tapes of their voices, given or played at night, often bring a response from an owl, which may call or fly in close to the source of the call, or both; in daytime, the same sounds may bring crows, jays, and songbirds, which usually mob roosting owls they discover.

GREAT HORNED OWL
Bubo virginianus
OWL FAMILY

L 23"; WS 4'7". Dark brown with black spots above; underparts pale brown with heavy dark brown bars; dark streaks on upper chest; facial disks rich rusty brown, ringed in black. Head large; eyes yellow; fluffy ear tufts. VOICE 3–8 deep hoots, 2nd and 3rd rapid and doubled. HABITAT Woods, parks. RANGE Resident in FL.

BARN OWL
Tyto alba
BARN OWL FAMILY

18″. Pale orange wash with gray above; white flecked with black dots below; head large, round, without ear tufts; disks form white, heart-shaped face; eyes dark. Legs long, feathered; feet yellow. Superb "mouser" with acute hearing. Strictly nocturnal; perches on poles along back roads at night. **VOICE** Variety of harsh screams, hisses, and clicks. **HABITAT** Woods, fields, towns. **RANGE** Resident in FL.

EASTERN SCREECH-OWL
Otus asio
OWL FAMILY

9″. 2 color morphs: gray and rufous. Facial disks pale gray or orange, ringed in black; dark streaks on breast; row of white spots on shoulder. Tail short; eyes yellow; fluffy ear tufts. **VOICE** Mournful whinny, rising then falling in pitch; also fast, even-pitched series of *hu* notes. **HABITAT** Woods, wooded swamps, cemeteries, towns. **RANGE** Resident in FL.

BURROWING OWL
Speotyto cunicularia
OWL FAMILY

9″. Body brown above, spotted with white; white below, scaled brown; head rounded, no ear tufts; facial disks light brown; eyes yellow. Legs long, grayish; tail short. Digs burrow nest in field, in small colonies; sentinel may stand by burrow in day. **VOICE** Mellow *coo-coo* at night. **HABITAT** Open fields, airports, golf courses. **RANGE** Resident in peninsular FL.

BARRED OWL
Strix varia
OWL FAMILY

L 21″; WS 3′8″. Dark brownish gray with black spots above; heavily striped underparts; dark bars on upper chest; facial disks gray, ringed in black. Eyes brown; lacks ear tufts. Feeds at night; some sit conspicuously on horizontal limbs by day. **VOICE** 2 sets of *hoo* notes: *Who cooks for you? Who cooks for you-all?* **HABITAT** Swamps, woods. **RANGE** Resident in FL.

COMMON NIGHTHAWK
Chordeiles minor
NIGHTJAR FAMILY

10″. Dark brown, heavily gray-spotted; throat white; legs very short. Flight reveals long, pointed, black primaries with prominent white bar; tail long, notched. Flies high and erratically. Hunts at night for insects. **VOICE** Nasal *peeent*. **HABITAT** Fields, ballparks, towns. **RANGE** Apr.–Oct.: all FL, ex. Keys. **Antillean Nighthawk** *(C. gundlachii)* identical by sight; lives Apr.–Sept. from Key West to Homestead in fields, airports; call is *pity-pit-pit.*

CHUCK-WILL'S-WIDOW
Caprimulgus carolinensis
NIGHTJAR FAMILY

12″. Dark tawny brown above and below, with blackish spots; throat buffy; white foreneck half-collar above blackish chest; bill and legs tiny; tail long, banded rufous. Flight reveals dark rounded wings, white outer tail. **VOICE** Oft-repeated *chuck-will's-widow.* **HABITAT** Open woods and clearings. **RANGE** Apr.–Sept.: all FL. A few winter in s FL. **Whip-poor-will** *(C. vociferus)* smaller (10″); throat black; in all FL Sept.–Apr.

CHIMNEY SWIFT
Chaetura pelagica
SWIFT FAMILY

5½″. Sooty gray; bill tiny; wings extend beyond tail when perched; clings upright with very small feet. In flight: dark, with pale gray throat; wings long and pointed; tail squared off. Flies fast, fairly high, in arcs. For nest, cements sticks with saliva to vertical spaces inside buildings, tree hollows. **VOICE** Rapid *chitter* and *chip* notes, frequently given in flight. **HABITAT** Towns, houses, fields. **RANGE** Apr.–Oct.: all FL, ex. Keys.

BELTED KINGFISHER
Ceryle alcyon
KINGFISHER FAMILY

13″. Male blue above, with tiny white spots; head blue; throat, neck, and belly white, with blue belt on chest. Female (pictured) similar; belly has 2nd (rufous) belt extending onto sides. Head large, with ragged fore- and rear crests; bill very long, thick, pointed, black; white spot before eye. Active, calls often; dives headfirst to seize small fish. **VOICE** Loud woody rattle. **HABITAT** Rivers, lakes, coasts. **RANGE** Resident in n half of FL. Sept.–Apr.: all FL.

RUBY-THROATED HUMMINGBIRD

female (left), male (right)

Archilochus colubris
HUMMINGBIRD FAMILY

3½". Male upperparts and crown iridescent green; chest and vent white; sides green; black line below eye; iridescent red throat often appears black; tail black, forked. Female green above, white below; tail corners tipped black and white. Bill long, needle-like, black; small white spot behind eye. Hovers at feeders and flowers, preferring red or orange tubular ones. Beats wings dozens of times a second; male wings can make humming sound. Hummingbirds are the only birds that can fly backward. **VOICE** High *chips*, squeaks. **HABITAT** Woodland edges, fields, gardens. **RANGE** Mar.–Oct.: n FL. Sept.–May: s FL (uncommon).

Woodpeckers

Woodpeckers, which range in size from small to medium, cling to the trunks and large branches of trees with their sharp claws (on short legs) and stiff, spine-tipped tails that help support them in the vertical position. Their long, pointed bills are like chisels, able to bore into wood. Curled inside the woodpecker head is a narrow tongue twice the length of the bill, tipped with spear-like barbs that impale wood-boring insects. Members of this family laboriously dig out nest holes in living or dead tree trunks and limbs. The sexes are very much alike, but the red patches on the heads of the males are reduced or lacking in the females of many species. In spring, males rapidly bang their bills against resonant wood on trees and buildings in a territorial drumming that is louder and more rapid than the tapping made while feeding. Most Florida woodpeckers are year round residents.

RED-HEADED WOODPECKER

Melanerpes erythrocephalus
WOODPECKER FAMILY

9". Adult back and wings black, ex. for white secondaries; clear white below; head and neck all red. Rump white; tail black. Imm. back, much of wings, and head brown. Caches acorns in tree cavities; will feed on ground and catch large insects in air. **VOICE** Loud high *chuurr*. **HABITAT** Open pine and oak woods, sandhills, towns. **RANGE** Resident in all FL north of Everglades (uncommon).

RED-BELLIED WOODPECKER
Melanerpes carolinus
WOODPECKER FAMILY

9″. Back and wings barred black and white; face and underparts clear pale gray; virtually no red on belly. Male forehead, crown, and hindneck red. Female crown gray; forehead spot, nape, and hindneck red. Flight reveals large white spot in black primaries, white rump. **VOICE** Rolling *chuurr;* double *chiv chiv;* drum is brief. **HABITAT** Open woods, towns. **RANGE** Resident in FL. **Yellow-bellied Sapsucker** *(Sphyrapicus varius)* is 8½″, has striped face, scaly back, white shoulder; Oct.–Mar: all FL.

DOWNY WOODPECKER
Picoides pubescens
WOODPECKER FAMILY

6½″. Back white; wings black, white-spotted; underparts white; outer tail feathers white, with black spots; head boldly pied, male with red nape patch. **VOICE** Rapid descending whinny; flat *pick;* long drum. **HABITAT** Woods, orchards, towns. **RANGE** Resident in FL. **Hairy Woodpecker** *(P. villosus)* larger (9″); has longer bill, unspotted white outer tail feathers; all FL, ex. Keys.

RED-COCKADED WOODPECKER
Picoides borealis
WOODPECKER FAMILY

8″. Back and wings black, barred white; white below, with fine black streaks on sides; large white cheek patch encircled by black crown, nape, and "mustache." Male has tiny red spot ("cockade") at rear of crown. Nests in colonies. Threatened species due to early harvesting of pines. One of largest populations in U.S. at Apalachicola N.F. **VOICE** Sharp *kyik,* and a rattle. **HABITAT** Mature open pinewoods. **RANGE** Resident in inland FL south locally to Big Cypress area (east of Naples).

PILEATED WOODPECKER
Dryocopus pileatus
WOODPECKER FAMILY

18″. Black; crest pointed, red; neck thin; bill heavy, silver; white and black stripes on face and down sides of neck. Male forehead and "mustache" red. Female forehead and "mustache" black. Flight reveals white underwing linings contrasting with black flight feathers. **VOICE** Rapid irregular series of *cuk* and *wucka* notes. **HABITAT** Woods, towns. **RANGE** Resident in mainland FL.

NORTHERN FLICKER
"Yellow-shafted Flicker"
Colaptes auritus
WOODPECKER FAMILY

13". Male back brown, with blackish bars; belly pale buff, with heavy black spots; crown gray; red crescent on nape; face buffy, with thick black "mustache"; wide black crescent on chest. Female similar, but lacks black "mustache." Bill long; legs short. Flight reveals white rump, bright yellow underwing and tail. Often feeds on ground. **VOICE** Rapid series of *wic* and *woika* notes; loud *klee-err;* drums softly. **HABITAT** Woods, farms, towns. **RANGE** Resident in mainland FL.

Songbirds (Passerines)

The birds described from here to the end of the birds section belong to a single order called Passeriformes. Known as passerines or, more commonly, songbirds or perching birds, they are the most recently evolved of the 25 bird orders; members of this order comprise more than half the world's birds. Their sizes range from 3½" kinglets to 18" crows, but they are generally small land birds with pleasing songs; among the finest songsters are the wrens, mockingbirds, and thrushes. Songbirds give call notes year-round, while most give their songs only during the breeding season (spring and early summer). In some species, the male has a particularly colorful summer breeding plumage that is changed in winter to drabber, female-like coloration. In the spring, migrant males generally arrive in Florida seven to ten days before the females and stake out breeding territories, which they defend against neighboring males. After a male shows a female around his territory, she may be satisfied (especially if the vegetation and insect life are plentiful) and stay with him, or search for another singing male whose territory is more to her liking. Most songbirds build open-topped, rounded nests of grasses, sticks, vegetable fibers, and rootlets in the fork of a tree, in a shrub, or tucked under tall grass. Some eat insects year-round, while others focus on seeds, grains, or fruit; all feed insects to their hatchlings. In the fall, the sexes may migrate south together, the adults often several weeks or more before the young born that year.

EASTERN WOOD-PEWEE
Contopus virens
TYRANT FLYCATCHER FAMILY

6". Dark grayish brown above, dingy white below; sides of chest gray; 2 narrow white wing bars; head often appears pointed; lower mandible dull orange; lacks eye ring. Late-returning migrant. Hard to see; stays high in trees. **VOICE** Slurred *pee-ah-weee.* **HABITAT** Broadleaf and mixed woods. **RANGE** Apr.–Oct.: w and n FL. Apr.–May, Aug.–Oct.: all FL.

EASTERN PHOEBE
Sayornis phoebe
TYRANT FLYCATCHER FAMILY

7". Back gray-brown; dingy white below; wings and tail dark brown. Some fall birds show yellowish wash on belly. Bill black; lacks eye ring and wing bars. Wags tail often. Early-returning migrant; easy to see; perches low. **VOICE** Hoarse *fee-bee.* **HABITAT** Scrublands, woods, towns, watersides. **RANGE** Oct.–Mar.: all FL.

ACADIAN FLYCATCHER
Empidonax virescens
TYRANT FLYCATCHER FAMILY

5½". Back, head, and sides olive; 2 buffy wing bars on dark brown wings; belly yellowish white; eye ring white; bill small; tail narrow, brown. Builds hammock-like nest in tree fork 8–13′ up. **VOICE** Song: emphatic *peet-SEET.* Call: even *peet.* **HABITAT** Swamps, riverine woods. **RANGE** Apr.–Oct.: n half of FL. Apr.–May, Aug.–Oct.: s half of FL.

GREAT CRESTED FLYCATCHER
Myiarchus crinitus
TYRANT FLYCATCHER FAMILY

8". Upperparts and crown dull brown; throat and chest grayish white; belly bright yellow; primaries and tail edged rufous; 2 thin white wing bars. Head a bit fluffy, but no true crest; bill heavy, pointed; tail fairly long. **VOICE** Loud rising *wheeep.* **HABITAT** Swamps, woods, scrub, towns. **RANGE** Resident in s FL. Apr.–Sept.: n and c FL.

EASTERN KINGBIRD
Tyrannus tyrannus
TYRANT FLYCATCHER FAMILY

9". Back and wings slaty; throat and underparts white, with grayish wash on sides of chest; head black; tail black, with white terminal band. Often flies slowly, with quivering wings. Perches on ends of tree branches and wires. **VOICE** Rapid agitated *kit-kit-kittery;* nasal *tzeer.* **HABITAT** Trees near fields, waterways, roads. **RANGE** Apr.–Sept.: mainland FL. Sept.–Oct.: Keys.

GRAY KINGBIRD
Tyrannus dominicensis
TYRANT FLYCATCHER FAMILY

9". Gray above, white below; wing bars very faint; head large; black eye mask above white throat; bill black, heavy, long; tail notched, slaty, without white edges. Chases insects from telephone wires and treetops. In U.S., occurs mainly in FL, and only in summer. **VOICE** Song: rapid *chee cheer-ree.* **HABITAT** Coastal woodland edges, mangroves, towns. **RANGE** Apr.–Oct.: all coastal FL.

PURPLE MARTIN
Progne subis
SWALLOW FAMILY

8″. Male mainly dark iridescent blue-purple; flight feathers black. Female upperparts and head dull purplish; throat and chest dusky gray, with darker fine scales and streaks; belly and vent white. Tail forked. Glides more than other swallows; often circles with short flaps then a glide. **VOICE** Song: low gurgling series. Call: throaty *chew chew.* **HABITAT** Fields, marshes, towns. **RANGE** Mar.–Aug.: breeds in n two-thirds of FL. Mar.–Apr., July–Sept.: migrant in all FL.

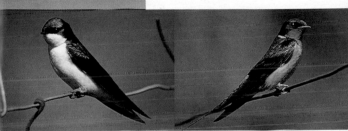

TREE SWALLOW
Tachycineta bicolor
SWALLOW FAMILY

6″. Adult male dark iridescent green-blue above; female duller. Tail notched; entirely snowy white below. Imm. all brown above, white below. Slow flier; short flapping circles and a climb. Often in massive flocks. **VOICE** Song: *weet-trit-weet.* Call: *cheat cheat.* **HABITAT** Fields, marshes, waterways. **RANGE** Oct.–Mar.: all FL.

BARN SWALLOW
Hirundo rustica
SWALLOW FAMILY

7″. Adult glossy blue above; chestnut forehead; throat dark orange, with thin blue necklace; rest of underparts buffy orange. Tail forked; outer tail streamers very long. Fast flier. Nest is open cup of mud pellets and grass inside or under overhang of barn or bridge. **VOICE** Song: long twittering. Calls: soft *vit vit* and *zee-zay.* **HABITAT** Fields, farms, waterways. **RANGE** Apr.–Oct.: n third of FL. Apr., Aug.–Nov.: all FL.

BLUE JAY
Cyanocitta cristata
CROW AND JAY FAMILY

12″. Crest and back blue; dingy white below; face whitish, with black necklace; wings and long rounded tail bright blue, banded black, edged in white. Brash; conspicuous. More common in winter. Feeds on acorns, insects, small rodents, lizards and nesting birds. **VOICE** Noisy; harsh *jaay;* liquid *queedle;* imitates hawks. **HABITAT** Woods, towns. **RANGE** Resident in mainland FL.

FLORIDA SCRUB JAY
Aphelocoma coerulescens
CROW AND JAY FAMILY

11". Back, wings, and rump turquoise blue; triangular gray midback patch; belly grayish white; crown uncrested, blue; white forehead above black eye-mask; throat white above purplish necklace; bill black, sturdy; legs black; tail long, rounded, uniform blue. Young of previous year help parents raise next year's brood. **VOICE** Song: trills and high warbles. Call: loud harsh *shreep*. **HABITAT** Scrub oaks, pine scrub, sandhills. **RANGE** Resident in peninsular FL south to n edge of Everglades.

AMERICAN CROW
Corvus brachyrhynchos
CROW AND JAY FAMILY

18". All glossy black; bill heavy, black. Flight reveals rounded wings, "fingered" wingtips, squarish tail. Bold, noisy. Huge night roosts in nonbreeding season. Less common than Fish Crow in coastal areas and larger lakesides. **VOICE** Loud descending *caw*. **HABITAT** Woods, farms, roadsides, towns. **RANGE** Resident in mainland FL.

FISH CROW
Corvus ossifragus
CROW AND JAY FAMILY

17". All glossy black; bill heavy, black; wings rounded, wingtips "fingered"; legs black; tail longish, flat. More common along coasts than American Crow; call is different; has faster wingbeats. **VOICE** Hoarse, high, nasal *cah* and double *uh-oh*. **HABITAT** Coasts, rivers, lake edges, nearby woods, towns. **RANGE** Resident in FL; sparse on Keys.

CAROLINA CHICKADEE
Parus carolinensis
CHICKADEE FAMILY

4½". Back, wings, and long, narrow tail gray; dusty white below; crown and throat black; cheeks white; bill very short, black. Family parties glean insects off branches. **VOICE** Song: *fee-bee fee-bay*. Call: high fast *chick-a-dee-dee-dee*. **HABITAT** Pine and broadleaf woods, towns. **RANGE** Resident south to Lake Okeechobee.

TUFTED TITMOUSE
Parus bicolor
CHICKADEE FAMILY

6". Adult upperparts, pointed crest, and tail gray; underparts dull white; sides washed rusty; forehead black; white area around beady black eye. Imm. forehead gray. Cheerful, active. **VOICE** Song: whistled *peter-peter-peter*. Call: nasal scolding. **HABITAT** Woods, towns. **RANGE** Resident south to c FL.

BROWN-HEADED NUTHATCH
Sitta pusilla
NUTHATCH FAMILY

4½". Back and wings blue-gray; white below, washed pale buff; crown brown; white patch on lower nape; thin dark line through eye; bill small, chisel-like. Tail short. Creeps over branches and headfirst down trunks. **VOICE** High rapid *kik-kik-kik;* squeaky *kee-day.* **HABITAT** Open tall pinewoods. **RANGE** Resident south to c FL.

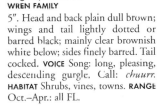

HOUSE WREN
Troglodytes aedon
WREN FAMILY

5". Head and back plain dull brown; wings and tail lightly dotted or barred black; mainly clear brownish white below; sides finely barred. Tail cocked. **VOICE** Song: long, pleasing, descending gurgle. Call: *chuurr.* **HABITAT** Shrubs, vines, towns. **RANGE** Oct.–Apr.: all FL.

CAROLINA WREN
Thryothorus ludovicianus
WREN FAMILY

6". Upperparts and crown dark rufous-brown; light orange below; fine black bars on wings and tail; long white eyebrow bordered in black; throat white. Head large; tail fairly long. **VOICE** Song: rollicking repeated *tea-kettle.* Call: harsh *jeer.* **HABITAT** Shrubs, gardens. **RANGE** Resident in all FL; local on Keys.

RUBY-CROWNED KINGLET
Regulus calendula
OLD WORLD WARBLER SUBFAMILY

4". Drab olive all over, but paler below; 2 white wing bars; large white eye ring. Male rarely raises red midcrown patch. Tail has short notch; no black stripes on head. **VOICE** Song: high warbles ending with 3 *look-at-me's.* Call: scolding *je-dit.* **HABITAT** Mixed woods, shrubs. **RANGE** Oct.–Apr.: all FL; less common in s FL.

BLUE-GRAY GNATCATCHER
Polioptila caerulea
OLD WORLD WARBLER SUBFAMILY

4½". Blue-gray above, white below; tail black with white outer tail feathers; eye ring white. Male has black line over eye in summer. Often wags tail sideways. **VOICE** Song: thin wheezy warble. Call: inquiring *pwee.* **HABITAT** Open woods, thickets. **RANGE** Mar.–Oct.: mainland FL. Oct.–Mar.: c and s FL.

EASTERN BLUEBIRD
Sialia sialis
THRUSH SUBFAMILY

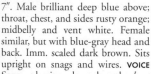

7″. Male brilliant deep blue above; throat, chest, and sides rusty orange; midbelly and vent white. Female similar, but with blue-gray head and back. Imm. scaled dark brown. Sits upright on snags and wires. **VOICE** Song: pleasing downslurred *cheer cheery charley.* Call: musical *chur-lee.* **HABITAT** Pine flatwoods, pastures with few trees. **RANGE** Resident in FL south to n edge of Everglades.

WOOD THRUSH
Hylocichla mustelina
THRUSH SUBFAMILY

8″. Crown and upper back rich reddish brown; snowy white below, with heavy black spots; wings, lower back, and tail brown; thin white eye ring. Tail short. **VOICE** Song: flute-like *ee-oo-lay?* Call: *wit-wit-wit.* **HABITAT** Woodland floor. **RANGE** Apr.–Oct.: n FL. **Hermit Thrush** *(Catharus guttatus)* winters in FL (Oct.–Apr.); crown and back brown; tail rusty; smaller brown chest spots.

Attracting Birds to Your Yard

Many people enjoy attracting birds into their yards, and feeding helps some birds when natural food is scarce. In the birds section, species that will come into a yard to feed are indicated by the icon 🏠.

Birdfeeders come in many designs. Hanging, clear seed feeders with short perch sticks are popular with goldfinches, siskins, and other finches. Window boxes and platforms on a pole are best for such small and medium-size birds as cardinals, chickadees, titmice, and jays, while doves, thrashers, towhees, and many sparrows prefer to feed on the ground. In most cases, mounting a birdfeeder requires also installing anti-squirrel devices, such as baffles mounted on a pole or fixed on the line that holds a feeder.

Grains and seeds are the best all-purpose fare for feeders. Most species like sunflower seeds, but your local birds may have particular preferences. Thistle seed is popular with goldfinches, white millet seed is a good choice for small species, and cracked corn is appreciated by large, ground-feeding birds. Many seed mixes are available at supermarkets and garden supply stores.

Birds also like fruit. You can lay out orange slices on a platform for orioles and tanagers; apples, oranges, grapes, and raisins can also be put out on a platform or the lawn or mounted on feeders. The fat and protein in nuts makes them disappear quickly. Suet, in a mesh holder suspended from a branch or mounted on a tree trunk,

adult (left), immature (right)

AMERICAN ROBIN
Turdus migratorius
THRUSH SUBFAMILY

10″. Male breast and sides rufous-orange; back and wings gray-brown; head blackish, with broken white eye ring; throat striped; bill yellow; tail black, with tiny white corners; vent white. Female head and back duller brown. Tail fairly long. Imm. paler; heavy spots below. In spring and summer, an earthworm specialist; in fall and winter, roams in berry-searching flocks, forms large communal roosts. **VOICE** Song: prolonged, rising and falling *cheery-up cheery-me*. Calls: *tut tut tut* and *tseep*. **HABITAT** Woods, shrubs, lawns. **RANGE** Mar.–Oct.: rare breeder n FL. Oct.–Apr.: all FL.

attracts birds such as nuthatches and woodpeckers that feed on insects in tree bark and bushes. Suet use should be discontinued in hot weather, when it spoils quickly and tends to mat feathers. Hummingbirds will come to specially designed red plastic dispensers of sugar water.

Water is important, especially during periods when natural water sources dry up. Many species are attracted to a bird bath, which should be regularly scrubbed with a brush to rid it of algae and prevent diseases from spreading.

You might want to make or purchase a nest box to attract breeding birds. The most popular—inviting to woodpeckers, chickadees, nuthatches, wrens, bluebirds, Great Crested Flycatchers, and even some owls—is an enclosed nest box with a square floor area 4–7″ wide and deep, and about twice as high as it is wide (8–12″). Specifications for such a box vary depending on the species you want to attract, and include floor area, the size of the entrance hole, the height from the base of the box to the hole, and proper siting of the box. Other birds will nest in open-fronted boxes, on platforms or shelves, in bowl-type baskets, or in martin houses. Information on building and siting nest boxes and feeders is available at your local Audubon Society or nature center. In the birds section, the icon 🐦 denotes species that have been known to use nest boxes in yards in the right habitat.

GRAY CATBIRD
Dumetella carolinensis
MOCKINGBIRD FAMILY

9". All slaty gray ex. for black crown and rusty vent. A skulker; often cocks or swings tail. **VOICE** Song: mimics other birds; doesn't repeat songs. Calls: cat-like *meeow;* sharp *check.* **HABITAT** Dense shrubs; woodland edges, and gardens. **RANGE** Resident in n FL. Oct.–May: all FL.

NORTHERN MOCKINGBIRD
Mimus polyglottos
MOCKINGBIRD FAMILY

10". Back, head, shoulder, rump gray; paler grayish white below; 2 slender wing bars and large wing patch white; tail blackish, with white outer tail feathers; bill short, thin. Chases other birds; mobs cats, snakes. **VOICE** Song: mimics other birds, repeats each song 3–6 times; sings day and night. Calls: loud *chack;* softer *chair.* **HABITAT** Shrubs, fields, towns. **RANGE** Resident in FL.

BROWN THRASHER
Toxostoma rufum
MOCKINGBIRD FAMILY

11½". Bright rufous-brown above, buffy white below, with dark brown stripes; white wing bars; gray cheeks around yellow-orange eyes; bill sturdy, downcurved. Tail very long, rounded. **VOICE** Song: mimics other birds, repeating each song twice. Call: loud *chack.* **HABITAT** Thickets, stunted oak woods. **RANGE** Resident in FL; less common in s FL.

CEDAR WAXWING
Bombycilla cedrorum
WAXWING FAMILY

7". Adult back and laid-back crest brown; soft brown chest grades to yellow belly; wings gray, with waxy red tips to secondaries; black line, edged in white, through eye. Yellow band at tip of gray tail. Imm. striped brown, with white eye line. Often seen in flocks. **VOICE** Call: high thin *zeee.* **HABITAT** Woodland edges, shrubs, gardens. **RANGE** Oct.–Apr.: all FL; less common in s FL.

LOGGERHEAD SHRIKE
Lanius ludovicianus
SHRIKE FAMILY

9". Back, crown, and rump silvery; wings black, with white spot on base of primaries; white below; head large, with wide black mask; bill heavy, hooked; feet short, black; tail black, edged white. Spots insects, lizards, small birds from open perches. **VOICE** Song: repeated phrases, mockingbird-like. Call: harsh *shack.* **HABITAT** Shrubby grasslands, farms. **RANGE** Resident in FL.

EUROPEAN STARLING
Sturnus vulgaris
STARLING FAMILY

summer adult (left), winter adult (right)

8″. Dark; wings short, pointed, rusty-edged; bill sturdy, pointed; legs dull red; tail short, square. Summer: glossy green-purple; bill yellow. Winter: blackish, heavily speckled with white; bill dark. Usu. in flocks. Successful species introduced from Europe, but very detrimental to native birds. Boldly takes over most nest holes and birdhouses, occupied or not. **VOICE** Song: mix of whistles, squeals, and chuckles; will mimic other birds. Calls: rising, then falling *hoooeee;* harsh *jeer.* **HABITAT** Towns, farms, fields. **RANGE** Resident in FL.

WHITE-EYED VIREO
Vireo griseus
VIREO FAMILY

5″. Vireos have thicker, hooked bills and move more slowly than warblers (see below). This species: olive green above, white below; sides yellowish; 2 pale wing bars; yellow spectacles; eyes white. Furtive skulker. **VOICE** Song: enunciated *chick-per-wee-o-chick.* Call: *chick.* Mimics other bird songs. **HABITAT** Swampy thickets, scrub. **RANGE** Resident in FL.

RED-EYED VIREO
Vireo olivaceus
VIREO FAMILY

6″. Olive green above, white below, with yellow wash on belly in fall; no wing bars; gray crown bordered by black; eyes red; black line through eye; white eyebrow. **VOICE** Song: monotonous *cher-eep cher-oop;* repeated up to 40 times a minute, all day long. Call: scolding *meew.* **HABITAT** Broadleaf woods. **RANGE** Apr.–Oct.: mainland FL, ex. Keys.

BLACK-WHISKERED VIREO
Vireo altiloquus
VIREO FAMILY

5½″. Olive green above; white below; no wing bars; crown gray, white eyebrow, gray eye line; eyes red; black "mustache" on white throat. In U.S., occurs mainly in FL, and only in summer. **VOICE** Song: repeated *whip-Tom-Kelly.* **HABITAT** Mangroves, low broadleaf woods. **RANGE** Apr.–Sept.: coastal FL from panhandle and Merritt Is. south; most common in s FL and Keys.

Wood Warblers

As there is a bird subfamily called Old World warblers, those in the New World are often called wood warblers or just warblers; they are the subfamily Parulinae, part of the Emberizidae family. While some warblers breed and others winter in Florida, most pass through quietly in spring and fall as they migrate between northern breeding areas and West Indian wintering grounds. Many adult males have the same plumage year-round, but a few have breeding (summer) and nonbreeding (winter) plumages. Females, a few fall males, and immature birds have a trace of the summer male pattern. Each species has a distinct song, while the warbler call tends to be a simple *chip*. During the summer, these birds breed in a variety of woodland and scrub habitats. Most nests are cups on small forks of branches. Warblers glean insects from leaves with their thin unhooked bills.

NORTHERN PARULA
Parula americana
WOOD WARBLER SUBFAMILY

4½". Male upperparts and head dull blue; olive patch on back; belly white; yellow throat and upper breast crossed by blue and orange band; white wing bars; incomplete white eye ring. Female lacks breast band. Tail short. **VOICE** Song: rising trill, with sudden lower ending: *zeeeeeeee-up*. **HABITAT** Broadleaf woods, often near water. **RANGE** Mar.–Sept.: n and c FL. Aug.–May: s FL.

BLACK-THROATED BLUE WARBLER
Dendroica caerulescens
WOOD WARBLER SUBFAMILY

5". Male dark blue above; white squarish patch on primaries; face, throat, and sides black; midbelly and vent white. Female plain brownish olive above, buff below, with same pale wing patch. **VOICE** Song: lazy *sir sir sir please?* **HABITAT** Woods, scrub, mangroves. **RANGE** Mar.–May, Sept.–Oct.: all FL. Oct.–Mar.: a few in s FL.

YELLOW-RUMPED WARBLER
"Myrtle Warbler"
Dendroica coronata
WOOD WARBLER SUBFAMILY

5½". Rump bright yellow. Summer male: gray above, with black streaks on back and white wing bars; white below; chest patch and side streaks black; yellow patches on crown and sides of chest; black mask. Female: mask and upperparts brown. Nicknamed "Butter-butt." Common in fall and winter. **VOICE** Song: musical trill, ending a bit higher or lower. Call: loud *check*. **HABITAT** Woods. **RANGE** Oct.–Mar.: all FL.

YELLOW-THROATED WARBLER
Dendroica dominica
WOOD WARBLER SUBFAMILY

5½". Slaty gray above; throat bright yellow; 2 white wing bars; sides streaked black on white; white eyebrow and neck spot; cheeks black. Creeps along trunk and branches. **VOICE** Song: descending *teeeuw teeuw teew-tew-tew-twee*. Call: loud *churp*. **HABITAT** Floodplain woods, pine-oaks with Spanish Moss, palms (winter). **RANGE** Mar.–Sept.: n half of FL. July–Apr.: s half of FL.

PINE WARBLER
Dendroica pinus
WOOD WARBLER SUBFAMILY

5½". Adult upperparts and cheeks plain olive green; belly and wing bars white; throat and chest yellow; faint olive stripes on sides. Imm. plain brown above, dingy white below, with 2 white wing bars. **VOICE** Song: slow musical trill on one pitch. **HABITAT** Pine woods. **RANGE** Resident in mainland FL.

PRAIRIE WARBLER
Dendroica discolor
WOOD WARBLER SUBFAMILY

4¾". Male olive green above; red stripes on back; underparts and face yellow; black lines on face and sides; pale yellow wing bars. Female duller; lacks red back stripes. Wags tail. **VOICE** Song: 8–10 buzzy *zee* notes, each one higher. **HABITAT** Brushy fields. **RANGE** Resident: s half of coastal FL; Keys. Apr.–Sept.: n half of FL.

PALM WARBLER
Dendroica palmarum
WOOD WARBLER SUBFAMILY

5½". Summer: olive above; crown rufous; underparts and eyebrow yellow; rusty stripes on sides. Winter: faintly brown-striped; vent yellow. Wags tail more or less constantly. Usu. in small groups. **VOICE** Song: slow buzzy trill. **HABITAT** Brushy fields. **RANGE** Nov.–Mar.: all FL; more common in s FL.

BLACK-AND-WHITE WARBLER
Mniotilta varia
WOOD WARBLER SUBFAMILY

5¼". Male body striped black and white; cheeks and throat black; crown black, with median white stripe; white eyebrow and "mustache." Female cheeks gray; throat white. Creeps down trunks like nuthatch. **VOICE** Song: 6 high double *wee-zy* notes. **HABITAT** Woods, towns. **RANGE** Sept.–Apr.: all FL.

female (left), male (right)

AMERICAN REDSTART
Setophaga ruticilla
WOOD WARBLER SUBFAMILY

5". Adult male mainly black; midbelly white; large orange patches on wings, sides of chest, and basal corners of tail. Female olive-brown above, white below; yellow or yellow-orange patches on wings, sides of chest, and basal corners of tail; head gray, with narrow white "spectacles." Often fans tail, chases flying insects. **VOICE** Songs: variable; 4 double *teet-sa's*, ending with *teet*, and 4 single *zee's*, ending with rising *zwee* or falling *tsee-o*. **HABITAT** Broadleaf woods, shrubs, mangroves. **RANGE** Aug.–May: all FL.

PROTHONOTARY WARBLER
Protonotaria citrea
WOOD WARBLER SUBFAMILY

5½". Male head and breast orangy yellow; back olive; wings, rump, and tail blue-gray; vent white. Female crown olive; breast yellow. Lacks stripes. **VOICE** Song: long series of *sweet* notes. Call: loud *tink*. **HABITAT** Swamps, riversides. **RANGE** Mar.–Oct.: breeds south to Lake Okeechobee.

OVENBIRD
Seiurus aurocapillus
WOOD WARBLER SUBFAMILY

6". Upperparts and sides of head brownish olive; white below, with black stripes; crown stripe orange, bordered by black; eye ring white; legs pink. Walks on forest floor. **VOICE** Song: *TEACH-er*, repeated 3–6 times; usu. silent in FL. **HABITAT** Mixed woods with dense undergrowth. **RANGE** Aug.–May: all FL; less common Nov.–Mar.

NORTHERN WATERTHRUSH
Seiurus noveboracensis
WOOD WARBLER SUBFAMILY

6". Upperparts and head plain brown; underparts and eyebrow (tapers to rear) yellowish white; throat dotted; breast striped brown; legs pink. Bill short, thin compared to sparrow look-alikes. Often bobs tail. **VOICE** Song: rapid *wit wit wit sweet sweet sweet chew chew chew*. **HABITAT** Swamps, moist woods, watersides. **RANGE** Aug.–May: all FL; most common in s FL.

female (left), male (righ.

COMMON YELLOWTHROAT
Geothlypis trichas
WOOD WARBLER SUBFAMILY

5″. Male upperparts and sides uniformly olive green; throat and chest yellow; midbelly white; black mask over forehead and cheeks; broad white line above mask. Female olive-brown above; pale eye ring; throat yellow. Feeds low; often raises tail at angle. Nicknamed "Lone Ranger" bird. **VOICE** Song: rollicking *witchity-witchity-witchity-witch*. Call: flat *chep*. **HABITAT** Swamps, marshes, shrubs. **RANGE** Resident in mainland FL. Oct.–Apr.: also Keys.

KENTUCKY WARBLER
Oporornis formosus
WOOD WARBLER SUBFAMILY

5½″. Olive green above, all yellow below; yellow lores and "spectacles"; forecrown and patch below eye black (slaty in female and imm.); legs long, orange. **VOICE** Song: rapid *shur-ree*, repeated 4 times. Call: low *chuck*. **HABITAT** Wooded and scrubby ravines. **RANGE** Apr.–Sept.: panhandle. Apr., Aug.–Oct.: all FL.

HOODED WARBLER
Wilsonia citrina
WOOD WARBLER SUBFAMILY

5½″. Male olive green above, clear yellow below; black hood encircles yellow face and beady black eyes; white stripes in fanned tail. Female olive above, yellow below. **VOICE** Loud *wee-ta wee-ta wee-tee-oo*. **HABITAT** Shrubs in wooded ravines. **RANGE** Apr.–Oct.: n FL. Apr., Aug.–Oct.: all FL.

YELLOW-BREASTED CHAT
Icteria virens
WOOD WARBLER SUBFAMILY

7″. Olive green above; throat and breast yellow; belly and vent grayish white; white "spectacles"; lores black in male, gray in female. Tail long. Sings in low fluttering flight, day or night. Usu. shy. **VOICE** Song: long series of scolds, whistles, and soft, crow-like *caw* notes. Call: loud *hack*. **HABITAT** Dense thickets, riverine scrub. **RANGE** Apr.–Oct.: n FL. Nov.–Mar.: a few in s FL.

SUMMER TANAGER
Piranga rubra
TANAGER SUBFAMILY

7½″. Adult male entirely rosy red, head and underparts brightest. Female and imm. yellowish olive above, bright olive-yellow below. Bill thick, whitish, conical. Lives in treetops. **VOICE** Song: varied melodious phrases; often continuously repeated *ur wee sue weet*. Call: fast *trick-ee dick-ee*. **HABITAT** Swamp and upland woods. **RANGE** Apr.–Oct.: all FL. **Scarlet Tanager** *(P. olivacea)* similar; adult male shiny red, wings and tail black; adult female like Summer, but wings black; migrant Apr.–May, Sept.–Nov.

NORTHERN CARDINAL
Cardinalis cardinalis
GROSBEAK SUBFAMILY

9″. Male grayish red to red above; underparts, crest, and cheeks red; black face encircles swollen, pointed, red bill. Female buffy brown; top of crest red; face black; bill red; wings and tail dusky red. Sought-after feeder bird that likes sunflower and safflower seed, cracked corn. **VOICE** Song: pleasing clear whistles; variations on *wait wait wait cheer cheer cheer*. Call: short *chip*. **HABITAT** Woodland edges, shrubs, yards, gardens. **RANGE** Resident in FL.

ROSE-BREASTED GROSBEAK
Pheucticus ludovicianus
GROSBEAK SUBFAMILY

8″. Male back, head, wings, and tail black; large white patches on wings; rosy triangular patch on chest; sides, belly, and rump white. Female and imm. dark brown above, buffy white below with dark streaks; wing bars white; most of head solid brown; eyebrow and median crown stripe white. Bill thick, pale gray. **VOICE** Song: melodious deep warbling; robin-like, but faster. Call: sharp *squeak* or *chink*. **HABITAT** Broadleaf woods and edges. **RANGE** Mar.–Apr., Sept.–Oct.: all FL.

BLUE GROSBEAK
Guiraca caerulea
GROSBEAK SUBFAMILY

7″. Adult male dark blue above and below, into black stripes on back; shoulder and wing bar chestnut; black feathers at base of bill. Female and imm. dull brown, with 2 buffy wing bars. Bill thick, silvery. Feeds on ground; often twitches tail. **VOICE** Song: sweet warbled phrases. Call: loud *chink*. **HABITAT** Brushy pastures, thickets. **RANGE** Apr.–Oct.: n half of FL. Sept.–Apr.: s half of FL.

INDIGO BUNTING
Passerina cyanea
GROSBEAK SUBFAMILY

female (left), male (right)

5½". Summer male: rich deep blue all over; wings and tail partly black; often appears all dark, ex. in very good light. Winter male and female uniformly dark brown above, pale dusky brown below; trace of blue on primaries. Bill medium-size, slaty, conical. Male sings conspicuously from exposed perch in summer. **VOICE** Song: paired *sweet sweet chew chew sweet sweet*. Call: sharp *spit*. **HABITAT** Woodland edges, shrubby fields. **RANGE** Apr.–Oct.: n half of FL. Sept.–May: s half of FL.

PAINTED BUNTING
Passerina ciris
GROSBEAK SUBFAMILY

male (left), female (right)

5½". Summer adult male: back yellow-green; wing coverts green; underparts, rump, throat, and eye ring red; head blue-violet. All other plumages green above, paler green or yellowish green below. Bill small, slaty, conical. Feeds on ground; will visit ground feeders. **VOICE** Song: high musical warble. Call: sharp *chip*. **HABITAT** Brushy pastures, woodland edges, towns. **RANGE** Apr.–Sept.: ne FL south to Orlando. Sept.–Mar.: s half of FL.

EASTERN TOWHEE
"Rufous-sided Towhee"
Pipilo erythrophthalmus
AMERICAN SPARROW SUBFAMILY

male (left), female (right)

8". Male back, head, throat, and wings black; sides rufous; midbelly white. Female head, throat, and upperparts brown; sides rufous; breast and belly white. White wing patches; outer tail feathers and terminal half of undertail white; eyes red; bill conical. FL race: eyes white; less white on wing and tail. Finds insects in dead leaves. **VOICE** Song: loud *DRINK your teeeeee*. Call: loud *che-wink* or *tow-whee*. **HABITAT** Brushy areas, oak barrens, open woods. **RANGE** FL white-eyed race resident in mainland FL. Red-eyed birds of several northern races winter south to c FL.

BACHMAN'S SPARROW
Aimophila aestivalis
AMERICAN SPARROW SUBFAMILY
6″. Rusty stripes on gray back, nape, and crown; shoulder rusty; plain pale gray below; tail dusky, rounded. Shy; can be hard to see ex. when singing from a bushtop. **VOICE** Song: clear whistle, then a trill *seeeee tip-tip-tip-tip*. **HABITAT** Dry open pinewoods. **RANGE** Resident in FL south to Naples and Ft. Pierce.

CHIPPING SPARROW
Spizella passerina
AMERICAN SPARROW SUBFAMILY
5½″. Summer: brown above, with black streaks; clear pale gray below; white wing bars; rufous cap; white eyebrow; black eye line; narrow notched tail. Winter: striped brown crown. **VOICE** Song: long, run-together series of about 20 dry *chip* notes. **HABITAT** Open woods, fields, towns. **RANGE** Oct.–Apr.: all FL; more common in n FL.

SEASIDE SPARROW
Ammodramus maritimus
AMERICAN SPARROW SUBFAMILY
6″. Adult slaty gray above; gray stripes on sides; yellow lores; blackish "mustache"; tail short, pointed. Imm. brown above; brown stripes on sides. Restricted to wetter sections of salt marshes; sings from tall grass; usu. hard to see. Cape Sable race: back olive; in w Everglades N.P. **VOICE** Song: *hut-hut hiiiike*. Call: hard *jack*. **HABITAT** Salt marshes. **RANGE** Resident along coasts north of Tampa and Daytona; w Everglades.

SAVANNAH SPARROW
Passerculus sandwichensis
AMERICAN SPARROW SUBFAMILY
5½″. Brown-and-white-striped above and below, ex. for white belly; breast may have central blackish dot; front of eyebrow yellow; bill and legs pink. Tail short, notched. Often secretive; if flushed, flies low. **VOICE** Call: light *tsip*. **HABITAT** Grasslands, marshes, sandy areas. **RANGE** Oct.–Apr.: all FL.

SONG SPARROW
Melospiza melodia
AMERICAN SPARROW SUBFAMILY
6¼″. Dark brown stripes on warm brown back and on white under parts; grayish-brown eyebrow; dark brown spot on chest; tail fairly long, unpatterned, rounded. **VOICE** Song *sweet sweet sweet towhee tri-tri-tri-tr* **HABITAT** Shrubs, marshes, fields, watersides. **RANGE** Oct.–Mar.: all FL.

SWAMP SPARROW
Melospiza georgiana
AMERICAN SPARROW SUBFAMILY

5½". Brown above, striped black on back; breast clear gray; midbelly whitish; sides buffy; wings and crown rufous; eyebrow gray; thin black "mustache"; throat white. **VOICE** Song: slow musical trill on one pitch. **HABITAT** Freshwater swamps and cat-tail marshes; shrubs. **RANGE** Oct.–Mar.: all FL; more common in n half.

male (left), immature (right)

BOBOLINK
Dolichonyx oryzivorus
BLACKBIRD SUBFAMILY

7". Summer male black with large golden yellow nape patch; rump and base of wings white. Female, fall male, and imm. buffy, sparrow-like, with brown stripes on head, back, and sides. Usu. in flocks during migration. **VOICE** Call: clear *pink*. **HABITAT** Hayfields and grasslands; perches on nearby fences, shrubs, trees. **RANGE** Apr.–May, Sept.–Oct.: all FL.

male (left), female (right)

RED-WINGED BLACKBIRD
Agelaius phoeniceus
BLACKBIRD SUBFAMILY

9". Male all glossy black, with red shoulder epaulets bordered by yellow; yellow and much of red less visible in late summer and fall. Female heavily streaked brown: crown and eye line dark brown; eyebrow buffy white. Bill fairly long, pointed; eyes black; tail fairly long and rounded. **VOICE** Song: gurgling *conk-a-ree*. Calls: harsh *check*, high *tee-eek*. Calls from trees, shrubs, tall reeds. **HABITAT** Marshes, swamps, fields. **RANGE** Resident in FL.

EASTERN MEADOWLARK
Sturnella magna
BLACKBIRD SUBFAMILY

9″. Speckled brown above and on sides; yellow throat and breast, with black V on chest; dark brown and whitish head stripes. Bill long, pointed, gray. Flight reveals white outer tail feathers; flies with flaps and glides. Perches on fence posts and telephone wires. **VOICE** Song: slurred whistles *tee-you tee-yerr*. Call: harsh *serrt*. **HABITAT** Grasslands. **RANGE** Resident in FL.

RUSTY BLACKBIRD
Euphagus carolinus
BLACKBIRD SUBFAMILY

9″. Summer male dull purplish black; wings and tail glossed green. Summer female dull dark gray. Winter: both sexes blackish or brown with rusty scaling. No red on shoulder; bill long, thin; eyes yellow; tail flat. Often in flocks. **VOICE** Song: creaky *cush-a-lee cush-lay*. Call: harsh *shaq*. **HABITAT** Bogs, wooded and grassy watersides. **RANGE** Nov.–Mar.: n half of FL.

male (left), female (right)

BOAT-TAILED GRACKLE
Quiscalus major
BLACKBIRD SUBFAMILY

Male 16″; female 13″. Adult male body and head black, glossed purple; wings black; eyes yellow in ne FL, black in rest of FL; bill long, pointed, black; tail very long, carried in a V, with wedge-shaped tip. Female dark brown above; buffy-brown eye line and underparts; eyes dark; tail long, flat, black. Imm. male black; tail flat. Cheeky; visits dumpsters, feeders, shores. **VOICE** Song: harsh high *jeep jeep jeep*. Call: harsh *check*. **HABITAT** Fresh and salt marshes, farms, towns. **RANGE** Resident in mainland FL.

COMMON GRACKLE
Quiscalus quiscula
BLACKBIRD SUBFAMILY

13″. Male often appears black, but has iridescent blue-green head, dark purple wings, bronzy green back and breast; long, wedge-shaped tail is held flat, or carried in V in courtship. Female very dark gray. Bill heavy, long, pointed; eyes yellow. Usu. in small to very large flocks outside breeding season. **VOICE** Song: short high *gurgle-eek*. Call: loud *shack*. **HABITAT** Farms, watersides, gardens, fields, shade trees. **RANGE** Resident in mainland FL; in Keys Mar.–Oct. only.

BROWN-HEADED COWBIRD
Molothrus ater
BLACKBIRD SUBFAMILY

female (left), male (right)

7″. Adult male dark, shiny, greenish black with brown head. Adult female uniformly dull dark brown. Bill medium-size, gray, conical. Flips wings out and back to body quickly in flight. Brood parasite; causes great losses in numbers of native songbirds; female lays single eggs in several nests of native songbirds; baby cowbird pushes out other eggs and babies, is raised by foster parents. **VOICE** Song: bubbly creaking, *bubble-lee come seee.* Flight call: high *weee teetee.* **RANGE** Resident in FL; more common Nov.–Apr.

SPOT-BREASTED ORIOLE
Icterus pectoralis
BLACKBIRD SUBFAMILY

9″. Back black; primaries black with orange shoulder; secondaries white; head and nape bright orange; throat and central chest patch black; lines of black spots on sides of orange breast. Tail black, long, wedge-tipped. Builds woven, sock-shaped nest of palm fibers and grass. **VOICE** Song: loud varied whistles. Call; loud *check.* **HABITAT** Towns, parks, gardens; often in palms. **RANGE** Resident in se FL (Palm Beach to Miami).

BALTIMORE ORIOLE
"Northern Oriole"
Icterus galbula
BLACKBIRD SUBFAMILY

8¾″. Male back, head, throat, wings, and tail black; underparts and shoulder bright orange; white patches on wing; yellow tail corners. Female brownish or olive-gray above; face, underparts, and rump yellowish. Bill thin, pointed. **VOICE** Song: 4–8 pleasing whistles. Call: low *tee-tew.* **HABITAT** Broadleaf woods, shade trees in towns. **RANGE** Aug.–Apr.: all FL. **Orchard Oriole** (*I. spurius*) smaller (7¼″); adult male black and chestnut; in n FL Apr.–Sept.

HOUSE FINCH
Carpodacus mexicanus
FINCH FAMILY

female (left), male (right)

5½". Male back, midcrown, wings, and tail brown; sides and belly whitish, streaked brown; 2 pale wing bars; wide eyebrow, throat, and chest rosy red. Female upperparts and head plain dull brown; dusky below, with brown streaks. **VOICE** Song: musical warbling ending with a downslurred *jeer*. **HABITAT** Towns, garden trees. **RANGE** Resident in n FL; may expand southward on peninsula.

AMERICAN GOLDFINCH
Carduelis tristis
FINCH FAMILY

summer male (left), winter male (right)

5". Summer male brilliant yellow; cap, wings, and notched tail black; rump white. Summer female olive green above; throat and chest yellow. Winter male brown above; face and shoulder yellow. Winter female grayish with or without trace of yellow on throat. All have white wing bars on black wings. **VOICE** Song: canary-like; long, pleasing, rising and falling twittering. Call: rising *sweee-eat*. Flight call: *per chicory*. **HABITAT** Fields, woodland edges, farms, yards. **RANGE** Nov.–Apr.: all FL.

HOUSE SPARROW
Passer domesticus
OLD WORLD SPARROW FAMILY

male (left) female (right)

6". Male back and wings rufous; underparts, crown, cheeks, and rump gray; 1 white wing bar; throat and upper chest black (only chin black in winter); wide chestnut stripe behind eye. Female: plain brown above, ex. for blackish back streaks; pale dusky eyebrow and underparts. Abundant European import and follower of human activities. Kills nestlings, removes eggs of other birds at birdhouses. **VOICE** Song: frequently given *chereep* notes. Call: *chir-rup*. **HABITAT** Cities, malls, parks, towns, farms. **RANGE** Resident in FL.

Mammals

All members of the vertebrate class Mammalia are warm-blooded and able to maintain a near-constant body temperature. Males generally have an external penis for direct internal fertilization of the female's eggs. Almost all mammals are born live rather than hatching from eggs (exceptions are the platypus and the echidnas of Australia). Mammary glands, unique to mammals, produce milk that is high in nutrients and fat and promotes rapid growth in the young. Mammals have abundant skin glands, used for temperature regulation (sweating), coat maintenance, territory-marking, sex and species recognition, breeding-cycle signals, and even defense, as in skunks and others that can repel predators with their powerful secretions.

Eleven mammalian orders are represented in Florida, including primates—humans and feral Rhesus Monkeys, which live on the Silver River near Silver Springs. Opossums (order Didelphimorphia) give birth to young in an embryonic state; they then develop in a separate fur-lined pouch on the mother's belly. The tiny energetic shrews and moles (Insectivora), which eat insects and other invertebrates, have long snouts, short dense fur, and five toes on each foot. Bats (Chiroptera), with their enlarged, membrane-covered forelimbs, are the only mammals that truly fly. Armadillos (Xenarthra) have bodies encased in hard plates, and peg-like teeth.

Hares and rabbits (Lagomorpha) resemble large rodents but have four upper incisor teeth—a large front pair and a small pair directly behind them—that grow continuously, and five toes on their front feet and five in back; digits on all feet are very small. Rodents (Rodentia—including squirrels, pocket gophers, mice, rats, muskrats, and the Nutria) have two upper incisor teeth that grow continuously, and most have four toes on their front feet and five in back.

Carnivores (Carnivora)— bears, Coyote, foxes, weasels, raccoons, and cats— have long canine teeth for stabbing prey, and most have sharp cheek teeth for slicing meat. The even-toed hoofed mammals (Artiodactyla), in Florida represented by the pig and deer families, have two or four toes that form a cloven hoof. The whales, dolphins, and porpoises (Cetacea) are hairless, and the legs have evolved into flippers. The manatees (Sirenia), which live in both fresh and salt water, are nearly hairless and vegetarian; they have front flippers and a rounded, flat, paddle-shaped tail.

Most mammals have an insulating layer of fur that allows them to maintain a fairly constant body temperature independent of their surroundings, thus making them among the most successful animals in cold climates. Many molt twice a year, and some have a thicker coat in winter. Whales, porpoises, dolphins, and manatees have thick layers of insulating blubber instead of hair. The ability to maintain a high body temperature allows many mammals to be active in cold weather, unlike reptiles and amphibians, which are cold-blooded.

The body parts and appendages of mammals exhibit a wide and adaptive variety of sizes, shapes, and functions. Most have well-developed eyes, ears, and noses that provide good night vision, hearing, and sense of smell. Mammalian teeth range from fine points for capturing insects (bats and insectivores) to chisel-like gnawing teeth (rabbits, rodents, and hoofed mammals), wide plant-crushers (rodents, hoofed mammals, and manatees), and heavy pointed instruments for flesh-ripping (carnivores). Mammals generally have four limbs. In many rodents, in some carnivores, and in primates, the ends of the forelimbs are modified into complex, manipulative hands. Solid hooves support the heavy weight of grazing or running ungulates, such as pigs and deer.

In the species accounts, the typical adult length given is from the tip of the nose to the end of the tail, followed by the tail length; for larger mammals, shoulder height is also given. Wingspan is given for bats, when known.

Mammal Sign and Tracks

The evidence that a particular animal is or has been in a certain area is called its "sign." The sign can be scat (fecal matter), burrow openings, nutshells, tracks, or other evidence. Tracks are a useful aid in confirming the presence of mammal species. Impressions vary depending on the substrate and whether the animal was walking or running. Animals can leave clear tracks in mud, dirt, and sand, usually larger ones in wet mud. Because animals come to ponds or streams to drink or feed, tracks are likely to be found on their shores; damp mud often records tracks in fine detail, sometimes showing claws or webbing. Prints can often be followed for a long distance, and may show the pattern of the animal's stride. The track drawings below, of selected mammals that live in Florida, are not to relative scale. The upper left track is the foreprint; the right track is the hindprint; the small formation in the lower left shows the pattern in which the tracks usually occur.

Virginia Opossum

Nine-banded Armadillo

Eastern Cottontail

Eastern Gray Squirrel

Brown Rat

Nutria

Coyote

Common Gray Fox

Black Bear

Common Raccoon

Long-tailed Weasel

Mink

Striped Skunk

Northern River Otter

Florida Panther

Bobcat

White-tailed Deer

VIRGINIA OPOSSUM
Didelphis virginiana
OPOSSUM FAMILY

L 32″; T 15″. Grizzled grayish (a few blackish), with mix of black underfur and longer white guard hairs. Head pointed; nose long; face white, with long whiskers; ears small, round, black with white tip. Legs short, black; feet have 5 digits each; hindfeet have opposable, grasping inner thumbs. Tail long and tapered, naked, pink with black base. Omnivorous: eats fruits, nuts, bird eggs, large insects, carrion. Hangs from branches using wraparound, prehensile tail. If surprised at close range, may "play possum" (play dead). **BREEDING** 1–14 (avg. 8) pea-size young attach themselves to nipples in mother's pouch for 2 months; 2–3 litters per year. **SIGN** Tracks: hindprint 2″ wide, 3 middle toes close, outer toes well spread; foreprint slightly smaller, star-like. **HABITAT** Woods, watersides, farms, towns. **ACTIVITY** Nocturnal; less active in cold weather.

SOUTHERN SHORT-TAILED SHREW
Blarina carolinensis
SHREW FAMILY

L 4¾″; T 1″. Body and head grayish black. Nose long, conical. Jaws long; open wide, exposing many fine teeth. Eyes tiny; ears tiny, hidden in fur. Legs short; 5 toes on each foot. Tail nearly hairless, short for a shrew. Very active; heart can beat up to 700 times a minute. Eats its weight daily; attacks worms, snails, insects, and mice, paralyzing them with poisonous saliva. **CAUTION** Poison not fatal to humans, but bites can result in intense, painful swelling. **BREEDING** 2–3 litters of 4–8 young year-round. **SIGN** Nest of shredded grass and leaves under a log. **HABITAT** Woods, watersides, brush. **ACTIVITY** Intensely active day and night, year-round. **RANGE** All FL, ex. Keys.

EASTERN MOLE
Scalopus aquaticus
MOLE FAMILY

L 7″; T 1″. Fur short, velvety, pale brown or tan. Snout long, pink, flexible; eyes and ears not visible. Legs very short; front feet have wide, round, fleshy palms that are turned out, and 5 long white claws. Tail short, few hairs. Feeds on earthworms and beetle larvae in shallow tunnels under soil surface. **BREEDING** 2–5 young born in tunnels Apr.–May. **SIGN** Low raised ridges on soil surface. **HABITAT** Fields, lawns, well-drained woods. **ACTIVITY** Near dawn and dusk, year-round. **RANGE** All FL, ex. Keys.

Bats

Bats are the only mammals that truly fly (the flying squirrels g…
The bones and muscles in the forelimbs of bats are elongated; t…
usually black wing membranes are attached to four extremely lo…
fingers. When bats are at rest, the wings are folded along the for…
arm; they use their short, claw-like thumbs for crawling about.
Small insectivorous bats beat their wings six to eight times a second.

Bats are mainly nocturnal, though some species are occasionally
active in the early morning and late afternoon. Their slender,
mouse-like bodies are well furred, and their eyesight, while not excellent, is quite adequate to detect predators and general landscape
features. Most use echolocation (sonar) to locate flying insects and
avoid obstacles. In flight, they emit 30 to 60 high-frequency calls
per second that bounce off objects and return to their large ears.
Bats interpret these reflected sounds as they close in on prey or
evade an obstacle. Echolocation sounds are mainly inaudible to humans, but bats also give shrill squeaks most humans can hear. By
day, most bats hang upside-down from the ceilings of caves, tree
hollows, and attics, using one or both feet. Members of solitary
species may roost alone under a branch or among the foliage of a
tall tree. In other species, large colonies gather in caves and under
natural and man-made overhangs.

Most Florida bats are insect-eaters. By night, they pursue larger
individual insects through the air or glean them from trees, and
skim open-mouthed through swarms of insects. A bat will trap a
large flying insect in the membrane between its hindlegs, then seize
it with its teeth. Because Florida has fewer flying insects in winter,
bats are less active or dormant then.

Watch for bats overhead on warm evenings, especially around
water, where insects are abundant and where bats may skim the
water surface to drink.

Parts of a Bat

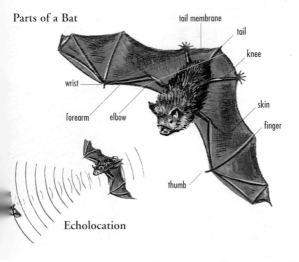

tail membrane
tail
knee
wrist
skin
forearm
elbow
finger
thumb

Echolocation

NORTHERN YELLOW BAT
"Eastern Yellow Bat"
Lasiurus intermedius
VESPERTILIONID BAT FAMILY

L 5"; WS 12". Fur long, silky, pale yellowish brown. Nose pointed; ears medium-small, rounded, pinkish. Basal third of tail membrane furred. Captures insects in flight. Roosts alone, ex. females when breeding.
BREEDING Females form small loose colonies in trees; 2–4 young in June.
HABITAT Pine (esp. Longleaf Pine) and oak woods; often roosts and nests in Spanish Moss. **ACTIVITY** Nocturnal, year-round. **RANGE** All FL, ex. Keys.

SEMINOLE BAT
Lasiurus seminolus
VESPERTILIONID BAT FAMILY

L 4"; WS 12". Fur on upperparts and entire head rich mahogany brown; belly white. Head rounded, face flat; ears medium-small, rounded, pinkish. Tail membrane entirely furred. Solitary; captures insects in fast steady flight. **BREEDING** 2–4 young in June. **HABITAT** Broadleaf woods, often in Spanish Moss; roosts low in trees. **ACTIVITY** Nocturnal, year-round. **RANGE** All FL, ex. Keys.

EVENING BAT
Nycticeius humeralis
VESPERTILIONID BAT FAMILY

L 3½"; WS 11". Fur silky; reddish brown above, whitish below. Head rounded; face and nose pointed; ears medium-small, rounded, black. No fur on tail membrane. Flight slow and straight. **BREEDING** 1–2 young in July. **HABITAT** Feeds over woods, cornfields, open areas; roosts in hollow trees; maternity colonies in buildings and tree hollows. **ACTIVITY** Spring–fall: nocturnal. Winter: range and roosting sites unknown. **RANGE** All FL, ex. Keys.

RAFINESQUE'S BIG-EARED BAT
"Eastern Big-eared Bat"
Plecotus rafinesquii
VESPERTILIONID BAT FAMILY

L 4"; WS 12". Head and upperparts brown; belly has white-tipped black hair. Face small; 2 large glandular lumps on nose. Ears very large, long (1"), blackish, with pink base inside. Hovers in flight; takes insects, esp. moths. **BREEDING** 1 young in May; small maternity colonies in buildings. **SIGN** Tiny black droppings on attic floors. **HABITAT** Feeds in woods; roosts in buildings, caves, trees. **ACTIVITY** Nocturnal, year-round.

NINE-BANDED ARMADILLO
Dasypus novemcinctus
ARMADILLO FAMILY

L 28″; T 12″. Only FL mammal with an exoskeleton: body, top of head, and tail covered with silver-brown, bony plates. 9 flexible, overlapping, armored bands encircle midsection, allowing body to twist or curl. Head small, elongated; nose long; eyes small. Teeth peg-like. Oval ears and underparts soft, unprotected. Legs short; feet have heavy digging claws. Tail almost as long as body. Feeds mainly on ants and other insects by digging and using its long sticky tongue; also eats crayfish, frogs, snakes, bird eggs, carrion. Runs rapidly; burrows efficiently in most soils; swims well. Introduced from Texas. **BREEDING** Mates in summer; quadruplets born in Mar., follow mother like piglets. **SIGN** Burrows: often by streams, with entrance holes 6–8″ wide. Scat: resembles clay marbles. Tracks: bird-like; 2″ long, 5-toed hindprint, middle 3 toes longer; smaller foreprint 4-toed, with long middle toes, short outer toes. **HABITAT** Woods, scrub, and fields with soft soil and rotting wood. **ACTIVITY** By night in hot weather, by day in cool; year-round. **RANGE** All FL, ex. Keys.

EASTERN COTTONTAIL
Sylvilagus floridanus
HARE AND RABBIT FAMILY

L 17″; T 1½″. Fur grayish brown, mixed with black hairs; belly white. White eye ring and rusty wash on nape; many have white spot on forehead. Ears to 2½″ long, with thin black stripe on upper edges. Legs buffy; hindlegs heavily muscled. Tail fluffy; underside white. Raises tail when bounding away, displaying white "cottontail." Those in s FL smaller, grayer, less washed with black. **BREEDING** 4–5 young born blind, nearly naked; several litters a year. **SIGN** Clean-cut woody sprigs; stripped bark on young trees. Tracks: 3″ oblong hindprints in front of smaller, round foreprints. Scat: piles of dark brown, pea-size pellets. **HABITAT** Fields, woodland edges, thickets, gardens. **ACTIVITY** Late afternoon through morning; spends midday in nest-like "form" in grass or thickets; year-round. **RANGE** All FL, ex, Keys

MARSH RABBIT
Sylvilagus palustris
HARE AND RABBIT FAMILY

L 16″; T 1½″. Fur coarse; dark brown above; belly white; indistinct rusty nape patch. Head and eyes large; ears short and broad for a rabbit, dark gray inside. Feet small, reddish brown above. Tail all brown. Sometimes walks on hindlegs; runs more slowly than a cottontail. Swims well, often with just eyes and nose exposed. **BREEDING** Mates from Feb. on; 2–5 young per litter, several litters per year. **SIGN** Trails in marshes. Tracks: hindprint about 3½″. **HABITAT** Fresh- and saltwater marshes and swamps. **ACTIVITY** Day and night, year-round.

Rodents

Rodentia is the world's largest mammalian order; more than half of all mammal species and many more than half of all mammal individuals on earth are rodents. In addition to the mice and rats (a family that also includes the mouse-like but chubbier voles, the pocket gophers, and the muskrats), other rodent families in Florida are the squirrels and the Nutria. Florida species range from mice weighing roughly an ounce to the Nutria, which may weigh up to 25 pounds, but most rodents are small. They are distinguished by having only two pairs of incisors—one upper and one lower—and no canines, leaving a wide gap between incisors and molars. Rodent incisors are enameled on the front only; the working of the upper teeth against the lower ones wears away the softer inner surfaces, producing a short, chisel-like, beveled edge ideal for gnawing. The incisors grow throughout an animal's life (if they didn't they would be worn away), and rodents must gnaw enough to keep the incisors from growing too long. Rodents have bulbous eyes placed high on the side of the head, enabling them to detect danger over a wide arc.

SOUTHERN FLYING SQUIRREL
Glaucomys volans
SQUIRREL FAMILY

L 9″; T 3″. Brown above: darker and redder in summer, paler fawn in winter; white below. Eyes large, black; ears rounded. Tail flat, bushy, narrow-based. Folds of furred skin connect fore- and hindlimbs, allowing glides up to 200′. Will visit birdfeeders at night, but eats mainly insects most of year. **BREEDING** 2–6 blind naked young; several broods a year. Nests in tree cavities, attics, birdhouses. **SIGN** Piles of nuts with fine tooth marks around a circular opening. **HABITAT** Broadleaf and mixed woods. **ACTIVITY** Nocturnal. **RANGE** South to Lake Okeechobee.

EASTERN FOX SQUIRREL
Sciurus niger
SQUIRREL FAMILY

L 24″; T 11″. Coat variable: grayish black, reddish brown, or all black above and on sides. Front half of face, incl. nose, often white. Legs, feet, underparts, and edges of bushy tail often buff or white. Caches nuts in tree cavities. **VOICE** A loud *que-que-que.* **BREEDING** 2–4 young Feb.–Mar.; sometimes a 2nd litter June–Aug. Young remain in leaf nest 2 months. **SIGN** Mounds of nutshells under feeding branch.; large leaf nest high in trees. **HABITAT** Mixed woods, esp. oak, pine, hickory, cypress; mangroves. **ACTIVITY** By day, year-round. **RANGE** All FL, ex. Keys.

EASTERN GRAY SQUIRREL
Sciurus carolinensis
SQUIRREL FAMILY

L 19″; T 9″. Summer: coat gray; head, legs, and sides tawny brown; white below. Winter: gray above, white below. Head rounded. Eye ring and edges of snout buffy; long bushy tail grizzled blackish and white. **VOICE** Gives variety of chattering and clucking calls. **BREEDING** 2 litters of usu. 2–3 young; mainly spring and summer, in nest in tree cavity. **SIGN** Summer: stick platform in tree; gnawed nutshells and corncobs. Winter: spherical leaf nest in tree. Tracks: longer hindprints in front of smaller foreprints. **HABITAT** Broadleaf and mixed woods, esp. oak and hickory, parks, towns. **ACTIVITY** By day, year-round.

MARSH RICE RAT
Oryzomys palustris
MOUSE AND RAT FAMILY

L 10″; T 5″. Grayish brown above, some washed dull brownish yellow; belly pale gray or tawny. Head large; whiskers long; ears round, medium-size. Feet short, whitish. Tail scaly, longer than body. Dives and swims easily; eats soft plants, fungi, fruits, snails, crustaceans, insects. **BREEDING** Several litters of 3–6 young year-round in grapefruit-size nest of woven grass. **SIGN** Runways in marsh; flat feeding platforms of bent-over marsh plants. Tracks: hindprint ⅜″ long, with 5 splayed toes. **HABITAT** Marshes, moist meadows. **ACTIVITY** Day and night, year-round. **RANGE** All FL, ex. Keys. **Round-tailed Muskrat** (*Neofiber alleni*) is larger (L 14″, T 6″), dark brown; tail naked, scaly, round; feeds in marshes of peninsular FL.

EASTERN HARVEST MOUSE
Reithrodontomys humulis
MOUSE AND RAT FAMILY

L 5″; T 2½″. Rich brown above, darkest on midback; dusky below. Head long, pointed; ears medium-size. Upper incisors grooved. Feet whitish. Tail equal to body length, thin. Stores surplus sprouts and seeds in cache or nest. **BREEDING** Several litters of 3–5 young spring through fall. **SIGN** 3″ round woven nest in low grass or bush. **HABITAT** Fields, meadows. **ACTIVITY** Day and night, year-round.

COTTON MOUSE
Peromyscus gossypinus
MOUSE AND RAT FAMILY

L 7"; T 3½". Tawny brown above, white below. Snout long; ears fairly large, narrow-based. Feet white. Tail equal to body length, short-haired, often bicolored (dark with pale underside). Climbs trees and swims well. Host, with White-tailed Deer, of Lyme disease tick and parasite. **BREEDING** Several litters of 1–7 young Aug.–May. **SIGN** Nests in or under logs or low in palmettos. **HABITAT** Swamps, bottomland woods, beaches, buildings. **ACTIVITY** Nocturnal, year-round.

FLORIDA MOUSE
Podomys floridanus
MOUSE AND RAT FAMILY

L 8"; T 3½". Brown above, white below. Bottom half of pointed head white; ears large, naked. Rear legs, hindfeet large. Tail slightly shorter than body, narrow. Nests, sleeps in burrows of other rodents, armadillo, Gopher Tortoise. **BREEDING** Several litters of 2–4 young July–Feb. **SIGN** Tracks in sand. **HABITAT** Sandy ridges of oaks, palmetto. **ACTIVITY** Day and night; year-round. **RANGE** nc and e peninsular FL; Franklin Co. in panhandle.

GOLDEN MOUSE
Ochrotomys nuttalli
MOUSE AND RAT FAMILY

L 6"; T 2½". Bright golden-cinnamon above, white below. Head pointed; ears medium-size. Feet short, white. Tail slightly shorter than body, prehensile. Runs along branches of trees and shrubs. **BREEDING** Several litters of 1–4 young year-round. **SIGN** Round nests of leaves, moss, shredded bark sometimes high in tree. **HABITAT** Woods, swamps. **ACTIVITY** Nocturnal, year-round. **RANGE** n and c FL.

HISPID COTTON RAT
Sigmodon hispidus
MOUSE AND RAT FAMILY

L 12"; T 5". Fur coarse; blackish brown, grizzled gray and tawny above; dusky below. Nose pointed; ears small, partly hidden. Feet dusky. Tail short, nearly hairless. Climbs vegetation, consuming seeds, greenery. **BREEDING** Many litters of 1–12 young year-round; can breed at 6 weeks. **SIGN** Ball-shaped woven nests; runways with cut-grass stems. Tracks: hind- and foreprints overlap; toes splayed in mud; ½" wide and long. **HABITAT** Fields. **ACTIVITY** Mainly nocturnal, year-round.

EASTERN WOODRAT
"Florida Woodrat" "Packrat"
Neotoma floridana
MOUSE AND RAT FAMILY

L 15"; T 7". Grayish brown above, whitish below. Head wide, blunt; ears large, rounded. Feet whitish. Tail furred, slightly shorter than body; brown above, white below. Each adult has own waterproof nest. **BREEDING** 2–3 litters of 2–4 young year-round. **SIGN** Nest of sticks, rocks, bones, rubbish in burrow, rocks, building, tree. **HABITAT** Woods, swamps, palmetto scrub. **ACTIVITY** Nocturnal, year-round. **RANGE** n and c FL; Key Largo.

BROWN RAT
"Norway Rat"
Rattus norvegicus
MOUSE AND RAT FAMILY

L 15"; T 7". Grayish brown above; belly gray; ears partly hidden in fur; tail long and scaly, a bit shorter than body. Excavates network of tunnels 2–3" wide in ground near buildings, dumps, water. Eats insects, stored grain, garbage. Introduced from Eurasia. **BREEDING** Avg. 5 litters of 7–11 young a year. **SIGN** Dirty holes in walls; droppings in houses; pathways to steady food supplies. Tracks: long, 5-toed hindprint forward of rounder foreprint. **HABITAT** Towns, buildings, farms. **ACTIVITY** Mostly nocturnal, year-round.

NUTRIA
Myocastor coypus
NUTRIA FAMILY

L 4'; T 15". Long-haired. Dark brown above, paler brown below. Head large; whitish patch at base of long whiskers on dog-like muzzle; orange incisors often protrude; ears small, partly hidden. Feet blackish; hindfeet webbed. Tail long, scaly, black, rounded. Introduced from Argentina, for fur; damages crops and embankments. **VOICE** Call: pig-like grunt. **BREEDING** 1–11 young twice a year. **SIGN** Nest in reeds; burrow near water; large floating feeding platforms in marsh. Tracks: webbed hindprint 3¾" long. **HABITAT** Marshes, waterways. **ACTIVITY** Mainly nocturnal, year-round. **RANGE** All FL, ex. Keys. **American Beaver** (*Castor canadensis*; L 4', T 16") is rich dark brown, with scaly, black, paddle-shaped tail; recolonized in n FL.

Carnivores

Members of the order Carnivora mainly eat meat, though many also eat a variety of fruit, berries, and vegetation. Carnivores vary greatly in size, from tiny weasels to massive bears. They have long canine teeth for stabbing prey, and most have sharp cheek teeth for slicing meat. None truly hibernates, but several den up and perhaps sleep in well-insulated logs and burrows during colder parts of the winter, especially in northern Florida. Most live on land, although otters spend most of their time in water. Most carnivores have a single yearly litter of offspring, which are born blind and receive many months, sometimes even a year or more, of parental care. Florida carnivore families include the bears, dogs (the Coyote, wolves, and foxes), weasels (the Mink, skunks, otters), raccoons, and cats. St. Vincent National Wildlife Refuge in northwestern Florida is currently being used as a place where captive-bred endangered Red Wolves *(Canis rufus)* can gain wilderness experience before being released at designated mainland areas.

COYOTE
Canis latrans
DOG FAMILY

H 25″; L 4′; T 13″. Coat long, coarse; grizzled gray, buffy, and black. Muzzle long, narrow, brownish; ears rufous; legs long; tail long, bushy, black-tipped. Runs up to 40 mph. Eats small mammals, birds, frogs, snakes, berries. 20th-century invader from w U.S. Only large carnivore to persist in heavily settled areas. **VOICE** Bark; flat howl; series of *yip* notes followed by wavering howl. **BREEDING** 4–8 pups Mar.–Apr. **SIGN** Den mouths 24″ wide, on slopes. Tracks: dog-like, but in nearly straight line; foreprint larger, 2⅜″ long. Scat: dog-like, but usu. full of hair. **HABITAT** Woods, brush, fields. **ACTIVITY** Mainly nocturnal, year-round. **RANGE** n and c FL.

COMMON GRAY FOX
Urocyon cinereoargenteus
DOG FAMILY

H 15″; L 3′2″; T 13″. Coat grizzled silvery gray above; throat and midbelly white; collar, lower sides, legs, sides of tail rusty; top and tip of tail black. Eats rabbits, rodents, birds, grasshoppers, fruit, berries. Often climbs trees. **BREEDING** 2–7 young Apr.–May. **SIGN** Den hidden in natural crevice in woods; often has snagged hair and bone scraps near entrance. Tracks: foreprint 1½″ long; hindprint slightly narrower. **HABITAT** Wooded and brushy areas. **ACTIVITY** Day or night, but secretive; year-round. **Red Fox** (*Vulpes vulpes*) is rusty orange above, with lower legs black, tail white-tipped; recently expanded into peninsular FL.

BLACK BEAR
Ursus americanus
BEAR FAMILY

H 3′4″; L 5′; T 4″; male much larger than female. Black, long-haired; often has white patch on chest. Head round; muzzle long, brownish; ears short, rounded. Legs long. More vegetarian than most carnivores; eats inner layer of tree bark, berries, fruit, plants, fish, honeycombs, insects in rotten logs, and vertebrates, incl. small mammals. Powerful swimmer and climber; can run up to 30 mph. Most common in Ocala N.F. and Big Cypress area. **CAUTION** Will usually flee, but can cause serious injury. **BREEDING** 1–2 cubs, about ½ lb. at birth, born in den in Jan. **SIGN** Torn-apart stumps; turned-over boulders; torn-up burrows; hair on shaggy-barked rubbing trees. Tracks: foreprints 5″ wide; hindprints up to 9″ long. Scat: dog-like. **HABITAT** Woods, swamps, dumps. **ACTIVITY** Mainly nocturnal; active by day in protected areas.

COMMON RACCOON
Procyon lotor
RACCOON FAMILY

L 32"; T 9". Coat long and thick, grizzled grayish brown. Black mask below white eyebrow; white sides on narrow muzzle. Legs medium-length; paws buffy; flexible toes used for climbing trees and washing food. Tail ⅓ body length, thick, banded yellow-brown and black. Swims well; can run up to 15 mph. **BREEDING** Usu. 4 young in Apr. **SIGN** Den in hollow tree or crevice. Tracks: flat-footed; hindprint much longer than wide, 4" long; foreprint rounded, 3" long; claws show on all 5 toes. **HABITAT** Woods and scrub near water; towns. **ACTIVITY** Mainly nocturnal, but sometimes seen in daytime.

LONG-TAILED WEASEL
Mustela frenata
WEASEL FAMILY

L 20"; T 6"; female smaller. Brown above, white below; face darker than body; feet and outside of legs brown. Neck long; legs short. Tail thin, furred, with brown base, black tip. Wraps sinewy body around prey as it kills by biting base of skull. Good swimmer and climber. **BREEDING** 4–8 young Apr.–May. **SIGN** Cache of dead rodents under log. Tracks: hindprint ¾" wide, 1" long; foreprint a bit wider, half as long. **HABITAT** Woods, brush, fields. **ACTIVITY** Mainly nocturnal, year-round.

MINK
Mustela vison
WEASEL FAMILY

L 21"; T 7"; female smaller. Lustrous blackish brown above and below; chin white. Muzzle pointed; ears tiny; legs short; tail fairly long, bushy. (Weasels are white below; have thinner tails.) Swims often; feeds mainly on fish, some birds, rodents, frogs. **BREEDING** 2–10 young in Apr. **SIGN** 4" burrow entrance in stream bank. Tracks: round, 1¼" wide; 5 well-separated toe pads with claws, inverted V heel pad. **HABITAT** Freshwater shores. **ACTIVITY** Late afternoon to early morning, year-round. **RANGE** n and c FL; Everglades.

EASTERN SPOTTED SKUNK
Spilogale putorius
WEASEL FAMILY

L 18"; T 7". Black with irregular white horizontal stripes on foreparts, vertical stripes on hindquarters. Head black with small white spots; ears tiny. Legs and feet black. Tail short for a skunk; fluffy; black with white tip. If threatened, stands on forepaws; can spray foul-smelling liquid up to 13′. Faster, more agile than Striped Skunk; climbs trees. **BREEDING** 2–6 young Apr.–May in burrow or log. **SIGN** Lingering stench. Tracks: hindprint 1¼" long; heel shows many small spots; stride irreg. **HABITAT** Woods, scrub, farms. **ACTIVITY** Nocturnal, year-round. **RANGE** All FL, ex. Keys.

STRIPED SKUNK
Mephitis mephitis
WEASEL FAMILY

L 24"; T 9". Coat thick, fluffy, mainly black; large white nape patch continues as 2 stripes along sides of back to tail, usu. reaching tail; narrow white forehead stripe. Head pointed; ears and eyes small. Legs short; rear large; tail long, bushy. In some individuals, most of upper back and tail white. If threatened, may emit foul-smelling, sulphurous spray that travels up to 15', stings eyes of predators, pets, humans. Eats insects, rodents, bird and turtle eggs, fruit, roadkills, garbage. **CAUTION** Can turn and spray in an instant. **BREEDING** 5–6 young in May. **SIGN** Foul odor if one has sprayed or been run over recently; scratched-up lawns and garbage bags. Tracks: round foreprint 1" long; hindprint broader at front, flat-footed, 1½" long. **HABITAT** Woods, fields, towns. **ACTIVITY** Dusk to dawn; may den up and sleep some of winter in n FL.

Rabies

Rabies is a serious viral disease that is carried and can be transmitted by bats, foxes, raccoons, skunks, and other mammals, as well as domestic animals; it can make humans deathly ill. Infected animals may be agitated and aggressive, or fearless and lethargic; nocturnal animals who are diseased may roam about fearlessly in daytime. As the disease drives infected individuals to bite others, rabid animals must be avoided. Stay away from any animal that is acting strangely, and report it to animal-control officers. The disease, which attacks the central nervous system, has an incubation period of 10 days to a year. If you are bitten by a possibly rabid animal, you must immediately consult a doctor for a series of injections that will save your life. There is no cure once symptoms emerge.

NORTHERN RIVER OTTER
Lutra canadensis
WEASEL FAMILY

L 3'7"; T 16". Fur dense, dark brown, often silvery on chin and chest. Ears and eyes small. Tail long, thick-based, tapering to a point. Legs short; feet webbed. Swims rapidly, stops with head raised out of water. Eats fish, frogs, turtles, muskrats. Runs well on land; loves to exercise and play. **BREEDING** Mates in water; 1–5 young born blind but furred in Mar. **SIGN** 12"-wide slides on sloping muddy riverbanks, in flat areas; vegetation flattened in large patch for rolling, feeding, defecating; trails between bodies of water. Tracks: 3¼" wide, toes fanned. **HABITAT** Clean rivers, wood-edged ponds and lakes. Eats in water and on land; rests and wanders ashore. **ACTIVITY** Day and night, year-round.

FLORIDA PANTHER
"Mountain Lion" "Puma" "Cougar"
Felis concolor
CAT FAMILY

H 30"; L 8'; T 30"; male larger than female. Golden brown to brownish above, whitish below. Head fairly small; dark spot at base of whiskers; ears small, erect, blackish on back. Neck fairly long. Legs long; paws wide; claws long, sharp, retractile. Tail long, blackish at end. Young longer-tailed than Bobcat; dark-spotted. Feeds on deer, pigs, rabbits, rodents, birds. Solitary, territorial hunter ex. for mother with older cubs and during 2-week breeding period; good climber. Normally very shy of humans; no recorded attack in FL. Race endangered. **VOICE** Screams, hisses, growls. **BREEDING** 2–4 young in any season every 2 years; young stay with mother 18 months. **SIGN** Scratch marks left 6–10' up on tree; piles of dirt and leaves urinated on by male. Tracks: round; 4 toe prints show no claws. **HABITAT** Woods, scrub, swamps. **ACTIVITY** Mainly nocturnal, year-round. **RANGE** sw FL.

BOBCAT
Lynx rufus
CAT FAMILY

H 20"; L 33"; T 4". Orange-brown in summer, paler grayish in winter; black spots and bars on legs and rear. Face wide and flat; black lines radiate onto facial ruff; ears slightly tufted, backside black. Underparts and insides of long legs white; many black spots on long legs. Tail bobbed. Stalks and ambushes small mammals and birds at night. **VOICE** Yowls and screams (though mostly silent). **BREEDING** 2 young in May. **SIGN** Tracks in mud at scent posts and scratching trees. Tracks: like domestic cat, but 2" wide vs. 1". **HABITAT** Woods, scrub, swamps. **ACTIVITY** Mainly nocturnal, year-round.

FERAL PIG
"Wild Boar" "Wild Hog" "Razorback"
Sus scrofa
PIG FAMILY

H 30"; L 5'; T 9"; female smaller than male. Coat coarse, bristly; brown or black. Head large; nose pad round with flat tip; ears triangular. Shoulders high; hindquarters sloping. Tusks (upper canines) curved, curl out and up; 3–6" long. 4 toes on each foot. Tail long, straight, bushy. Young have coat of dark brown and buffy stripes. Omnivorous, with excellent sense of smell; roots in soft soil. Swims well; runs fast; sometimes roams in herds. Ancestor of domestic pig; introduced from Europe as game animal; interbreeds with escaped domestic pigs. **CAUTION** If harassed or wounded, can cause serious injury with tusks. Flesh often full of parasitic worms. **BREEDING** 3–8 young, often 2 broods a year in Jan.–Feb., June–July. **SIGN** Rooted-up earth; hair and mud stuck to rubbing trees; muddy wallows. Tracks: cloven, more rounded and splayed than deer; 2½" long. **HABITAT** Woods, scrub, swamps. **ACTIVITY** Day or night, year-round.

WHITE-TAILED DEER
Odocoileus virginianus
DEER FAMILY

H 30″; L 5′6″; T 7″; male much heavier than female. Rich reddish brown in summer, some gray-brown in winter. Neck long; ears large; legs long; tail fairly long. Nose and hooves black. Ring around nose, eye ring, throat, midbelly, and underside of tail white. Summer male develops antlers with main beam curving out and up, points issuing from it. Fawn reddish orange, with many white spots. Communicates danger by loud whistling snort; flees with white undertail prominently erected. Can run 35 mph, clear 8′ tall obstacles, and leap 30′. Host, with several mice species, of Lyme disease tick and parasite. Wipes out many valuable plants when allowed to overpopulate in area free of predators and hunting. Those in s Fl. smaller. Key Deer race of pinewoods, palmetto thickets, and mangroves of Big Pine and nearby Keys; similar in body and antlers, but much smaller (H 25″; L 3′2″); browses tender shoots and leaves. **BREEDING** Mates Aug.–Oct. in s Fl., Oct.–Dec. in n Fl.; bucks with swollen necks wander widely to find receptive does. Fawns (mainly 1–2, rarely 3–4) born in spring; nibble greens at 2–3 weeks; weaned at 4 months. **SIGN** Raggedly browsed vegetation along well-worn trails; worn tree trunks where male rubs bark off with antlers; flattened beds in grass. Tracks: "split hearts," with narrow pointed end forward, 2–3″ long; dots of dewclaws behind. Scat: ¾″ cylindrical dark pellets. **HABITAT** Broadleaf and mixed woods and edges, hammocks, fields, swamps, marshes. **ACTIVITY** Day and night, year-round.

BOTTLE-NOSED DOLPHIN
Tursiops truncatus
OCEAN DOLPHIN FAMILY

10′. Slaty bluish gray above; paler gray on sides; whitish gray on throat and belly. Bump on forehead; beak fairly long and broad, gray above, white below. Back fin large, swept-back, pointed. Flippers blackish. Travels in small parties; curious, often friendly. Very intelligent; interacts with humans in wild. Will ride ships' bow waves. Feeds on fish, especially mullet, often chasing them onto shoreline. **BREEDING** 1 young every 2–3 years. 3′ long at birth; family helpers push newborn to surface for first breath of air. **HABITAT** Shallow brackish inshore waters, lower reaches of rivers, ocean waters.

STRIPED DOLPHIN
Stenella coeruleoalba
OCEAN DOLPHIN FAMILY

8′. Blue-black above, white below; black stripe from eye to anus; 1 or 2 black stripes from eye to flipper. Forehead sloping; beak fairly long, all black. Back fin large, black, swept-back. Often travels in herds of hundreds. Will ride ships' bow waves and jump clear of water. **BREEDING** 1 young every 2–3 years. **HABITAT** Warm ocean waters.

ATLANTIC SPOTTED DOLPHIN
Stenella frontalis
OCEAN DOLPHIN FAMILY

7′. Slaty black above, with many small white spots; paler gray below, with many dark spots. Forehead sloping; beak fairly long and narrow, with white tip. Black eye ring and black line from eye to black front flipper. Back fin large, black, swept-back, sharply pointed. Often travels in herds of 100–1,000. Will ride ships' bow waves and jump clear of water. **BREEDING** 1 young every 2–3 years. **HABITAT** Warm ocean waters.

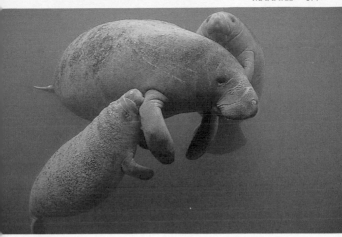

MANATEE
Trichechus manatus
MANATEE FAMILY

7–13′. Cylindrical, tapered. Grayish black, shading to pink on underparts; hide thick, strong, wrinkled, with a few sparse bristly hairs. Head rounded; neck short, thick. Lips thick, fleshy, disk-like, covered with bristles; upper lip deeply cleft. No external ears; eyes tiny. Front limbs large, paddle-like, with embedded fingers and 3 exposed nails. No external hindlimbs. Tail broad, paddle-shaped, horizontal. Entirely aquatic; unable to move on land; swims by slowly flapping tail up and down. Seeks water warmer than 46° F; suffers in cold spells. Grazes only on water plants; eats 60–100 lbs. a day. Docile and defenseless. Protected, but suffers injuries from motorboat propellers; dies from blooms of red tide toxins when in salt water. **VOICE** High-pitched chirps and squeals. **BREEDING** Mates and gives birth to 1 young underwater at any time of year, every 2–3 years. Baby suckles while mother swims on surface on her back. **HABITAT** Fresh and brackish waters; also shallow ocean waters. **RANGE** All FL coasts; rivers, lakes with outlets to sea. Winter: warm springs and other warm-water outfalls, mainly along c and s FL coasts. Major wintering sites: Crystal River, Homosassa River, Tampa Bay, Ft. Myers–Boca Grande, Port Everglades, Riviera Beach (near Titusville), and St. Johns River, esp. near Blue Spring.

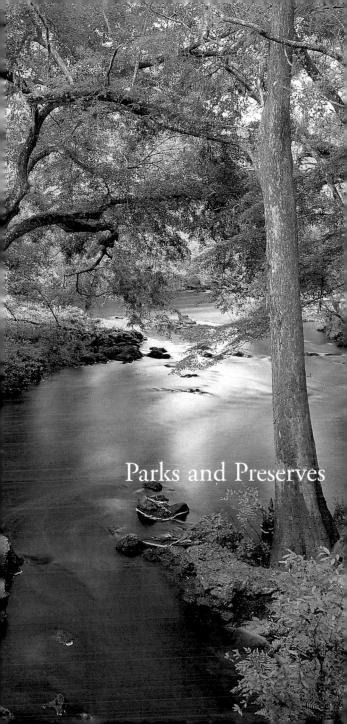

Parks and Preserves

Introduction

The longest peninsula in the mainland United States, with more than 1,200 miles of coastline and thousands more miles along numerous bays, sounds, and inlets, Florida has more saltwater shore than any other state.

Although Florida is often envisioned as a subtropical paradise, with swaying palms and white sandy beaches, its landscape is quite varied. Oriented essentially north-south, Florida bridges two climatic and biotic zones. At its northern reaches it is temperate, while its southern extreme is variously referred to as semitropical, subtropical, or tropical. Nearly 900 vertebrate species and at least 4,000 plants are native or naturalized in the state, and the number of naturalized species grows annually as humans introduce nonnative plants and animals.

Florida contains three national forests, three national parks, two national seashores, several national wildlife refuges, and a growing list of state parks, forests, and recreation areas. The Florida National Scenic Trail, with about 1,300 miles of main footpath and nearly 800 miles

St. Joseph Peninsula State Park

of scenic side loops, crosses much of the state, and is referred to numerous times in the descriptions that follow. Though some sections of the trail traverse private land, many miles weave through some of Florida's most picturesque public areas.

This section provides introductions to 50 of the most important natural locations in Florida, plus annotated listings of dozens of others. Mailing addresses and telephone numbers are given for all sites (most will send brochures and other information), and driving directions are given for the 50 featured sites. If a preserve has a visitor's center its location is noted. Since fees and exact hours of operation change frequently, they are not included in the listings, though seasonal access is noted.

This guide highlights some of the predominant plants and animals you may see as you visit the parks and preserves, but always ask if local lists of flora and fauna are available, as these can help pin down identifications.

In the text that follows, we have divided the state into four geographical regions: **Northwestern,** stretching from northwestern-

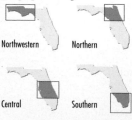

Northwestern   Northern

Central   Southern

most Florida east across the panhandle to the Suwannee River; **Northern,** from the Suwannee River east to the Atlantic Ocean and south to the Ocala National Forest; **Central,** from the Ocala area south to include Lake Okeechobee; and **Southern,** from the southern edge of Lake Okeechobee to the Keys.

Northwestern Florida

The panhandle, Florida's most lightly traveled region, claims some of the state's most beautiful natural areas. Situated 100 and 200 miles west of Interstates 75 and 95, respectively, Florida's two most important north–south arteries, the panhandle is easily bypassed by southbound visitors. Unlike the central and southern parts of the state, the panhandle has only a single interstate highway, I-10. Its Gulf coast beaches are not as developed as those along the Atlantic seaboard, and its major cities are few and relatively small in comparison to many of Florida's other urban areas.

Much of the landscape here is not what you might expect from the Sunshine State. Along its northern reaches the panhandle is composed of hilly terrain with discernible changes in elevation and relief; the town of Lakewood, Florida's highest point at 345 feet, is in the northern panhandle. At its western extreme, northeast of Pensacola in the Blackwater River area, lies a deep mantle of coarse, glacier-deposited quartz sand. Farther east, especially in the Tallahassee Red Hills region, the land is characterized by rounded hills and gentle valleys. Steep-sided ravines, moist woodlands, and scenic bluffs dot the eastern side of the upper Apalachicola River, while rich, mixed forests and longleaf pinelands clothe the uplands.

Along the panhandle's coast, a string of barrier islands lines much of the mainland shore from Pensacola to Apalachicola. Some of these islands are relatively stable landforms that exhibit little change, while others are in a nearly continuous state of flux from the pushing and tugging of coastal currents. East of Apalachicola, beaches and barrier islands give way to an expansive and luxuriant swath of Needlerush salt marsh that some refer to as the "wilderness coast."

One of the region's most unusual areas lies at the panhandle's eastern and southeastern extremes. Especially eastward along and north of U.S. 98 through Wakulla, Jefferson, and Taylor Counties, the landscape is pockmarked by freshwater springs, limestone sinkholes, and twisting, rock-lined rivers, including the Suwannee River, which flows south for 235 miles from the Okefenokee Swamp in Georgia to the village of Suwannee on the Gulf of Mexico. This distinctive terrain is home to myriad plant and animal communities and attracts snorkelers, divers, hikers, and canoeists.

ST. MARKS NATIONAL WILDLIFE REFUGE

St. Marks

The 67,000-acre St. Marks National Wildlife Refuge on Apalachee Bay due south of Tallahassee is the panhandle coast's most important natural treasure. Approximately 20 miles across and spanning three counties, the refuge is divided into three distinct regions: from east to west, the St. Marks (the refuge's administrative center), the Wakulla, and the Panacea units. The Wakulla and Panacea units have fewer amenities and are less visited than the St. Marks unit, but they also offer opportunities for exploration. Wakulla Beach Road, which leads through the Wakulla unit to a salt marsh on the shores of Apalachee Bay, affords access to a trailhead for the 40-mile St. Marks portion of the Florida National Scenic Trail, and the Panacea unit includes Otter Lake, an excellent place to see Ospreys and cormorants.

The St. Marks unit, which features a large assortment of freshwater impoundments (man-made bodies of water), a wildlife drive, and 75 miles of marked trails, is a mecca for birders, offering them the possibility of seeing many of the refuge's 270-plus species, including the Vermilion Flycatcher and the Western Kingbird. Waterfowl, shorebirds, and long-legged waders are especially plentiful and easy to spot here. The refuge also supports about 50 mammal species and a large number of reptiles and amphibians, including American Alligators, which are readily seen in the St. Marks unit impoundments at any time of year.

Amateur naturalists and lepidopterists will certainly want to visit this refuge in the fall, when huge populations of Monarch butterflies migrate southward through the area on their way to Mexico for the winter. Spring and summer are also good times to see many species of swallowtails, fritillaries, skippers, and buckeyes.

LIGHTHOUSE ROAD This 6¾-mile-long drive starts at the visitor center (which also serves as refuge headquarters, staffed by rangers and knowledgeable volunteers; recommended as your first stop) and ends at the 80-foot-high St. Marks Lighthouse overlooking

Apalachee Bay. For most of its length, the roadway parallels a series of managed impoundments that allow easy viewing of waterfowl, long-legged waders, hawks, and Bald Eagles. All the gated roads that turn off Lighthouse Road are open year-round for hiking, birding, wildlife observation, and botanizing.

PRIMITIVE WALKING TRAILS The Stoney Bayou (7 miles) and Deep Creek (13 miles) trails both start on Lighthouse Road. Both follow old logging roads and pass through a variety of habitats, including the tops of the levees that form barriers around refuge pools. The best time for extensive walks is winter, when birding and other wildlife observation along the trails are outstanding.

MOUNDS INTERPRETIVE TRAIL This 1-mile-long trail, located about 5 miles south of the visitor center, originates at a sharp curve in the road near a restroom facility, then crosses an old Indian midden (refuse) mound and encircles Tower Pond. The pond hosts wintering waterfowl, and the marsh vegetation along its edges supports a surprising variety of nesting species later in the year. An observation deck overlooks the pond as well as the salt marsh and remnant pine islands beyond.

MOUNDS POOL OBSERVATION TOWER Located across from the Mounds Pool trailhead, this deck provides an excellent vantage for viewing both the salt marsh and Tower Pond. Bald Eagles are often seen here, as are many species of wintering waterfowl.

ST. MARKS LIGHTHOUSE St. Marks Lighthouse was built in 1829, rebuilt in 1842 after the soil began eroding away, and has been in continuous use ever since. This National Historic Site is 80 feet tall with walls 4 feet thick at the base and 18 inches thick at the top. First tended by lighthouse-keepers, it became automatic in 1960. The lighthouse area is a favorite birding spot and features a covered observation deck with an enchanting view of the salt marsh and Lighthouse Pool.

Monarch

SEA KAYAKING The marshy shore of Apalachee Bay, below the lighthouse, is excellent for launching sea kayaks. Paddling east along the coastline allows exploration of numerous shallow coves, which often contain flocks of shore- and wading birds. Biologically productive and ecologically significant sea-grass meadows carpet the floor of the bay. Plan trips around high tide to avoid being stranded.

CONTACT St. Marks N.W.R., P.O. Box 68, St. Marks, FL 32355; 850-925-6121. **HOW TO GET THERE** Take Rte. 363 south from Tallahassee, then take U.S. 98 east through Newport to Rte. 59 south. **SEASONAL ACCESS** Year-round. **VISITOR CENTER** Three miles south of U.S. 98 on Rte. 59.

APALACHICOLA NATIONAL FOREST   Bristol

The forested interior of Florida's Big Bend—the region between the Apalachicola and Suwannee Rivers, where the peninsula joins the panhandle—lies atop the subterranean remnants of a 24-million-year-old seafloor. This region is a mosaic of wetland forests dominated by swamps, flatwoods, and magnificent herbaceous bogs and savannas. More than 600,000 acres of this wildly beautiful natural system are contained within the sprawling Apalachicola National Forest, which is divided into the Apalachicola and the Wakulla Ranger Districts.

The plant and animal life here are testimony to the region's biological productivity. More than 50 species of mammals and nearly 70 species of reptiles make their homes in the area, and about 170 bird species visit for at least part of the year. The forest is home to the world's largest population of the endangered Red-cockaded Woodpecker as well as stable populations of the hard-to-find Bachman's Sparrow. Grassy, treeless savannas support carnivorous pitcher plants, sundews, dew threads, and butterworts, as well as a plethora of colorful wildflowers.

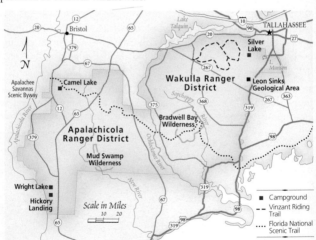

APALACHEE SAVANNAS SCENIC BYWAY Beginning 9 miles south of Bristol on Route 12, then continuing south along Route 379 and Route 65, this delightful driving tour extends from one forest boundary to the other. The savannas that border the roadway in many places are naturally treeless and are outstanding for botanizing—if you don't mind getting your feet wet. Old pines with large white bands painted around them mark Red-cockaded Woodpecker colonies.

BRADWELL BAY AND MUD SWAMP WILDERNESS AREAS These wildernesses, Bradwell Bay on the east side of the Ochlockonee River and Mud Swamp on the west, are large, remote wetlands. Bradwell Bay is crossed east to west by the Florida National Scenic Trail; the New

River runs north and south through Mud Swamp. Exploring either area requires a calm presence of mind, significant wilderness skills, and a willingness to slog through waist-deep water. The reward for this diligence includes the sight of virgin pines, towering Black Tupelo and ancient cypresses, and the stillness that comes only from being insulated from the sounds of civilization.

CANOE ROUTES Several canoeing streams are accessible. The tiny, twisting Sopchoppy River is one of the most ruggedly charming. It begins on Forest Road 365 at Oak Park Bridge, continues 5 miles to the Mount Beeser Bridge on Forest Road 343, then runs another 5 miles to Route 375. The New River canoe route begins on Forest Road 13 and continues south for about 5 miles to Forest Road 182. Both are small waterways that require expertise in maneuvering a canoe. Backwaters of the Apalachicola and Ochlockonee Rivers also offer quiet paddling.

Savanna

FLORIDA NATIONAL SCENIC TRAIL This trail traverses Apalachicola National Forest for about 60 miles from east to west and is one of the best ways to experience the forest's natural habitats. Road crossings and trailheads are well marked; the trail is blazed with rectangular swabs of orange paint at eye level. The route is marked on the official Apalachicola National Forest map.

LEON SINKS GEOLOGICAL AREA This fascinating area 7 miles south of Tallahassee off U.S. 319 offers 6 miles of hiking through sandy uplands and along the edges of limestone sinkholes. Interpretive exhibits explain the area's origin.

MUNSON HILLS OFF-ROAD BICYCLE TRAIL This 7½-mile off-road bike trail along the eastern edge of the forest can be reached from Route 363, just south of Tallahassee.

VINZANT RIDING TRAIL These developed, well-marked trails off Route 20, about 6 miles west of Tallahassee, offer some 30 miles of scenic horseback riding.

CAMPGROUNDS There are 15 designated campgrounds. Developed sites include Silver Lake in the eastern portion, and Camel Lake, Hickory Landing, and Wright Lake in the west. Drinking water and toilet facilities are available at all four sites.

CONTACT Apalachicola N.F., c/o Apalachicola Ranger District Office, P.O. Box 579, Bristol, FL 32321; 850-643-2282. **HOW TO GET THERE** Rte. 20 borders the northern edge; U.S. 319 the eastern and southeastern; Rte. 65 cuts through the center of the Apalachicola Ranger District; Rte. 67 and Rte. 375 run parallel on either side of the Ochlockonee River in the forest's midsection. **SEASONAL ACCESS** Year-round.

TORREYA STATE PARK   **Bristol**

Apalachicola River

Torreya State Park, situated on a series of high bluffs overlooking the eastern side of the Apalachicola River north of Bristol, is a botanist's paradise. Two of the United States' rarest large plants, the Florida Yew and the Florida Torreya (also called the Stinking-cedar but actually a member of the yew family), occur here, as do a large number of other rare or disjunct species. Such plants as Leatherwood, Squawroot, Doll's-eyes, Beech-drops, Wild Comfrey, Atamasco Lily, and Bloodwort dot the ground, while a variety of flowering trees and shrubs reach into the forest overstory.

HIKING TRAIL Torreya's 15-mile double loop hiking trail is the best way to experience the park's natural features. Beginning at either the Gregory House picnic area or near the main park entrance, the trail encircles the park and constitutes a full-day outing. Those expecting typical flat Florida terrain should be aware that several portions of the trail traverse steep bluffs and ravines. Be sure to climb up to the Rock Bluff primitive camp to enjoy the river view, and to

make your way into Rock Creek primitive camp to see one of the park's best populations of Florida Yew. Both of these campsites are excellent for overnight backpacking. Don't forget to investigate the old Confederate gun pits along the access trail below Gregory House.

GREGORY HOUSE Now a museum but originally a plantation home, Gregory House was built in 1849 on the west bank of the Apalachicola River. In the 1930s the state acquired the home, dismantled it, floated it across the river, and reassembled it in its current location. The house is furnished with articles from the 1850s. Call for tour schedule.

CONTACT Torreya S.P., HC 2 Box 70, Bristol, FL 32321; 850-643-2674. **HOW TO GET THERE** Take exit 25 off I-10 southwest to Greensboro, then take Rte. 12 southwest for approximately 19 miles to Rte. 1641; turn right (west) onto Rte. 1641 to park. **SEASONAL ACCESS** Year-round.

BLACKWATER RIVER STATE FOREST   Munson

At 184,000 acres—the largest state forest in Florida—Blackwater River is part of the world's biggest contiguous Longleaf Pine/wiregrass ecosystem and supports populations of carnivorous plants, Eastern Fox Squirrels, and Red-cockaded Woodpeckers. With the tea-colored Blackwater River, creeks, and several large lakes, the forest offers a variety of opportunities for canoeing, recreation, and wildlife observation. The 21½-mile Jackson Red Ground Trail, 5½-mile Wiregrass Trail, and 4½-mile Sweetwater Trail offer enjoyable hiking. Coldwater Recreation Area includes 50 miles of horseback riding trails and a campground for riders; call 904-957-4012 for reservations.

CONTACT Blackwater River S.F., 11650 Munson Hwy., Milton, FL 32570; 904-957-4201. **HOW TO GET THERE** From U.S. 90 at Milton, follow Rte. 191 northeast for 22 miles to forest headquarters in Munson. **SEASONAL ACCESS** Year-round. **VISITOR CENTER** Blackwater Forestry Center is at the intersection of Rte. 191 and Rte. 4.

FLORIDA CAVERNS STATE PARK   Marianna

Situated in a limestone-studded landscape sculpted by thousands of years of surface and subsurface erosion, this 1,300-acre park protects Florida's only publicly accessible cave in the only region of the state that has air-filled underground caverns. In prehistoric times, when the water level here was much nearer the land surface, the caverns were underwater. Daily tours follow a 1,640-foot path as far as 50 feet below ground. Narrow passageways give way to underground rooms containing beautiful limestone formations known as rimstones, flowstones, draperies, and soda straws. Hiking and horseback riding trails outside are noted for rare and unusual plants, especially Bloodwort and Wild Columbine.

CONTACT Florida Caverns S.P., 3345 Caverns Rd., Marianna, FL 32446; 850-482-9598. **HOW TO GET THERE** From I-10 near Marianna, take Rte. 71 north to Rte. 166 and follow signs. **SEASONAL ACCESS** Year-round. **VISITOR CENTER** Adjacent to main parking area.

EDWARD BALL WAKULLA SPRINGS STATE PARK

Wakulla Springs

Forming the headwaters of the Wakulla River, this mammoth natural spring's flow averages 400,000 gallons per minute. Guided sightseeing and glass-bottom boat tours allow visitors to peer into the spring's main vent or to look for alligators, Limpkins, Ospreys, Anhingas, wading birds, and water snakes. The 1-mile-long Sally Ward nature trail allows walkers to explore some of the 3,000 acres of pristine forest surrounding the spring run (a clear stream that runs from a spring).

CONTACT Edward Ball Wakulla Springs S.P., 550 Wakulla Park Dr., Wakulla Springs, FL 32305; 850-922-3632. **HOW TO GET THERE** From I-10, take Tallahassee exit 28 and follow Rte. 263 (Capital Circle) south to Rte. 61; go 1½ miles to fork, staying to left on Rte. 61, then drive 8 miles to Rte. 267; turn left (east) to park. **SEASONAL ACCESS** Year-round. **VISITOR CENTER** At park's center.

SUWANNEE RIVER STATE PARK

Live Oak

Two of Florida's finest canoeing streams join forces here: the Withlacoochee and the Suwannee. Several paddle trails begin north of the park and terminate at the park's landing. The park holds 1,800 acres of hardwood hammocks, bottomland forests, and upland sandhills. Five trails offer ample opportunities for wildlife- and plant-lovers; for more ambitious hikers, the Florida National Scenic and Big Oak Trails pass through the park. Specimens of Cedar Elms, one of the few populations of this species in Florida, are scattered

along the trails. The park also contains Civil War earthworks and a historic cemetery. A shaded campground, developed boat landing, and picnic area are also available.

CONTACT Suwannee River S.P., 20185 County Rd. 132, Live Oak, FL 32060; 850-362-2746. **HOW TO GET THERE** Just off U.S. 90, 15 miles west of Live Oak. **SEASONAL ACCESS** Year-round.

ST. ANDREWS STATE RECREATION AREA

Panama City Beach

This 1,260-acre park bordering the Gulf of Mexico along the state's northwest coast is best known as a summer beach destination. In late fall, winter, and spring, however, it is almost deserted, and hosts nearly 160 species of wintering and migrating birds, including shorebirds, gulls, and terns. Two nature trails allow exploration of typical coastal habitats, and a large jetty that juts into the Gulf provides opportunities for birding, fishing, and meditation. An excellent campground is situated along a lagoon, and several beach-side picnic sites are available.

CONTACT St. Andrews S.R.A., 4607 State Park La., Panama City Beach, FL 32408; 850-233-5140. **HOW TO GET THERE** From Panama City, take U.S. 98 across Hathaway Bridge; turn left (south) on Thomas Dr. (Rte. 392), then continue several miles to park; watch for signs. **SEASONAL ACCESS** Year round. **VISITOR CENTER** Pavilion and beach store at swimming area.

ST. JOSEPH PENINSULA STATE PARK

St. Joseph Peninsula

St. Joe Spit is one of the Gulf coast's premier hawk-watching spots. The Broad-winged Hawk and other migrating raptors congregate along this ribbon of beautiful white-sand beaches during fall migration. Throughout the fall and spring, birders come here to see migrating songbirds, including more than 20 species of warblers,

and specialty shorebirds like Piping and Snowy Plovers. This park also has a 1,650 acre wilderness preserve attached to it. Two excellent campgrounds and some cabins (which require reservations) in this 2,516-acre park offer plenty of overnight accommodations.

CONTACT St. Joseph Peninsula S.P., 8899 Cape San Blas Rd., Port St. Joe, FL 32456; 850-227-1327. **HOW TO GET THERE** From Port St. Joe, take U.S. 98 south for 3 miles; take Rte. 30 south for 8 miles; make sharp right (north) onto Cape San Blas Rd. (Rte. 30E) and continue for 9 miles, following signs. **SEASONAL ACCESS** Year-round.

GULF ISLANDS NATIONAL SEASHORE

Gulf Breeze

Located on about 135,000 acres of mainland areas, adjacent submerged lands, and offshore barrier islands along the Gulf coast, the Gulf Islands National Seashore protects an endangered natural and cultural landscape. Birders, hikers, and historians will find activities of interest here. Fort Pickens preserves American Civil War history, and Fort Barrancas preserves Florida's Spanish influence. More than 280 bird species, including shorebirds and migrating warblers, visit here, and Johnson Beach offers miles of unspoiled beaches lined with salt-tolerant plants along sparkling green Gulf waters.

CONTACT Gulf Islands N.S., 1801 Gulf Breeze Pkwy., Gulf Breeze, FL 32561; 850-934-2600. **HOW TO GET THERE** Follow I-10 to I-110 south to Pensacola; take U.S. 98 east to Gulf Breeze; continue east to park. **SEASONAL ACCESS** Year-round. **VISITOR CENTERS** One is located at Naval Live Oaks Area on U.S. 98, another at Fort Pickens, and another at Fort Barrancas.

ST. GEORGE ISLAND STATE PARK
St. George Island

This classic Gulf coast barrier island off Apalachicola Bay offers hiking, boating, swimming, fishing, outstanding birding opportunities, and car-side and primitive camping. **CONTACT** St. George Is. S.P., 1900 E. Gulf Beach Dr., St. George Is., FL 32328; 850-927-2111.

St. George Island State Park

ST. VINCENT NATIONAL WILDLIFE REFUGE   St. Vincent Island
Hiking, biking, fishing, and swimming are available on this pristine barrier island with beach and dense woods. Accessible only by boat. **CONTACT** St. Vincent N.W.R., 479 Market St., Apalachicola, FL 32320; 850-653-8808.

APALACHICOLA BLUFFS AND RAVINES PRESERVE   Bristol
See rare plants and unique habitats, including mature woodlands, at this Nature Conservancy preserve. The Garden of Eden hiking trail leads to a scenic overlook on the Apalachicola River. No camping or pets allowed. **CONTACT** Apalachicola Bluffs and Ravines Preserve, P.O. Box 393, Rte. 270, Bristol, FL 32321; 850-643-2756.

BIG BEND WILDLIFE MANAGEMENT AREA   Perry
This area has nearly 70,000 acres of coastal habitats. Hickory Mound Impoundment, with its observation tower and wildlife drive, is the best place to see wading birds and other waterfowl, as well as Bald Eagles. **CONTACT** Big Bend W.M.A., 663 Plantation Rd., Perry, FL 32347; 850-838-1306.

Big Bend Wildlife Management Area

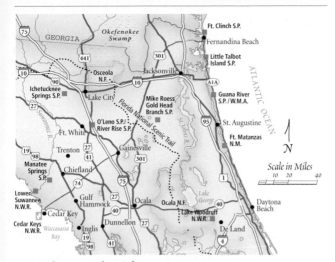

Northern Florida

Northern Florida is bounded by the Atlantic Ocean on the east, the Suwannee River on the west, the Georgia state line on the north, and the massive Ocala National Forest on the south. This part of the state is replete with interesting natural areas, many of which are unknown to the typical Florida visitor. Such places as Mike Roess Gold Head Branch State Park, Guana River State Park, O'Leno State Park, and Lower Suwannee National Wildlife Refuge are relatively undiscovered.

Though northern Florida is crossed by three major interstates—east to west by I-10 and north to south by I-75 and I-95—the discriminating naturalist should follow the older and more picturesque back roads, such as U.S. 98 down the west coast; Route A1A and U.S. 1 down the east coast; U.S. 441 from the Georgia state line through Gainesville to Ocala; U.S. 90 from the Suwannee River east to the Atlantic coast; and old U.S. 301 from Jacksonville to Tampa.

Northern Florida's central ridge is composed of sandy uplands pockmarked with moist pine flatwoods, forested wetlands, and moist hardwood hammocks. Down the western edge, the Suwannee River courses in a wide arc from its headwaters in the Okefenokee Swamp to the vast expanses of Needlerush salt marsh where it empties into the Gulf of Mexico. On the eastern edge, the narrow, sandy Atlantic Coastal Ridge that once bordered the ocean's pounding surf parallels the more recent coastline. Just west of the ridge, the St. Johns River follows the valley of an ancient saltwater bay from its origin in the Kissimmee prairie southwest of Melbourne to its mouth northeast of Jacksonville. The St. Johns River once served the naturalist William Bartram as a passage into Florida's interior and prompted some of his most vivid and sensational tales of the American wilderness. The sites described below allow modern-day visitors to glimpse images of Bartram's Florida.

OCALA NATIONAL FOREST

Silver Springs

The Ocala National Forest is the largest publicly accessible land-holding in northern Florida and the state's second largest national forest. Established in 1908, it is both the oldest national forest east of the Mississippi River and the southernmost in the mainland United States. With approximately 2 million visitors annually, it is also one of the nation's most frequently visited. It encompasses 384,000 acres and contains an array of habitats, including flatwoods, sandy uplands, swamps, spring-run woodlands, and numerous lakes.

A main attraction for naturalists is the Big Scrub region on the eastern side of the forest—a dry, sandy upland known for natural stands of Sand Pine and scrubby woods. In prehistoric times, when sea levels were much higher than they are today, the ancient dune field that constitutes much of the scrublands was all that separated the Atlantic Ocean from the Gulf of Mexico.

Juniper Springs Recreation Area

OCALA NATIONAL RECREATION TRAIL A local portion of the Florida National Scenic Trail, this trail offers approximately 65 miles of hiking, backpacking, and backcountry camping. Perhaps the most scenic stretches are the grassy wetlands through the Juniper Prairie Wilderness Area and along Hopkins Prairie.

SALT SPRINGS This large inland salt spring, located along Route 19, is perfect for fishing, scuba diving, snorkeling, and swimming. The 4-mile Salt Springs Run is canoeable to Lake George, the state's second largest lake. The salty content of the spring's waters comes from remnant subsurface salt beds laid down by an ancient sea.

CANOEING In addition to the Salt Springs Run, Juniper Creek and Alexander Springs Creek offer pleasant paddling excursions. For the more adventurous, the 19-mile Oklawaha Canoe Trail on the Oklawaha River, which runs along the forest's western edge, is the forest's longest canoe run.

HORSEBACK RIDING Ocala's 100-mile horse trail, divided into two 40-mile loops and one 20-mile loop, is an excellent way for equestrians to experience the forest.

CAMPING Nineteen campgrounds dot the forest. The campground within Juniper Springs Recreation Area is one of the most developed and most popular. It is just south of Juniper Prairie Wilderness Area and offers swimming, a concession area, and tent and trailer sites.

WILDERNESS AREAS There are four designated wilderness areas within Ocala. The easily accessible Juniper Prairie and Alexander Springs Wilderness Areas are the most popular, with Billies Bay coming in third. Little Lake George Wilderness, in the forest's northeastern corner, is difficult to reach and is less often visited. Though not a designated wilderness area, the dense woodland around Morman Branch, just southeast of the Juniper Creek Bridge on Route 19, is rugged and quite beautiful.

FAUNA Bird life includes populations of Bachman's Sparrows, Brown-headed Nuthatches, Bald Eagles, Wild Turkeys, and Red-cockaded Woodpeckers. The Florida Scrub Jay is a specialty here as its closest relatives live in the western United States. Its loud, raspy call is unmistakable in the scrub oak regions where it makes its home. Black Bears and White-tailed Deer are also plentiful, though the former are secretive and therefore seldom seen. Alligators are present in some of the streams and wetlands. Ocala is also an outstanding butterfly area.

Wild Turkey

FLORA Scrub plants, including Chapman and Myrtle Oaks, Sand Pine, Scrub Morning-glory, and Garberia, are of special interest in this forest. Another botanical draw here is the Yellow Anise, a Florida endemic naturally found only in wet hammocks and along spring runs in Marion, Lake, and Volusia Counties, now widely used as an ornamental shrub because of its easy cultivation and the distinctive aroma of its leaves. Large populations of Atlantic White Cedars can also be found in Ocala.

CONTACT Ocala N.F., Lake George Ranger Station, 17147 E. Hwy. 40, Silver Springs, FL 34488-5849; 352-625-2520. **HOW TO GET THERE** From I-75 at Ocala, take Rte. (Hwy.) 40 east toward Daytona Beach. Rte. 40 traverses the forest from west to east; Rte. (Hwy.) 19 crosses it from north to south. **SEASONAL ACCESS** Year-round; fall and winter are hunting season. **VISITOR CENTERS** Highway 40 V.C. (352-625-7470) is about 2 miles east of Silver Springs at 10863 E. Hwy. 40; Salt Springs V.C. (352-685-3070) is at 14100 N. Hwy. 19 at Salt Springs; Pittman V.C. (352-669-7495) is at 45621 S. State Rd. 19 near the forest's southern edge at Altoona; Lake George Ranger Station, which offers camping information, is 18 miles east of Ocala.

LAKE WOODRUFF NATIONAL WILDLIFE REFUGE

De Leon Springs

Located outside the southeastern corner of Ocala National Forest, Lake Woodruff National Wildlife Refuge contains about 19,500 acres, nearly 12,000 of which are in freshwater marshes, 5,400 in hardwood swamps, 1,000 in lakes, streams, and canals, and 445 in managed impoundments (man-made bodies of water). Only about 1,200 acres are in uplands such as pine flatwoods. Situated just east of the St. Johns River and containing two large lakes and numerous streams and rivulets, this refuge is a haven for wintering waterfowl and supports such threatened or endangered species as Bald Eagles, Manatees, Indigo Snakes, American Alligators, and Wood Storks.

Though a canoe or a motorized boat is required to get around much of this refuge, several miles of walking trails are available at the designated public-use area at the end of Mud Lake Road, just south of the refuge headquarters. Two short nature trails pass through hardwood hammocks, and the 6-mile, round-trip Jones Island Trail leads to Pontoon Landing on Garden Run. The latter trail is a particularly good place to look for White-tailed Deer and Bobcats. Impoundments at the public-use area are lined with dike roads that make for excellent walking (especially in winter), and offer outstanding wildlife observation. Alligators are common year-round, as are herons, egrets, Glossy and White Ibises, and Sandhill Cranes. Snail Kites might be seen at any time of year, Bald Eagles nest in late winter and spring, and Swallow-tailed Kites are regular visitors in summer. Thirty warbler species have been recorded during spring and fall migrations.

Sandhill Crane

Paddling enthusiasts can launch (and rent) canoes at nearby De Leon Springs State Park, take the spring run to Spring Garden Lake, and go on to Garden Run around the northwestern edge of Jones Island. It is also possible to paddle (or motor) the much greater distance to Lake Woodruff.

CONTACT Lake Woodruff N.W.R., P.O. Box 488, De Leon Springs, FL 32130; 904-985-4673. **HOW TO GET THERE** From De Land, take U.S. 17 north 6 miles to De Leon Springs; turn west onto Retta St., then south onto Grand Ave. to refuge. **SEASONAL ACCESS** Year-round. **VISITOR CENTER** At refuge headquarters.

OSCEOLA NATIONAL FOREST   Lake City

Florida National Scenic Trail

The nearly 200,000 acres of the Osceola National Forest are tucked away in the northernmost reaches of the Florida peninsula. Frequented mostly by weekend campers and hunting and fishing enthusiasts, Osceola is not as well known by naturalists as are the state's two larger national forests. Nevertheless, it contains outstanding natural areas, plenty of hiking and canoeing, and primitive and developed camping areas. For a day visit, drive along Route 250 from just north of Lake City about 30 miles northeast to Taylor, a diagonal route across the forest that passes through most habitats. Numerous primitive and improved roads turn off Route 250 and provide interesting walking. For overnight stays, 50 camping sites are located on the shore of Ocean Pond, a large freshwater lake that is good for swimming, fishing, and boating.

FLORIDA NATIONAL SCENIC TRAIL Twenty-two miles of the trail pass through the forest, with the most convenient trailheads located along U.S. 90 at the Olustee Battlefield State Historic Site and on the access road to Ocean Pond Campground. Leave your car at either of these trailheads and enjoy a leisurely 6-mile, one-way day hike through bay swamps and pine flatwoods, with many boardwalks offering drier views of the wetlands.

BIG GUM SWAMP WILDERNESS The interior of this 13,000-acre wetland in the north-central section of the forest, accessible only on remnants of earthen trams (rights of way for old logging railroads), is forested with mature woodlands of Black Tupelo, Loblolly Bay, Sweetgum, cypresses, hickories, and numerous other wetland trees and shrubs. Black Bears, White-tailed Deer, Feral Pigs, and Bobcats live in this swamp, although the secretive nature of bears makes them difficult to see. Experience in hiking through swampy terrain, and skill with a map and a compass, are required of those who venture into this fascinating area.

Sweetgum

CONTACT Osceola N.F., c/o U.S. Forest Service, P.O. Box 70, Olustee, FL 32072; 904-752-2577. **HOW TO GET THERE** From I-10 just north of Lake City, drive northeast on Rte 250. Numerous access roads are available off Rte. 250. **SEASONAL ACCESS** Year-round. **VISITOR CENTER** Osceola Ranger District office on U.S. 90 at Olustee, about 10 miles east of Lake City.

GUANA RIVER STATE PARK AND GUANA RIVER WILDLIFE MANAGEMENT AREA

South Ponte Vedra Beach

Although Guana River State Park and Guana River Wildlife Management Area are two separate sites (the former is managed by the Florida Park Service, the latter by the Florida Game and Fresh Water Fish Commission), they share a common boundary—the state park is south of the Guana Dam, the wildlife management area is north of it—and are treated as a single location. It should be noted that hunting is permitted in the wildlife management area; other recreational activities are not advised during hunting season.

Both sites are on a barrier island that is bounded on the east by the Atlantic Ocean and on the west by the Intracoastal Waterway and the Tolomato River. The ocean side is popular for seashore activities and also offers opportunities for naturalists; North Beach and South Beach provide public access. Loggerhead marine turtles and Least Terns nest on the beach in spring and summer; Common Loons and Northern Gannets are sometimes seen offshore in winter months.

The inland side of the island is a collection of hammocks, pine flatwoods, and freshwater marshes. The only facilities are a short boardwalk, three observation platforms, and many miles of marked hiking and biking trails. Enter on foot from the Guana Dam Recreation Site at the south end of Guana Peninsula; after crossing the dam, pick up an area map, a bird list, and a trail guide from the outdoor kiosk. Guana Lake is located just north of the dam and is excellent for shorebirding. Marbled Godwits, Solitary Sandpipers, Black-necked Stilts, and a variety of common shorebirds are often seen. Bald Eagles nest here and are sometimes seen flying over the lake.

CONTACTS Guana River S.P., c/o Florida Park Service, 2690 S. Ponte Vedra Blvd., Ponte Vedra Beach, FL 32082; 904-825-5071. Also Guana River W.M.A., c/o Florida Game and Fresh Water Fish Commission, 2690 E. Ponte Vedra Blvd., Ponte Vedra Beach, FL 32082; 904-825-6877. **HOW TO GET THERE** On Rte. A1A about 13 miles north of St. Augustine. **SEASONAL ACCESS** Year-round; check with the Florida Game and Fresh Water Fish Commission about hunting dates before visiting the wildlife management area.

LOWER SUWANNEE
NATIONAL WILDLIFE REFUGE   Chiefland

The floodplain wetlands, hardwood hammocks, and freshwater marshes of the lower Suwannee River are wild and untamed. This area is largely protected by the 51,000 acres of the Lower Suwannee National Wildlife Refuge, which is just 10 miles north of Cedar Keys National Wildlife Refuge (see below), and little development adjoins this historic stream in its lower reaches. Wildlife is abundant: More than 250 bird species visit here, including Bald Eagles, Osprey, and Swallow-tailed Kites, and at least 90 species nest here.

White-tailed Deer are easily seen, and Manatees visit the river annually from March to November. The wildflower blooming season is spectacular; take the 9-mile drive through the heart of the refuge during spring.

CONTACT Lower Suwannee N.W.R., 16450 NW 31st Pl., Chiefland, FL 32626; 352-493-0238. **HOW TO GET THERE** Off Rte. 347, about 13 miles southwest of Chiefland. **SEASONAL ACCESS** Year-round. **VISITOR CENTER** Refuge headquarters is off Rte. 347.

CEDAR KEYS
NATIONAL WILDLIFE REFUGE   Cedar Key

Cedar Keys National Wildlife Refuge is just 10 miles south of the Lower Suwannee National Wildlife Refuge (see above), which administers it. The refuge, which today consists of 12 offshore islands in the Gulf of Mexico, was established in 1929 to protect

colonies of nesting herons on Snake, Bird (Deadman's), and North Keys. In the 1960s and 1970s, more than 200,000 colonial birds used these nesting grounds; the number today is closer to 50,000. White Ibises, Great and Snowy Egrets, Double-crested Cormorants, Brown Pelicans, Great Blue Herons, and Tricolored Herons are the most populous species. This wildlife refuge lives up to its name: Only limited human use is permitted and access is only by boat. Seahorse Key and a 300-foot buffer zone around it, in particular, are completely closed from March to July during breeding season.

CONTACT Cedar Keys N.W.R., 16450 NW 31st Pl., Chiefland, FL 32626; 352-493-0238. **HOW TO GET THERE** By commercial or private boat from the city of Cedar Key. **SEASONAL ACCESS** Beaches of all islands except Seahorse Key are open year-round; interiors of all islands are closed year-round.

MANATEE SPRINGS STATE PARK   Chiefland

Manatee Springs

This 2,300-acre park is located along the Suwannee River and protects one of the state's 27 first-magnitude springs (those whose average discharge equals or exceeds 64 million gallons per day). More than 80,000 gallons of water per minute flow from its limestone crevices into a short, crystal-clear run to the Suwannee River. The water is 72° Fahrenheit year-round and has long attracted a variety of visitors, from aboriginal peoples of Florida to the naturalist William Bartram to modern-day swimmers, snorkelers, and canoeists. The endangered Manatee, a gentle, warm-water sirenian, occasionally visits the spring run and can be seen from a boardwalk that overlooks the Suwannee River (November to April is the best time to see Manatees). A boat ramp is located within the park, and rental canoes are available.

CONTACT Manatee Springs S.P., 11650 NW 115th St., Chiefland, FL 32626; 352-493-6072. **HOW TO GET THERE** On Rte. 320, 6 miles west of Chiefland. **SEASONAL ACCESS** Year-round.

ICHETUCKNEE SPRINGS STATE PARK   Fort White

This 2,200-acre park, which surrounds the springs that give rise to the Ichetucknee River, is one of Florida's most-visited state parks. On weekends from late spring through early fall it can be overrun with visitors tubing a 3½-mile stretch of the river's crystal-clear 7-mile length, although the park

limits the number of people allowed to tube on and swim in the river each day. During the winter and on weekdays, however, it is an excellent place for amateur naturalists to paddle or walk along one of Florida's most enchanting spring runs or to snorkel or scuba in the translucent waters. Moist hardwood hammocks and sandhill uplands provide exploration opportunities for walkers and hikers, and guided moonlight canoe trips are offered seasonally. Day-paddlers should arrive early for the best chances of seeing Limpkins, Wood Ducks, Northern River Otters, and American Beavers.

CONTACT Ichetucknee Springs S.P., Rte. 2, Box 5355, Ft. White, FL 32038; 904-497-4690. **HOW TO GET THERE** The south entrance is off U.S. 27 about 5.5 miles northwest of Ft. White. The north entrance is off Rte. 238. **SEASONAL ACCESS** Year-round.

O'LENO STATE PARK
AND RIVER RISE STATE PRESERVE   **High Springs**

Santa Fe River

This 6,000-acre park and preserve offers possibilities for exploring virtually all of northern Florida's major habitat types, as well as paddling or walking along the tannin-stained Santa Fe River, which disappears and flows underground for more than 3 miles before resurfacing at River Rise. A tributary of the Suwannee River and designated by the state as an Outstanding Florida Water (legally protecting it from pollution), the Santa Fe is one of the state's most pristine streams. Miles of trails, some of which follow historic wagon roads, pass through the park and adjacent preserve, meandering among sinkholes, sandhills, hammocks, and limestone-studded terrain. Primitive campsites allow for overnight backpacking excursions and provide access to numerous shorter loop trails. A suspension bridge constructed in the late 1930s spans the river near the park's swimming area and affords entry to some of the trails. Canoes are also available to rent at the park.

CONTACT O'Leno S.P. and River Rise S.P., Rte. 2, Box 1010, High Springs, FL 32643; 904-454-1853. **HOW TO GET THERE** From I-75, take exit 80, then Rte. 441 west for 5 miles. **SEASONAL ACCESS** Year-round. **VISITOR CENTER** At ranger station near entrance.

MIKE ROESS GOLD HEAD
BRANCH STATE PARK   **Keystone Heights**

The deep ravine that cuts through the sandhills of this 2,099-acre park constitutes the main natural attraction here. It is remarkable to realize that the tiny stream at the bottom of this steep-sided gorge, which is eroding the lowest portions of the ravine slope from below as it makes its way down toward Little Lake Johnson, could have carved out such a chasm. Botanists and native plant enthusiasts will be intrigued by the diversity of plant communities at the park. Surrounding the ravine are sandy woodlands with species typical of northern Florida's sandhills, including Longleaf Pines, wiregrass, and Turkey Oaks. Along the ravine slopes and at its bottom is a moist forest that includes hickories, oaks, and heaths, as well as numerous herbaceous plants and several species of ferns.

CONTACT Mike Roess Gold Head Branch S.P., 6239 State Rd. 21, Keystone Heights, FL 32656; 352-473-4701. **HOW TO GET THERE** On Rte. 21, 6 miles northeast of Keystone Heights. **SEASONAL ACCESS** Year-round.

FORT CLINCH STATE PARK   Fernandina Beach

This 1,153-acre park in the extreme northeastern corner of Florida covers 12,400 feet of shoreline along Cumberland Sound and the Atlantic Ocean. The park is outstanding for its towering sand dunes and its birding. Several of Florida's most unusual and sought-after species can be seen at various times of the year. Painted Buntings are common in summer; Northern Gannets, Great Black-backed Gulls, Oldsquaws, and all three species of scoters (Black, White-winged, and Surf) are sometimes seen off the pier in winter; Purple Sandpipers are occasionally observed on the rock jetty; Merlins and Peregrine Falcons are regular visitors in late fall and winter.

The park is named for a federal fort built in 1847; park rangers dress in Union uniforms and carry on the daily activities of garrison soldiers as visitors wander the grounds. Self-guided and ranger-led candlelight tours of the fort are available for a small fee.

CONTACT Fort Clinch S.P., 2601 Atlantic Ave., Fernandina Beach, FL 32034; 904-277-7274. **HOW TO GET THERE** In Fernandina Beach, on Atlantic Ave., which is perpendicular to the northern terminus of Rte. A1A. **SEASONAL ACCESS** Year-round. **VISITOR CENTER** At the old Fort Clinch; also houses a museum.

LITTLE TALBOT ISLAND STATE PARK   Jacksonville

This 2,500-acre park is part of the Talbot Islands State Parks, which encompass both Big and Little Talbot Islands, as well as part of Long Island and the southern tip of Amelia Island. It preserves an array of coastal habitats, including Needlerush salt marshes, coastal flatwoods and hardwood hammocks, and Atlantic dunes and beaches. Nearly 200 birds are on the park's species list. Seabirds such as Northern Gannets, Greater Shearwaters, Caspian Terns, and Common

Loons are sometimes seen from the observation platform. Many miles of nature, hiking, and canoeing trails pass through the various components of the park. A 40-site family campground makes the park an excellent base for exploring the northeastern Florida coast, one of Florida's least-spoiled shorelines.

CONTACT Little Talbot Island S.P., c/o Talbot Islands S.P.'s, 12157 Heckscher Dr., Jacksonville, FL 32226; 904-251-2320. **HOW TO GET THERE** On Rte. A1A about 20 miles northeast of Jacksonville. **SEASONAL ACCESS** Year-round. **VISITOR CENTER** At ranger station near entrance.

FORT MATANZAS
NATIONAL MONUMENT Summer Haven

This 298-acre park preserves a Spanish fort constructed in 1742 on Rattlesnake Island, which is across the Matanzas Inlet from Anastasia Island. For naturalists, the free ferry ride across the river to Rattlesnake Island and the marshes and hammocks on Anastasia Island are the main attractions: Brown Pelicans, Ospreys, Bald Eagles, Belted Kingfishers, Wood Storks, and rarely Roseate Spoonbills are seen on the boat ride over, and the woodlands on Anastasia Island shelter numerous songbirds during their migration. Florida Scrub Jays also reside in the park. Just south of the ferry landing on the mainland bank of the Matanzas River, a spit of sand that juts out into the inlet serves as both a nesting and resting site for several species of sea- and shorebirds.

CONTACT Fort Matanzas N.M., 8635 A1A South, St. Augustine, FL 32086; 904-471-0116. **HOW TO GET THERE** On Rte. A1A, 14 miles south of St. Augustine. **SEASONAL ACCESS** Year-round. **VISITOR CENTER** On Anastasia Island.

HUGUENOT MEMORIAL PARK Jacksonville

This outstanding coastal birding site has hosted several Florida rarities. **CONTACT** Huguenot Memorial Park, 10980 Heckscher Dr., Jacksonville, FL 32226; 904-251-3215.

E. DALE JOYNER NATURE PRESERVE
AT PELOTES ISLAND Jacksonville

Hike more than 3 miles of nature trails through coastal hammocks and along saltmarsh creeks. **CONTACT** E. Dale Joyner N.P. at Pelotes Island, 11201 New Berlin Rd., Jacksonville, FL 32226; 904-751-7856.

ANDREWS WILDLIFE MANAGEMENT AREA Trenton

Hike along the Suwannee River floodplain and see several Florida champion trees such as the Southern Sugar Maple and the River Birch. **CONTACT** Andrews W.M.A., Rte. 1, Box 741, Trenton, FL 32693; 352-493-6020.

CEDAR KEY SCRUB STATE RESERVE Cedar Key

Meander along trails through excellent examples of ancient coastal dune scrub; foot traffic only. **CONTACT** Cedar Key Scrub S.R., P.O. Box 187, Cedar Key, FL 32625; 352-543-5567.

WACCASASSA BAY STATE PRESERVE
Gulf Hammock

Paddle or boat along this 30,000-acre northeastern Gulf coast preserve made up of salt marsh, wooded islands, and tidal creeks; boat access only. **CONTACT** Waccasassa Bay S.P., P.O. Box 187, Cedar Key, FL 32625; 352-543-5567.

Waccasassa Bay State Preserve

GOETHE STATE FOREST Dunnellon

Drive, walk, or horseback ride along many miles of roads in this 44,000-acre forest of flatwoods, hammocks, and wetlands. **CONTACT** Goethe S.F., 8250 SE County Rd. 336, Dunnellon, FL 34431; 352-447-2202.

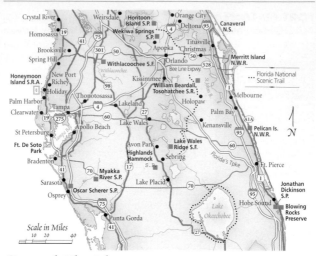

Central Florida

The fuzzy line between temperate and tropical Florida is most evident in central Florida. Along the coastal edges of this singular region, which stretches from the Ocala area south to include Lake Okeechobee, the remnants of tropical vegetation extend as far north as Tampa Bay on the west and Merritt Island on the east. In between is a fascinating landscape characterized by an ever-shrinking expanse of deep sand scrub that was left as ice age seas retreated.

In prehistoric times of higher seas, the central ridge was a narrow strip of sandy dunes separating the Atlantic Ocean from the Gulf of Mexico. Ocean waves washed up on what today are dry, sandy hills, while the current coastline was far out to sea. The scrubby terrain that is preserved at Highlands Hammock State Park, Lake Wales Ridge State Forest, Archbold Biological Station, and Tiger Creek Preserve contains fascinating remnants of the central ridge's ancient history and waterside origins.

Visitors driving south along either coast (U.S. 1 on the east, U.S. 41 on the west) will see the vegetation become more tropical, while those traveling through the center of the state (U.S. 27) will be surrounded by a landscape more typical of temperate regions. This land is an often overlooked region of Florida, and for many years its scrub regions were considered wastelands fit only for clearing and development. Intense study during the last two decades has revealed that this scrubland harbors an impressive variety of endemic plants and animals.

Along both coastlines the influence of warm tropical waters is evident: Mangroves appear along lagoons and bays, and the few remaining coastal hammocks—ridges of ground elevated above wet terrain that support dense hardwood forests—take on a more tropical aspect. The sites in this region provide ample opportunities to study these varied natural communities.

FORT DE SOTO PARK

Tierra Verde

This 900-acre park, which takes its name from the old fort built in 1898 and named for the Spanish explorer Hernando De Soto, is located on Florida's western coast, primarily on Mullet Key, an island of green in the Tampa–St. Petersburg metropolis. Jutting out into Tampa Bay, its inland woods and mangrove shore constitute a beacon for incoming songbirds. On a good day in spring, just a few hours of observation can yield sightings of 20 species of warblers and other migrant songbirds. The best birding spots are the campground overlooking Mullet Key Bayou, Arrowhead Picnic Area, the low shrubbery around the administrative area just west of the end of Route 679 (Pinellas Bayway), the East Beach Swim Area, and the wooded picnic area near North Beach. Low-growing Sand Live Oaks here may be full of birds. Park in one of the pull-outs along the access road and begin walking. The assemblage of bird species here can change throughout the day, so either stay here for an extended period or check back periodically throughout your visit.

East Beach is a good location for gulls, terns, and shorebirds: Long-billed and Short-billed Dowitchers, American Oystercatchers, several species of "peeps," Double-crested Cormorants, and an occasional Magnificent Frigatebird can be seen here. The gulls at East Beach are often seen taking hermit crabs from the water, then flying

Short-billed Dowitcher

high above the parking lot and dropping their prey onto the pavement to dislodge the crabs from their shells.

The park offers an excellent waterside camping area for tents and RVs. However, reservations are taken only from walk-in traffic.

CONTACT Fort De Soto Park, 3500 Pinellas Bayway South, Tierra Verde, FL 33715; 813-866-2484. **HOW TO GET THERE** From I-275 (traveling south), take exit 4 (Pinellas Bayway S.) to second stoplight; turn left (this road is still Pinellas Bayway S.), and follow signs. **SEASONAL ACCESS** Year-round. **VISITOR CENTER** Near park entrance.

MERRITT ISLAND NATIONAL WILDLIFE REFUGE AND CANAVERAL NATIONAL SEASHORE   Titusville

Merritt Island National Wildlife Refuge and Canaveral National Seashore, located on the Atlantic coast just east of Orlando and Titusville, are separate sites that share a common boundary (Route 402) and a common bond. Though each is distinct—the former is managed by the U.S. Fish and Wildlife Service, the latter by the National Park Service—it is difficult to visit either without visiting both. Both are birding hot spots, especially during winter and spring migrations. At least 310 bird species have been identified in the area, including 27 kinds of wintering shorebirds and concentrations of winter waterfowl that sometimes exceed 100,000 individuals. Be sure to check for Florida Scrub Jays along the scrubby roadsides between the visitor center and Playalinda Beach. Small flocks are sometimes seen along this stretch; once found, they are easy to observe. Plants, too, are plentiful: approximately 1,050 species of plants, including coastal species such as Beach Sunflower and Sea Daisy, have been identified at the two sites.

BLACK POINT WILDLIFE DRIVE Leading off Rte. 406 just northwest of the visitor center, this 6-mile, one-way, self-guided drive meanders through flatwoods and impounded marsh, affording excellent views of wildlife and easily consuming most of a day for ardent observers. This is the best place to see large concentrations of waterfowl and shorebirds in winter, Roseate Spoonbills and Black-necked Stilts in summer, and herons, ibises, and egrets year-round. Alligators are also common. The turnoff for the 5-mile Cruickshank Trail, named for the wildlife photographer, writer, and naturalist who helped establish the refuge, is located about halfway around the drive. The trail encircles a picturesque marsh and includes an observation tower just a few yards from the parking lot. A blind is available for photographers who want to get close to their quarry.

OAK HAMMOCK AND PALM HAMMOCK TRAILS Located off Rte. 402 about a mile east of the visitor center, these ½-mile and 2-mile trails pass through typical coastal oak-palm hammocks.

PLAYALINDA BEACH Situated at the eastern end of Route 402, Playalinda Beach is a popular spot for swimmers and sunbathers. There are paved parking areas and boardwalks that lead across the huge dunes and down onto the Atlantic shore. This undeveloped beach (as well as others within the

Green Turtle

confines of the seashore) is also known as a nesting site for marine turtles such as Loggerheads and Green Turtles during the summer. Females of these species arrive at night, lumber up the beach to the edge of the dune line, scratch out a nest cavity in the sand, lay their eggs, then return to the ocean. Visitors on early-morning walks sometimes see the V-shaped pathway of tracks leading from the water to the nest site and back.

KLONDIKE BEACH North of Playalinda Beach and accessible only by foot, bicycle, or horseback (in deference to sea turtles, horses are allowed only from November 1 to April 30), this is one of the longest stretches of undeveloped beach on Florida's eastern coast. The trail that follows behind the dune is good birding territory. Backcountry camping is allowed on parts of the beach during winter and early spring; permits are required.

TURTLE MOUND, ELDORA HAMMOCK, AND CASTLE WINDY TRAILS These short walks are located near the Apollo Beach area, which is accessible only by driving north on U.S. 1 to New Smyrna Beach, then back south on Rte. A1A. Turtle Mound Trail crosses an old Indian shell midden (refuse pile) and offers a panoramic view of the Atlantic Ocean.

MOSQUITO LAGOON This inland waterway, some 20 miles long, is lined with mangroves and dotted with small, sometimes marshy islands. Canoes can be launched just north of Turtle Mound Trail.

CONTACT Merritt Is. N.W.R., P.O. Box 6504, Titusville, FL 32782-6504; 407-861-0667. Canaveral N.S., 308 Julia St., Titusville, FL 32796-3521; 904-428-3384. **HOW TO GET THERE** The Apollo Beach area and the Canaveral N.S. Visitor Information Ctr. are located on Rte. A1A, 7 miles south of New Smyrna Beach; the southern part of the seashore and the Merritt Is. N.W.R. are reached on Rtes. 406 and 402, east of Titusville. **SEASONAL ACCESS** Year-round; both sites are closed during launchings at nearby Kennedy Space Center. **VISITOR CENTER** Canaveral's V.C. is 7 miles south of New Smyrna Beach on Rte. A1A; Merritt Is.'s V.C. is located on Rte. 402.

MYAKKA RIVER STATE PARK   Sarasota

Covering an approximately 45-square-mile area east of Sarasota, Myakka River is Florida's largest state park. The Myakka River and Upper Myakka Lake are the main attractions for day visitors. The 7-mile entrance road that runs along the river and lake on one side and an oak-palm hammock on the other is an outstanding scenic drive. Hikers and backpackers will especially enjoy the park in winter and early spring, when the trails are driest.

Nearly 40 miles of trails meander through a variety of natural communities, including pine flatwoods, dry prairies, an oak-palm hammock, and freshwater marshes. A 15-mile horse trail meanders through the park as well, but riders must bring their own horses. Canoeing is another way to experience the area's natural beauty; rentals are available at the concession store. Guided airboat tours of Upper Myakka Lake are also offered.

The park's wildlife list includes more than 250 bird species, including Limpkins, Peregrine Falcons, Purple Gallinules, Black-necked Stilts, and a variety of waders and shorebirds. The boardwalk extending onto the lake is an excellent birding spot.

South of Route 72, the 7,500-acre Myakka Wilderness Preserve provides access to Lower Myakka Lake. The preserve is mostly pine flatwoods and wetlands. Winter waterfowl are abundant on the lake, and White-tailed Deer and Wild Turkeys are common along the shore. Sightings are often reported of Sandhill Cranes, Wood Storks, Bald Eagles, Ospreys,

Purple Gallinule

and Roseate Spoonbills. Permits, which may be obtained at the entrance station, are required to enter and to backpack through the park. Hiking and canoeing are also allowed. Myakka River is one of only a handful of Florida parks that offer rustic cabins as well as a campground. Call the park for reservations.

CONTACT Myakka River S.P., 13207 State Rd. 72, Sarasota, FL 34241; 941-361-6511. **HOW TO GET THERE** From I-75, take exit 37 onto Rte. 72, then head east for 9 miles. **SEASONAL ACCESS** Year-round. **VISITOR CENTER** Near entrance.

HIGHLANDS HAMMOCK STATE PARK   Sebring

Cypress Swamp Trail

Highlands Hammock is one of Florida's first four state parks. Originally set aside by local residents in 1931, it remains one of the best-preserved parks in the system: what visitors see here is what the landscape looked like before development, not a restored replica. One of the few large virgin Cabbage Palmetto hammocks in Florida can be explored here. The Cypress Swamp Trail includes nearly 2,000 feet of boardwalk through magnificent scenery that begins on the main road and meanders through a canopied cypress and gum swamp. A number of short trails pass through the nearly 5,000-acre park.

At least seven plant communities are represented in the park, from dry scrub to wetlands. Such scrub specialties as Florida or Scrub Hickory, Scrub Holly, Tough Bumelia, and the Florida endemic Scrub Oak are all found here or nearby. Tree-lovers in particular will want to walk the Ancient Hammock, Big Oak, and Hickory Trails to see a variety of beautiful specimens, including huge 1,000-year-old oaks, mature mulberries, Pignut Hickory, Sweetgum, and Sugarberry. Those who prefer keeping their gaze closer to the ground will enjoy the Fern Garden Trail, with its lush ground cover. More than 30 species of native ferns can be found at the park.

The park's bird list includes 177 species: Florida Scrub Jays, Wood Storks, Sandhill Cranes, Brown-headed Nuthatches, Pileated Woodpeckers, Wild Turkeys, and Swallow-tailed Kites are among the possible sightings. Ranger-led tram rides through remote areas allow visitors the opportunity to see some of these birds as well as other wildlife such as White-tailed Deer and rarely a Bobcat.

Pileated Woodpecker

A picnic area and a paved loop bicycle trail are available. Camping facilities include 138 drive-up sites with both water and electricity, 16 primitive sites, and five equestrian sites. The latter are situated at the head of an 11-mile trail; riders must bring their own horses.

CONTACT Highlands Hammock S.P., 5931 Hammock Rd., Sebring, FL 33872; 941-386-6094. **HOW TO GET THERE** Take Rte. 634 west 4 miles from U.S. 27 in Sebring. **SEASONAL ACCESS** Year-round. **VISITOR CENTER** Ranger station at entrance.

BLOWING ROCKS PRESERVE   Hobe Sound

The rocks at this 76-acre preserve north of Palm Beach on Jupiter Island constitute the largest outcropping of Anastasia limestone along the Atlantic coast. Lining the shore for approximately 5,000 feet, this unique landscape dates from an ancient era when sea levels were much higher than today, and Jupiter Island was a completely submerged offshore bar. As the oceans retreated to current levels, a subsurface cliff produced by years of marine sedimentation emerged that now parallels the shoreline just a few feet from the water's edge. During extreme high tides and winter storms, the salty waves that break against the shore force their way through crevices and blowholes in the limestone and send dramatic plumes of water spiraling skyward.

Four plant communities are found here: oceanfront dune, coastal scrub, interior mangrove wetland, and tropical hammock. Approximately 250 native plants are found within these communities, and the Nature Conservancy, which owns and manages the site, has worked diligently to restore the area to its natural aspect. The 7-acre tropical hammock includes such southern Florida specialties as Mastic, Gumbo Limbo, Lime Prickly Ash, Willow Bustic, Marlberry, Necklace Pod, Pigeonplum, and Jamaica Caper Tree. Sea Grape and Myrsine are found along the coastal scrub; all three mangroves—Red, Black, and White—line the edges of Hobe Sound; and Sea Oats, Bay Bean, Bay Cedar, and Beach Creeper are found on the dunes.

Marlberry

This area also hosts a wide variety of aquatic birds and other wildlife. Three species of marine turtles—Green Turtle, Leatherback, and Loggerhead—nest here in the summer. Manatees frequent the preserve's bayside shore in winter.

The landscape at this preserve is quite fragile, so visitors should walk only on designated trails. Food, beverages, and coolers are not permitted.

CONTACT Blowing Rocks Pres., 574 S. Beach Rd., Hobe Sound, FL 33455; 561-744-6668. **HOW TO GET THERE** From I-95, take the Indiantown Rd. exit east to U.S. 1, drive north to Rte. 707, then drive 2 miles east to preserve. **SEASONAL ACCESS** Year-round.

JONATHAN DICKINSON STATE PARK

Hobe Sound

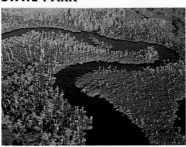

This 11,500-acre state park, located near the Atlantic coast and across U.S. 1 from Blowing Rocks Preserve, is the second largest in Florida. As with most large parks, the developed areas make up only a small portion of the total land area, leaving much territory for exploration. About one-fifth of the park consists of one of the best remnants of the extremely rare and endangered coastal Sand Pine scrub communities. The short trail to Hobe Mountain, a huge relict sand dune, provides access to the scrub. An observation tower sits atop Hobe Mountain and provides an enchanting view of the park, Hobe Sound, Jupiter Island, and the Atlantic.

Part of the Florida National Scenic Trail passes through the park and offers about 20 miles of hiking. Two primitive camping areas make the trail good for overnight backpacking excursions. For shorter walks, the Kitching Creek and Wilson Creek Trails provide a firsthand look at a southeastern Florida cypress swamp community. Two full-facility drive-up campgrounds are also available.

For history enthusiasts, there are two items of interest here. First, the origin of the park's name comes from a Quaker merchant who was shipwrecked near here in 1696. With the help of local natives, he and his stranded family made their way on foot to St. Augustine, more than

Green Heron

200 miles to the north. Second, the 44-passenger *Loxahatchee Queen II* takes visitors up the Loxahatchee River to the Trapper Nelson Interpretive Site. Nelson settled in the area in the 1930s and lived off the land by trapping and selling furs. The boat trip includes a tour of his rustic establishment. Naturalists will enjoy the ride up the Loxahatchee, a designated National Wild and Scenic River; watch for herons, Anhingas, and Ospreys. The river also offers outstanding canoeing, and canoe rentals are available at the concession store.

CONTACT Jonathan Dickinson S.P., 16450 SE Federal Hwy., Hobe Sound, FL 33455; 561-546-2771. **HOW TO GET THERE** From I-95, take exit 59A east on Indiantown Rd. to U.S. 1, then continue north for 5 miles. **SEASONAL ACCESS** Year-round.

WEKIWA SPRINGS STATE PARK

Apopka

To the Creek Indians, *Wekiwa* means "spring of water," which is an apt appellation both for the magnificent springs and river system that are the main attractions at this park. Encompassing approximately 8,000 acres, the park, just 15 miles northwest of Orlando, offers hiking and backpacking on nearly 14 miles of foot trails, with two primitive campsites; canoeing (rentals available at the concession store) and canoe camping on Rock Springs Run and the Wekiva River; and riding on 8 miles of horse trails. Birders will see Limpkins, Bald Eagles, Ospreys, and many long-legged waders. Plant enthusiasts can explore an excellent example of Sand Pine scrub as well as seven other plant communities. The lowland swamp is home to cypress and Sweetgum trees, as well as alligators, turtles, and Northern River Otters. Black Bear sightings are also possible.

CONTACT Wekiwa Springs S.P., 1800 Wekiwa Circle, Apopka, FL 32712; 407-884-2009. **HOW TO GET THERE** From I-4, take exit 49 west onto Rte. 434; follow signs. **SEASONAL ACCESS** Year-round.

HONEYMOON ISLAND STATE RECREATION AREA

Dunedin

This Gulf coast park—an island consisting of 385 upland acres, plus 2,400 submerged acres—is crowded with beachgoers during the summer but is a great birding spot in the fall, winter, and spring. A variety of migrants stop here in both spring and fall, and gulls, terns, and shorebirds—including godwits, Whimbrels, dowitchers, and Black Skimmers—use the shoreline in winter; Least Terns, American Oystercatchers, and Ospreys nest here. The Pelican Cove and Osprey Trails provide nearly 4 miles of walking, traversing the edge of Pelican Cove, coastal pine woodlands, and a typical Gulf coast salt marsh. Egrets (including an occasional Reddish Egret), herons, and ibises frequent the cove.

CONTACT Honeymoon Island S.R.A., c/o Gulf Islands GEOpark, 1 Causeway Blvd., Dunedin, FL 34698; 813-469-5942. **HOW TO GET THERE** Turn west off U.S. 19 (west of Tampa) onto Rte. 586; follow signs. **SEASONAL ACCESS** Year-round.

OSCAR SCHERER STATE PARK — Osprey

The Florida Park Service has done an excellent job of restoring this 1,384-acre park, situated about 10 miles south of Sarasota, to more natural conditions. Due to the reintroduction of prescribed fire, a practice whereby fires are intentionally set to mimic the natural process and to help restore land to its native appearance, the park now supports four of Florida's threatened or endangered species: the Indigo Snake, Gopher Tortoise, Crawfish Frog, and Florida Scrub Jay; the last is most easily found in the flatwoods just northwest of Lake Osprey. A 5-mile hiking trail allows access to the scrub and flatwoods, and a full-facility campground makes this park a perfect base for an extended exploration of Florida's southwestern coast. Many fossil shark teeth can be found on nearby beaches.

CONTACT Oscar Scherer S.P., 1843 S. Tamiami Trail, Osprey, FL 34229; 941-483-5956. **HOW TO GET THERE** Two miles south of Osprey off U.S. 41. **SEASONAL ACCESS** Year-round.

HONTOON ISLAND STATE PARK — De Land

The vistas of the St. Johns River and the palm-oak hammocks and marshes viewed from the 80-foot-high observation tower are just an example of the magnificent attractions of this 1,650-acre park. Canoeists can enter the park from nearby Blue Springs State Park, about 3 nautical miles to the southeast. Canoes can be rented at

the park, and a small campground is available. Late afternoons and evenings on the island are less crowded and perfect for exploring. Manatees visit the river, and bird life includes Limpkins, Common Moorhens, waders, and Ospreys.

CONTACT Hontoon Island S.P., 2309 River Ridge Rd., De Land, FL 32720; 904-736-5309. **HOW TO GET THERE** Accessible only by boat. For the free public ferry, drive west from De Land on Rte. 44, then left (north) onto Rte. 4110 (Old New York Rd.), and left again on Hontoon Rd.; dockage for private boats is also available. Vehicles are not allowed on the island. **SEASONAL ACCESS** Year-round.

WILLIAM BEARDALL TOSOHATCHEE STATE RESERVE

Christmas

This 30,000-acre reserve protects one of central Florida's largest and best-preserved natural areas. Pine uplands, cypress swamps, hardwood hammocks, and riverine marshes are all easily accessible by many miles of hiking, bike, and horse trails along dirt roads as well as along developed paths. Bordering 19 miles of the St. Johns River, the reserve is an excellent place to see Bald Eagles, Ospreys, Northern River Otters, Eastern Fox Squirrels, Wild Turkeys, Black Bears, Gopher Tortoises, a variety of hawks, and large congregations of wintering waterfowl. Overnight backpacking trips of 7 to 17 miles may be arranged by reservation. This is a hunting reserve, so be sure to wear bright orange clothing or visit in the off-season (late spring or summer).

CONTACT William Beardall Tosohatchee S.R., 3365 Taylor Creek Rd., Christmas, FL 32709; 407-568-5893. **HOW TO GET THERE** From Rte. 50 at Christmas (east of Orlando), turn south onto Taylor Creek Rd. **SEASONAL ACCESS** Year-round.

PELICAN ISLAND NATIONAL WILDLIFE REFUGE

Sebastian

Wildlife enthusiasts should visit this refuge just for its historical significance: In 1903 it became the first installment in the national wildlife refuge system. Approachable only by boat and encompassing nearly 5,000 acres of submerged bottomlands, grass beds, adjacent shoreline, and tiny Pelican Island, the refuge is lo-

Brown Pelicans

cated in a tidal lagoon just south of Sebastian Inlet State Recreation Area (south of Merritt Island and Melbourne). Originally set aside to protect important bird rookeries as well as the nesting grounds of Brown Pelicans, it is now designated a National Historic Landmark. Though not as plentiful as in the late 1800s, the nesting populations of long-legged waders are still impressive and include a variety of species from Wood Storks to Snowy Egrets, Black-crowned Night-Herons, Anhingas, and Brown Pelicans. Spring is the best time for viewing nesting birds.

CONTACT Pelican Is. N.W.R., c/o Merritt Is. N.W.R., P.O. Box 6504, Titusville, FL 32782-6504; 561-589-2089. **HOW TO GET THERE** Charter boat tours are available by calling 407-589-6161; boats may not land on the island. **SEASONAL ACCESS** Year-round.

LAKE WALES RIDGE STATE FOREST   Frostproof

During the last two decades, the Lake Wales Ridge—a 100-mile-long ridge of elevated land that ends just north of Lake Okeechobee—has become famous among botanists and naturalists as one of Florida's most unusual natural ecosystems. Once considered a mere scrubby wasteland, it is now recognized as a repository of many rare and endangered species. The more than 10,000 acres of this forest and nearby Lake Arbuckle State Park protect at least 15 listed (threatened or endangered) animal species and more than 20 listed plants. Such scrub plant specialties as Scrub Plum, Pygmy Fringe Tree, Scrub Morning-glory, Lavender Basil, and Beargrass are found here, as are Florida Scrub Jays and Red-cockaded Woodpeckers. More than 20 miles of the Florida National Scenic Trail pass through the area.

CONTACT Lake Wales Ridge S.F., 452 Schoolbus Rd., Frostproof, FL 33843; 941-635-7800. **HOW TO GET THERE** From U.S. 27 at Avon Park, go east on Rte. 630; turn right onto Lake Reedy Blvd. and follow signs. **SEASONAL ACCESS** Year-round.

WITHLACOOCHEE STATE FOREST   Brooksville

Nearly 145,000 acres of pine uplands, cypress swamps, and river-bottom woodlands are contained within this state forest west of Orlando. The forest is divided into five main disjunct tracts, some with limited use. Hiking and wildlife observation are the most popular activities within the forest. The Withlacoochee State Trail and the Croom and Richloam Trails, three of the longer walks, offer opportunities for backpacking and primitive camping. Horse and bicycle trails are also available. The northward-flowing Withlacoochee River (South) State Canoe Trail provides 83 miles of paddling, 13 miles of which pass through the state forest. (The state forest does not rent canoes, but they can be rented in the nearby town of Nobleton.) A short, scenic loop trail at McKethan Lake affords opportunities for viewing one of the few known populations of Cooley's Water-willow. White-tailed Deer, Common Raccoons, rabbits, Eastern Fox Squirrels, Wild Turkeys, Bobcats, and Red-cockaded Woodpeckers are sometimes seen along the roads and walking trails.

CONTACT Withlacoochee S.F., c/o Withlacoochee Forestry Center, 15019 Broad St., Brooksville, FL 34601; 352-754-6777. **HOW TO GET THERE** Eight miles northeast of Brooksville on Rte. 41. **SEASONAL ACCESS** Year-round; caution is advised during the fall hunting season. **VISITOR CENTER** Forest headquarters is at entrance.

HOMOSASSA SPRINGS STATE WILDLIFE PARK
Homosassa

Winding trails and interpretive programs highlight native Florida wildlife. **CONTACT** Homosassa Springs S.W.P., 4150 S. Suncoast Blvd., Homosassa, FL 34446; 352-628-2311.

CHASSAHOWITZKA NATIONAL WILDLIFE REFUGE
Crystal River

Canoe through charming coves and coastal marshes and along a forested spring run. **CONTACT** Chassahowitzka N.W.R., 1502 SE Kings Bay Dr., Crystal River, FL 34429; 352-563-2088.

HILLSBOROUGH RIVER STATE PARK
Thonotosassa

Stroll through Live Oak and palm hammocks or paddle the gentle Hillsborough River. **CONTACT** Hillsborough River S.P., 15402 U.S. 301 North, Thonotosassa, FL 33592; 813-987-6771.

BLUE SPRING STATE PARK
Orange City

Visit this park during winter to observe large congregations of Manatees. **CONTACT** Blue Spring S.P., 2100 W. French Ave., Orange City, FL 32763; 904-775-3663.

TIGER CREEK PRESERVE
Lake Wales

Follow self-guided trails through an endangered Florida scrub community. **CONTACT** Tiger Creek Preserve, c/o The Nature Conservancy, 225 E. Stuart Ave., Lake Wales, FL 33853; 941-678-1551.

Hillsborough River State Park

CRYSTAL RIVER STATE BUFFER PRESERVE
Crystal River

This park comprises 36,000 acres in western Citrus County. Habitats include vast areas of tidal marsh and pristine examples of hydric hammock further inland. **CONTACT** Crystal River State Buffer Preserve, 5990 N. Tallahassee Rd., Crystal River, FL 34428; 352-563-1136.

TRIPLE N RANCH WILDLIFE MANAGEMENT AREA
Kissimmee

Crabgrass Creek runs through 7,000 acres of flatwoods, dry prairie, scrub, and depression marsh. **CONTACT** Triple N Ranch W.M.A., 1420 Simons Rd., Unit A, Kissimmee, FL 34744; 407-436-1818.

HOBE SOUND NATIONAL WILDLIFE REFUGE
Hobe Sound

Visit sea-turtle nesting grounds along a pristine southeastern Florida shore. **CONTACT** Hobe Sound N.W.R., 13610 SE Federal Hwy., Hobe Sound, FL 33455; 561-546-6141.

FORT PIERCE INLET STATE RECREATION AREA
Fort Pierce

Meander through maritime hammocks (seaside hardwood forests) and along the edges of mangrove swamps. **CONTACT** Fort Pierce Inlet S.R.A., 905 Shorewinds Dr., Fort Pierce, FL 34949; 407-468-3985.

CALADESI ISLAND STATE PARK
off Honeymoon Island

Accessible only by public ferry from Honeymoon Island, this charming park consists of several Gulf coast barrier islands, where fishing, shelling, and swimming are popular activities. **CONTACT** Caladesi Island S.P., c/o Gulf Islands GEOpark, 1 Causeway Blvd., Dunedin, FL 34698; 813-469-5942.

JAY B. STARKEY WILDERNESS PARK New Port Richey
Hike, bike, backpack, horseback ride, and primitive camp in western
Florida's pineland and sandhill communities. **CONTACT** Jay B. Starkey W.P.,
7750 N. Congress St., New Port Richey, FL 34653; 813-834-3247.

UPPER TAMPA BAY COUNTY PARK Tampa
Canoe and hike among mangroves, salt marshes, and hammocks, or check
out the interpretive exhibits at the nature center. **CONTACT** Upper Tampa Bay
C.P., 8001 Double Branch Rd., Tampa, FL 33635; 813-855-1765.

LOWER WEKIVA RIVER STATE PRESERVE Apopka
Explore pristine bottomland woods along the Lower Wekiva River, designated by the state as an Outstanding Florida Water. **CONTACT** Lower Wekiva
River S.P., c/o Wekiwa Springs S.P., 1800 Wekiwa Circle, Apopka, FL
32712; 407-884-2009.

LAKE KISSIMMEE STATE PARK Lake Wales
Situated along the marshy edges of Florida's third largest freshwater lake,
this park comprises more than 5,000 acres. **CONTACT** Lake Kissimmee S.P.,
14248 Camp Mack Rd., Lake Wales, FL 33853; 941-696-1112.

SEBASTIAN INLET STATE
RECREATION AREA Melbourne Beach
Three miles of undeveloped Atlantic beaches and dunes offer picnicking,
swimming, surfing, snorkeling, scuba, boating, and camping. **CONTACT** Sebastian Inlet S.R.A., 9700 S. A1A, Melbourne Beach, FL 32951; 407-984-4852.

BULL CREEK WILDLIFE MANAGEMENT AREA Holopaw
Take a self-guided, 8½-mile drive through several central Florida habitats.
CONTACT Bull Creek W.M.A., c/o Florida Game and Fresh Water Fish Com-
mission, 1239 SW 10th St., Ocala, FL 34474; 352-732-1225.

CHARLOTTE HARBOR
ENVIRONMENTAL CENTER Punta Gorda
See American Alligators, Bald Eagles, Gopher Tortoises, and Florida Softshell Turtles along a self-guided wetland trail. **CONTACT** Charlotte Harbor
Environmental Ctr., 10941 Burnt Store Rd., Punta Gorda, FL 33955; 941-
575-4800.

LETTUCE LAKE PARK
Tampa
Observe Lettuce Lake and the Hillsborough River with its abundance
of birds from a 35-foot-tall observation tower. **CONTACT** Lettuce Lake
Park, 6920 E. Fletcher Ave.,
Tampa, FL 33637; 813-987-6204.

Lettuce Lake Park

SAWGRASS LAKE PARK
St. Petersburg
Meander along an elevated boardwalk through a maple swamp and a Live
Oak hammock. **CONTACT** Sawgrass Lake Park, 7400 25th St. North, St. Pe-
tersburg, FL 33702; 813-527-3814.

TAMPA ELECTRIC COMPANY
MANATEE VIEWING CENTER Apollo Beach
Visitors here will experience one of the state's best Manatee viewing areas.
CONTACT Tampa Electric Company Manatee Viewing Ctr., 6990 Dickman
Rd., Apollo Beach, FL 33572; 813-228-4289.

COQUINA BAYWALK AT LEFFIS KEY Bradenton Beach
Follow footpaths and boardwalks along a mangrove swamp and tidal lagoon.
CONTACT Coquina BayWalk at Leffis Key, c/o Sarasota Bay National
Estuary Program, 5333 N. Tamiami Trail, Suite 104, Sarasota, FL 34234;
941-359-5841.

JOHN CHESTNUT, SR., PARK   Palm Harbor
Cypress swamps, pine flatwoods, three nature trails, Lake Tarpon, and Brooker Creek are the main attractions at this park. CONTACT John Chestnut, Sr., Park, 2200 E. Lake Rd., Palm Harbor, FL 34685; 813-784-4686.

ANCLOTE RIVER PARK   Holiday
Take a driving tour of mangrove wetlands and tidal coves. CONTACT Anclote River Park, 1119 Baillie's Bluff Rd., Holiday, FL 34691; 813-938-2598.

CREWS LAKE PARK   Spring Hill
Enjoy an array of Florida habitats, including a Live Oak hammock with more than 300 old-growth trees. CONTACT Crews Lake Park, 16739 Crews Lake Dr., Spring Hill, FL 34610; 813-856-6742.

CECIL M. WEBB WILDLIFE MANAGEMENT AREA   Punta Gorda
Marshes and wet prairies full of showy wildflowers make this site a botanist's delight. CONTACT Cecil M. Webb W.M.A., 29200 Tucker Grade, Punta Gorda, FL 33955; 941-575-5768.

HILLSBOROUGH COUNTY'S WILDERNESS PARK   Thonotosassa
Canoe, hike, or bicycle along enchanting creeks and in floodplain forests in six separate parks near the junction of I-75 and U.S. 301. CONTACT Hillsborough County's Wilderness Park, 1101 E. Rivercove, Tampa, FL 33604; 813-975-2160.

ORLANDO WETLANDS PARK   Christmas
Hiking and bike trails afford birding opportunities in these managed wetlands. CONTACT Orlando Wetlands Park, c/o City of Orlando Recreation Bureau, 649 W. Livingston St., Orlando, FL 32801; 407-246-2288.

SUNNYHILL RESTORATION AREA   Weirsdale
This 4,000-acre area has many miles of levee roads and hiking trails near the upper Ocklawaha River where thousands of Sandhill Cranes spend the winter. Boating is available and camping is by permit only. CONTACT Sunnyhill Restoration Area, 19561 SE Hwy. 42, Umatilla, FL 32784; 352-821-1489.

THREE LAKES WILDLIFE MANAGEMENT AREA   Kenansville
Red-cockaded Woodpeckers, Burrowing Owls, Crested Caracaras, and Sandhill Cranes are this area's main attractions for birders. CONTACT Three Lakes W.M.A., 950 Sunset Ranch Rd., Kenansville, FL 34739; 407-436-1818.

ARCHBOLD BIOLOGICAL STATION   Lake Placid
This private research facility in the middle of pristine Florida scrub has a self-guided nature trail that emphasizes plant identification. CONTACT Archbold Biological Sta., Old State Rd. 8, Lake Placid, FL 33852; 941-465-2571.

Lake Okeechobee

TURKEY CREEK SANCTUARY
Palm Bay
This Audubon Society sanctuary has boardwalks through wet hammocks and scrub. CONTACT Turkey Creek Sanctuary, 1502 Port Malabar Blvd. Northeast, Palm Bay, FL 32905; 407-952-3433.

LAKE OKEECHOBEE   Okeechobee
The 110-mile Hoover Dike Trail circles this 730-square-mile lake in south-central Florida; call the Florida Trail Association at 352-378-8823 for details. Daily private tours into the National Audubon Society's 28,500-acre wildlife sanctuary on the lake allow observation of birds, plants, and other wildlife. CONTACT Swampland Tours, 10375 Hwy. 78 West, Okeechobee, FL 34974; 941-467-4411.

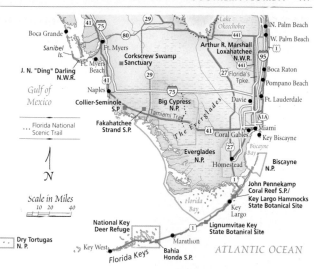

Florida National
Scenic Trail

Gulf of
Mexico

Dry Tortugas
N.P.

Scale in Miles
10   20   40

ATLANTIC OCEAN

Southern Florida and the Keys

Florida's southern tip is a land like no other in the continental United States. Angling eastward along the western reaches of the Tamiami Trail (U.S. 41)—the old two-lane, 245-mile Tampa-to-Miami highway and one of the earliest routes across the Everglades—visitors are almost immediately immersed in a fascinating terrain of tropical habitats. Familiar roadside plants mingle with those more typical of the Caribbean than of temperate North America. Sawgrass prairies stretch toward the horizon, punctuated with isolated stands of Cabbage Palmetto, Florida's state tree and one of its eight species of native tree-size palms.

At the southern tip of Lake Okeechobee, U.S. 27 turns due south, then connects with U.S. 1 in the Miami area before crossing a short bridge onto the Florida Keys. Overrun annually in winter by throngs of tourists, the Keys are less bustling in early fall and late spring. The more than 200 islands and islets that make up the Keys are less than 5,000 years old. They are composed of a thin sand and shell layer perched on young limestone formations, many of which are the remains of coral reefs. Averaging less than 10 feet above sea level, they are barely raised above the waters that surround them.

North of the Keys, the pounding surf of the Atlantic Ocean on the east contrasts with the gentle waves that are characteristic of the western shore. Unbridled development has taken over much of the natural landscape along the Atlantic coast, but a few natural remnants survive in places like Biscayne National Park, Tree Tops Park, Gumbo Limbo Environmental Complex, and John D. MacArthur Beach State Park. The much less developed Gulf coast mainly consists of swamps, mangroves, and thousands of small islands barely above water.

EVERGLADES NATIONAL PARK   Homestead

As Marjory Stoneman Douglas points out in the first line of her book, *Everglades—River of Grass*, "There is no other Everglades in the world." Certainly no other national park in North America preserves such a singular—and threatened—ecosystem. Situated at the southern tip of the state, this 1½-million-acre park encompasses less than 20 percent of the Everglades' original extent, with much of the remainder having been diked and drained or otherwise cut off from the inches-deep and miles-wide sheet of surface water that flows across the area and gives it life. What remains of the area has present-day environmentalists and land managers scurrying to find ways to ensure its conservation for the future.

Royal Palm, Anhinga Trail

Wildlife in Everglades National Park is abundant: The Roseate Spoonbills at Flamingo, the Smooth-billed Anis at Royal Palm, the Snail Kites soaring over Shark Valley, and the hard-to-find Mangrove Cuckoos are birds of special interest. Birders are treated to approximately 350 species, some of which are rarely found elsewhere in the United States.

The most important mammal here is the Florida Panther. The tragic population decline—fewer than 50 are left—of this large, golden-brown, long-tailed cat symbolizes the environmental deterioration that has plagued one of the country's fastest-growing states. Casual visitors rarely get a glimpse of this impressive and elusive creature, which is sometimes confused with the much smaller and shorter-tailed Bobcat. The American Crocodile, an essentially saltwater reptile that is very secretive and not easily seen, is another of the Everglades' unique and endangered animals. The current population is estimated at fewer than 600 individuals.

It is impossible to fully explore or appreciate this area in only a few hours, so visitors to Everglades National Park should come prepared to stay several days. However, for those with limited time, Royal Palm and Flamingo are the most accessible destinations. The park's 37-mile driving road (Route 9336) travels from the main park entrance off U.S. 1 to Flamingo, with several scenic stopping points and short hiking trails along the way.

For those with more time, the route along the Tamiami Trail described below begins at Everglades City, 35 miles southeast of Naples via U.S. 41 and Route 29, and follows an approximately 80-mile course that's generally west to east, then southerly. Fall, winter, and spring are the most popular with visitors; summer can be quite hot and humid, and there are many more mosquitoes and other biting insects at that time.

Roseate Spoonbill

TAMIAMI TRAIL To observant naturalists, the long, gentle curve in U.S. 41 south of Naples begins an immediate transition into a fresh and distinctive landscape. Huge expanses of Sawgrass marsh become visible on either side of the roadway. Though most of the Tamiami Trail passes through Big Cypress National Preserve (see below), it provides an excellent introduction to subtropical Florida and the Everglades ecosystem, as well as access to some of the park's most beautiful and delightful areas, such as the Ten Thousand Islands and Shark Valley.

TEN THOUSAND ISLANDS This area, named for the numerous small mangrove islands that line the coast southwest of Everglades City, is used primarily by canoeists and sea kayakers. The 99-mile mangrove-lined Wilderness Waterway begins at Everglades City and terminates at Flamingo, at about the southern tip of the peninsula. Several days are required to make this trip, and only seasoned paddlers should attempt it. Permits are required, and plans should not be made haphazardly because wind, weather, and inaccessibility of fresh water can become significant obstacles. For those with less time or more modest ambitions, a variety of shorter overnight or day trips can be planned, with Everglades City as both the departure and return point; permits are required for overnight outings, though not for day trips. Canoe rentals and boat tours are available at the concession store at Flamingo Lodge and Marina and in Everglades City.

Aerial view of Wood Stork rookery

SHARK VALLEY On the Tamiami Trail in the northeastern corner of the park, Shark Valley Visitor Center provides access to a shallow, slow-moving, 50-mile-wide body of water known as the Shark River Slough, a critical link to the preservation of the fragile Everglades ecosystem. The currents that creep through its channel supply much of the water that keeps the park healthy. The area also offers ranger-led programs and hikes, nature and bike trails, and an observation tower (a good place to see wading birds). The 15-mile Lookout Tower Road takes visitors to Shark River Slough and the observation tower, but only park-operated trams, bicycles (rentals available; call 305-221-8455), and foot traffic are allowed on the roadway.

ROYAL PALM The first stop along the main park road to Flamingo, this area features a boardwalk through a forested wetland of Button Bushes, willows, and Pond Apples. The boardwalk is part of the Anhinga Trail, which runs along Taylor Slough. Alligators are also abundant and easily seen. The Gumbo Limbo Trail, a ½-mile jaunt through a tropical hammock, begins near the end of the parking lot.

LONG PINE KEY This excellent recreation area and campground (no showers available), which is not really a key but a large pine island surrounded by wetlands, is on the main park road less than 4 miles from the entrance. The many miles of hiking trails accessible from here pass through rimrock pines and tropical hammocks and provide outstanding botanizing and wildlife observation.

Sunset over hammocks and alligator trails

PINELANDS AND OTHER TRAILS The ½-mile Pinelands Trail, the first stop west of Long Pine Key, offers a good introduction to southern Florida's rimrock pine habitat. Several miles beyond the Pinelands, the Pa-hay-okee Overlook Trail leads to an observation tower with a spectacular view of the seemingly endless marshy glades from which the Everglades takes its name. A boardwalk here passes just above a sawgrass marsh and allows close observation of the mucky substrate. The Mahogany Hammock Trail, about 7 miles past Pa-hay-okee, offers a fascinating walk along a ½-mile-long boardwalk that passes through a mature tropical hammock. The site takes its name from the Mahogany trees that line the trail; look for the base-ball-size, woody, gray-brown pods that constitute the fruit of this species. Colorful Florida Tree Snails are also found here. The next stop is Paurotis Pond, an artificial lake with an easily seen population of the dainty, thin-trunked Everglades Palm, also known as Paurotis Palm. West Lake Trail, approximately 30 miles from the main gate, is a leisurely ½-mile walk through a mangrove forest that supports all three of Florida's true mangrove species—Red, Black, and White—as well as a large population of Buttonwood. Snake Bight Trail, known mostly for its views of birds, an occasional American Crocodile, and swarms of mosquitoes, is a nearly 2-mile

Gumbo Limbo

walk to an observation deck overlooking Florida Bay. Mrazek Pond, the last main stop before Flamingo, is a popular birding spot with great photographic opportunities.

FLAMINGO RECREATION AREA Flamingo is situated on the edge of Florida Bay and offers a campground (only in late fall, winter, and early spring), marina, lodge, museum, boat tours, canoe rentals, visitor center, and plenty of opportunities for wildlife watching. Several canoe trails begin here or nearby. In addition to the Wilderness Waterway, mentioned above, paddling opportunities include Nine Mile Pond, Noble Hammock, Hell's Bay, Coot Bay, and Bear Lake. Walking opportunities near Flamingo include the Bear Lake, Christian Point, Rowdy Bend, Eco Pond, and Coastal Prairie Trails. Sea kayakers will enjoy paddling portions of Florida Bay and visiting the closest of the mangrove islands that dot the horizon.

CONTACT Everglades National Park, 40001 State Road 9336, Homestead, FL 33034-6733; 305-242-7700. **HOW TO GET THERE** There are four entrances to the park: Homestead and Florida City, Shark Valley, Everglades City, and Chekika. The main entrance is at Homestead, on the east coast. From the west coast, follow U.S. 41 (Tamiami Trail) along the park's northern border to Rte. 997 (Krome Ave.), then south to Homestead. From Miami, take U.S. 1 or Florida's Turnpike to Homestead; take the Florida City exit from the Turnpike, then the first right on Rte. 9336 (Palm Dr.), then follow signs. **SEASONAL ACCESS** Year-round. **VISITOR CENTERS** From west to east, then south: Gulf Coast, Shark Valley, Ernest F. Coe, Royal Palm, and Flamingo visitor centers.

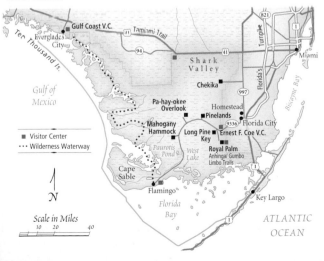

CORKSCREW SWAMP SANCTUARY   Sebastian

The towering stand of old-growth Bald Cypress trees—the largest known old-growth cypress population in North America—is enough to entice most naturalists to this 11,000-acre National Audubon Society preserve located east of Bonita Springs between Fort Myers and Naples. Some specimens here are more than 500 years old and are well over 120 feet tall. Follow the self-guided, 2-mile Boardwalk Trail through the sanctuary and see the landscape of a Florida from long ago.

The imposing giant trees are certainly not the only attraction. A variety of birds, reptiles, mammals, and plants are easily seen from the boardwalk, including the United States' largest nesting colony of Wood Storks. Beginning as early as November and continuing into early spring, an entire range of nesting activities may be observed as young storks move from egg to fledgling under their parents' watchful gaze. The sanctuary's bird list totals about 200 species: Limpkins and an array of herons and egrets are common year-round, large populations of Swallow-tailed Kites reside here in summer, and American Bitterns are seen in winter. A feeding station near the visitor center attracts Painted Buntings in winter and various migrants in spring.

Lush populations of Giant Leatherfern and Swamp and Boston Ferns add greenery to the ground cover. Epiphytic orchids and lichens dot the tree trunks, while Spanish Moss hangs from branches. The conspicuous white flowers of Swamp-lilies appear in the spring and are joined in the summer by the large, showy red and pink flowers of two of Florida's native hibiscus species. Stately Florida Royal Palms are easily seen here, and the lattice-like roots of Strangler Figs are visible on some of the Cabbage Palmettos and cypresses. Be sure to watch out for the whitish masses of BB-size Florida Apple Snail eggs on vegetation; they typically appear above water level from March through September and provide food for the Limpkins.

Wood Stork

CONTACT Corkscrew Swamp Sanct., 375 Sanctuary Rd., Naples, FL 34120; 941-657-3771. **HOW TO GET THERE** From Naples, take U.S. 41 (Tamiami Trail) north for 9 miles, then Rte. 846 (Immokalee Rd.) east for 17 miles. **SEASONAL ACCESS** Year-round. **VISITOR CENTER** Near boardwalk entrance.

J. N. "DING" DARLING NATIONAL WILDLIFE REFUGE   Sanibel

Situated along the northern edge of tiny Sanibel Island, which is off the Gulf coast south of Fort Myers, this refuge's 6,200 acres sometimes seem as crowded with people as with wildlife. One of the most frequently visited sites in the National Wildlife Refuge System, it is a place that no visitor to southwestern Florida should miss.

Great Egret with Roseate Spoonbills

WILDLIFE DRIVE This 5-mile drive off Sanibel–Captiva Road leads through the heart of the refuge. Low tide in conjunction with sunrise or sunset is the best time to visit: low tide provides increased foraging areas for shorebirds and waders, and sunrise is when the large flocks of herons and egrets take flight. About 250 species appear on "Ding" Darling's bird list: Roseate Spoonbills, Mottled Ducks, Ospreys, Red-shouldered Hawks, Brown Pelicans, Royal and Sandwich Terns, Anhingas, and all of south Florida's herons, egrets, and ibises are seen year-round. Black-bellied, Snowy, Wilson's, Semipalmated and Piping Plovers are seen in season. Sought-after species include the elusive Mangrove Cuckoo and the Black-whiskered Vireo, both of which are easiest to find in late spring and summer. The drive is also a good place to spot basking alligators at any time of the year, but it is closed on Fridays.

The Bailey Tract, located on the south side of Sanibel–Captiva Road and separate from the rest of the refuge, is a likely place to see Smooth-billed Anis, rails, and spring migrants. A short trail system (1¾ miles) provides access to the area. Other walking trails include the ⅓-mile Shell Mound Trail off Wildlife Drive and the 2-mile Indigo Trail near the visitor center.

Two mangrove-lined canoe trails run through the refuge. The 2-mile Commodore Creek Trail is accessible from the marina east of the visitor center; the 4-mile Buck Key Trail is across Roosevelt Channel on the east side of Captiva Island. Canoes can be rented in the refuge at Tarpon Bay (941-472-8900).

CONTACT J. N. "Ding" Darling N.W.R., 1 Wildlife Dr., Sanibel, FL 33957; 941-472-1100. **HOW TO GET THERE** From Fort Myers, take Rte. 867 (Sanibel Causeway) to the island; turn right onto Periwinkle Way, take another right onto Tarpon Rd., and then left onto Sanibel–Captiva Rd. **SEASONAL ACCESS** Year-round. **VISITOR CENTER** On Sanibel–Captiva Rd.

JOHN PENNEKAMP CORAL REEF STATE PARK AND KEY LARGO HAMMOCKS STATE BOTANICAL SITE

Key Largo

If the island of Key Largo is the gateway to the Florida Keys, then John Pennekamp Coral Reef State Park and Key Largo Hammocks State Botanical Site constitute the prelude to these magnificent islands' natural history. John Pennekamp was established in 1960 as the United States' first underwater park, and these two sites combined include representative samples of most of the Keys' major natural habitats. Together with the adjacent Florida Keys National Marine Sanctuary, the park and botanical site protect approximately 178 nautical square miles of coral reefs, mangrove swamps, and seagrass beds, as well as an impressive collection of mature tropical hammocks.

DIVING AND SNORKELING Most visitors to John Pennekamp come to see the offshore coral reefs. Glass-bottom boat tours and snorkeling excursions allow close observation of the sponges, shrimps, lobsters, crabs, and nearly 600 species of fish that inhabit the reefs. Scuba diving is also popular, and lessons are offered on site.

Coral reef with Longspine Squirrelfish

CANOEING AND KAYAKING A 2½-mile marked trail leads over crystal-clear water and through a maze of mangrove swamps. Boat rentals are available. Tent and RV camping is available in a full-facility campground.

BIRDING The park's bird list of nearly 200 species includes Roseate Spoonbills in summer, Scissor-tailed Flycatchers, Bonaparte's Gulls, Common Terns, and Caspian Terns in winter, and Reddish Egrets year-round.

BOTANIZING At John Pennekamp, the Wild Tamarind and Mangrove Trails offer tropical hammock and mangrove swamp vegetation, respectively. The main entrance to the botanical site, at Port Bougainvillea on North Key Largo, also passes through tropical hammock vegetation. Tropical trees and shrubs such as Lime Prickly Ash, Satin Leaf, Gumbo Limbo, Poisonwood, Tamarind, Florida Fish Poison Tree, Joewood, Sea Grape, and Buttonwood are common and easy to find.

CONTACT John Pennekamp Coral Reef S.P., Mile Marker 102.5, Key Largo, FL 33037; 305-451-1202. Key Largo Hammocks State Botanical Site, Cardsound Rd., State Rd. 905, Key Largo, FL 33037; 305-451-1202. **HOW TO GET THERE** At mile marker 102.5 on U.S. 1 in Key Largo. **SEASONAL ACCESS** Year-round. **VISITOR CENTER** Next to the main concession area.

NATIONAL KEY DEER REFUGE

Big Pine Key

Key Deer

It's difficult to resist the urge to feed or pet the tiny deer that are often seen foraging along the main roads through this refuge; nevertheless, the impulse should be controlled at all costs. In the 1940s the total population of this diminutive mammal had dropped to fewer than 50. Thanks to the refuge, it has now rebounded to nearly 300, about 200 of which are located on Big Pine Key. Today, the main enemy of the Key Deer is the automobile; in an average year up to 15 percent of the current population may be killed by careless drivers. Visitors who stop to feed or approach these trusting animals only encourage them to loiter too long in the roadside danger zone.

At first glance, observers might think that a full-grown Key Deer is merely a fawn. The shoulder height of the species ranges from 24 to 28 inches, and mature bucks weigh less than 75 pounds. Considered a race of the White-tailed Deer, the Key Deer is found no other place in the world. The best places to observe them are along Key Deer Boulevard and across the bridge on No Name Key.

BLUE HOLE Located 1¼ miles north of the intersection of Key Deer and Watson Boulevards, this is the only natural source of fresh water in the Lower Keys (those Keys stretching from Big Pine Key to Key West), so it is most attractive to wildlife. The hole is the remains of an old rock quarry that is now filled with salt water at its depths, with a layer of fresh water floating on top. Alligators, turtles, and freshwater fish inhabit the hole and are visible from an observation deck. Mangrove Cuckoos, Antillean Nighthawks, White-crowned Pigeons, and Black-whiskered Vireos can also be seen here.

THE WATSON TRAIL 1½ miles north of the intersection of Key Deer and Watson Boulevards, this 1-mile-long trail passes through a southern Florida Slash Pine woodland that also includes both Silver and Key Thatch Palms.

CONTACT National Key Deer Refuge, Mile Marker 30.5, P.O. Box 430510, Big Pine Key, FL 33043-0510; 305-872-2239. **HOW TO GET THERE** Off U.S. 1 at mile marker 30.5. **SEASONAL ACCESS** Year-round. **VISITOR CENTER** In the shopping plaza between Key Deer Blvd. and Wilder Rd.

DRY TORTUGAS NATIONAL PARK

A collection of seven islands encompassing nearly 65,000 acres and composed of coral reef and sand, the Dry Tortugas are surrounded by a natural system of shoals and reefs. Situated nearly 70 miles west of Key West, this is one of North America's most remote natural preserves. There is no fresh water on the islands—hence the name "Dry" Tortugas—and resident park staff still use the historic catchment system as well as a small desalinization unit for their water supply.

Fort Jefferson and Bush Key

FORT JEFFERSON Begun in 1846, essentially to control navigation and shipping in the Gulf of Mexico and to protect ship traffic bound for the Atlantic from the Mississippi River, Fort Jefferson was under construction for nearly 30 years. It was designated a national monument in 1934 and redesignated a national park in 1992. A seawall that forms a moat around the fort is bordered on both sides by crystal-clear water and is an excellent place to look for sea life.

WILDLIFE Approximately 100,000 Sooty Terns and 2,500 Brown Noddies nest on Bush Key from April to September. Other special-interest species include Magnificent Frigatebirds, Masked Boobies, Brown Boobies, and Roseate Terns. Spring and fall are outstanding for migrants, especially after storms. Marine turtles like the Green Turtle, Hawksbill, and Loggerhead are regularly seen.

SNORKELING AND SCUBA DIVING Colorful tropical fish and other reef life provide beautiful underwater scenery for snorkelers and scuba divers. Snorkeling sites include the shallow waters north and south of Loggerhead Key and the reefs and wrecks just southwest of Garden Key. Snorkeling equipment is available at the visitor center; scuba equipment is not.

Camping is available on Garden Key, but campers must provide their own food, fuel, supplies, and fresh water, and must carry their trash out.

CONTACT Dry Tortugas N.P., P.O. Box 6208, Key West, FL 33041-6208; 305-242-7700. **HOW TO GET THERE** Commercial sailboats, charter boats, and air taxis are available (most commercial departures are from Key West); a list of approved operators is available from the park. **SEASONAL ACCESS** Year-round; Bush Key is closed during tern nesting season; some islands are closed at night during turtle nesting season. Hospital and Lawn Keys are closed year-round. **VISITOR CENTER** In Fort Jefferson on Garden Key.

ARTHUR R. MARSHALL LOXAHATCHEE NATIONAL WILDLIFE REFUGE **Boynton Beach**

The primary purpose of this 221-square-mile refuge is to provide habitat for wildlife of the northern Everglades. The refuge is hemmed in by a canal and dike system that is designed to impound and protect the marshlands within. Large numbers of waterfowl, especially Blue-winged Teal and Ring-necked Ducks, congregate in the pools during winter. The Mottled Duck, a southern Florida and Gulf coast specialty that closely resembles the more widespread American Black Duck, is abundant year-round. Fulvous Whistling-Ducks are common in fall and winter, and the Masked Duck, a tropical vagrant, has been seen on rare occasions. A variety of shorebirds visit here, including large populations of Black-necked Stilts, Spotted Sandpipers, and both Greater and Lesser Yellowlegs. By far the most sought-after bird is the Snail Kite. The kite nests in the refuge and is seen in all seasons foraging for Florida Apple Snails over the marshes. Ask at the visitor center about recent sightings.

Loxahatchee is mostly water, but two short nature trails provide access for walkers. The nearly ½-mile Cypress Swamp Boardwalk passes through a lush cypress swamp, and the nearly 1-mile Marsh Trail circles around a freshwater impoundment and leads to an observation tower. Limpkins, rails, bitterns, and a variety of long-legged waders are easily observed along the Marsh Trail.

Greater Yellowlegs

The circular 5½-mile Everglades Canoe Trail begins near the visitor center and provides an introduction to the northern Everglades ecosystem. No motorized boats are allowed on this trail. Canoeists are also permitted on the canals but must compete with motorboats there.

CONTACT Arthur R. Marshall Loxahatchee N.W.R., 10216 Lee Rd., Boynton Beach, FL 33437-4796; 407-734-8303. **HOW TO GET THERE** From I-95, take the Boynton Beach exit, then head west to U.S. 441; drive south for 2 miles and turn right onto Lee Rd. **SEASONAL ACCESS** Year-round. **VISITOR CENTER** Headquarters Recreation Area is near the parking lot just off U.S. 441. The V.C. is open weekdays mid-Oct.–mid-Apr., but closed Mondays and Tuesdays the rest of the year.

BIG CYPRESS NATIONAL PRESERVE   Ochopee

Big Cypress, adjacent to Everglades National Park, is a 2,400-square-mile collection of subtropical habitats that includes sandy Slash Pine islands, hardwood hammocks, wet and dry prairies, marshes, and estuarine mangrove forests. Though most of the original virgin forest succumbed to the axe during the logging-crazed 1930s and 1940s, a few 700-year-old Bald Cypresses are still extant. Today, most of the preserve's namesake trees are dwarf Pond Cypresses. Thirty-one miles of the Florida National Scenic Trail, the Tree Snail Hammock Nature Trail, and the 15-mile Loop Road Scenic Drive provide access. Nine campgrounds are available but provide no water or facilities.

CONTACT Big Cypress N.P., HCR 61 Box 11, Ochopee, FL 34141; 941-695-4111. **HOW TO GET THERE** From I-75, exit onto State Rd. 951 heading south, then turn left (east) on U.S. 41 (Tamiami Trail). **SEASONAL ACCESS** Year-round. **VISITOR CENTER** Just off U.S. 41 in Ochopee.

FAKAHATCHEE STRAND STATE PRESERVE   Copeland

The Fakahatchee Strand is an elongated cypress and hardwood swamp forest, or strand, about 20 miles long and 3 to 5 miles wide, that drains Big Cypress Swamp near the western end of the Tamiami Trail. The 2,000-foot-long Big Cypress Bend boardwalk through the preserve is one of southern Florida's most delightful walks. Originating atop an old roadway along the Tamiami Trail, the path quickly joins a boardwalk lined with Strangler Fig, Wild Coffee, Myrsine, cypress trees, and an array of other plants. The strand also contains the largest stand of Royal Palms in North America. For a driving tour with an opportunity to see

Big Cypress Swamp

wildlife—Fakahatchee is home to several endangered or threatened mammals, including the Black Bear, the Everglades race of Mink, and the Florida Panther—the W. J. Janes' Memorial Scenic Drive offers 11 miles of improved dirt roads. Old gated tram roads turn off Janes' Drive here and there, leading into the wilder parts of the preserve; the trails beyond gates 2, 7, 12, 16, 19, and 20 have been partially cleared and provide excellent opportunities for exploration.

CONTACT Fakahatchee Strand S.P., 137 Coastline Dr., P.O. Box 548, Copeland, FL 34137; 941-695-4593. **HOW TO GET THERE** From I-75, exit onto Rte. 29, then head south for about 14 miles. **SEASONAL ACCESS** Year-round.

COLLIER-SEMINOLE STATE PARK   Naples

The 13½-mile canoe trail that meanders through this park, a beautiful 6,423-acre wilderness inland from Marco Island and just west of Fakahatchee Strand State Preserve, is an excellent way to explore southwestern Florida's magnificent mangrove swamp habitat. The Blackwater River, which flows through the park, provides paddling or motorboat access to the Gulf of Mexico and the Ten Thousand Islands. Private boat tours of the mangrove area are also

available. For landbound explorers, a 6½-mile hiking trail and nature trail and boardwalk allow close observation of the hardwood hammock, pine flatwoods, cypress swamp, and saltmarsh communities. From mid-spring to mid-fall, the biting insects can be bothersome.

CONTACT Collier-Seminole S.P., 20200 E. Tamiami Trail, Naples, FL 34114; 941-394-3397. HOW TO GET THERE On U.S. 41 (Tamiami Trail), about 17 miles southeast of Naples. SEASONAL ACCESS Year-round. VISITOR CENTER At the blockhouse near the campground.

BISCAYNE NATIONAL PARK   Homestead

Located just east of Miami's Cutler Ridge community, this 181,500-acre park includes a mangrove-lined mainland shore, several undeveloped islands, or keys, and a number of offshore and close-to-shore coral reefs. A park concession offers glass-bottom

boat tours of the bay and reefs, as well as snorkeling and scuba diving excursions. Primitive camping and a self-guided nature trail are available on Elliott and Boca Chita Keys, the former being the largest of the islands, but you must arrange for a boat at mainland marinas. All of the keys are accessible by boat, but only Elliott Key has drinking water.

Biscayne Bay

CONTACT Biscayne N.P., 9700 SW 328th St., Homestead, FL 33030; 305-230-7275. HOW TO GET THERE Take Florida's Turnpike south to exit 2 (Campbell Dr.), bear right, take first right turn onto Kingman Rd., continue to the light, then turn left (east) on SW 328th St. to the park. SEASONAL ACCESS Year-round. VISITOR CENTER At Convoy Pt. on the mainland.

BAHIA HONDA STATE PARK

Bahia Honda Key

Great White Heron

Its crystal-clear waters and white sand beaches make Bahia Honda State Park, located on the key of the same name, one of the most popular recreation areas in the Keys. Though many visitors come here to swim, sun, and snorkel (a dive shop operates in the park), naturalists will also find much to explore. The large observation deck built high atop the remains of the defunct Flagler railroad offers a breathtaking view of the neighboring keys. Amateur botanists will want to walk the Silver Palm Trail to see one of the largest remaining stands of this diminutive species along with such tropical specialties as Seven-year Apple, Beach Creeper, and Black Torch. Two Florida specialties, Florida Silver Palm and Yellow-wood, are both found in the park.

CONTACT Bahia Honda S.P., 36850 Overseas Hwy., Big Pine Key, FL 33043; 305-872-2353. **HOW TO GET THERE** On U.S. 1, 12 miles southwest of Marathon on Bahia Honda Key. **SEASONAL ACCESS** Year-round. **VISITOR CENTER** Ranger station at park entrance.

LIGNUMVITAE KEY STATE BOTANICAL SITE

Upper Matecumbe Key

Lignumvitae Key, a 280-acre island just southwest of Islamorada on Upper Matecumbe Key, is one of the largest and best examples of coastal tropical hammock left in Florida. The Key takes its name from the *Lignum vitae*, or Tree of Life. Once treasured for its use in ship-building and its supposed medicinal value, this plant is now listed as endangered in Florida as a result of overcollecting by early explorers. Visitors may see it and such hammock plants as White Stopper, Pigeon-plum, Lancewood, Marlberry, and Black Ironwood along the trails. Guided walks are available.

CONTACT Lignumvitae Key State Botanical Site, P.O. Box 1052, Islamorada, FL 33036; 305-664-4815. **HOW TO GET THERE** One mile west of U.S. 1 at mile marker 78.5; accessible by private or charter boat. Reservations for tour boat access may be arranged by calling 305-664-9814. **SEASONAL ACCESS** Year-round. **VISITOR CENTER** Historic Matheson House Museum and ranger station on the island.

THE CONSERVANCY'S BRIGGS NATURE CENTER **Naples**
Visitors can enjoy guided canoe trips of a mangrove community, guided boat explorations of Rookery Bay, and a 2,500-foot boardwalk. **CONTACT** The Conservancy's Briggs Nature Ctr., 401 Shell Island Rd., Naples, FL 34113; 941-775-8569.

GUMBO LIMBO ENVIRONMENTAL COMPLEX **Boca Raton**
Explore the canopy of a tropical hammock from the observation deck or follow the self-guided boardwalk. **CONTACT** Gumbo Limbo Environmental Complex, 1801 N. Ocean Blvd., Boca Raton, FL 33432; 407-338-1473.

TREE TOPS PARK **Davie**
This 358-acre park features four self guided nature trails, a 1,000-foot boardwalk over a freshwater marsh, and canoeing on 15 acres of waterways. **CONTACT** Tree Tops Park, 3900 SW 100th Ave., Davie, FL 33328; 954-370-3750.

SANIBEL–CAPTIVA
CONSERVATION FOUNDATION **Sanibel Island**
This 1,100-acre nature center has 4 miles of loop trails through coastal habitats. **CONTACT** Sanibel–Captiva Conservation Foundation, P.O. Box 839, 3333 Sanibel–Captiva Rd., Sanibel, FL 33957; 941-472-2329.

JOHN D. MACARTHUR
BEACH STATE PARK
North Palm Beach
Mangrove estuary, subtropical coastal hammock, and nearly 2 miles of beach are accessible by a nature trail and a boardwalk. **CONTACT** John D. MacArthur Beach S.P., 10900 State Rd. 703 (A1A), N. Palm Beach, FL 33408; 407-624-6950.

Cayo Costa State Park

FERN FOREST NATURE CENTER **Pompano Beach**
A meandering trail offers observation of open prairie and Cabbage Palmetto hammock. **CONTACT** Fern Forest Nature Center, 201 Lyons Rd. South, Pompano Beach, FL 33068; 954-970-0150.

MATHESON HAMMOCK PARK **Coral Gables**
Easy-to-follow trails wind through the remnants of a tropical hammock. **CONTACT** Matheson Hammock Park, 9610 Old Cutler Rd., Coral Gables, FL 33156; 305-666-6979.

CAPE FLORIDA STATE RECREATION AREA **Key Biscayne**
This Lighthouse Historic Site offers tours as well as biking and nearly 1½ miles of Atlantic beaches. **CONTACT** Cape Florida S.R.A., 1200 S. Crandon Blvd., Key Biscayne, FL 33149; 305-361-5811.

SIX MILE CYPRESS PRESERVE **Fort Myers**
Stroll along a 1¼-mile self-interpretive boardwalk trail through a 2,000-acre wetland preserve. **CONTACT** Six Mile Cypress Preserve, 7751 Penzance Crossing, Ft. Myers, FL 33912; 941-432-2004.

CAYO COSTA STATE PARK **Boca Grande**
An outstanding shorebirding site on an unspoiled barrier island, accessible only by private boat or ferry. **CONTACT** Cayo Costa S.P., c/o Barrier Islands GEOpark, P.O. Box 1150, Boca Grande, FL 33921; 941-964-0375.

The Authors

Peter Alden, principal author of this volume, is a naturalist, author, and tour guide who has lectured and led nature tours all over the world for Harvard's Friends of the Museum of Comparative Zoology, Massachusetts Audubon Society, Overseas Adventure Travel, Lindblad Travel, and many cruise lines. He has written books on North American, Latin American, and African wildlife. Alden lives in Concord, Massachusetts.

Rick Cech wrote the habitats and conservation sections of this book. He is a nature writer, consultant, and photographer; past president of the Linnaean Society of New York; and founder of the North American Butterfly Association's newsletter, *The Anglewing.*

Richard Keen, author of the weather and night sky sections, is a freelance science writer, nature photographer, and public speaker. He has published many books, articles, and photographs on the topics of meteorology and astronomy.

Amy Leventer, author of the geology and topography portions, is a visiting assistant professor at Colgate University's Geology Department. She has published many articles on geology and co-authored the *National Audubon Society Pocket Guide to the Earth from Space.*

Gil Nelson, regional consultant and author of the parks and preserves section, is a naturalist, writer, and educator who has written several books on Florida as well as many articles for national and regional magazines. He lives in Tallahassee.

Wendy B. Zomlefer, Ph.D. wrote the flora section of this guide and has published numerous books and journal articles on botany. She is a postdoctoral associate in the botany department at the University of Florida and courtesy assistant curator of the University of Florida Herbarium.

Acknowledgments

The authors thank the thousands of botanists, zoologists, and naturalists we have worked with over the years and whose books and papers provided a wealth of information for this guide. The staff and members of the following organizations were most helpful: National, Florida, and Massachusetts Audubon Societies, the Nature Conservancy, the North American Butterfly Association, the American Birding Association, Harvard's Museum of Comparative Zoology, and the many federal and state land, game, and fish departments.

We thank all of the experts who contributed to this book. Carter Gilbert of the Florida Museum of Natural History reviewed the fish species accounts, Gary Mechler examined the weather and night sky spreads, Chuck Keene reviewed many species photographs, Thomas M. Scott of the Florida Geological Survey and Rick Oches consulted on the topography and geology text, Marc S. Frank and Roger W. Portell of the Florida Museum of Natural History consulted on the fossils section, and Jon Blanchard of the Florida Natural Areas Inventory reviewed the parks and preserves section.

Special thanks go to Maria Abate, James Baird, Richard Carey, Holly DePaula, the late Richard Forster, Ted and Florence Glass, Karsten Hartell, Vernon Laux, the late C. Russell Mason, Roger and Virginia Peterson, Jeff Stone, Michael Sylvan, Guy Tudor, and Tom Tynning.

We are grateful to Andrew Stewart for his vision of a regional field guide encompassing the vast mosaic of Florida's topography, habitats, and wildlife, and to the staff of Chanticleer Press for producing a book of such excellence. Editor-in-chief Amy Hughes provided conceptual guidance and constant encouragement. The success of the book is largely due to the skills and expertise of series editor Patricia Fogarty and project editor Lisa Leventer. Editors Miriam Harris and Pamela Nelson examined and refined the flora and invertebrates sections, respectively. Managing editor Edie Locke shepherded the book through the editorial process. Assistant editor Kristina Lucenko and editorial assistant Michelle Bredeson fact checked, copyedited, and proofread the book through all stages. Publishing assistant Karin Murphy and intern Tessa Kale offered much assistance and support. Editor Holly Thompson and database consultant Dan Hugos made valuable contributions to the project. Art director Drew Stevens and designer Vincent Mejia created a visually beautiful and eminently usable volume. The design contributions of interns Anthony Liptak and Enrique Piñas and designer Sandra Louro were invaluable. Howard S. Friedman created the beautiful illustrations. Ortelius Design made the many detailed maps. The tree silhouettes were contributed by Dolores R. Santoliquido, and the animal tracks by Dot Barlowe. Photo directors Zan Carter and Teri Myers and photo editor Christine Heslin sifted through thousands of photographs in their search for the stunning images that contribute so much to the beauty and usefulness of this guide. Linda Patterson Eger, Lois Safrani, Yvonne Silver, and Anita Dickhuth of Artemis Picture Research Group, Inc., brought considerable skills and experience to the researching and editing of many of the species photographs. Permissions manager Alyssa Sachar facilitated the acquisition of photographs. Kate Jacobs, Leslie Fink, Jennifer McClanaghan, and Mee-So Caponi helped sort and traffic photographs and offered endless additional support. Director of production Alicia Mills and production assistant Philip Pfeifer saw the book through the complicated production and printing processes to ensure the excellent quality of these books.

In addition, we thank all of the photographers who gathered and submitted the gorgeous pictures that make this book a delight to view.

—Peter Alden, Rick Cech, Richard Keen,
Amy Leventer, Gil Nelson, Wendy B. Zomlefer

Picture Credits

The credits are listed alphabetically by photographer. Each photograph is listed by the number of the page on which it appears, followed by a letter indicating its position on the page (the letters follow a sequence from top left to bottom right).

Kevin Adams 106d, 175a, 203c

William H. Allen, Jr. 93e, 100g, 122e

Tony Arruza 18b, 44a, 61e, 160a, 416, 430b

Ron Austing 310b, 313a, 318b & e, 328b, 329f, 331a, 335b, 336b & c, 337a, b & c, 338a, 340b, 343d, 347d, 355a, 356a, b & c, 369b

Noella Ballenger 415, 422a

Robert E. Barber 372b

Roger W. Barbour/ Morehead State University 364a & b

Kevin Barry 39c, 88b & e, 97a, 135d, 183c, 212b, 395a, 406a, 411a, 412a

Steve Bentsen 319c, 320a, 393

Susan E. Blanchet/ Blanchet Photographics 264a, 265b & d

Bob Bowdey 262d

Wayne & Karen Brown/

Brown & Co. Photography 200d, 204b, 259a, 267a

Fred Bruemmer 33a, 208b

Sonja Bullaty & Angelo Lomeo 98e, 99a, 100f & h, 104c, 108a & b, 116c, 118f, 122d, 132d

Gay Bumgarner 352d, 373b

Frank Burek 261c, 262b, 271d

Joyce Burek 261d, 268c & d

Index

Florida Counties

Northwest Panhandle

Converting to Metric

Limited space makes it impossible for us to give measurements expressed as metrics. Here is a simplified chart for converting inches and feet to their metric equivalents:

	MULTIPLY BY
inches to millimeters	25
inches to centimeteres	2.5
feet to meters	0.3
yards to meters	0.9
miles to kilometers	1.6
square miles to square kilometers	2.6
acres to hectares	.40
ounces to grams	28.3
pounds to kilograms	.45
Farenheit to Centigrade	subtract 32 and multiply by .55

Prepared and produced by Chanticleer Press, Inc.

Founder: Paul Steiner
Publisher: Andrew Stewart

Staff for this book:

Editor-in-Chief: Amy K. Hughes
Series Editor: Patricia Fogarty
Project Editor: Lisa Leventer
Managing Editor: Edie Locke
Editor: Miriam Harris
Contributing Editor: Pamela Nelson
Assistant Editor: Kristina Lucenko
Editorial Assistant: Michelle Bredeson
Photo Directors: Zan Carter, Teri Myers
Photo Editor: Christine Heslin
Photo Research and Editing: Artemis Picture Research Group, Inc.
Rights and Permissions Manager: Alyssa Sachar
Art Director: Drew Stevens
Designer: Vincent Mejia
Design Interns: Anthony Liptak, Enrique Piñas
Director of Production: Alicia Mills
Production Assistant: Philip Pfeifer
Publishing Assistant: Karin Murphy
Illustrations: Howard S. Friedman
Maps: Ortelius Design

Series design by Drew Stevens and Vincent Mejia

All editorial inquiries should be addressed to:

Chanticleer Press
665 Broadway, Suite 1001
New York, NY 10012

To purchase this book or other National Audubon Society Field
Guides and Pocket Guides, please contact:

Alfred A. Knopf
201 East 50th Street
New York, NY 10022
(800) 733-3000

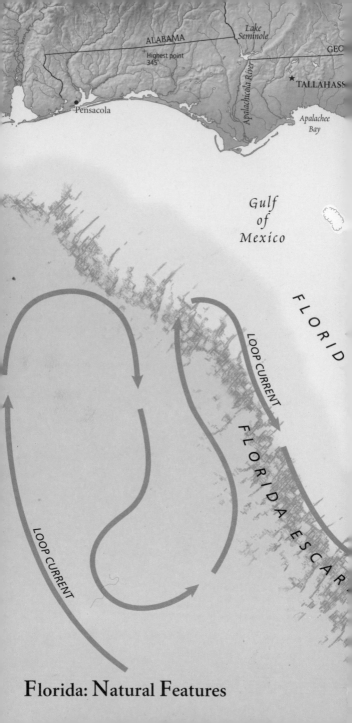

ALABAMA

Highest point
345'

Lake
Seminole

GEO

★ TALLAHASS

Apalachicola River

Pensacola

Apalachee
Bay

Gulf
of
Mexico

FLORID

LOOP CURRENT

FLORIDA ESCAR

LOOP CURRENT

Florida: Natural Features